Alfonso Gálvez

Waiting for
Don Quijote

New Jersey
U.S.A. – 2022

CATALOGING DATA

Author: Gálvez, Alfonso, 1932–1922
Title: Waiting for Don Quijote

Library of Congress Control Number: 2022913369

ISBN: 978-1-953170-22-4 (hardcover)
      978-1-953170-23-1 (e-book)

**Published by
Shoreless Lake Press
P.O. Box 157
Stewartsville, New Jersey 08886**

Many therefore of his disciples, hearing it, said: This saying is hard, and who can hear it? But Jesus, knowing in himself, that his disciples murmured at this, said to them: Doth this scandalize you? If then you shall see the Son of man ascend up where he was before? It is the spirit that quickeneth: the flesh profiteth nothing. The words that I have spoken to you, are spirit and life. But there are some of you that believe not. For Jesus knew from the beginning, who they were that did not believe, and who he was, that would betray him. And he said: Therefore did I say to you, that no man can come to me, unless it be given him by my Father. After this many of his disciples went back; and walked no more with him. Then Jesus said to the twelve: Will you also go away? And Simon Peter answered him: Lord, to whom shall we go? thou hast the words of eternal life. And we have believed and have known, that thou art the Christ, the Son of God. Jesus answered them: Have not I chosen you twelve; and one of you is a devil? Now he meant Judas Iscariot, the son of Simon: for this same was about to betray him, whereas he was one of the twelve.

(Jn 6: 60–71)

PROLOGUE

Since the first time they were uttered, the words of Jesus Christ have sounded both wonderful and strange at the same time. They were too wonderful for some people and too strange for others. But, in general, His words were incomprehensible for all. More than twenty centuries have passed, and His Message continues to appear, more and more, as something strange, even to those who consider themselves Christian —as if It were a doctrine of madmen and for madmen. And the truth is that if one looks at this issue with purely human eyes, the World's rejection of the Gospel seems almost logical; just as it happens with delectable delicacies, which are not precisely the most suitable thing for a coarse palate... and so much the more in our case, since the World is increasingly far from being a first–class *gourmet*. The wisdom of the Cross, which in the early days of Christianity caused scandal, has never seemed to hold as much madness as it does now.

The Gospel is the doctrine of true Love, or perfect Love, which, inexplicably, has been offered to man. And although it is true that man was created in the image and likeness of God —Who is Love, according to Saint John (1 Jn 4:8)— and, therefore, was created by Love and for love, nevertheless, since the Fall, the human creature has become significantly too diminished to attain a deep understanding of many concepts; Love is one of them. One could even say that Love is the least understood of them all; and yet It is the greatest reality existing in Heaven and on Earth: that which fills everything. As Dante said in his *Divine Comedy* with words that conclude his immortal Poem:

> Love, which moves the sun and the other stars.

Once the human mind and heart were made small by sin, their possibility of opening themselves to perfect Love faced serious risks and no less severe difficulties. Jesus Christ did not have to wait long to see that His words were rejected: *From that time many of his disciples drew back, and walked no more with him.*[1] The truth is that openness and correspondence of self–surrender to perfect Love, through faith, are a true gift from Heaven that can never be based on so–called human wisdom: *That your faith might not stand in the wisdom of men, but in the power of God.*[2]

It is clear that the Gospel is a matter of madness; although it must be taken into account, as strange as it may seem, that madness is one of the most obscure and controversial concepts in existence. At first glance it seems that everyone is in agreement as to its meaning: namely, unsound reasoning, which can also be termed as *that which is irrational*. Yet, one does not need to examine this description too closely to realize immediately that it is simplistic. Quite some time ago now, people began to consider mistrusting reason as

---

[1] Jn 6:66.
[2] 1 Cor 2:5.

something increasingly normal; and, in addition, the claim that reason can comprehend objective truth was seen as abnormal and crazy. Contrary to popular thought, the truth is that the modern world frequently considers as rational only that which is irrational —so much so that it is becoming increasingly more difficult for people to agree upon what is reasonable and what is not.

Thus, according to some people, today's world has gone mad; others, instead, consider crazy those who say such a thing. It is also undeniable that both a divine and a human concept of wisdom and madness, which are not only different from each other but are even contradictory and opposite, do co–exist. *For the wisdom of this world is foolishness with God. For it is written: 'I will catch the wise in their own craftiness.' And again: 'The Lord knows the thoughts of the wise, that they are vain.'* [3] And again it is said in another place, as if there could be any doubt: *For the preaching of the cross, to them indeed that perish, is foolishness; but unto us which are saved it is the power of God. For it is written: 'I will destroy the wisdom of the wise, and the prudence of the prudent I will bring to nothing.' Where is the wise? Where is the scribe? Where is the disputer of this world? Has not God made foolish the wisdom of this world?*[4] Certainly, the Bible does not mince words. It presupposes that human wisdom —which by human reason is regarded as opposite to madness— is distinct and different from divine wisdom —which is true wisdom for the Bible—; even more, the Bible uses very strong language in referring to human wisdom: *This wisdom does not descend from above, but is earthly, sensual, and devilish.*[5] Therefore, even assuming that men could agree on

---

[3] 1 Cor 3: 19–20.

[4] 1 Cor 1: 18–20.

[5] Jas 3:15.

the concepts of what is reasonable and what is madness —which is far from given—, both concepts should then be compared to the understanding that God has of those two realities. And one would surely see that they are in contradiction, because what is wisdom to man is foolishness to God, and vice versa.

Nevertheless, this contradiction is understandable; for it is true that the world has its own wisdom which everybody accepts, even if only in a merely practical way, in spite of disagreement as to which things either concept should be applied. A wisdom, of course, which is totally contrary to the Gospel: *The wisdom of the flesh is death, but the wisdom of the Spirit is life and peace. Because the wisdom of the flesh is an enemy to God.*[6] There is, therefore, a code of conduct which, being wisdom for God, is, simultaneously, madness and folly for men. And because that code is precisely the Gospel, it can be affirmed with absolute certainty that the Gospel is, at least in the eyes of the world, suitable only for madmen. And surely to God as well, for it is very probable that He considers the Gospel as a lovely and joyful madness, which is, on the other hand, the only safely sane route that man can follow.

We have already seen that the connotations of "reasonable" and "unreasonable" frequently depend on whether one takes the point of view of God or of man: what is wisdom to the former is folly to the latter; besides, as I have said above, men not only disagree about what is and what is not reasonable, they also hold —as their exclusive point of agreement— the incontrovertible truth that the Gospel is madness... raving madness if we speak clearly. In the eyes of God, however, things are quite clear: the alleged wisdom of the world is folly, and the Gospel is the only reasonable madness; that is to say that, to God, the only attitude of reasonableness is precisely the very attitude that we define as *being mad.*

---

[6]Rom 8: 6–7.

It is probably foolish to consider what we have just said as a mere play on words. The problem is far too serious to simply dismiss it in that way. It is still discussed to this day whether Don Quixote was really insane or the madmen were those who lived around him. It is uncertain whether Cervantes proceeded in the best way when he had Don Quixote die in his bed, surrounded by relatives, after having regained his right mind. Some people even question whether such *right mind* was any more reasonable than his madness. At any rate, do not we also feel some nostalgia when we read that Cide Hamete Benengeli definitively leaves his quill to tell us, as if in a happy ending, that Don Quixote died after having recovered his sanity, thus bringing us back by doing so, and as if he did not intend it, to the world of sane people? All of us have probably sensed in some way, in view of the purported wisdom of this world, that there must be a more reasonable kind of madness than what we see every day. A madness which, also, is more necessary for man than what the world usually considers as intelligence. Maybe that is why the audacity of Erasmus in writing *The Praise of Folly* seems almost logical. The truth is that man became crazy because of sin, which was, in turn, caused by lack of love. Since then, only another madness —this time one caused by a superabundance of love— could bring man back to the path of sanity. Or, put another way, an alternative madness of love which is able to cure the supreme folly of the lack of love: *For seeing that in the wisdom of God, the world by wisdom knew not God, it pleased God by the foolishness of our preaching to save them who believe.*[7] It seems clear that it is impossible to determine what is really reasonable and what is not without taking into account what God has done for man and taught him.

---

[7] 1 Cor 1:21.

I

LOGIC, THE GREAT UNKNOWN

Anyone with common sense would suppose that it is impossible to be a good pastoralist if one has never (or almost never) had the responsibility of caring for souls, including, of course, the necessary experience of having ministered to some difficult parish (assuming that there is an easy parish). Similarly, one cannot be a good carpenter if he has never worked with wood, nor a good electrician if he has never done anything in the field of electricity. However, truths of simple common sense, which people call "platitudes," barely have a place in the ecclesiastical world, where everything is different; as if that world were some kind of *Wonderland*, in which, like Alice, one finds himself suddenly living in.

In the sixties of the last century, I was required to spend fifteen days in Madrid attending a preparatory course for priests who were destined to carry out their ministry in South America. No matter how many times I asked myself the same question (there was no one else I could ask without causing scandal), I was unable to figure out what rare sort of mysterious training a Spanish priest could possibly need in order to carry out his ministry in South America.[1] The study and practice of what was then called *revision of life* —an ineffable discovery of pastoralists of the time, that was believed to be the closest thing to the philosopher's stone of Evangelization— took up almost the entire course. Later on I did have the opportunity to verify the use that these new methods could add to my work with the Indians of the Andes. Although, most awe–inspiring to me was the extraordinary confidence[2] with which those socio–pastoral formulas (rather almost magical, I would say) were explained and accepted.

I was not yet aware of what was happening, although I vaguely sensed it. This was perfectly normal given my young age, my scarce formation, and the great difficulty entailed in assessing what goes on during moments of great transition in History. Without knowing it, we were witnessing quite a transcendental change: the Church founded by Jesus Christ, alive through the Holy Spirit, governed by the law of charity, guided by Faith, directed by the Magisterium, nourished by the Sacraments, walking under the *blessed Hope* (Tit 2:13), sheltered under the banner of the Cross of her Lord in which she was given the opportunity to partake (Rom 8:17; Gal 2:19), was being replaced by the sociological Church, world peace, and purely human well–being. The road she began to tread was the path that led from the Celestial Paradise to the Earthly Paradise. The Church of Shepherds of souls was a thing of the past, giving way to the Church of Experts and qualified bureaucracy. The

---

[1]The unwinding of the course, along with the years that went by after it, confirmed my belief in the almost insubstantial use of it all.

[2]The almost infallible effect that seemed to be attributed to this new recipe was astonishing. I was overwhelmed by the thought of the amazing survival of the Church for twenty centuries without it: another unmistakable proof of her divinity.

Good Shepherd was going to be replaced by the Good Administrator or the Good Politician: *One woe is past; and, behold, there come two woes more hereafter.*[3]

However the short story of what happened at that *Course* has not yet reached its climax, and, don't forget, I am still referring to the strange absence of logic that seemed to be the norm in that gathering.

Most extraordinary was that none of the *teachers* in charge of mentally preparing us for our new destiny had ever been in America, North or South. And to make matters worse, this didn't seem to catch anyone's eye, nor arouse anybody's surprise.

The truth is that my memories of that course, or whatever it was, are not very pleasant. In order to attend it, I had to leave behind many activities in my parish that I thought were important, and, needless to say, the knowledge received in return did not compensate for the painful sacrifice of my time. I was quite young when this took place, and probably quite anxious, so I found myself in awe at the apparent nonchalance of the other sixty priests that were attending. They behaved as if they had absolutely nothing else to do, and they seemed convinced of the great importance and essential significance of the course. The entire time I could not free myself of the sickening feeling that we were wasting our time. Now that many years have gone by, and I have become more knowledgeable on the whole, I must confess that what was then a feeling is now an absolute certainty.

At that time, my limit of bewilderment had not yet been reached, so there were many things that forcefully caught my eye. One of

---

[3]Rev 9:12. This phenomenon coincided, in all logic, with the so–called promotion of the laity. Especially in the USA, it was already clear that things were quickly moving towards a lay Church (managed by a battery of lay bureaucrats and expert nuns); a situation made even worse by the shortage of priests and the lethargy to remedy the grave problem of vocations.

them, for example, was the incredible, and comic, affair of the *notes*.
With praiseworthy interest, everyone was tirelessly taking notes, as
if they were taking down words from Above. Strangely enough, even
the teachers were writing down anything that the students would
say, no matter how bizarre; one of us would hardly begin to speak,
and the teacher would already be taking notes on the subject with
such enthusiasm that it disconcerted me. Needless to say, most of
the observations that we, as students, offered did not stand out as
exceedingly bright. This did not stop the teacher from writing them
down with admirable enthusiasm, making it seem to all of us that the
importance of what was being said was on par with the salvation of
the world. Many times I have asked myself what might have come
of such and so many notes that were taken; and although I have
never found out —perhaps The Historical Archives in Simancas, in
Spain? The Library of Congress, maybe?—, I always suspected that
it was none other than the wastepaper basket. A conclusion which
I reached due, most likely, to my malicious nature. The passing of
time brought to my attention that this practice was quite extended
throughout ecclesiastical circles of the time; and for this reason, I
have come to terms with the thought that there were complex reasons that I, in my simplicity, was never able to comprehend. I have
even thought of the possibility that the *experts* intended nothing
else than to fill simple commoners like myself with confidence; and
this is why they strove to show us the importance that they gave
to, and the great respect deserved by, our insignificant conjectures
despite their lack of consequence. Nonetheless, because tomfoolery
is always tomfoolery, and I have never believed in its fruitfulness, I
still think that the wastebasket was their final end. And because of
this, I am a convinced advocate of simplicity, that we simply show
ourselves as we are, without ever leaving mutual respect aside. I

have never been able to believe that nonsense like the ones I have often heard at events like this could ever be interesting to anyone. And this is why I do not like it when someone tries too hard to *show* me respect; I am content with their simply *being* respectful. However, it is evident that being natural is not the dominant virtue in the ecclesiastical milieu; it seems that when supernatural stature is lost, even the purely natural is less than satisfactory.

What surprised me most, of all the things that went on during our distinguished course, was the exceedingly verbose explanation of a new, astounding, and revolutionary pastoral method. It was presented to us under the title of *revision of life*; although, to be exact, I should say that it was not the method, precisely, that spurred my amazement. The truth is that I could not understand how this discovery could ever be considered revolutionary; and in addition, I had already known about this method for some time in its pastoral application (I was aware of its results as well). One way or the other, we dedicated the larger portion of our time and classes to it. And I am sure that, by the end of the fifteen days, each and every one of us attending the course had reached the same conclusion, invariably: Among the proofs of the divinity of the Church, we finally had one that was conclusive which consisted, basically, in the unbelievable fact that it had been able to survive for twenty centuries without the *revision of life* method. Apologists could now be at ease. This method, in case someone is not familiar with it, is nothing other than (what follows is not a joke) a simple reflection in which the deduction is replaced by induction: a simple everyday fact is chosen, and general principles would be applied to it. Considering the reason for the course, now we really were able to confirm beyond any doubt that we were witnessing the authentic *discovery of America,* not just of the Mediterranean Sea. Now, finally, the New World could be evangelized, thanks to this revolutionary method.

Surely someone will think I am exaggerating. It is completely understandable insofar as I would too if I myself had not experienced it. This disbelief is one of the dangers that must be faced by anyone who dares to make something like this known: there is no other option than to admit how story–like and difficult to believe these things are for normal people. Once again, as happens so often, reality outdoes imagination. And anyhow, everyone winds up finding out that what is usually understood to be *normal* is not exactly normal among some people, especially in certain, well–known and typical environments.

As far as I am concerned, I confess that I feel incapable of understanding how so much importance is given to the use of a series of simple didactic methods, whose relative value, on the other hand, I am not going to deny. This excessive value given to such things may have been influenced by the mirage of novelty. I tend to think, nonetheless, that there is an even deeper and more concerning reason. I believe it is entirely due to a loss of the sense of the supernatural —we might as well say that it is a lack of faith— that has, in turn, led to an overrating of the means, on the one hand, and to an error in the evaluation of their proper place in the hierarchy of things, on the other. As anyone could have guessed, I, logically, did not have anything against the *revision of life*, and my uneasiness came simply from my unwillingness to believe that this method could ever be the panacea for all evils.[4]

---

[4]Through the years, I often have had the occasion to experience, and with no little curiosity, the strange tendency of many clerics to attribute a *magical* —one could even say *infallible*— nature to certain purely natural pastoral procedures.

In my opinion, the greatest problem with this method does not consist in giving too much importance to the means, because the ensuing failures always take care of putting things into perspective. The worst thing about this error of evaluation is that it leads to the neglect of, or at least the disregard for, the supernatural means, which cannot be absent in any pastoral method. If prayer and sacrifice (for example) are practiced with both sincerity and generosity, any amount of *revision of life* can be added; it can't do any harm; but if none at all is added, the outcome will very possibly be exactly the same.[5] Pastoral work should be done with unchanging, constant values that are, above all, of supernatural content. Using those values as a foundation, all convenient methods can then be put into practice —as long as their status as *methods* is not forgotten—, with the assurance that good results will come forth. Nonetheless, when the supernatural is forgotten or left aside, nothing but failure can be expected; along with the deception and disgust that follow and lead to who–knows–where. Avant–garde theology, which for a long time criticized an alleged *objectification* of the sacraments, has itself fallen into this phenomenon in an even greater way: yesterday it was the revision of life and today it is the commitment to the marginal-

---

[5]Even though this last comment may scandalize *expert* pastoralists and sociologists, I stand firm in what I have said. On the other hand, I imagine that someone may object that supernatural life is always a given, and that no one tries to set it aside when using these methods. This is most likely true. And this is exactly what may be said —and I am not going to judge intentions—, *but it is not, in fact, what is done*; as I myself can testify according to what I have seen in forty years of pastoral life. Reality demonstrates that these methods are abused, while those of a supernatural nature are ignored. And people, including the clergy, end up giving credence exclusively to that which is the only thing they hear. Besides, who, today, remembers anything about the *revision of life*?

ized, pacifism, consumerism, or machismo, just to state a few.[6] I am ready to believe that Christian existence is compatible with the exercise of multiple and frequent revisions of life —the more the better—, and with what is understood today as the commitment with the marginalized. But to think that everything depends on *one of these approaches* seems to me dangerous. If this attitude also implies leaving aside other elements of Christianity that are just as necessary, the danger level rises. The Gospel is too rich and diverse to try to enclose it in just one container. In principle, anything can be used to make it known to men: all things human, and all things created by God;[7] but no one should be allowed to try and limit it to the narrow–mindedness of certain idealistic notions that, being purely human, are always partial and fragmentary.

---

[6]This machismo is one of the most puzzling traits that I have seen on the list of worries of today's Church in North America; however, this Church suffers so many real and serious problems, but they do not seem to bother anyone. Afterwards, with the passing of the years, other, even greater problems have appeared; perhaps as a result of not having dealt with the truly important ones from the very beginning.

[7]Tertullian was proud to proclaim that what is Christian is also human.

II

POWER TO THE LAITY

One of the most disquieting phenomena in the years after the Council, whose full consequences for the Church are known only by God, was the earthquake caused by the so–called *promotion of the laity.* After the first moments of commotion, everyone became convinced that, after a long history of belittlement and unjust discrimination, at last the hour had arrived for lay people to be put in the place they properly deserved.

Some time ago, a priest friend of mine told me something that he had learned from a prestigious ecclesiastical figure. The anecdote, according to this person, clearly showed the high regard the Church currently gives to the laity. He proceeded to explain that the Vatican Swiss Guard now gives a martial salute to bishops and lay people, but not to priests. Logically, I did not give credence to my friend's report; for, although it is true that not all crazy people are in mental institutions, it is difficult to believe that the Swiss Guard has reached such an extreme, however much in tune they may be with the findings of the new theology. But what is most surprising of all is not so much the story in itself —which is absolutely unbelievable— but the fact that sensible people can have accepted it and told it to others as if it were true. It seems as if our illustrious cleric not only considered it to be true, but even granted it an uncontroversial demonstrative value (as always, *Roma locuta,* etc.). I told my friend my profound conviction that, in the incredible case that this preposterous tale were true, the only thing it would prove was the idiocy of either the Swiss Guard or, in any case, the Monsignor who had ordered such an absurdity.

The truth is that I have never fully understood the problem of the promotion of the laity; probably because I also could never understand the need for the laity *to be promoted.* My naiveté has always led me to the belief that the laity have a specific and fundamental place in the Church, so well defined and specified that it does not at all have any need to be promoted *from above*; and even less by ascribing to them clerical attributes and competencies. For simple people like me, it is difficult to understand why lay people need to take on the duties of a cleric or a sacristan in order to become more like lay people. I must admit that, even from its inception, this endeavor of the experts and trendy theologians sounded to me like a new type of clericalism. Now I am convinced of something else: the grievances in favor of the laity have always bothered the clergy more than the laity themselves. In those years, at least in Spain, common people lived Christianity better or worse —undoubtedly with more faith than now— without caring too much about the theological concerns of *avant-garde* experts. I myself think that the anxiety was born, not in the area of normal Christian life, but in the laboratories of pastoral alchemy. This proves, once again, the admirable capacity of human nature to manipulate problems: either by inventing false or non-existent ones or by ignoring the truly important ones. The reasons for all this may not be easy to explain, and I am certainly not the right person to do so. But it is possible that they have something to do with that strange schizophrenic *complex of clerical-*

ism which seems to be an endemic evil of so many churchmen. The undeniable fact is that the *promotion* was accomplished by making the laity more clerical, which may be an indication of support for what I am saying.

That is how a shower of *ministries* fell upon laymen, disrupting forever the tranquility of their Christian existence.

Undoubtedly, the phenomenon was advanced as a remedy to the serious problem of the shortage of priestly vocations; one of the most serious challenges the Church is facing today. I, for one, have always entertained serious doubts as to whether authorizing *lay ministers* was the right solution to the problem. Leaving aside the question of their utility where they were really needed (as this and no other was the intention with which they were established), it must be admitted that the result was an abuse of immeasurable and widespread proportions which is still occurring.[1]

Among other possibly more important effects, it is clear that lay ministries (or the abundance of them) may partially efface in the minds of the faithful the notion of and the absolute necessity for the priesthood. I have always thought that big problems can not be solved with short–lived solutions. What we really need, in my humble opinion, is a great renewal of Christian life, with the consequent promotion of prayer life and authentic spirituality, along with the promotion —truly necessary in this case— of the ministerial priesthood. For, as incredible as it is, some irresponsible theological reasoning actually came to believe that the promotion of the laity could not be accomplished except on the basis of demeaning the image of the priest. In the years following the Second Vatican Council, there already were those who were saying that if this was the Coun-

---

[1]It is not infrequent today to find a parish in the USA *with more than one hundred Eucharistic ministers.*

cil for Bishops and the laity, then a day should probably come when another would be held to dignify the ministerial priesthood and its place within the Church. A commendable suggestion that today hardly anyone seems to remember. The fact is that, given the need to elevate the status of the laity, it seems that the best method they could think of to achieve this was to make the laity share, as much as possible, the status of clerics. Of course things were not presented in this way: *participation of the laity in the liturgy,* and *active lay presence in the sacraments* and, in general, in the life of the Church, were worn–out phrases in those years. But the goal pursued was, in fact, to make lay people more like clerics. Many years have passed since the end of the Council and it cannot be said that the results have been encouraging.

It was a great loss to the Church that the great intuition of Saint Josemaria Escrivá de Balaguer, the founder of *Opus Dei,* was thwarted. He could have laid the doctrinal foundation for the true consecration or sanctification of the laity. His bright idea was easily understood by the genius mind of Pius XII, who quickly encouraged and implemented it.[2] The issue was too important, since at stake was the birth of a new association for the laity to channel their legitimate desires for sanctification and consecration. I mean, of course, the Secular Institutes. Two things were quite clear in Saint Josemaria's mind: that the laity had to sanctify themselves as lay people, and that the Secular Institutes were to be precisely *secular,* no more no less. The founder of *Opus Dei* was able to see clearly the consequences of the separation between *secular* and *religious,* by marking a net distinction between them which the doctrine considers final: on one hand the secular priests and lay people —both

---

[2]To that time belong the Constitution *Provida Mater Ecclesia,* on February 2, 1947, and the Motu Proprio *Primo Feliciter,* on March 12, 1948.

subsumed under the concept of *secularity*—, on the other hand, the religious.

Saint Josemaria developed a good body of doctrine about sanctification and consecration of the laity in which he also included the theology of the vows. The legal structure of *Opus Dei* evolved in later years; only now it seems to deny that the purpose of the vows was in the founder's mind.[3] Anyway, as I have no intention of undertaking any discussion in this regard, I will only say that it is clear to me that Saint Josemaria wanted to incorporate all the elements of the consecration of the religious to secular life; but in such a way that lay people and secular priests *would not lose any of the features provided by their own charisma.* His purpose contained this undisputable vision: stressing the fact that the laity should never lose their character and status as such, neither in substance nor in form. One must admit, to his credit, that he succeeded; thus establishing the basis for making progress in structuring definitely what may have been Secular Institutes.

But post–Pius XII theology did not know, or would not understand, the problem,[4] and Secular Institutes ceased to be *secular*

---

[3]I do possess conclusive evidence that he had such a purpose and that he actually carried it out; which, on the other hand, and given the historical context in which the events unfolded, was something entirely reasonable and logical. In my opinion, Saint Josemaria did the best he could within that context.

The events that took place during the following years were the reason behind the founder's abandonment of the legal form as Secular Institutes; and rightly so, in my opinion. Today, Personal Prelature is the canonical configuration of *Opus Dei.*

[4]Perhaps the decision of Pius XII to place the newly born Secular Institutes under the jurisdiction of the Sacred Congregation for Religious was not very felicitous. The fact is that Secular Institutes have continued in that status until the present. The little hopes harbored by some people that the Council, or the new Code, would arrange things differently were dashed.

shortly after they came into existence. Since then the promotion of the laity in the Church has been done by way of their clericalization. If we add to this the strange manipulations to which this doctrine has been subjected, then we must recognize that the effective commitment of the laity to a true Christian life has been often reduced, in fact, to a political dedication, more or less disguised with religious labels. Just when it seemed that Catholic Action had become obsolete,[5] there appeared the phenomenon of lay people who did not limit themselves to *participate*; they even *intervened,* and very actively indeed, in the hierarchical apostolate performing tasks that once were considered exclusive of and proper to the clergy. It was the beginning of an era in which many laypeople were to become part of a new hybrid entity (half clergy and half laity) whose mysterious legal status has not been fully explained yet by canonical doctrine.

I must clarify that I have nothing against the laity carrying out clerical occupations, in so far as these are accomplished according to Law and in response to genuine pastoral needs. Here, as in any other case, it is the Church who has the last word and it is my duty

---

[5]Catholic Action, or *participation of the laity in the hierarchical apostolate of the Church,* lives its heyday under the pontificates of Pius XI and Pius XII. It virtually disappeared afterwards. In its later years, at least in Spain, the various specialized branches that resulted from its fragmentation, particularly the area of evangelization of the working force, fell to the infiltration of Marxist ideology, whose adherents finally gained total control of all of them. This was the destiny of the J.O.C. (Catholic Workers Youth) and the HOAC (Brotherhood of Catholic Action Workers), for example; even the Spanish Communist Union, Workers Commissions, was born in that milieu. The well–intentioned *participation in the hierarchical apostolate* was reduced first to a series of social demands, then to leverage for political demands. Most of these associations were used by Marxists agents with the pretext of fighting the dictatorship of Franco, and under the shadow and blessings of more or less naive and well–meaning bishops and priests.

to accept her decisions. Nevertheless, it is worrisome that, taking advantage of the search for answers to particular problems, there is a real possibility that we may achieve a promotion of the laity that perhaps is not the best; and, in doing so, deprive them —which would be its most dire consequence— of an authentic participation in the mysteries of the Christian life proper to their own *status*. For example, it is difficult for me to believe that the laity *participate* more in the Mass because they do the readings or administer the Eucharist. Even admitting the possibility that such practices could be good sometimes for fostering Christian life, it is evident that there is the danger of walking only half of the way. In the first place, it could be plausible that we are only creating a new kind of sacristan; secondly, perhaps we are allowing the need that the laity have of savoring the mystery of their authentic participation in the life and destiny of Christ to fall into oblivion. Authorizing[6] a good family man to distribute Communion is undoubtedly an interesting experience; but everybody will agree that it is much more important that he become a Christian family man (for it is evident that he is not going to become a better Christian due only to the fact that he is distributing the Eucharist). His true *promotion* as a Christian layman will become a reality when he fulfils his proper and specific obligations: carrying out as a Christian his professional duties, along with his no less delicate and important obligations as husband and father of his children. It would be regrettable that, perhaps because he is too imbided in the duties originated by the faculties he receives in his *promotion* to clerical occupations, or because he is excessively conscious of the importance of his new *status*, this aforementioned family man would forget or would not under-

---

[6]The very word speaks volumes, for it suggests that something is allowed which does not correspond by law to the *status* of the person in question.

stand properly the meaning of his authentic participation in the life and death of Christ: a mission that he must accomplish *as a layman*, in form as well as in content.

Some may think that these things are not incompatible —which could be true, at least in principle. But what everyday life shows is that people dedicate themselves more intensely to what is more dazzling or colorful and, of course, to what demands less effort. Participation in the Liturgy of the Word, for example, requires much less effort than daily fulfilling one's intricate professional duties faithfully or the no less difficult responsibilities towards one's family. Though both tasks are clearly not incompatible, you do not have to be too down–to–earth or knowledgeable of human nature to guess what is going to happen. And if you add to what has been said the possibility —a fact, really— that the doctrine taught has insisted on the first task and has systematically forgotten the second, the danger of deviation becomes even greater: serenity and balance are not usually common attitudes. Also, as we said before, the laity must sanctify themselves as lay people *also in form*, which is an important requirement that is often forgotten. And everyone will agree that administering a sacrament or participating in the Liturgy of the Word, for example, though sometimes convenient, *are not tasks proper to and peculiar to laymen*; or, to say it more technically, *they cannot be considered as constituting their specific form of sanctification.*

I believe it is interesting that nuns occupy themselves, among other things, with giving out the Eucharist in liturgical gatherings; provided that the need for it is demonstrated. But I am afraid that such varied and new tasks are going to make the nuns forget what is essential; as it happened to Martha in the Gospel. Nevertheless, I am convinced that what they urgently need at this moment is to foster their interior life by practicing prayer and sacrifice, in addition to dedicating themselves to the charitable and apostolic works proper to their Institute or Congregation, and always according to their religious spirit. In my opinion, and despite current triumphal statements to the contrary, we are witnessing the greatest crisis in religious life ever before known in the history of the Church. A multitude of religious women have abandoned their convents and have gone to parishes where they could put into practice *pastoral* works: distributing the Eucharist, teaching catechism, and other activities of the same sort. And they do these things with the purpose, so they say, of simultaneously giving testimony of Christian life. It also seemed convenient that they live outside their religious houses, for there are many who consider this the most appropriate measure in order to stay abreast of the problems and concerns of the world. Undoubtedly, these are interesting and revolutionary innovations relative to the customs of the former world. The only objection one could introduce here has to do with the proven fact that whenever too much emphasis is placed on testimony for testimony's sake, we risk forgetting the important detail that testimony must be of *something* or of *somebody*. But he gives a poor testimony of Christian life who has lost or relaxed all interior life and his own religious spirit. In addition to this, and in spite of the official documents and statistics to the contrary, the real–life facts are well patent: empty convents, the tactical withdrawal of Religious Orders and Institutes due to lack of personnel, the absence of vocations, the abandonment of the life of prayer and of ascetic life, the lack of interest for the classical virtues which are the basis for religious vows, as well as the general tepidity and relaxation of religious life. These are clear symptoms that we are experiencing a crisis the likes of which has never been seen before in the Church.

On the other hand, it has not been clearly demonstrated that priests are being relieved from their everyday duties, and thus more available for other activities, because of the ministerial help they may be receiving from the nuns —administering the Eucharist, for instance, or even preaching in some cases. What is actually occurring is a loss of the sacred sense of the Eucharist and a decrease in belief in the Real Presence— among the faithful as well as among consecrated people. Perhaps the presence of nuns intervening in the worship of the Church has meant a great advance; if so, we must rejoice. One last thing remains to be done now: the nuns dedicating themselves to prayer must be present again. They are the nuns who, in spite of never going out to the streets or to parishes and, therefore, not being in any position to give testimony, are, nevertheless, those who pull the Church through. And we should not forget either those nuns who expend their lives, out of love for God, in hospitals, nursing homes, leprosaria, teaching institutions, and other charitable activities. They are the ones who appear as authentic women consecrated to God: more concerned with living their self–giving in love to God (in prayer, in sacrifice, in poverty, in chastity and obedience) than in demanding women's *rights* in the Church; they do not even care about going around proclaiming their commitment to the marginalized.

As for Secular Institutes, I mentioned earlier that, despite the name, they do not appear in any way secular. I think that this is due in part to the fact they are a mixed bag in which everything fits; which may be good in order to simplify classifications, but that is no longer so when the mixture almost eliminates the possibility of the Secular Institutes having a specific spirit and according to the purpose for which they were born. As for me, I smile sympathetically when Secular Institutes announce gatherings for their Congresses;

for example: first of all, their members are warned not to forget to bring the right books to pray the Divine Office. Personally, I love the Divine Office very much, which I have prayed daily for almost forty years, with the exception of few occasions when illness has prevented me. But I can not imagine, though I do try, an executive or a mother praying or chanting the canonical hours. The same could be said of certain customs —praiseworthy in other contexts— which are practiced in many of these institutes. I mean, for example, the practice of lay people being silent at meals, in order to allow for the reading of lives of saints or other pious writings in the so–called *refectory.* Such practices are proper and specific to religious life; some of them are legitimately shared with the secular clergy, as the recitation of the Divine Office. But they have very little to do with the style of sanctification proper to the laity.[7] There is even the legal absurdity of Secular Institutes of *contemplative life,* probably created with the good intention of complicating things further. No matter how very supportive one may be of contemplative life — moreover, it would be nice if this life were more common among Christians—, it is difficult to think how a good secular priest or a true layman *could possibly dedicate themselves officially to contemplative life* without disrupting the responsibilities inherent to their status and condition. Even if we admit that any Christian can be contemplative in the midst of the world, we must not forget that one thing is prayer or contemplative life, and quite another thing

---

[7]I have nothing against the laity praying the Divine Office, although it is clear that this is a ministry very unique to religious and priests. And, while encouraging its practice among the laity can only be good, it can not reasonably be expected that such a practice becomes a general one or a pious devotion characteristic of the laity. It is regrettable, however, that devotions, to which the Christian people has always been healthily attached, are no longer practiced, as the recitation of the rosary and fervor for the saints.

the state of contemplative life. We must concede that the latter is in itself a situation difficult to fit with a secular state of life. Some timely clarifications from the Magisterium to shed light on these issues may also be needed.

Anyway, I have the impression that the problem had barely started, and that the praised *promotion of the laity* would have much more serious implications for the Church than those listed here. I have always been fearful that far greater evils await us: *The second woe is past; and, behold, the third woe cometh quickly.*[8] It is certainly not good to sow the wind because we will surely reap the whirlwind. And this is precisely what seems to have happened in the Church.

The much–hyped *promotion of the laity* was to bring about too important consequences in the Church; such as probably no one could have predicted or imagined.

It would be difficult to try to explain the meaning and scope of such promotion. Probably no one has ever known it. But this is precisely what happens with happy expressions, or lucky if you want: they are well liked and warmly welcomed; but nobody calmly ponders what they mean. Topics, for example, are but a subspecies of felicitous expressions (except for those too boring which are typically used by the clergy), and, of course, they are not expected to have any conceptual content: it is enough that they sound good.[9]

But why was it necessary that the laity be *promoted*...? And what exactly would such a promotion be?

---

[8]Rev 11:14.

[9]True human folly not only opposes, of course, the folly of divine wisdom; it also completely ignores all vestiges of human rationality. The folly of men is but a war to the death against anything that involves a hint of rationality or wisdom; whether it be divine wisdom itself or a participation of it as far as the human reason is capable.

Everyone knows that the simple formulation of these questions is a trigger for scandal. Although scandal in this case, as happens in many cases, *is but one way of trying to conceal the failure to provide a convincing answer*; that is, irrationality once again against rationality.

A dispassionate examination of this issue cannot but conclude that *to promote* means nothing other than *to raise a person of rank or status*. This sounds easy and simple. The problem comes when you apply that concept to the laity; a multitude of questions immediately arise whose answer is hard, if not impossible, to find.

III

THE PROMOTION OF THE PRIESTHOOD

(THE GREATEST STORY EVER TOLD)

Much has been said and written about Cervantes' intentions in writing his *Don Quixote*, postulating the existence of a certain philosophy in the book. This implies that Cervantes was impelled to write it due to reasons deeper than what appears at first sight.

Simplest explanations, however, are often the truest or at least the ones that most closely approach reality. In spite of this, if anyone dares to hold to a simple and obvious explanation, disregarding profuse and unnecessary deeper explorations, he will automatically join those ignored by High Critics. But this is a problem only for those who want to make it so and who forget the simple principle that ignorance is the aspect most congruent with and peculiar to an ignoramus.

And what seems most obvious and simple at first sight (or at least what I believe) is that Cervantes intended nothing other than to end what he thought to be a horrible plague: books about knight errantry.

It is also necessary to recognize that great literary works, whether prose or verse, often go far beyond the purpose intended by their authors. And it would fitting here to mention (using a subtle and distant analogy) what happens to the so–called charism of prophecy, where the content and meaning of the visions far exceed the cognizance of those to whom they are addressed —and even of the seer himself aside from the prophetic statements made by Jesus Christ.

Be that as it may, we will opt for what is simple and obvious, despite the risks this stand entails, and assume that Cervantes wanted to put a definitive end to lore about knight errantry... which suggests that he was moved by his lack of faith, rather than by his personal enmity, with respect to the Order of Knight Errantry.

As for the particular character of Don Quixote, universal criticism has always agreed, with strange unanimity, that Don Quixote was a madman, a raving lunatic. Therefore, no one has ever doubted that what the priest and the barber with the complicity of the Bachelor Sansón Carrasco achieved was certainly a good deed. I mean bringing poor Don Quixote back home and getting him started in the process of recovering his right mind before he died.

That I am surprised at the consensus of opinion about the madness of Don Quixote will indeed be shocking. Thus it seems to me that some kind of explanation may be in order; especially if I am to avoid (if possible) someone becoming too severe and applying to my mind the same epithet used in reference to Don Quixote's.

It is obvious, though not to everybody, that the world has gone mad: governments, politicians, institutions, the world of intellectuals, arts, and culture, the mass population... and apparently even the Church herself —or at least many churchmen, for I do not wish to shock anyone. But if this is so, who can claim that he is qualified to determine that Don Quixote was mad? The mental patients inside an insane asylum (mental hospital, today), for instance, are considered insane; in turn, probably all of them deem the people outside crazy. The only *judicious* affirmation to be made, of course, is that the lunatics are, no doubt, the tenants of the asylum. However, if one is willing to apply logic seriously, one could always ask (possibly leaving much room for discussion): Since when are madmen capable of categorizing other men as any particular variety of madmen? Are we witnessing crazy people with an array of madness diagnosing the diverse madness (purportedly worse ones) of other madmen? But if this is so, as it seems, then we would have to admit that applying the term *madman* exclusively to the patients of a psychiatric facility is merely a social convention commonly accepted by those who are on the outside.

Let us focus on the character of Don Quixote. How can it be explained that everybody, including Cervantes, has always agreed that Don Quixote was mad as a hatter? In reality, Alonso Quijano *the Good*, also known by the moniker that he gave himself: Don Quixote or the Knight of the Woeful Countenance, only wanted to *right all wrongs*. And there undoubtedly are in this world many wrongs to be put in right order. Therefore, anyone who attempts to undertake this task may be called idealistic, romantic, or something similar, but it does not seem right to call him mad for that reason alone. For that matter, even Jesus Christ said of Himself that He had come to seek and save what was lost (Lk 19:10) —although perhaps that is why they also thought that He was a madman (Lk 23:11; Jn 10:20). The truth is that if you emphasize intentions, this issue will not be easily resolved, unless you agree with the world about Jesus Christ not being in His right mind.

Perhaps the practices whereby Don Quixote decided to accomplish his intentions are the only possible justification for determining the madness of our Knight Errant. Intentions aside, it is difficult to believe that the way to right the many wrongs which fill up the world would be the Order of Knight–Errantry.

I, master barber, am not Neptune, the god of the waters, nor do I try to make anyone take me for an astute man, for I am not one. My only endeavor is to convince the world of the mistake it makes in not reviving in itself the happy time when the order of knight-errantry was in the field. But our depraved age does not deserve to enjoy such a blessing as those ages enjoyed when knights–errant took upon their shoulders the defense of kingdoms, the protection of damsels, the succor of orphans and minors, the chastisement of the proud, and the recompense of the humble.[1]

Truly it is not enough that the world consider this or that dreamer a madman in order for him to be taken as such, without further ado. Men have been wrong too many times about this, and it seems that they have not done much to learn their lesson. The same must be said, more specifically, about the procedure followed to reach the conclusion that somebody is mad; therefore, one must be careful before issuing judgements of this sort. For instance, we must never forget that the world has always considered folly the means used by God to redeem man (1 Cor 1: 18–25). Men tend to take little time and use little reflection before discerning between sanity and insanity. However, since the dividing line between rationality and insanity is so vague and open to debate, who can claim to be competent enough to draw it exactly?

However, in order to avoid running into a dead end, we must adopt a safe starting point. So let's admit —maybe it would be

---

[1]*Don Quixote*, II, 1.

better to state a hypothesis we can work with?— that Don Quixote really was a madman; at least in regard to his intention of reviving the Order of Knight–Errantry. That would be easier to reach an agreement, as we have said before, when it comes to his intention of righting all wrongs. This established, and leaving aside, at least for the moment, any related discussions, we can move on to our main topic.

Much has been said and much progress has been made regarding the so–called *promotion of the laity.* So much so, that this promotion almost seems to have been already accomplished, even if there is still room for improvement. Unfortunately, it has happened here what often occurs when one —and only one— of the terms of any relationship is emphasized, namely that the other is forgotten. On the occasion of the celebration of Vatican II and during the turbulent times of its aftermath, voices were heard (admittedly few and timid) which dared to claim the promotion of the priesthood. The Council —it was said— had dealt enough about the Pope, Bishops, new ecumenism, the promising dawn of the Church (*Gaudium et Spes...*); and, of course, it had also spoken abundantly about the laity. Maybe that was why it barely had any time left for mere priests.[2] Consequently, there were those who even suggested that there could be a need for a future Council which would address this apparently omitted issue.

It seems, however (and everyone will agree on this), that the chances of holding another Council in the near future are very slim. In fact, many years have passed since the last one, and no one thinks about it any more, neither in a short, nor medium nor long term. And the odds that this possible new Council would focus on this

---

[2] It must be admitted that the Decree *Presbyterorum Ordinis* was probably the most inconsequential of conciliar documents.

specific issue are even more remote yet. Meanwhile, for one reason or another, priests have reached this deplorable situation which they live at the beginning of this century. Many, no doubt, will want to qualify this statement; others will not be so benevolent and will reject it outright.[3] Truly speaking, toward the middle of the past century, when enthusiasm for the Pastoral Guidelines for Workers was in full swing, it was very fashionable to talk about *poor priests* (the only ones, it was said at the time, capable of providing valid testimony). There was so much talk about this issue that in the end, as it usually happens, nobody paid attention to the *poor priests*, or thought about the wretched priests; and this last affront was really serious; which is another reason that could have endorsed the need for a new Council.

It is not my intention here to make a detailed exposition of the so–called *crisis of priestly identity*, of which much has been said (I have addressed the issue in other works). But since it is useless and impossible to deny its existence, posing the need for *some* promotion of the priesthood does not seem a trivial matter. And I think it is fair to add, although it may sound shocking, that the even stranger fact is that nobody seems to feel the need to bring this promotion to the table.

Anyone who is fair–minded will agree with me about the (urgent) need to *promote the promotion* of the priesthood. Who could oppose such an endeavor or who would find anything wrong with it?

---

[3]Priests can rightly be referred to as *poor curés* when one takes into account what is happening, for example, in countries like the United States of America. It is a sad and unfortunate situation; nevertheless, one can neither justify the crime nor fail to admit that the perpetrators must be punished. And yet, one must refer to those priests as poor curés. The offenses are so serious that they demand an inquiry to uncover their deepest causes and to learn who the true and ultimate guilty parties are.

Presumably, it would not be difficult, therefore, to find candidates willing to enlist in this new Crusade.

But before going forward, some particulars must be made clear. The identity crisis of the priesthood became more acute with the occasion of the Second Vatican Council, but it had begun before then, and some attempts to mitigate it had been already made.[4] Efforts to tackle the problem intensified throughout the ensuing decades, but without satisfactory results; worse yet, these efforts were the main contributors to the worsening of the crisis.

Why? In my opinion, because the wrong approach was used; indeed, *the method chosen was at the opposite pole to the one really needed.*

Precisely the same thing happened with Don Quixote. While everyone could agree on the need to redress the wrongs (let us also establish this as a working hypothesis), in this case the mistake was made in tackling the task at hand by reviving the Order of Knight–Errantry. Put more clearly: while intentions might have been good, the methods used were by far inappropriate.[5] Thus the idea of adapting the priesthood to the demands of the modern world, presented as an agonizing and urgent need, became indisputable dogma for conciliar and post–conciliar theology; although this was but one more draft of the many that blew at the time (and are still blowing) along with the winds of reform.

To be totally precise, there is one statement to be made which could seem astonishing: Christian Priesthood does not need to be

---

[4]Let us remember the missionary initiative of the *worker–priest* established for the so–called *Missions of Paris* and approved during the pontificate of Pius XII.

[5]I have said that I am using a working hypothesis, one that is necessary to analyze the problem we are dealing with. It would take us too far (or nowhere at all) to examine in detail the intentions of those who supported such a tremendous change of bearing. Besides, judging intentions is not our undertaking.

promoted: it was sufficiently instituted by Jesus Christ as participation in His own Priesthood and having its same characteristics
(Jn 17:18; 20:21). The Priesthood, therefore, has been *constituted*
for men, once and for all and forever, according to the Order of
Melchisedech (Heb 5: 1 ff.). To speak about the need for a future
Council in order to confront this problem would not make any sense.
The alleged promotion of the Priesthood —should words have any
meaning at all— would imply the need to elevate its *status*, which
would lead to the admission of strange conclusions: that the Priesthood, for example, had not already been given its proper place by
Jesus Christ; or that the Church can discover in the Priesthood a
new identity or characteristic which had gone unnoticed for more
than twenty centuries; or, and which is even more absurd, that the
Church can *elevate* the Priesthood to a higher dignity and position
than it has already been given.[6]

Even more: If the Catholic Priesthood, given its present crisis
situation, must be promoted, such promotion must be attempted in
a manner contrary to what is commonly thought and practiced, as
we have said before. In other words, to increase the dignity of the
Priesthood *does not mean to consider its elevation in rank, dignity,
or significance according to worldly standards* (Jn 5: 41–44; 7:18;
8:50), *but rather to insist upon the way which leads to humility,
acceptance of persecution, and loathing on the part of the world. It
cannot be otherwise if we accept that the Priest is another Christ*

---

[6] A similar argument could be made about the so–called promotion of the laity.
But the baptism instituted by Jesus Christ already promotes *sufficiently* those who
are not part of the clerical establishment. And while it is clear that one can always
delve further into the characteristics of a simple Christian, this has not been the
path followed by modern theology. It is absurd to think that the social conditions
of any given time can delete, or even blur, the ontological *status* of the sacrament
of baptism.

and that his mission is but a continuation of the mission and work of the Master (Mt 20:28; Mk 10:45; Lk 22: 26–27; Phil 2: 7–8). The most effective way, in fact the only one, of promoting the Priesthood is to place it into its proper condition of permanent *kenosis*.

There were many post–conciliar theologians who claimed/held the identity crisis in the Priesthood as an indisputable truth. The idea that a Priest ought to appear no different from other men — his dress, his social condition, questioning the need for celibacy— became widespread. The existence of the crisis could not be denied, but much more could have been said about its causes. For my part, I have always been convinced that it was artificially induced, finding support, above all, in the rabid secularist environment which had overtaken the ecclesiastical ambience. I have always believed, likewise, that the determination to suppress all signs of differentiation of the Priest relative to the surrounding world is an idea contrary to the doctrine of the New Testament.

In reference to the artificial causes of the crisis and, consequently, the fallacious manner in which the problem has been laid out, one has only to remember what was said above about the identification of the Priest with Jesus Christ, Whose mission the Priest continues. If it is admitted that the identity crisis affects one of the two members of this partnership, one must then acknowledge that the other integral part is also affected; the result could be a total disdain for the purpose of the Incarnation as well as for the mission of the Word Made Flesh and His coming into the world. The character of *co–redemptor* cannot be considered alien to the office of the Priest, for he continues and *consummates* the mission of Jesus Christ (the Virgin Mary also being co–Redemptrix, and more properly so). There is no participation in the Priesthood of Jesus Christ without co–redemption (Heb 9:22) if one admits that redemption is the chief reason for the Incarnation and the anointing of Jesus Christ as High and Only Priest. Hence, the tremendous importance of the passage of Colossians 1:24, and of other texts: 2 Corinthians 1: 5.7; Philippians 3:10; 1 Peter 4:13.

We should add that Scripture passages about the distancing (estrangement) of the Priest from the world are very clear; and that Tradition is just as forceful and far from hesitation.

In Hebrews 5:1 we must take both expressions *ex hominibus assumptus* and *pro hominibus constituitur* at face value; that is, each of them with its most profound meaning. There is no reason not to proceed in this way, since both are parallel and interdependent. But if it can be admitted that the Priest has been *taken from* among men, we must also admit that he is somehow different from them. Once again we find ourselves before another of the numerous antithesis of Christian existence which, in this case, leads to a double phenomenon that we may consider centrifugal and centripetal at the same time. The former, which would be determined by an *outward* movement expressed by *ex hominibus assumptus*, confirms the idea that the Priest has been separated from men to make him different from other people —by attributing to or bestowing upon him something that others do not possess—, but he is still one of them. The efficient cause of this displacement or separation comes from Above (Heb 5:4) and is just what makes this situation possible and, simultaneously, legitimate. At the same time, this distancing would make no sense without a concurrent *centripetal* movement, expressed by *pro hominibus constituitur*. This is the same as saying that the Priest is someone who has been separated from men so that he can be sent back to them. This separation, which necessarily implies attributing to the chosen one an unmistakably distinctive character with regard to his brothers, not only does not estrange him from them but, in fact, it does just the opposite, for it makes him more intimate and close to his brethren. The first movement of separation is necessary to distinguish the Priest as a man of God and witness to Jesus Christ; otherwise, he would have *nothing* to give or communicate to his brothers. It is important to emphasize the fact that his distancing or separation from other men does not diminish the human condition of the Priest; on the contrary, it elevates and highlights it. It is similar to what happens to Jesus Christ in the Hypostatic Union: His Divinity does not diminish the fullness or authenticity of his Humanity —true *God* and true *Man*. And it may be convenient to mention, in passing, that the antithetical separation–return is a paradigm of Christian existence (Jn 14: 3.28; 16:28).

It is beyond doubt that the expression *ex hominibus assumptus* implies an authentic *separation* from the world: *If the world hates you, know ye that it hath hated me before you. If you had been of the world, the world would love its own: but because you are not of the world, but I have chosen you out of the world, therefore the world hates you...*[7] *I have given them your word, and the world has hated them because they are not of the world, as I also am not of the world.*[8] That is why it makes no sense to insist that the Priest, the closest disciple of Christ whose role it is to be *another Christ*, should appear as being identified with the world. Some people talk about *incarnationism* as a means of being accepted by the world, in order to make it possible for them to fulfill the mission entrusted to them. However, it must be emphasized that the Incarnation does not involve identification with the world: *Just as I am not of the world... He came to his own, but his own did not receive him.* Here

---

[7] Jn 15: 18–19.

[8] Jn 17:14.

again the estrangement–approximation antithesis, which is so specifically Christian, appears; without it the Incarnation would be void
of content and intelligibility —and the same could be said about the
mission of the Priest. That is why the *separation* and differentiation
from the world is so essential to the Catholic Priesthood. But we
must not confuse this with a mere *distinction*, which rather indicates
a difference of degree but not one of quality. When this is not taken
into account, when more emphasis is placed on identification with
the world, then, and only then, is when the identity crisis appears.
If the Priest is no different from other men, then who is he and
what does he have to say to them? For that is precisely the tragedy
of Protestantism: a man of the community, chosen and appointed
by the community, *is not capable of giving to the community anything that it does not already have or does not know.* Nothing can
come from the community that is not previously of the community,
since from the wanting of something you cannot get even so much as
another wanting. The community in itself is *incapable* of giving to
anyone the supernatural means that lead to heaven for the simple
reason that it does not have them. Ignorance, doubt, and hesitation
about his own identity is the tragedy in which the Priest immerses
himself when he tries not to feel different from the world. If a drop
of water in the middle of the ocean does not try to be anything but
part of the same water —really becoming one with it— how can
someone even ask if that drop is different from the rest of the water? But the Priest, even though he is among men (Jn 17: 11.15),
has been at the same time chosen from among men. It is true that
the Word came to those who were His own, but *His own people
did not receive Him,*[9] as we have just seen. What men could not
understand when they rejected Him was that they were fulfilling

---

[9]Jn 1:11.

God's plan. The paradox or antithesis —revelation/concealment, wisdom/foolishness, greatness/smallness— became a reality.

Although Cervantes himself probably did not perceive it, there was no doubt that the (authentic) insanity of Don Quixote is the manifestation of the (even more authentic) insanity of those around him. At least Don Quixote was committed to righting all wrongs, while the men of his time (just like those of today) lived in harmony with them and showed no intention of righting them.

Forgetting what is fundamental is what leads Christians to make the mistake of not realizing that Christian existence is a paradox. The greatest project of Divine omnipotence and wisdom, the Incarnation, is at the same time the greatest emptying and lowering possible for anyone driven by love. The mystery in itself which in its double aspect would have been unimaginable for mankind is, at the same time, a display of the infinite magnificence of Divine Glory. As for the Priest in particular, who can do nothing but follow in the footsteps of the Archetype, he cannot achieve *promotion* except by humbling himself. In the present state of the Economy of Salvation, that which is greatest cannot manifest itself except through that which is smallest, just as the greatest sanity does not manifest itself except through the greatest insanity —as can be seen abundantly in the texts of Saint Paul and throughout the New Testament. If the Priest is to be a testimony before men, he must necessarily appear as distinct from them; a differentiation which cannot come about by *rising to a higher level* but rather just the opposite; if his testimony refers and points to Christ, the Priest has no other way except the one that is already drawn and marked, which is the one Christ followed from the *emptying* of Himself in the Incarnation until His death on the Cross: *and where I am going you already know the way.*[10]

In Jesus Christ, God's revelation in concealment reaches perfection, and not only in the events of the Passion but in the Incarnation itself —already in the very fact that the Word becomes flesh. This is an inconceivable paradox on which all the paradoxes of creation and of salvation history converge. For, to be sure, what is fulfilled superabundantly in the Incarnation is what creation had begun: God's expressing and representing Himself, the infinite and free Spirit's creating for Himself an expressive body in which he can, first of all, manifest Himself but, even better, in which He can conceal Himself as 'the one who is ineffably exalted above everything which is outside Him and which can be conceived' (Dz 1782). And there is likewise fulfilled in a superabundant manner what God Himself had introduced into Israel: the fact that, in His own Word, spoken into history and into the hearts of the people, He explains Himself to them ever more deeply and abandons Himself to them ever more defenselessly, and that precisely in this manner He reveals Himself more and more as He who remains inconceivably concealed. All particular considerations aside, the Incarnation of the Word indicates the most extreme manifestness within the deepest concealment. It is manifestness because here God is explained to man by no means other than Himself —not primarily through words and instructions, but by His own being and life. What is most familiar to man is suddenly turned for him into a word and a teaching about God: how could he 'not' understand! But it is concealment because the translation of God's unique, absolute, and infinite Being into the ever more dissimilar, almost arbitrary and hopelessly relativized reality of one individual man in the crowd from the outset appears to be an

---

[10] Jn 14:4.

undertaking condemned to failure. For, if 'man' is truly to become the language of God, this cannot occur by straining man's nature toward the super–human, or by his wishing to stand out by becoming greater, more splendid, more renowned and stupendous than all others. He will have to be a man like every one because he will be a man for everyone, and he will exhibit his uniqueness precisely through his ordinariness: 'He will not wrangle or cry aloud, nor will anyone hear his voice in the busy streets' (Is 42:2; Mt 12:19). The insignificant must be manifested in the appearance of what is most significant.[11]

The opposition between these two statements which refer to being in the world without belonging to the world, a necessary characteristic of any Christian, is particularly prominent in the Priest, according to Hebrews 5:1, which asserts both positions. Unless the Priest *is in* the world, he cannot be a living testimony of Jesus Christ; but such a Priest is in no condition to bear that witness if he has not been *taken from* the world.

The problem becomes even more serious when the necessity of being in the world is confused with the (supposed) need of belonging to the world: *I do not ask you to take them out of the world but to protect them from the Evil One.*[12] It is true that the Priest must be in the world; otherwise he would not be able to get close to his brothers and share their existence or even to become all things to all men (1 Cor 9:22). However, at the same time, he must appear to his brothers as somebody different from them, because of the need that weighs upon him to give testimony of Him Who, having become

---

[11]Hans von Balthasar, *Herrlichkeit: Eine theologische Ästhetik*, I: *Schau der Gestalt*, Einsiedelm, 1961. The quotation has been taken from the English translation, *The Glory of the Lord: A Theological Aesthetics*, I, Ignatius Press, San Francisco, 1982, pp. 456–458.

[12]Jn 17:15.

one of us (Jn 1: 11.14; Phil 2:7), remained, however, the *Absolute Other*.[13] It should be clear that it isn't enough for the Priest to appear as different from the world; he must also manifest himself as not belonging to it. Saint Peter, in his exhortation to all Christians, speaks of the obligation they have of appearing before men as *strangers and pilgrims* in the world (1 Pet 2:11; cf. Heb 11: 9.13); which obligation is especially pertinent to Priests.

All of this leads to living a new manifestation of that tense opposition. On the one hand, the Priest must be in the world as the living testimony of his Master; a charge which must be very clear (especially to him).[14] On the other hand, the Priest is forced to live in constant *absence* of his Master which may be described as an experience of Faith and which forces him to live in a continuous state of tension: *I am no longer in the world, but they are in the world.*[15] In spite of this reality —or precisely because of it— the enthusiasm of his faith must be patent before men, even to a level of resistance which does not exclude the shedding of his blood (Heb 12:4); or to a degree of intensity similar to the *insanity* of

---

[13]We must not forget what has been said earlier: the Incarnation is the supreme manifestation (revelation) of God and, at the same time, the absolute *kenosis* (hiding) of the Divinity.

[14]This is a most important truth which mysteriously goes unnoticed: the explicit reality of *being in the world* never becomes consciously effectual to many Priests. Here we are referring to an everyday expression that is practiced by very few: the necessity of having one's feet on the ground. Too many Priests do not know the reality in which they live; moreover, they do not even realize that there is a dilemma: hence the futility of their preaching. It is impossible to be open to that one reality if you are not equally open to the other element that causes tension. In other words, the Priest must be aware of the reality around him without ceasing to be receptive to the reality from above —or, one might say, without ceasing to possess a deep interior life.

[15]Jn 17:11.

Abraham's faith (Rom 4: 19–20) although even more so, since the type or figure cannot be superior to the reality signified. All of this would be impossible *if the Priest appears as just one more in the world and as belonging to it.* The Master was careful to point out that *no one lights a lamp to put it under the measure, but upon the lamp–stand, so as to give light to all in the house.*[16] Saint Paul, who had already spoken of hoping against all hope (Rom 4:18), could have equally spoken, in regards to faith, of a force that inspires belief in what is *invisible,* in spite of what is *visible* (in the sense of Heb 11:1).[17] In a post–Christian world as ours, the attitude of a Priest can be no other than accepting God's point of view, so frequently contrary to the world's, and *in spite of all that could seem evident.* According to Saint John, faith is precisely what overcomes the world (1 Jn 5: 4–5). This victory, especially for a Priest, given the situation of the world today, cannot become real without the sacrifice of his own life, whether we understand this in a metaphorical or in a very real sense.[18] For the Minister of Jesus Christ cannot adopt any other position in the presence of the world than appearing before it as crucified (Gal 6:14); which becomes more problematic if it is interpreted in a figurative sense rather than a literal one. The text from Galatians 6:17, *stigmata Iesu in super corpore meo porto, I bear the marks of the Lord Jesus in my body,* has always

---

[16]Mt 5:15.

[17]Faith, as the text says, is the *proof of the things you do not see,* which is the same as saying that the proof is indeed proof *in spite of what we do see;* which is what happens, for example, with the Mystery of the Church. In this way, faith can become the anti–evidence of what is evident (or the evidence of the anti–evidence): the proof that the Wisdom of God reaches much further than the wisdom of man, and also that God's insanity is wiser than human sanity.

[18]The offering of his own life bears no resemblance to a metaphor for a Priest; at least in the sense that his immolation, in one way or another, will always require a suffering that must find its consummation in his death.

seemed obscure to the commentators. It is evident that it can only refer to the fact that the signs of the sufferings of Christ —the most convincing testimony of all— are perceptible in the Apostle. This means that *his testimony of Christ is a true testimony*. The necessity of sharing in the death of Jesus Christ, induced at the moment of baptism, is an experience that must become reality during the life of any Christian, though it will not be consummated until the moment of his death. In the Priest, however, *it is already a reality* from the moment of his consecration by the Sacrament of Holy Orders: since the testimony he must give to the death of his Master is not destined to manifest itself in a constant process of slow maturing, but it must be an evidence that necessarily shows itself *already here and now*.

Whatever sense you give to Galatians 6:17, what clearly is derived from the text is that the living testimony of Jesus Christ, given by the Priest, must be as strong and as clear as the one the Apostle refers to. The textual expression *in super corpore meo*, added to the *stigmata* (whatever these stigmata entail), both point to a perceptibility that tends to acquire the level of evidence. Also, since the context shows that Saint Paul refers here to himself as an Apostle and not as a simple Christian, we must conclude that the appearance of the Minister of Jesus Christ must be distinctive enough so as to *show himself* as somebody different from others. This is why the desire to appear before the world without any difference from other men is contrary to the doctrine of the New Testament and any correct theology of the Priesthood.

Of course what we have said here does not refer mainly to the merely external aspect of the Priest or the way he dresses. Affirming this would minimize and misinterpret the sense of these state-

ments.[19] What has happened here is really a conceptual displacement that has caused a serious problem of profound importance;
namely, the fundamental issue has been replaced by a superficial
approach in order to replace the supernatural context with a purely
natural one. This is an important subject and merits a more careful
consideration.

According to Saint Paul, *God has set forth us the apostles last of*
all, as men doomed to death: for we are made a spectacle unto the
world, to angels, and to men.[20] The Apostle is specifically speaking
of *we the apostles*, which makes us think that he is referring to the
ministerial Priesthood. Thus, the Priest is the lead actor in a performance that, having transcended drama, has entered the realm of
tragedy: *novissimos ostendit tamquam morti destinatos.* Calderón
assigns only to God the role of spectator,[21] reserving the status of
actor to humans —each in his own role; in this passage, however,
the Priest is assigned the role of the main and only actor. This undoubtedly produces within himself a situation of extreme tension,
similar to the actor who finds himself alone on stage, confronting
both the responsibility of his acting and the contemplation of an

---

[19] True, you cannot judge a book by its cover, but the cassock or clerical dress, like
the habit, are helpful to the priest or the monk. Besides, nobody has ever proven
that vulgar and even ridiculous clothing (often unbecoming the social status or
the age of the wearer) facilitates the practice of pastoral ministry. Putting too
much stress on the former way of dressing is as wrong as placing in on the latter.
Furthermore, the appearance of a clergyman donning layman's common clothes
easily suggests that he is somehow nostalgic and envious of the world.

[20] 1 Cor 4:9.

[21] Calderón, *The Great Theater of the World.* The solemn sentence *Act well, for*
God is God! is repeated regularly throughout the Mystery Play.

expectant public.[22] The spectators here are the collectivity of all men, good and bad (the world and men, as the text literally differentiates them), to which one must add all those who make up the supernatural realm (the angels).

Never has such performance been represented, neither so crowded (with Heaven and Earth in common contemplation), nor giving rise to such great suspense. The Greeks distinguished between the People —represented by the Chorus— and the tragic heroes; although the Chorus did partake in the action: Calderón will continue the same tradition in his plays. In contrast, the Scriptural texts of the *First Letter to the Corinthians* and the *Letter to the Hebrews* point to this very important fact: the Apostle is singled out as the only actor, clearly separated from all other rational beings —men and angels— to whom the position of mere spectator is assigned.

Under these conditions, it is difficult to claim that the Priest should not differentiate himself from the rest of men. In the drama to be represented in the Great Theater of the World (which, in this case, encompasses even Heaven as spectator), just as it occurs in the human theater, actors are never spectators.[23] On the other hand, it is not a question of deciding what must or must not be, for the content and signification of the Sacrament of Holy Orders have already been determined solely and exclusively by God. The Priest is

---

[22]The situation of the Priest is, if possible, more tragic because he has not chosen it; God does not consult beforehand with those concerned to carry out His *free* election (Mk 3: 13–14; Jn 15:16; Heb 5:4). This is an important subject to which we must return later.

[23]The so–called *Interactive Theater* is a hybrid product that has never prospered. In fact, it has been put into practice —just as attempts have been made to make the Priest perform tasks of the layman, and the layperson Priestly tasks. The results have always been the same in both cases: it is impossible to avoid the perception of witnessing a denaturalized product.

what he is, without his being able to structure himself as something different according to purely human parameters. Man would never have been able to configure, on his own, what pertains to the strictly supernatural order, such as the Christian Priesthood. He could not have even fathomed that the function of his ministry —his role as *alter Christus*— would be accomplished based on a contraposition of wills: the election by God and the compliant answer of a human will freely accepting a destiny which will end in tragedy: *God has set forth us the apostles last of all, as men doomed to death...*

If the role to be played by the Minister of Jesus Christ in accordance with the will of Him Who has summoned him develops itself within a tragic drama with an expected and consequent end, to speculate about the *promotion* of the Priesthood makes no sense —at least in the manner in which one usually understands this term. Hence, one can safely say that the Church will do nothing to foster that promotion, neither in a next Council nor in any other Council. Nor can it be expected that the Church will display any intention whatsoever to promote a condition which has already been set in its proper place by God. The drama–tragedy, along with its outcome proportional to the grandiosity and logic of the play, has already been written and revised by the Divine Author. Thus, the actor, in this case and always, cannot intend to do anything except perform his role well. The current crisis of the Priesthood within the Church has served to make it patently manifest that the post–Conciliar Priest has the possibility of reaching the loftiest point of his vocation and destiny, namely that, at the culminating moment in which the drama has reached its climax, he finds himself compelled to make his talents as an actor shine forth before an expectant public contemplating with eagerness, observing with curiosity, and anxiously awaiting a successful outcome. It makes no sense to

try to promote that which is destined to *descend* to its final destiny
of immolation and death. Saint Paul explains it to the Faithful in
Corinth: *We are fools for Christ's sake, but you are wise in Christ;*
we are weak, but you are strong; you are honorable, but we are de-
spised. Even unto this present hour we both hunger, and thirst, and
are naked, and are buffeted, and have no certain dwelling place; and
labor, working with our own hands: being reviled, we bless; being
persecuted, we suffer it: being defamed, we entreat: we are made
as the filth of the world, and are the offscouring of all things unto
this day.[24] Just as it happened with the Cross of Christ, those who
work to destroy the Priesthood are fulfilling, without intending it,
the saving plans of God, Who has wanted to align some men with
His own Passion in a particularly intimate way. For these men, this
is about the fulfillment of a co–redemptive destiny which escapes
human understanding and counts, in this particular case, on the
role and mission of the Priest as *alter Christus*. In the face of the
most difficult moment which the Church has suffered throughout
her history, this is the opportune time for the grain of wheat to fall
to the ground and die; never before has there been such a need to
carry this out nor such a fitting occasion to see it through.

Throughout the centuries, men have received in various ways the
Word of God addressed to them. Sometimes, they have welcomed It
with good will and as an indispensable way of salvation; more frequently, with skepticism and rejection (Jn 12:48, 15:22). As to how
to interpret It, methods have evolved from the strictly literal to the
most varied forms of allegory and, since the Age of Enlightenment
to modern times, to the liberal systems: rationalism, historicism,
and analysis of forms, etc. Most of them, however, have something
in common. They tend to excise the unquestionable fact that the

---

[24]1 Cor 4: 10 ff.

Word of God in the Bible, from the first verse of Genesis to the last of Revelation, is most certainly the Word of the Spirit directed at men about a single central theme, which is Christ. Currently, many of those who accept It and use It in good faith often do so in a superficial way. However, if we assume that the Word of God is the sword of the Spirit (Eph 6:17), alive and effectual and sharper than any two–edged sword (Heb 4:12), we must conclude that It can only be read, understood, and interpreted (up to certain layers of depth at least), in light of the Spirit to be led by Him (Jn 16: 12–13). The example of the famous (and unfortunate) liberal, rationalist distinction, now a commonplace in theology, between the *historical Christ and the Christ of faith*, is illuminating. The fact is that the historical Christ cannot be understood but through the Christ of faith; in turn, the Christ of faith is but a wisp of smoke if one ignores the historical Christ.

One of the most pernicious developments of modern Catholic Pastoral activity is its superficial use of the Word of God in Catechesis particularly in preaching. Certain issues contained in the Word are even spirited away because they may make present day men feel uncomfortable. Thus, sometimes the preaching is focused on pointless topics that are absolutely meaningless; at other times, which is much worse, the preaching never touches upon particular issues that men do not want to hear about. *There shall be a time when they will not endure sound doctrine; but having itching ears, shall they heap up to themselves teachers after their own lusts; and they shall turn away their ears from the truth, and shall be turned unto fables* (2 Tim 4: 3–4). The reasons for this phenomenon are mainly two. The first is the abandonment of prayer; to which one could also add the depreciation of study by the Shepherds at large (Bishops and Priests). From the moment one stops listening to the voice of the Spirit, he inevitably falls into the commonplace. Hence, the faithful are subjected to the annoyance (which develops into boredom) of listening to long speeches during which they have the opportunity of experiencing a real wonder performed by the preacher: *speaking without saying anything.* Another procedure frequently used is resorting to some slogan of the moment, which, though lacking in content and being usually false, overrun the media: the press, radio, television, and official speeches. People simply accept them, to the extent that they desperately want to be deceived and not have their lives mixed up in anything.[25]

The second reason, more important, if possible, is the loss of the supernatural sense within the Church. The ecclesial establishment has replaced the issues related to salvation with those of merely human content: human rights; social justice; pacifism; dialogue and understanding among men; along with plenty of modern theology jargon: pacifism and the union of nations; all men are good and Christian;[26] all religions are legitimate paths to salvation and possess some truth; and a long list that always leads to the same topic which the now–forgotten Maritain already pointed out: the inferiority complex of the Church and her kneeling before the world. This is how we came to accept a merely *human* morality (if one can consider human the acceptance of principles that go against what is most essential in human nature; for example, the attacks on the indissolubil-

---

[25]We could also speak of another more serious procedure: *the chattering of prejudicial flattery.* Not a few preachers, writers, and religious journalists think that the speeches or allocutions of many hierarchs of the Church are absolutely perfect, totally enlightening, beautifully crafted, quite timely, perfectly doctrinal, accurate in their analysis of current events, lacking any fault or defect or anything of that sort, and so on. It does not matter that those speeches lack content, often times are tiresome or deal with issues for which the ecclesiastics are not competent or, which is worse, they ultimately forget their main purpose, that of spiritually feeding the flock. What is the purpose of so much flattery? To perhaps obtain some advantage? Or maybe to be part of the list of possible candidates for promotion to this or that position? If so, we clearly contemplate an unquestionable search for *promotions*, but one whose intention is polar opposite to the true Christian meaning of priestly promotion.

[26]The so–called *anonymous Christianity* is one of the major findings of Karl Rahner that has been greeted and applauded by modern Theology. Preaching about utopias from rooftops is one of the worst plagues suffered by Western society since the nineteenth century. Utopias are one of the more subtle tools for deceiving peoples, ranging from the most cruel and bloody (like Marxism), to those which proclaim naiveties such as universal peace and human rights (whose implementation throughout is considered imminent), reaching to the stupid ideas of Rodríguez Zapatero, President of Spain, with his *Alliance of Civilizations.* When utopias are removed from their specific field (which is none other than mere literature), they become a dangerous, even deadly, weapon.

ity of Christian marriage or the *legitimizing* of sins such as homosexuality or contraception); the dissemination of false ecumenism claiming that all religions are valid; the manipulation of dogma by accepting the tenets of Protestant theology at the expense of sacrificing Catholic theology.

Hence, if we are willing to take seriously the text cited above from the First Letter Saint Paul wrote to the Corinthians, we come to the conclusion (confirmed by experience) that the Minister of Jesus Christ is nothing for the world today but a *fool*, weak, despised, suffering hunger, thirst, and nakedness (hunger and thirst can be experienced in many ways), *buffeted, having no certain dwelling place, working with his own hands, reviled, persecuted, defamed...*: in one word, somebody who is considered *the filth of the world and the offscouring of all things*. Can anybody say more...? For this is a collection of epithets replete with ponderous burdens. There are two possible interpretations of this passage that deserve our attention.

First of all, we must say that this issue seems to be true now more than ever. The crisis (quite real) of the priestly ministry appeared in the wake of the Second Vatican Council and reached its peak in the late twentieth and the early twenty–first centuries. Presently, it has spread throughout the entire Church, although it seems to be more acutely felt in countries like the United States of America, with problems like the scandal caused by the sexual abuse by the clergy; although this is not the most egregious matter that the Church in America must face, as we will show later.

This has contributed very effectively to the regarding of the Catholic Priest, today more than ever, as the *filth of the world and the offscouring of all things*. Moreover, this opinion has become generally admitted within the Church Herself, even more than outside Her.

Thus, from a merely human point of view, which some would call realistic, the discrediting of the Catholic priesthood cannot be greater. The defection of many Priests and the scandalous crimes committed by many others have contributed to deepening the crisis of faith that the Church is currently undergoing. Taking also into account that the so–called *promotion of the laity* was carried out mainly at the expense of minimizing the proper functions of the ministerial priesthood —thus reducing the character of the Priest to a nonentity—, and that the famous theory of the *crisis of the priestly identity* was widely publicized, we can say that the task of discrediting the priesthood was utterly accomplished. Never were the words of Saint Paul more pertinent.

Since we have alluded to the Church in America, it seems important to add that the issue with which we are dealing here poses in that Church an alarming and particular seriousness, for it seems to be more deeply rooted than first appearances may suggest.

Sexual crimes committed by ecclesiastics, although a real and extremely regrettable problem, are but the tip of the iceberg at whose bottom there are more serious issues. In this sense, the clergy scandal is actually acting as a cover to hide other more worrisome matters. I am referring to the tremendous crisis of faith that the American Church is suffering. The heroic faithful lay people who, rather isolated, are still left in this country are not able to analyze this reality.

Again, you cannot see the forest for the trees. The causes of the crisis are complex and varied, and this is not the place for their analyses. It may suffice to say here that, when it comes to seeking accountability for these actually committed crimes, one would have to lay the guilt at the door of those who have given rise to the present situation of abandonment and neglect of the clergy by their Shepherds; which, in turn, has led to an extraordinary state of *spiritual misery*; which is intimately related to the root causes that have brought about the crisis in the Church in the

American nation. A succinct and quick inventory[27] would include the bad *policy* (understood here in its fullest sense) connected with the election of Bishops; the *dollarization* of the parishes and dioceses; the lack of vigilance with regard to training in seminaries, including relaxation of the moral and spiritual life; the concessions and capitulation of the Vatican to the U.S. Bishops (partially determined by dependence of Rome on the American Church), which are leading to a *de facto* schismatic situation; the acceptance of Protestant theology and of all the rationalist, progressive, and neo–modernist ideas; the anarchy in dogma, morals, and liturgy; the practice of a false ecumenism; the increasing influence of Masonry in the Church; etc. All of the above can be summarized by referencing the loss of the supernatural element throughout the Church, which has hurt some places more than others.

Those who, immediately after the Second Vatican Council, called for the promotion of priests seemed to be right. But it is unlikely that anyone could have imagined then, even approximately, that things would go as far as they have. Hence, when we look at the present situation, we should be talking of restoration or reform rather than of promotion (which today would barely have any sense). The *identity crisis* has come to be regarded as something given, and the Church seems too busy with other issues to pay any attention to this one. Which has led to the incessant closing of seminaries and novitiates and, as a result, an increasing number of parishes. In the interim, thousands and thousands of young people cheer the Pope and attend the *Gatherings*; but these meetings are not translated into an increase of vocations, Sunday Mass attendance, practice of

---

[27]As I said, this is not the place to address this problem in depth. There are many American religious analysts (mostly lay people) who have already done so; but they have failed to reach the heart of the problem, something that cannot be criticized. To reach the core of this harmful situation it would be necessary, first of all, to be part of the ecclesiastical world in order to know it better; then, and above all, to have a sufficient regimen of prayer so as to receive light from the Holy Spirit in order to attain knowledge of *all truth* (Jn 16:13).

the sacraments, or boosting Christian life. This reminds me of what the ancients Greeks said in reference to the gay and noisy caravan that accompanied the god Bacchus: *Many are those who carry the thyrsus, but only few receive the favor of the god.* In short, it appears that the Apostle was far from exaggerating when he said, alluding to the Ministers of Jesus Christ, that they have become the filth of the world and the offscouring of all things.

It is remarkable, however, how often people forget that the foolishness of God is wiser than the wisdom of men; and that the weakness of God is stronger than all of them (1 Cor 1:25). For God has His own ways.

It is true that many have fallen and many have defected. However, there have always been cowards, deserters, and traitors in any army of the world. But this does not say anything against the army as such or against those who have remained bravely at their posts. Losing the battle —including one's life, even the lives of all the soldiers of one army— far from being a defeat, can reveal the most exalted heroism. An army never appears more glorious than when all its soldiers have fallen bravely in battle. The Three Hundred Spartans who fell defending the Pass at Thermopylae are still remembered today; or the immortal Sagunto and Numancia; or the response given by Francisco de Melo, Captain of the Spanish Tercios, to the French general who asked, after the battle of Rocroi (1643):

> —*How many were you...?*
> —*Count the dead!*

It could even be that the most glorious destiny of a soldier or an army does not become effective but through heroism in battle (including a possible unfavorable end), wounds suffered, and death itself if necessary. Besides, it is a known fact that *battles are always won by tired soldiers.*

Consequently, the priesthood needs no promotion. It is now, more than ever before, when the priesthood *is exactly in its appropriate place.* The destiny and glory of a Priest, who has been called to be an authentic testimony of Jesus Christ, cannot be but the Cross: *And whither I go ye know, and the way ye know.*[28] It should be a testimony so clearly perceivable as to become evident: *Glorify God in your body.*[29] Indeed, how could a testimony be effective were it not perceivable? The Apostle, therefore, emphasizes that the glorification of God accomplished by the Minister of Jesus Christ before men, his brethren, must also be *corporeal*, so that the strength of his convincing power can be ignored only by men of ill will. Applying this teaching to himself (clearly, he is not referring to the mass of Christians in general),[30] he goes so far as to say *that with all confidence, as always, so now also, shall Christ be magnified in my body, whether it be by life or by death.*[31]

Once more we are at the opposite pole to the theory according to which the Priest should not in any way differentiate himself from the rest of men. The priestly image as a representative of the community is a detritus produced by Protestant theology, adopted now by Catholic theology, thus doing away with the doctrine of the priesthood. No wonder the theory of the identity crisis of the Priest has appeared now. If an orange is committed to being an apple at all costs, a time most likely will come when the orange, because it

---

[28] Jn 14:4.

[29] 1 Cor 6:20.

[30] Although this doctrine can be applied to all Christians, there is no doubt that the passage, when its context is objectively examined, refers in this case directly and mainly to the Minister of Jesus Christ, that is to the Priest.

[31] Phil 1:20.

cannot turn itself into an apple and is beginning also to look less like an orange, is affected by an unfortunate crisis of identity.

The passage from the Letter to the Philippians that we have just quoted establishes that the real and living testimony leads to the glorification of Jesus Christ, which must be attained through the body of the apostle, *whether it be by life* —he said— *or by death.* And Christian death is but the culmination of a life that has been maturing in Jesus Christ (Gal 4:19); the corollary of which is that the testimony is destined to reach it zenith in death. This is what the passage seems to point to: that death is the capstone of the testimony because it becomes the very death of Christ (a patent testimony now for anyone who wants to see). The apostle —the Minister of Christ—, once he has been dispossessed of everything, has lost not only his own life (Mk 8:35) but also his death, for it does not belong to him now (Rom 14: 7–8): *None of us dieth to himself... whether we die, we die unto the Lord.* This does not mean that the death of the Minister of the Lord ought to be merely interpreted as the culmination of a testimony that has been given throughout his life; nothing could be further from the truth. The death of the apostle is the absolutely indispensable *sine qua non*: *Unless the grain of wheat falling into the ground die, itself remaineth alone.* This thought deeply moved Bernanos and underlies his work *Dialogue of The Carmelites,* playing an important role. In other words, the testimony of the apostle about Jesus Christ Resurrected must be preceded by the testimony of Jesus Christ Crucified (1 Cor 1:23; Gal 6:17).

We are now beginning to penetrate the hidden mysteries of the theology of the priesthood. One must realize that the urgency of ministerial testimony, since it must necessarily be accomplished in the *already*, does not allow waiting until the death of the apostle.

The Minister of Christ has to renounce his life —he has to begin to die— *right now*, at this very moment and continuously, as something that is necessary so that others may live; as Saint Paul stated clearly: *Ergo mors in nobis operatur, vita autem in vobis: so then death worketh in us, but life in you.*[32] And so, he could add that death for him was a gain; which can be understood only when one considers that Saint Paul's life was Christ, according to his own testimony (Phil 1:21). However, one should take care not to interpret this text (in connection with the previous one) to mean that the high point of his death would essentially be to become a source of life for others, which would accord this text a rather shallow explanation. If life for the Apostle was Christ, then his death could be understood as profit in that through it he gives the last and only thing he still possessed: Christ Himself; that is, all his Love. It is, therefore, a total self–giving, an absolute and final dispossession: *Father, into thy hands I commend my spirit.* In this way, total dispossession and poverty, which renounces everything to give all and which consequently leads to an absolute death, becomes a source of life for others. But it is absolutely necessary, first of all, to be in love with Jesus Christ and then to be willing to surrender that Love —a terribly painful moment, beyond all comprehension, that depends entirely on that prior love. In effect, *this is the only self–giving that makes sense to the lover*, everything else is worthless: *For Him I have suffered the loss of all things and count them as dung.*[33]

For him who is in love, his *entire* life is his Beloved, the only one who counts for him; so much so that everything else is rubbish. The Beloved is thus the *only thing and everything* that he possesses; the only thing that matters to him, and the only thing that he can and

---

[32] 2 Cor 4:12.

[33] Phil 3:8.

wants to give. When the enamored soul does surrender the Beloved, he becomes lost in total and absolute dispossession: *I live; yet not I, but Christ liveth in me.* The greatest and most sublime proof of love that cannot be bested is that a man lay down his life for the one he loves (Jn 15:13). The Life of the lover is precisely his Beloved... but it was essential beforehand that only the Beloved mattered and that everything else were left behind:

> *Thy love is better than wine.*
> *Thy name is as oil poured out,*
> *Smelling sweet of the best ointments.*
> *Therefore do the maidens love thee.*[34]

>   ....

> *My beloved is radiant and ruddy,*
> *The chief among thousands.*
> *His head is as the finest gold,*
> *His locks are as branches of palm trees...*[35]

But, somebody might ask, to whom and why should everything be given? Of course, to Love and because of Love. But it happens that the Beloved cannot receive everything without previously having surrendered everything. Hence, the moment in which the Beloved is dispossessed of everything coincides with the instant when He receives all. *Through Nothingness to Everything*, said Saint John of the Cross. But then, does one give in order to receive? If yes, could then that self–giving be understood as a selfish giving? We must undoubtedly answer that nothing is further from the truth,

---

[34]Sg 1: 2–3.

[35]Sg 5: 10–11.

since he who is in love *thinks only of giving*. Hence Love is essentially a Gift (the most proper name of the Holy Spirit) and not a Reception. But we must immediately add that there cannot possibly be a Donation without a reciprocal and simultaneous Reception. How could it be otherwise? In the bosom of the Trinity, the Father *thinks* only of giving Himself to the Son; in turn, the Son, Who is equal to the Father, equally *thinks* only of giving Himself to the Father. The result is the essential law of bilateralism in Love. Thus the Holy Spirit is the reciprocal and mutual Love between the Father and the Son. The notable anonymous sonnet beautifully expresses the unselfishness in self–giving out of love:

> *What moves me, finally, is your love, and in such way,*
> *That even if there were no heaven, I would love You,*
> *And even if there were no hell, I would fear You.*

Truly speaking, it surpasses all human understanding that in created love as well as in divine–human love this reciprocity becomes a veritable struggle between the two lovers. Who will give more?

> *He brought me into the banqueting house,*
> *And his banner over me was love.*[36]

This combat shows what we have said before, that each lover *thinks only of self–giving*. The key to understanding this is that, in regard to divine–human love, the lovers —God and His creature— are always able to love more intensively. The latter evidently is; as for God, He is to the extent that He can always see in His creature

---

[36]Sg 2:4.

a more perfect image of His Son, Who is the ultimate subject and reason for His love.

But we said above, with respect to the priestly vocation, that God calls those and only those whom He wants. He chooses some and leaves others aside. But why such a choice? On the other hand, the call to be His minister —to become *another Christ*— is the greatest demonstration of love that God may grant to any of His creatures. And that is why we know that the ultimate answer to the question we have just formulated is Love. But we must immediately add that in the event that there were an explanation to the fact that God loves some individuals more than others, then we would have explained the mystery of love and, therefore, the mystery of God (Who is Love). Hence, as always, we can only try to inquire into the Mystery; with the certainty that we will always stay on its surface. However, such is the nature of the unfathomably deep Mysteries of our Faith that the little we are given to know of them is enough to fill our lives with enthusiasm (which some would rightly call *hope* of the highest degree) and substance (which has also been called *abundant life* in John 10:10).

Therefore, it does not make any sense to inquire why God chooses some men in preference to others —that is, why He loves some more than others. Or it might be better to say that the question has no answer. For if love is essentially free —*ubi Spiritus Domini, ibi libertas*—,[37] then Substantial Love is Infinite Freedom. But Infinite Freedom, in turn, cannot be determined by anything outside Itself, otherwise it would not be Infinite Freedom. And since it is impossible to admit the existence of any reason foreign to that Freedom that determines Its choice, it must be concluded that Infinite Freedom chooses *whom It wants only because It wants him.* Furthermore, if one takes into account that Infinite Freedom is simply Infinite Love, then one can conclude that Freedom's choosing is also an

---

[37] 2 Cor 3:17.

act of Infinite Love. Consequently, Perfect and Infinite Love cannot admit reasons other than Himself that might determine Him; otherwise, It would not be Infinite Freedom nor, therefore, Infinite Love.

The same does not apply in created love, of course. Here the lover is moved to love by the beloved object, in the first place, and only then by love itself. In the bosom of the Trinity (in Substantial Love), the Person of the Lover, the Person of the Beloved, and the Person of the Love Who unites them with infinite intensity are one and the same thing, but not one and the same Person. In divine–human love, Infinite Divine Love —term *a quo*— remains unchanged; but in the beloved creature love is limited due to the finite nature of the recipient —term *ad quem*.[38]

Keeping these considerations in mind, we can sketch some thoughts in connection with the issue we are analyzing, although we do not claim to have found the ultimate explanation. It is possible then to admit that God's election of a man for the priesthood has to do with the logical consequence that the Priest is to be considered as the filth and the offscouring of the world. *Ego autem sum vermis et non homo, opprobrium hominum et abiectio plebis. But I am a worm, and no man; a reproach of men, and the despised of the people* (Ps 22:7). Which seems to be the only way for his testimony about Jesus Christ to be a true and valid one —the notion of a Priest as *alter Christus* appears again. If we connect all of the data mentioned so far, we are ready to show that, also in the supernatural world, only some are apt to be chosen. I am referring to those who are destined to carry out missions where they make up the vanguard of the war or where special (even suicidal) exploits must be accomplished in battle.

This squares perfectly with what we have been saying. Indeed, the New Testament swarms with paradoxes: the entire Christian ex-

---

[38] In divine–human love, the term "*a quo*" in regard to Divine Love is not arbitrary. According to Saint John, *We love because he first loved us* (1 Jn 4:19).

istence is total madness when compared to the way the world thinks.
But when one conscientiously examines the pieces of the puzzle, he
discovers that the whole makes a logical and perfect picture. The
same thing happens here.

As regards Western Christianity, the status of the priesthood is
at its lowest point since mid–twentieth century. A proof that cannot
deceive is the numbers: there has never been such a shortage of vocations and never before have so many seminaries, novitiates, parishes,
and places of worship been closed.[39] It is true that statistics can be
manipulated (and indeed are), but reality is all too evident, rendering the attempt irrelevant. The crisis seems to be so severe that
no one talks about a possible promotion of the priesthood; nobody
even thinks about it. And although a reform would seem to be
the most logical and urgent task to undertake, apparently nobody
is concerned about this problem; which is further evidence of the
seriousness of the situation.

But God's ways, as is well known but often forgotten, are strange
and mysterious, and eventually they always lead to situations and
results which man cannot predict. It so happens that the Christian
priesthood, contrary to what was expected and to all attempts and
efforts carried out against it, is now in precisely the best state for
which it was established by God. The present situation of surviving
Priests, after more than a few turbulent movements and ideological
attacks and many trials that they have been forced to endure, cannot
be better, given the imminent, horrible, and dangerous situation in
which they are going to be immersed at the dawn of the twenty–first
century; a situation that perfectly fits the plans of God.

---

[39]Hardly anyone seems to have noticed that numerous cathedrals, including
many monumental ones, have been converted to museums or places for concerts
and cultural events.

First, because these survivors are prepared for battle, being in optimum condition and possessing those personal qualities that God wants them to have going into difficult and imminent battle (impossible to be won according to merely human standards). In this regard, we should listen again to the Apostle: *But the foolish things of the world hath God chosen, that he may confound the wise: and the weak things of the world hath God chosen, that he may confound the strong. And the base things of the world and the things that are contemptible, hath God chosen, yea, and things that are not, that he might bring to nought things that are.*[40]

And, indeed, God's thoughts are never the thoughts of men. Pastoral experts, in particular experts in fostering vocations, could have possibly planned a smart strategy to carry out the task. It is probable that their strategy, given the *modus operandi* of modern Catholic Pastoral activity, would have been based especially on the methods of action developed by current sciences and sociological techniques (whose ignorance of the supernatural is evident). I use the conditional tense because it is certain that no plans have been made; at least none that I am aware of.[41] Which, far from causing any sensation, should rather be subject to approval. The reason? Because it so happens that, for this specific need, the solution was already given by our Lord Himself (Mt 9: 37–38 and Lk 10:2); *unfortunately*, the answer was supernatural in nature: *Prayer.* Oh, the inventiveness of God! For it seems unlikely that the High Laboratories of Pastoral Alchemy would approve this kind of solution.

If it is true, therefore, that God chooses the foolish and weak things of the world, the base and contemptible things, and things

---

[40] 1 Cor 1: 27–28.

[41] The truth, as painful as it is to admit, is that probably nobody would have been found willing to carry out this experiment.

that are not... And since the Ministers of Jesus Christ —those who have survived the neo–modernist currents that have swept the Church after Vatican II, as well as those intrepid few who make up the Task Force added later— fit perfectly the epithets used by Saint Paul (in the eyes of the world, and perhaps also in the eyes of many members of the Catholic Church), presumably everything is ready for the fight ahead. The advantage this time is not on the part of the enemy, who walks off guard because he is convinced that his victory has been total and complete.

It is important to take into account, nevertheless, that the weakness to which we are referring is such only in the eyes of the world and of men, but not in the eyes of God Who regards it opposite to the world. The scriptural texts about this issue are quite clear.

It is equally important to remember that man —the Minister of Jesus Christ in the present case— must not only be aware of it, he must accept it and love it; for only thus will he be filled with strength from Above. Fortitude is also a matter of love, for the intensity of the strength received depends on one's faith in God: *Pro me autem nihil gloriabor nisi in infirmitatibus meis... But for myself I will glory nothing but in my infirmities...*[42] *Nam virtus in infirmitate perficitur. Libentissime igitur porius gloriabor in infirmitatibus meis, ut habitet in me virtus Christi. For power is made perfect in infirmity. Gladly therefore will I glory in my infirmities, that the power of Christ may dwell in me.*[43] Cum enim infirmor, tunc potens sum. *For when I am weak, then am I powerful.*[44]

After all that has been said, we are now ready to affirm that *there is no need to promote the priesthood. On the one hand, such*

---

[42]2 Cor 12:5.

[43]2 Cor 12:9.

[44]2 Cor 12:10.

a promotion would be harmful, for it would render the priesthood ineffective. On the other, it is now when the priesthood has the status in which and for which it was established: the very status desired by God. The System has plenty of reasons to be alarmed were it not oblivious, as indeed it is. It is providential and fortunate that Evil is always dwelling in lies, self–complacency, and self–admiration, which make It unable to conceive the mere possibility of defeat.[45]

The path to follow in order to attain a true *promotion* of the Priesthood has been perfectly delineated in Holy Scripture. It would be foolish to think that God would leave such a matter to the will of man. This path has nothing to do with the content of a particular formation which, while claiming to be able to confront the challenges of the modern world, is based on criteria of what many today understand as modernity. Educating priests as experts in anthropology, sociology, psychology, promotion of human rights and social justice, etc., does not seem to be the most pressing thing. This could be convenient (or even worthwhile) *as an additional tool* to whatever degree deemed necessary; as long as we seek first the Kingdom of God, according to the formula given to us by our Lord Himself (Mt 6:33).

If the Minister of the Lord is to be the light of the world, and given the nature of his work, it is evident that his formation must be built mainly on the solid columns of Philosophy and Theology. A

---

[45] Obviously, I do not mean to say by this that a thorough reform is not necessary, for indeed it is; starting, for example, with the Seminaries. I simply want to insist on the need to eradicate as soon as possible a whole jargon of words and concepts which, far from leading to anything positive, merely reflects the vain attempts of a progressive Pastoral activity made in Laboratories and of dubious faith. These attempts, say what you want, lead only to a superficial and useless approach to the problems, or to manipulations that seek only to discredit the priestly state.

number of genuine auxiliary sciences might be added to those two, most importantly, for example, History.

But even in this area we must remember the words of Saint Paul: *Scientia inflat, caritas vero aedificat. Knowledge puffeth up, but charity edifieth.*[46] They are not an indictment against science, but rather only a warning that science without charity is worthless: *And if I should have prophecy and should know all mysteries and all knowledge... and have not charity, I am nothing.*[47] Again, it would be absurd to interpret those words as if Saint Paul had a poor appreciation of wisdom: *I would have you all to speak with tongues, but rather to prophesy... that the church may receive edification... I thank my God I speak with all your tongues. But in the church I had rather speak five words with my understanding, that I may instruct others also.*[48] *That the God of our Lord Jesus Christ, the Father of glory, may give unto you the spirit of wisdom...*[49]

It is true that Saint Paul clearly distinguishes between wisdom and knowledge (Rom 11:33; 1 Cor 12:8; Col 2:3; etc.); he is aware that any supernatural wisdom or knowledge requires previous human knowledge as their base. This is a well–known topic: the supernatural not only does not destroy nature, the former demands the latter as its fundamental basis that is to be healed and elevated. Saint Paul expresses this notion very accurately by establishing the existence of a true Natural Theology (Theodicy) as the foundation and previous moment for Revelation (Rom 1: 19–22).

As we have always said, following sound Catholic doctrine, Theology does not make any sense and becomes devoid of content if

---

[46]1 Cor 8:1.

[47]1 Cor 13:2.

[48]1 Cor 14: 5.18–19.

[49]Eph 1:17.

it dispenses with reason. Much to Luther's regret, reason is not a prostitute. In his present condition, man needs the complement of Revelations as a *sine qua non* condition to manage himself in the supernatural world and, as a necessary tool, a security warrant, not to err in the natural world. In this connection, the perfect parallelism and interrelation between faith and reason (despite the infinite distance between them as a consequence of the difference between grace and mere nature) is a *given*, according to sound Theology, for the perfect functioning of the human being. We have referred many times to the deficiencies in the clergy with the practice of *human virtues*. These deficiencies, in my opinion, are but a consequence of flaws in the practice of *supernatural virtues*. We have said above that the supernatural demands the natural as its basis, restores it, and elevates it. But the *restored* natural, although carried out by grace, an instrument of the supernatural order, is still part of the natural world. This explains the frequent *alienation* of the Priest in regard to the world around him; an estrangement that has nothing to do with the *contemptus mundi* of the mystics and much to do with their disconnection from and ignorance of their milieu.[50]

Consequently, his *becoming–another–Christ* is the most important —the only important— thing for a candidate to the ministerial priesthood: his assimilation of the life of Christ (which the Apostle referred to as coming unto the measure of the stature of the fullness of Christ). Without this transformation into Christ, he would be but a mere official, a person without identity to himself or to others, having nothing of his own about which to give testimony before

---

[50]This is the reason behind the lack of authenticity of many homilies and documents issued by some sectors of the ecclesiastical hierarchy, and of their use and abuse of platitudes and inanities. Contrary to what many people might believe, abandonment or neglect regarding the supernatural world inevitably leads to ignorance of and disregard for the natural world.

the world; and this would explain the emergence of the mentioned *identity crisis of the priesthood.*

We have already said that the path has been well marked by Saint Paul for the priesthood of all ages, especially for the one that is living the troublesome times of the beginning of the twentieth century. The Apostle, of course, coincides with our description:[51] *Giving no offence to any man, that our ministry be not blamed. But in all things let us exhibit ourselves as the ministers of God, in much patience, in tribulation, in necessities, in distresses; in stripes, in prisons, in seditions, in labours, in watchings, in fastings; in chastity, in knowledge, in long suffering, in sweetness, in the Holy Ghost, in charity unfeigned, in the word of truth, in the power of God; by the armour of justice on the right hand and on the left; by honour and dishonor; by evil report and good report; as deceivers and yet true; as unknown and yet well known; as dying and behold we live; as chastised and not killed; as sorrowful, yet always rejoicing; as needy, yet enriching many; as having nothing and possessing all things.*[52]

Many books would be needed to comment on these words. Personally, I consider myself unable to even try. But let me state, for the record, that they are extremely consoling words for an old priest like me. Having lived two very different eras in the history of the World and the Church —from before the middle of the twentieth century until well into the twenty–first century—, it is impossible to dispel the impression that these words attempt to poignantly describe, not without grandeur, what could be a coherent depiction of a priestly existence: constant patience quite spattered with endless tribulations, necessities, distresses, stripes, tumults, labours, watch-

---

[51]The text and the context clearly imply that the Apostle is addressing himself directly to the Ministers of Christ.

[52]2 Cor 6: 3–10.

ing, fastings... Indeed, an old priest who had lived intensively his priestly life could hardly restrain his tears. It is evident that the Apostle is acting as a reporter of future realities, rather than as a chronicler of his own time; or, if you prefer, as a prophet, which indeed he was. Truly, many a book would be necessary to comment upon this. Some of the statements of the Apostle are so cutting as to wound the heart and bring tears to the eye. Tears caused undoubtedly by love, but which also inflict sorrow; a consoling sorrow certainly, as Tolkien rightly said: *not all tears are an evil*. More so these tears, for they spring from an enamored heart.

Some of the statements of Saint Paul are particularly important, as when he says that we have been branded as *impostors, and yet we are true*. Indeed, a life spent in love of truth, willing to spread it everywhere —in far and different places, among diverse peoples—, and always running the risk of losing it while exposing it, does not deserve the appellative *deceiver*; but the insult can be embraced out of love, knowing well that it is seen by God Who rewards those whom He loves with a share in the Cross of His Son. Therefore, what can one do but offer heartfelt thanks for such abuses?

Something similar happens with the next expression: *as unknown and yet well known*. The Apostle could as well have said that we are ignored, willfully forgotten, or perhaps silenced; for it is so true that the Powers of this world tend to ignore and silence those who do not please them. And yet, there is great joy in knowing that never is a man more present to God than when he is unfairly ignored by the world (or perhaps even by his own brethren): *The world knoweth us not because it knew him not.*[53] One must recognize that if being unknown to the world is the price to be paid for loving Jesus Christ and for working so that others love Him too, then it is a blessed cost: *One can say of men what is said about nations:*

---

[53] 1 Jn 3:1.

blessed are those who have no history. Men are what God knows about them; nothing more and nothing less.

Especially profound and mysterious is the Apostle when he says that we are considered *as dying and behold we live.* Here it appears that we are facing an abyss of unfathomable depth and amazing beauty. Can we do anything except fall into silence and allow the heart to expand beyond words and concepts which accomplish nothing but, in their inelegance, move us away from the intuition of a magic world able to give us the ineffable *already* first fruits of a *not yet?* It is true that the mere attempt to communicate these sublime words does not seem permissible (2 Cor 12:4). For it is evident that Life and everything It entails or the Life abundant of which Jesus Christ speaks (Jn 10:10) not only are forever unknown to the world, but the world considers them as death. That is why the world thinks that we Christians are dying beings. Yet the Master said of Himself that He is Life (Jn 14:6), and we do know that only He is our Life (Col 3:4). Therefore, what does it matter what the world might think? Can anybody on this Earth be joyful if he does not possess Life abundant, at least as first fruits? Besides, if the Minister of Jesus Christ is labeled by the world (and frequently by the Church herself) as garbage and offscouring, which is as nothing, what is so remarkable about his being considered a dead person? The fact that the world thinks us moribund does not mean anything to the Apostle; only the wonderful reality that we do live matters to him: *and behold we live.* For the authentic disciple of Jesus Christ, to mean nothing in this society is even yet not enough. The seal of authenticity is obtained only when he receives the death certificate. Consequently, and according to the proportion established by the Apostle, the more one is thought of as dying, all the more he lives. Jesus Christ clearly said it when He stated that it is necessary first to die in order to yield fruit (Jn 12:24).

The final part of Saint Paul's programmatic exhortation is arguably the most substantial and beautiful one. According to him, the world also thinks that the Ministers of Jesus Christ are poor, having nothing; in reality, they are enriching many, possessing everything: *Sicut egentes, multos autem locupletantes, tamquam nihil habentes et Omnia possidentes.* It is astonishing to see once more how incredibly profound, how ineffably grandiose are the paradoxes of Christian life. These epithets that the world hurls with contempt/scorn to the face of Jesus Christ's disciples are true praises. Poverty is a sublime virtue and probably the one closest to charity. And the condition of having naught is nothing short of the sublime situation of him who is stripped of everything because he has given up everything out of love. It follows, therefore, that we are in the presence of Love Himself; and also in the situation closest to Love.

According to this, why is the world then turning these concepts into insulting epithets and throwing them at the disciples? Because, according to the Apostle, the sensual man perceives not the things of the Spirit of God; he perverts them and thinks that they are foolishness: *Animalis autem homo non percipit, quae sunt Spiritus Dei, stultitia enim sunt illi, et non potest intellegere, quia spiritaliter examinantur. But the sensual man perceiveth not these things that are of the Spirit of God. For it is foolishness to him: and he cannot understand, because it is spiritually examined.*[54] There is a kind of poverty that the world surprisingly accepts, which we can term *advertising poverty*; for it goes about everywhere promoting itself with the applause of everybody. This poverty is a characteristic of some religious Families and it does not intend to enrich others but only to make itself wealthy. It would be immediately and easily recognized if the world would not love and prefer the lie; for true virtues never broadcast themselves. True poverty does not enjoy

---

[54]1 Cor 2:14.

a good reputation for the simple reason that it does not have any reputation.

It could be said that the world has three standards to determine poverty. There is first the promotional or false poverty, which the world applauds and cheers and totally approves.[55] Then there is poverty that the world considers vile and despicable solely because this poverty disregards the very things, criteria, and behavior that the world appreciates as the only authentic and valid ones. Finally, there is a third kind of poverty that in reality coincides with the one just mentioned: authentic poverty; perhaps its only characteristic is that the world does not even suspect it exists.[56]

---

[55]It would not be an easy task to inquire into the reasons for the world to adopt this behavior. A superficial analysis of things would suppose that the world has made a mistake and will not look further to find out if this mistake is the result of good or ill will. Another explanation would rather believe that the world tries to bribe God. As incredible as it might seem, there are in fact many who think that they can acquire their salvation by giving up some crumbs of their assets as alms. For my part, I rather suspect that the real reason is that the world *feels or guesses that it is a false poverty*, and that is why the world accepts and applauds it; once again, it is the option for the lie (Jn 3:19; Rev 22:15).

[56]It is easy to understand that Christian poverty is that poverty that the world despises and vilifies. Everything then depends on the approach one takes; but the poverty that the world first proclaims for all to hear and then applauds has nothing to do with the Christian virtue of poverty. Nothing to do with spiritual poverty or poverty of the spirit, and nothing to do with material poverty. The latter refers mainly to any kind of money, but it also embraces all types of influence or power, even the fame granted by the world: *Woe to you when men shall bless you: for according to these things did their fathers to the false prophets* (Lk 6:26). According to these words of Jesus Christ, there could be not only false poor but also false prophets —an issue of which He speaks more clearly in Matthew 7:15; 24:11 and other places in the New Testament. Evidently, the fame bestowed by the world, and which can easily be translated into influence and money, is yet another false form of poverty. We have already said that true poverty is recognized by the fact that nobody knows it, and nobody wants to know it.

This is how the taunts of the world become God's praise. *Blessed are the poor!*[57] If Christian poverty is the virtue that is nearer to and most clearly manifests charity, then it must be regarded as a fundamental element in the life of the apostle of Jesus Christ. In the eyes of God, he is poor who has agreed, out of love, to be deprived of everything. In this way, he testifies, visibly, that he only cares about God and that only He is his life. Hence, it is extremely important for the Minister of Jesus Christ to use supernatural means for his mission, and in such a way that he puts his trust only in them, according to the counsel of his Master: *Take nothing for your journey, neither staff, nor scrip, nor bread, nor money; neither have two coats.*[58]

Also, the contempt of the world for the Ministers of Jesus Christ because it thinks that they *have nothing* undoubtedly becomes the greatest praise that an apostle can receive. According to Saint Paul, as we have seen, those who have nothing are precisely the ones who *possess everything*; through Nothing to Everything. He who is truly in love has given *everything* to the beloved person, which is an essential feature of love. And as God in His madness of Love and devouring fire has completely given Himself to man, He equally expects that man repay Him in kind. For the real devouring fire of true Love cannot in any way be devouring —not even of love— if it is not fed by both lovers at the same time and in total reciprocity: *Quia*

---

[57]The speculations of the exegetes with regard to the distinction between the *poor in spirit* of Saint Matthew and the simply *poor* of Saint Luke do not make much sense. Christian poverty is one and the same in both cases. Poverty in Saint Luke is an authentic virtue that has to be determined by the spirit. And as for the passage of Saint Matthew, if we accept that it is really poverty *of spirit*, it must obviously be, first and foremost, true *poverty*. Put another way: either Christian poverty is, also and at the same time, poverty of spirit, or it is not poverty at all.

[58]Lk 9:3. Parallel places, Mt 10: 9–10 and Mk 6: 8–9.

Dominus Deus tuus ignis consumens est, Deus œmulator. Because the Lord thy God is a consuming fire, a jealous God.[59] This devouring fire can bring death. The Divine Lover already died; the human lover dies because he feels that he is dying until his death takes place: *I die because I do not die!* said Saint Teresa of Ávila, echoing the lamentation of the bride in the Song:

> *Stay me with flagon,*
> *Comfort me with apples,*
> *For I languish with love.*[60]

---

[59]Deut 4:24; cf Heb 12:29.
[60]Sg 2:25.

IV

UTOPIAS, SCOURGE OF HUMANITY

Unless either philosophers become kings in the cities,
or those who are now called kings and rulers
sincerely and adequately get to philosophize,
and there can be found in the same person both
political power and philosophy,
the crowd of those who are nowadays driven
by their nature toward either one exclusive of the other
having been forcibly set aside,
there can be no end, dear Glaucon,
to the evils in cities,
nor, methinks, to those of humankind.[1]

However, kings will never become philosophers, nor philosophers crowned kings. The astonishing fact is that very few people know that all utopias are false. We should make a distinction, for utopias may be presented as stories, fiction, or entertaining narrative, in which case they are innocent and inoffensive. But utopias

---

[1]Plato, *The Republic*, V, 473, c–d.

may also claim to be real and necessarily true, and then they become instruments capable of destroying humanity. The latter are precisely the ones that presently flood the world and dominate it.

The title of Chapter 6 of the first part of Don Quixote is rather amusing; it reads: *Of the diverting and important scrutiny which the curate and the barber made of the library of our ingenious gentlemen.* Of course, the action mentioned in this humorous title was something more than mere scrutiny, because it quickly becomes an inquisitorial fire.

It is odd that nearly all commentaries agree in cataloging this chapter as a mere hiatus in the sequence of the novel. It is almost unanimously described as mere literary criticism; through the commentaries of the priest, Cervantes gives his opinion about the popular literature of his time. Miguel de Unamuno himself said that it should be disregarded.[2] Vicente Gaos in his commented critical edition of *Don Quixote* asserts that *this chapter consists of literary criticism, written, in general, from the point of view of Cervantes, whose spokesperson is the priest.*[3]

We could accept this opinion with some reservations. Personally, I don't feel identified with it. Even if we admit the critics' opinion that this chapter is a digression, with which I do not agree, we should not forget that it is part of a work whose intention is clearly stated by the author, which is none other, as everybody admits, than ending the plague of the knight–errantry books. That is why it would seem natural that Cervantes should use this occasion to attack some of the more famous books of this kind in his time, clearly stating his opinion of them (this time through the housekeeper and the niece):

---

[2]Unamuno, *Vida de Don Quixote y Sancho.*

[3]Cervantes, *Don Quijote de la Mancha*, critical edition and commentaries by Vicente Gaos, Madrid, 1987, I, p.129. Martín de Riquer suggests the same in his critical edition with commentaries of *Don Quijote*, Madrid, 2004, p.69.

Here, your worship [holy water and the sprinkler], *senor li-
centiate, sprinkle this room; don't leave any magician of the
many there are in these books to bewitch us in revenge for
our design of banishing them from the world...No, said the
niece, there is no reason for showing mercy to any of them;
they have every one of them done mischief; better fling them
out of the window into the court and make a pile of them and
set fire to them; or else carry them into the yard, and there a
bonfire can be made without the smoke giving any annoyance.*

Vicente Gaos admits being confused by the lack of logical explanations for this chapter: *Despite the danger posed by knight–errantry
books* —he says— *so censured by moralists, Cervantes criticizes them
mainly for aesthetic reasons, which seems strange since the censor
is a priest.* He is right in terming this purge as *strange*; and it is not
surprising that experts may not have reached the possible heart of
the problem. The truth is that both are wrong, because Cervantes
does not criticize these books only for aesthetic reasons; at least that
is what I think. I tend to think that the error of the critics derives
from their lack of an in–depth study of this topic, as I am going to
try to explain following Cervantes himself.

During the scrutiny, grotesque heroes and absurd characters appear; all of them carrying on even more absurd adventures, which,
together, cause the drying up of the brain and the insanity of our
ingenious nobleman.[4] Here the Amadises of Gaula, and the one
from Greece, appear with the Esplandián, Don Olivante of Laura,

---

[4]The expression is used by Cervantes himself: cf. I, Chap. 1, where he also
states that *those intricate reasons seemed like pearls to him... With these reasons
the poor gentleman lost his wits, and used to lie awake striving to understand them
and worm the meaning out of them; something Aristotle himself could not have
made out or extracted had he come to life again for that special purpose.*

the Flormorte of Hircania, and the Knight of Platir, etc. Cervantes
clearly expresses his opinion of them, as clear as midday light, just
in case anyone thought he hadn't explained it clearly enough before:

> —*Then to the yard with the whole of them —said the curate—;
> for even at the risk of burning Queen Pintiquiniestra, and
> the shepherd Darinel and his eclogues, and the bedeviled and
> twisted discourses of his author, I will burn with them the
> father who begot me if he were going about in the guise of a
> knight–errant...*
>
> —*The next one is 'Florismarte of Hircania' —said the barber.*
>
> —*Is senor Florismarte there? —said the curate—; then by
> my faith he must take up his quarters in the yard, in spite of
> his bizarre birth and renown adventures, for the stiffness and
> dryness of his style deserve nothing else; into the yard with
> him...*
>
> —*This —said the barber— is 'The Knight Platir.'*
>
> —*That is an old book —said the curate—, but I find no reason
> for clemency in it; send it after the others without appeal.*

Can we easily admit that Cervantes' criticism is based on aesthetic reasons only, *even though the censor is a Priest* as Gaos says?
I fear that by not studying this issue in depth, we may be underestimating Cervantes' intelligence. It is true that philologists, as
authorities in their specialty, should give the final word; and more
so when they have the expertise of Gaos or Riquer. In their own
field they have no obligation to either study the question more profoundly, or speculate in areas that are not their own. That is why
we cannot reproach them if they do not enter into domains that may

border on Philosophy, since they go beyond the supposed intentions of the author. However, it is never a waste of time to seek a more profound knowledge of reality, whenever possible and as much as possible. This has always been man's concern and this has always been the flame that has continually fed Wisdom.

What Cervantes accomplished with his work was a ferocious invective on books of knight–errantry. In this chapter he goes through some of the best–known examples of his time, though he shows mercy by saving a few from the fire and leaving some others in suspense.[5] Rather than a parenthesis in Cervantes' diatribe, this salvage looks more like a continuation and accentuation of his purpose. What we have here is a direct and scathing attack on those responsible for the mess, without omitting the names of authors that were well known —some of them were still alive and quite prestigious— during Cervantes' lifetime.

It is evident that, if we stop where the language experts do, we must resign ourselves to going no further. But surely it is possible to go further and reach interesting considerations which, on the other hand, do not seem so hard to find, given the trend of the chapter. A mere digression of literary criticism...? One can admit this opinion if he so wishes. But the chapter does not show any sign of discontinuity either with the previous ones or with those

---

[5]Riquer seems to think it is important that some books are pardoned from the flames, and he focuses on the list of the acquitted; though he ends up attributing the different treatment to the literary tastes of Cervantes. That is probably the reason and there does not seem to be sufficient motives to give the incident more relevance. Either way, the general condemnation of such outreach tools is as firm as that of knight–errantry throughout the work. The bucolic and poetic works, also found in the library of Don Quixote, will be commented on later.

that come after. What Cervantes does here, in conformity with his general purpose of criticizing severely such ill–conceived knight–errantry books, is to mention expressly some of them and ridicule their authors. This is exactly what he did in previous chapters (although he adds here certain cruelty as a new ingredient), and what he keeps on doing later.

Everybody agrees that Cervantes had a veritable rancor against the knight errantry books, yet few ask themselves about the reason behind that acrimony. It is evident that Cervantes harbored something much deeper than a mere literary dissatisfaction. His critique against this sort of literature (Knight Errantry) is terribly harsh and pervades his entire work, for *Don Quixote* serves no other purpose. We must also take into account Cervantes' condemnation of the devastating damage which that literature caused among both noble and simple people:

> *...he so buried himself in his books that he spent the nights reading from twilight till daybreak and the days from dawn till dark; and so from little sleep and much reading, his brain dried up and he lost his wits... In fact, now that he had utterly wrecked his reason he fell into the strangest fancy that ever a madman had in the whole world. He thought it fit and proper, both in order to increase his renown and to serve the state, to become a knight errant...*[6]

This passage gives evidence of Cervantes' intention of not limiting the real danger posed by this kind of literature (of falling into

---

[6] *Don Quixote*, I, 1.

madness; that is, of ending up with a *dried–up* brain) to an isolated case: Alonso Quijano the Good.[7]

Cervantes takes direct aim at the lies and falsehoods of the Knight Errantry Literature as being the perpetrators of such dire consequences among common people. In my opinion, I cannot be accused of extrapolating the problem when I say that Cervantes aimed his artillery against knight errantry books as such; but more so, and above all, against the huge number of fantasies, falsehoods, and lies which they contained because they were narrated as if they held real and beneficial facts, in spite of being quite capable of *drying out* the brains of the people.[8]

Upon close examination of both the content and the ideology of knight errantry books, three conclusions can be drawn.

First, the details and adventures narrated in them are so imaginary and unreal, as well as outlandish, that they can be considered without any qualms as absolute falsehoods.

Second, in spite of their outlandishness, those adventures are presented as beneficial, as being accomplished by generous and courageous heroes and heroines whose only intention is to procure the

---

[7]The popular jargon, quite fashionable nowadays in Spain, uses the expression *brainwashing*; which describes remarkably well a phenomenon that is more widespread and of far more damaging consequences among ordinary people than what is commonly thought. That is going to be the theme of this present chapter: the problem of the *manipulation of the masses* by those who have the Power while staying in the background, which is precisely what Cervantes was then pointing at and denounced in such a superb way.

[8]It is possible that the *express* intention of Cervantes in writing *Don Quixote* was not so clear. But whether explicit or implicit, his intention cannot be denied by anybody. No one will happen to think that Cervantes meant to wipe out knight errantry books merely because they were just that. It must be accepted that his invective against such books had a purpose and was motivated *by something*, lest we think that Cervantes possessed a diminished intelligence.

welfare of their fellowmen and to restore peace and justice. In other words, they try to *right all the wrongs* that fill up the world: to assist orphans, to help the destitute, to protect pupils and widows, to punish evildoers, to restore justice, etc.

Third, in spite of staging such a nonsensical and unreal collection of events, characters, and purposes, they are presented to us *not only as real and possible, but also as the best and only way to achieve the restoration of justice and peace in human society.*

All of which can be equated to a particular kind of falsehood within the genre of lies: utopia. If we take into account that modern society (worldwide) is fed and led (misled) by utopia, while walking on the bed of a quicksand of lies, we can begin to understand the importance of this issue.

It must be emphasized that this problem, as it is posed here, was not alien to the mind of Cervantes; as can be suggested by what he says while he is weeding out books apropos Tirante the White, saved from the purifying flames:

> —*God bless me! —said the curate with a shout—. 'Tirante el Blanco' here! Hand it over, gossip, for in it I reckon I have found a treasury of enjoyment and a mine of recreation. Here is Don Kyrieleison of Montalvan, a valiant knight, and his brother Thomas of Montalvan, and the knight Fonseca, with the battle the bold Tirante fought with the mastiff, and the witticisms of the damsel Pleasureofmylife, and the loves and wiles of the widow Peaceful, and the empress in love with her squire Hipólito. In truth, gossip, by right of its style this is the best book in the world. Here knights eat and sleep, and die in their beds, and make their wills before dying, and*

a great deal more of which there is nothing in all the other books.

It is interesting to note here, besides Cervantes' blatant mockery and his rejoicing in making fun and bringing up ridiculous names of knights, maidens, and ladies, this clarification:

This is the best book in the world. Here knights eat and sleep, and die in their beds, and make their wills before dying, and a great deal more of which there is nothing in all the other books.

It is clear, therefore, that Cervantes' diatribe is not directed against knight–errantry books just because of the mere fact that they/there are such kinds of books. *Neither has he intended, ultimately, to put an end to the lies contained in them just because they are lies.* What he really tries —and which often goes unnoticed— is to denounce the damage that such falsehoods bring about, mostly to ordinary people. Because these falsehoods are offered as a solution against injustice, and even as the safest method to procure a better world, no one considers that they hide the fact of their being only utopias. They are, therefore, purely intellectual elaborations that in addition to not being helpful at all because their fantasies have no basis in fact, they deceive and harm many common people of good will who, consciously or unconsciously, yearn for a better world. De-hydration of the brain according to Cervantes —or *brainwashing,* for us— is a reality that is there. In our modern society, that possesses a technology which would have been unthinkable in Cervantes' time, this brainwashing manipulates with great effectiveness the minds of the masses.

Different treatment is dispensed by Cervantes in this chapter to books of poetry and pastoral novels.[9] The Prince of the Spanish Literature does not hesitate to grant them his favor and understanding: *These do not deserve to be burned like the others, for they neither do nor can do the mischief the books of chivalry have done, being books of understanding*[10] *that can hurt no one.*

The reason for such a benevolent treatment is not difficult to understand, taking into account that Cervantes himself points it out: These books *cannot hurt anyone.* At a closer look, it is easy to understand that poetry is located at the opposite pole of utopia. The latter is an enormous lie that becomes all the more serious when it seeks to leave its own milieu, literature, to present itself before the world as the solution and the cure of many problems and situations. On the contrary, poetry —to the extent that it is true poetry— *is always based in truth.* The essence of poetic expression is nothing other than to give testimony of the *pulchrum* by using words, which are the basis for its relationship with this transcendental,[11] which is to say with being and, therefore, with the other transcendentals: the *bonum* and the *verum.* Poetry, in prose or in verse, is but an agonizing attempt to at least insinuate that which simple prose is not able to express; it is like trying, in an attempt that seems to go beyond human possibilities, to reach a comprehensive understanding of being (an adventure which, although being doomed to failure

---

[9]This distinction is not important for our analysis. Pastoral novels (to the extent that they existed and may still exist) can be easily classified as poetic books.

[10]Some critics read here *entertainment.* But the most serious critics seem to support the first reading; either reading has no bearing on our theme. Besides, both readings do not appear to be incompatible.

[11]It is well known that for Saint Thomas and the classics beauty is perceived only through the senses of sight and hearing. Written poetry is essentially oral poetry; hence its proper field is the sense of hearing.

from the very beginning, still retains its wonderful character of being an ineffable and amazing mystery); thus poetry seeks to come out with intuitions (to express, insofar as it is possible, what is beyond words), to somehow fill the void that the poverty of mere prose cannot satisfy. In one way or another, poetry coincides with *truth*, and its search for a better and more complete understanding of being, through the beauty of language, cannot be described as other than commendable. Poetry is, therefore, at the most opposite pole of utopia, hence Cervantes' treatment of poetry is more than justified.[12] If poetry is an expression of *pulchrum* through language, and if poetry therefore, as the transcendental which it is, identifies itself with being (and with *bonum* and *verum* as well), then this means that poetry opposes lies (and, by the same token, utopias) to the same degree and in the same way as the two other transcendentals do.

It would be convenient, before going further, to establish an important distinction in the concept of utopia. There are two rather different species within the genre.

There is a utopia that is a merely literary fiction; it does not intend to present itself as true, let alone to offer (or to impose) itself as a remedy to the outrages or as a solution for a better world; it is absolutely harmless. Utopias of this sort are the universally known Plato's *Republic* and Thomas More's *Utopia*. Both are harmless because they do not claim to be real facts or infallible (or fallible)

---

[12]Some critics are confused by the ending of the paragraph —can hurt no one—, to the point that they do not find an easy way to explain it. But I do not understand their confusion; the fact that these books contain no harm to anyone reaffirms in a very clear and forceful way what we are saying.

medicine for the health of society.[13] Cervantes alluded to them when speaking of *works of entertainment*.

Of a different kind are what one could call "real" utopias, if one wants to use such an aberrant expression which is self–contradictory *in terminis*. Taking advantage of the wealth of possibilities offered by the Spanish language, it can be said that while it would be valid to talk about *real utopias*, it would be wrong to use the phrase *utopias that are true* because, by definition, all utopias are false. Nevertheless, it is reasonable and in accord with truth to brand as criminal even those utopias which claim to offer themselves as truthful, useful, and indispensable. And this indictment is far from being unfair or exaggerated, and we will try to explain.

Utopias like Marxism, Nazism, or pacifism —to name a few— have caused (and continue to cause) millions of deaths and have deceived entire nations. As expected, they present themselves as true doctrines, as the only truth; claiming to be the essential tool for the salvation of mankind, the irreplaceable way to implement paradise on Earth —which is the only paradise they admit as real and possible—; and they try to impose themselves by force, even at the cost of causing rivers of blood. It is easy to note in them a direct proportional relationship between their falsehood and their

---

[13]For a long time, critics have argued about the odd nature of this work of Thomas More. The island of *Utopia* is a pagan republic governed by merely rational laws and rules of ethics which are completely ignorant of Christian morality, although never contrary to it. The problem arises when we take into account that Thomas More is a saint canonized by the Church. As far as I am concerned, I think that the difficulty exists only in the minds of scholars. If we read his work carefully and calmly, we cannot possibly conclude with certainty (nor even with probability) that Sir Thomas More proposed as something feasible and desirable the happy society described by him. The most natural conclusion to be drawn from his work is that the author did not intend to create anything but a merely literary work.

dangerous aggressiveness. Hence the logic of Jesus Christ in placing in parallel lies and murder and in denouncing the devil as the father of both: *Ye are of your father the devil and the desires of your father ye will do. He was a murderer from the beginning, and abode not in the truth, because there is no truth in him. When he speaketh a lie, he speaketh of his own: for he is a liar and the father of lies.*[14]

But before going into more detail about some utopias, we may want to pay some attention to the text just quoted, given its enormous importance, significance, and relevance today of what it says. We are not at all turning aside from our subject. For the link that Jesus Christ establishes between the devil and those who have opted for lies (Rev 22:15) has nothing to do with a mere congruence of affinities (whether of ideas, feelings, or any other thing); that connection is a veritable parent–child relationship. We are not talking here, therefore, of followers or disciples, but of true children and their father, the devil. And given the size, influence, and topicality of lies in modern society (which is virtually ruled by falsehood and manipulation), is a fact whose importance cannot be ignored; it is indeed a serious statement which can be applied even to the Church herself.[15]

---

[14]Jn 8:44.

[15]There are many members of her Hierarchy whose faith and personal life are rather dubious. A common behavioral pattern has emerged within her: connivance with pagan and anti–Christian policies of many governments as something normal; guilty silence before sophisticated campaigns to de–Christianize the masses; pastoral procedures of doubtful effectiveness and even more questionable integrity; capitulation to the demands of *other churches* (the very term "churches" speaks for itself), etc. These statements cannot be scandalous to anyone, if one takes into account that self–serving silences may be as guilty as a lie declared; and if, moreover, one does not want to forget the words of Pope Paul VI, according to which the smoke of Satan has entered the Church.

All this, in turn, leads to another important conclusion. Human beings have become accustomed to regarding lying as one act of malice among many others; as a sin —more or less severe, depending on the damage it causes— among many other different sins that man is capable of committing. This opinion, though true, is too simplistic, for it does not take into account the special relationship, clearly pointed out in the passage, between lies and devilish malice. And although it may be said, indeed, that every sin has a diabolical nature, one cannot forget, however, that lying was the only sin about which Jesus Christ mentioned this particular relationship: the lie is the offspring of its father, the devil. He who opts for the lie (in whatever form it takes) cannot be merely considered as a weak victim of lust which has induced him to choose evil, but as a human being who, by making up his mind for the lie, does the will of his father, the devil; a will which from now on is also his own. This is how a diabolical filiation has become the perverted and caricatured opposite side of divine filiation; an option that instills in God's creature an unfathomable malice impossible to understand by the human mind even when aided by the lights provided by Revelation. Moreover, according to the teaching of Jesus Christ Himself, the devil did not keep himself in the truth *because there is no truth in him.* The fact that the lie has to pay the homage of servitude by always appearing wrapped with the trappings (disguise) of truth, and also given that utopias go even further and are presented as instruments of (human) salvation, poses a major problem.

Does the appearance of truth with which the lie has to present itself, and even the promise of salvation (always in the form of human welfare) that utopia strives to offer, mean that one or the other contains some truth? The importance of the question and of its possible answer has much to do with utopia. The promises of salvation that the latter offers, do they contain real elements usable in some way, or vestiges of goodness sufficient to be able to extract from it something useful? But since it has been established above both that utopia is just a lie and that it has an intimate relationship of filiation with the devil —in whom there is nothing real—, then we can advance a negative answer. And this would lead to the definite conclusion that there are no useful elements in utopia.

Oddly enough, this conclusion will not be accepted by the majority of people. They are willing to admit the existence of useful elements in utopias; moreover, they earnestly defend that utopias are true in their entirety, and even necessary. This compels men of our time —whether they are aware of it or not— to deal with highly sensitive issues.

In order to understand better what has been said, let us now say something about an issue which will be dealt with in greater depth later on: *pacifism*. According to this utopia, it is necessary to seek peace at all cost because *all wars are bad*. As one can see, the lie, an essential element at the core of utopia, has immediately made its appearance, for *it is absolutely not true that all wars are bad*. Otherwise, how could the mere mention of the centuries–old doctrine of a *just war* even be possible; a doctrine which Catholic Theology and the universal belief of all nations have never hesitated to maintain? Moreover, in every war there are always men that attack and others who defend; who would then venture to say that either the perpetrators or those who repel the aggression, always and in every case, are those who do wrong? In each particular case, who is acting unjustly, the former or the latter? And who is to decide, with sufficient moral certainty to be trusted, on whose belligerent side reason and justice are? Nobody can deny that, even if there were one instance in which this dispute could be resolved clearly enough, there would be many other occasions —most of them, in fact— where these questions would be difficult if not impossible to solve.

From about mid–twentieth century to modern times, many Shepherds of the Catholic Church have taken every opportunity possible to talk about peace: universal peace, peace among nations, and *no* to war. Although we will talk later more extensively about this issue, we may advance here that it probably would have been desirable if those Shepherds had clearly established *the distinction between mundane peace and the peace offered by Jesus Christ.* The distinction is far from being a subtlety, for it was accurately and forcefully pointed out by Jesus Christ Himself (Jn 14:27). And if He very carefully distinguished those two kinds of peace, to the point of excluding worldly peace from the content of His message, then it is dangerous for the Shepherds of His Church to wrap both in the same package; otherwise we would admit what is precisely happening nowadays: only world peace appears in the foreground, while Christian peace cannot even be distinguished as a hazy background which, truly speaking, does not exist. The indisputable fact here is that, regarding this problem, the Church's exclusive responsibility is to proclaim the doctrine of just war;[16] but she must teach that doctrine in a very general way, for it is impossible for the Church to be able to decide, in each and every instance, if a particular war is just

---

[16]They also are to preach peace; but the peace of Jesus Christ, and not that of the world. Notwithstanding a further more extensive dealing with this issue, since it is very important, it may suffice now to ask a question which is not easy to answer: What do the words of Jesus Christ, *Blessed are the peacemakers* (Mt 5:9) exactly mean? Or, what is He trying to tell us with that warning: *Do not think that I came to bring peace on earth. I have not come to bring peace but a sword* (Mt 10:34)? *Pax Christi* is, indeed, a key element in the Message of the Good News, and it cannot be treated lightly, let alone be spirited away and replaced by worldly peace.

or unjust. She will not always be able to rule on something which, because of the enormous complexity of the facts, human conscience will often find difficult to judge. As we shall see later, the peace of Christ is the only one that can give to the world the peace for which this world seems to be searching (or which this world understands as such); and not vice versa, as many Catholic Bishops seem to think. The pursuit of worldly peace, as if there were no other, has never managed to achieve it; let alone true peace, in which, on the other hand, this world is not interested because it simply does not believe in that peace.

The *Marxist utopia* in the world has caused millions of deaths, and many more millions of deceived people who have been destroyed as human beings. In his preface to *Ludwig Feuerbach and the End of Classical German Philosophy* of 1888, Engels considers the *Theses on Feuerbach* as the first document —so he says— that *contains the brilliant seeds of the new worldview.*

As you can imagine, we are not going to summarize Marxism or its consequences. Therefore, we will not talk about the *Gulag,* or the millions of victims of Communism (far superior in number to those of Nazism), or the countries that Communism has enslaved and deprived of liberty, or the cynicism with which Communism has made a mockery of human rights, or about its destruction of the individual human person as such, and so on. There are entire libraries on the subject. We are just going to point out some facts and circumstances which, despite their importance and relevance, and the tremendous damage they have caused and continue to cause, often go unnoticed. That is why we are going to briefly examine the influence of Marxist utopia within Catholicism whose consequences and outcomes are still in full force.

The doctrines of Engels, Feuerbach, and Marx, put into practice later on with blood and fire by Lenin and his followers (with over a hundred million people dead),[17] are summarized by one idea: the instauration of the Terrestrial Paradise as the only one which man can expect. We could go into details and discuss the abolition of social classes, the elimination of the concept of inequality of labor, the satisfaction of all needs —*to each according to his needs*—, the universal abolition of injustice,[18] the replacement of the person by the community and, in general, everything that follows the new man fashioned by Marxism. But everything boils down to what we have said: the reopening of the Earthly Paradise; regardless of the Bible's claim that man was permanently expelled from the Garden of Eden (Gen 3: 22–24), and despite the cherubim with flaming swords appointed by God to guard the entrance.[19]

About the years in which the Second Vatican Council was held, and before the fall of the Berlin Wall took place (along with other events that shook Europe at the time), a deep conviction became common among many theologians and Catholic leaders that Communism will finally triumph in the world. That this belief was shared by a great number of top officials in the Catholic world is very odd, more so if we consider some of the events that followed. One of

---

[17]These figures refer only to the first years of Communism. Other Communist characters came —and are still coming— after Lenin and Stalin, along with many more millions of dead and imprisoned people in their wake. In modern times one may think of Fidel Castro and the Communism in Asia.

[18]It should be noted that the concept of justice, by materialistic utopias, has nothing to do with justice based on Natural Law, which does not even exist for these ideologies.

[19]The text of Genesis, where God speaks with irony and even mockery, gives the lie, blatant and forceful, to every utopian aspiration of a better world *built by man*. As outlined below, too many Christians also have succumbed to the deception of this utopia.

them, by way of example, would be the Pact, signed by Khrushchev and by Popes John XXIII and Paul VI, agreeing to not condemn Communism at the Council, or the policy of the Vatican, difficult to explain, to comply with the treatment given by Communist Russia to some bishops persecuted in countries of the then–called Eastern Bloc.

However, it would not be smart to think that such a belief was completely wrong. The cancer of Marxist utopia was far from removed; and this situation continues even today. Communism's malignant cells continue to flourish in the body of mankind to such an extent that the Church herself has not managed to shake them.

Marxism, of course, does not believe in man's supernatural destiny. It thinks that the statement of the Bible claiming that *we have not here a permanent city, but we seek one to come,*[20] is but another falsehood. For Marxism, Religion does not aim but to the alienation of human beings. Hence the famous phrase of Marx that *religion is the opium of the people.*

The objective of Marxism, therefore, is to pull together everybody's efforts to create the Earthly Paradise, built entirely by man and the only one people can expect. Let us take into account that man's aspiration *to make himself* without God is as old as man himself; Marxism's only design was to put that longing into practice. On the other hand, we must recognize that Protagoras was right —to some extent, at least— when he said that man is the measure of all things; and so also was Petrarch when, initiating the incipient Humanism of the Renaissance, he saw himself —it is said— as the center of the world. Both were right in some way. But if we seriously strive to be objective, we must recognize that, to tell the

---

[20]Heb 13:14.

truth, man is neither the measure of all things nor is he the center of the universe.

However, neither Protagoras nor Petrarch ever tried to transform human beings into the *Homo Faber* creator of the Universe. At this point it is clear that Adam and Eve, through their attempt to be like God, greatly exceeded both: *And the Lord God said, Behold, the man is become as one of us, to know good and evil.*[21] The scientific systematization of such a diabolical intention came much later, when the Doctrine of Idealism burst into the world. The speculative aspect of this philosophy appeared long before Descartes, Kant, or Hegel. As a practical philosophy, however, attempting to make its speculative character more of a reality with a matter–of–fact projection in ordinary life, it appeared with Engels, Feuerbach, and, of course, Marx. But philosophies of Idealism began to emerge as early as the late Middle Ages, at the same moment when the metaphysical concept of being began to wane (fade away).

This said, we must add one more thing. Marxist utopia, like all philosophies of Idealism, is rooted in the dark background of the Gnosis; a breeding ground whose main tenet is its effort to *rationalize* the world, that is, the desire to do away with a God, who is considered as non–existent, and not accept as truth anything except what can be pigeonholed within the limits of human understanding. This axiom has always fed, and continues to feed, all heresies.

The Marxist utopia has influenced Catholic theology more than what might seem to those who do not want to think objectively. Its aftermath (although even now there are many who still believe

---

[21] Gen 3:22. Man's attempt to deny any *heteronomy,* in order to enforce his own *autonomy* in regard to the power to determine by himself what is good or what is bad, amounts to man's refusal to recognize himself as a creature. In this sense the evil of original sin is pure *diabolism,* and coincides, in the end, with the sin of Satan himself.

that Marxism is past history) still holds considerable weight in the Catholic world today. *Marxist utopia has been and will remain being a utopia, with no possibility of ever leaving the field of deceitful illusion, which is its own. But this kind of utopia is simultaneously, and paradoxically, a reality that cannot be taken as a joke because of its claim to impose itself in a dictatorial way to the world as the only means of salvation.* In this sense, Marxist utopia has caused severe damage in all areas of the Catholic world.[22]

As can be easily understood, we do not intend to develop here the comprehensive treatise that would be necessary to develop this issue. So we will limit ourselves to outlining some related themes —very few in fact— that, despite their importance and curious peculiarities, often go unnoticed.

The fundamental principle of Marxism —that man has to build a Paradise by himself and for himself— has left its imprinted mark in Catholic thought. This is certainly a statement which is no less true because it is capable of shocking many people.

But before we get deeper into this subject, an interesting observation should be brought forward. We found in Marxism a utopia which, in turn, calls for another utopia, even more false, if possible. To put it another way: we are dealing here with a lie (Marxism) which proclaims another even greater lie (earthly Paradise) as if it were absolutely true. And yet it is certain that *there will never be a new earthly Paradise.* Now, lie feeds on lies —*when he speaks a lie, he speaks of his own*— to the extent that it cannot act otherwise. In fact, lie deepens its roots into two realities at the same time: first of all, into itself, like a cancer that eats itself; secondly,

---

[22]Someone said that, despite the fall of the Berlin Wall, the tyrannical Powers that manipulate the minds of the citizens of the world, especially Europeans, have not fallen yet.

into the desire of many who long to be deceived at all costs. This second reality is well expressed in the Spanish saying: *If the mountain does not come to Mohamed, then Mohamed will come to the mountain*; that is, if the world is not willing to admit transcendence and what is supernatural, then one must be prepared to serve the world a bowl of purely natural food. Did Christians feel a failure after the events that culminated in the French Revolution, the Enlightenment, and the two World Wars...? For my part, I admit that I cannot decide. However, what I do see is the revival of Gnosticism. Nineteenth century Modernism and neo–Modernism of the twentieth and twenty–first century are but another attempt to rationalize Christianity, namely: to make it more human and more acceptable to modern man, even at the cost of emptying its entire transcendental content; since Celestial Paradise is unattainable, we must build the Earthly one, which is the only one man can look for. In this way, the Modernism and neo–Modernism in force within the Catholic Church coincided with and joined Marxist utopia: in view of the uselessness of philosophy and the failure of religions (whose inability to be accepted by the modern mind is a given), it only remains to be practical and build something that is useful and acceptable. So we finally have, at last, the basic and fundamental principle of Marxist doctrine: *orthodoxy replaced and displaced by orthopraxis.*[23]

---

[23]In reality, it is difficult to accept that Modernism is but a mere well–meaning attempt to build a Christianity acceptable to the world. To admit this would be a serious naiveté, for such a claim involves a loss of faith. Intentions aside, whose judgment belongs only to God, it must be recognized that a peaceful search for truth rather suggests that the mentioned attempt is a diabolical maneuver, whose purpose is none other than banishing all thoughts about God from the human mind. To which we must add something that no one will dare to deny: the high interest that Freemasonry is investing in this subject.

The wave of rationalism which, under the shape of neo–Modernism, has invaded theology and Catholic life has encountered a seemingly inescapable obstacle difficult to overcome. As expected, neo–Modernism has found it necessary to deny the Magisterium of the Church; or at least, since it was not possible to deny it clear and openly, neo–Modernism launched a campaign to distort and weaken it.

Unfortunately, this attempt has given rise, in turn, to further serious and extremely delicate problems. If we accept the assertion of Cardinal Ratzinger that the Second Vatican Council is a true *Anti–Syllabus*, then one will have to face the thorny problem of a possible *Anti–Magisterium* designed to nullify a legitimate Magisterium. How is this possible?

> *There are decisions of the Magisterium that cannot be considered as the last word on the subject, but are, according to a substantial expounding of the issues, mostly an expression of pastoral prudence, a sort of interim precept. Its essence remains valid, but the details, which have been influenced by the circumstances of the time, may be in need of more complex conclusions...*

> *In this regard, we could consider the statements of the Popes of the last century about religious freedom, the anti–Modernist decisions at the beginning of this century, and, above all, the decisions of the Biblical Commission at the time. They are still fully justified as a voice of alarm at the hasty and superficial adaptations that took place then. A character like John Baptist Metz said, for example, that anti–Modernist decisions of the Church were of great service in preserving her from becoming immersed in the liberal-bourgeois world. But the details contained in such determinations had become obsolete after having fulfilled their pastoral mission in due course.*[24]

---

[24]Joseph Cardinal Ratzinger, *L'Observatore Romano*, June 27, 1990.

In another place Cardinal Ratzinger wrote:

If you want a global analysis of this text [Gaudium et Spes] *it could be said (in connection with the sections on religious freedom and religions of the world) that it is a revision of Pius IX's "Syllabus," a sort of counter–Syllabus. It is well known that Harnack interpreted the "Syllabus" of Pius IX as a challenge to his century...*[25]

We could quote many more texts by Cardinal Ratzinger and other Catholic theologians; but it is not worth it, for this is not a polemic book. We only want to find a reassuring answer to questions that are still disturbing. There is no reason to believe that such a response does not exist. We have used the similarity between the surging of ideas to which modern theology gave rise and utopias because it seems to us that there is a close affinity between them which must be urgently dispelled.[26]

Are we in a situation of *Magisterium versus Magisterium?* Obviously, this question is meaningless. The Magisterium of the Church, assisted by the Holy Spirit, is unique and indefectible, without any possibility of contradiction or going against itself. Therefore, it seems to me that it may be possible to conclude that there are

---

[25] Joseph Ratzinger, *Principles of Catholic Theology*, San Francisco, 1987.

[26] The *Syllabus* accompanied the encyclical *Quanta Cura*, of Pope Pius IX (1846–1878). The encyclical and *Syllabus* were promulgated on December 8, 1864. The latter is a list of eighty condemned errors referring to Pantheism, Naturalism, Rationalism, Indifferentism, Socialism, Communism, Freemasonry, and various forms of religious Liberalism. This condemnation was upheld and reaffirmed by the encyclical *Pascendi* (1907), of Saint Pius X, which also refers explicitly to Modernism, specifically in relation to philosophy, apologetics, exegesis, history, liturgy, and discipline; not to mention its persistent warning about the contradiction between innovation and the faith of all times. The Second Vatican Council was held from 1962 to 1965.

only three possible positions before the issues raised by Cardinal Ratzinger:

Either the Magisterium before Vatican II was wrong. Or to put it best: perhaps its decisions have become obsolete and no longer have effect.

Or the Magisterium after Vatican II is the one that is not true, since it lacks any power to overrule the previous Magisterium.

Or perhaps, given that the ideas expounded by Cardinal Ratzinger are nothing more than the personal views of a theologian, his opinions are not very significant and, therefore, can be accepted or rejected.

However, the problem cannot be solved so easily. Cardinal Ratzinger is well known for his deserved reputation as a profound theologian, and he also holds such an important post as the Prefect of the Congregation for the Doctrine of the Faith. We cannot flippantly believe that the Guardian of Orthodoxy has strongly disavowed the pre–Vatican II Magisterium; or that he has come to think that it has become so obsolete that one cannot attribute to it any current relevance.

We can (and must) accept that. *But clearly, the Cardinal's statements give rise to an extremely delicate problem.* First, because everything in them seems to indicate that the Magisterium of the Church is *relative* the moment it is accepted that the Magisterium may have become obsolete. However, let us look carefully at the words of Cardinal Ratzinger: *There are decisions of the Magisterium that cannot be considered as the last word on the subject... they are an expression of pastoral prudence, a sort of interim precept. Its essence remains valid, but the details have been influenced by the circumstances of the time and need, therefore, new explanations.*

Now, who decides that certain dispositions of the Magisterium
are mere expressions of pastoral prudence? Which concrete dispositions can be termed as such? Which criteria should be used to
determine that those dispositions have been influenced by circumstances of time and, therefore, should be changed? And who decides
that? If the firmness of the teachings of the Magisterium, given at
a certain time in the past, depends on historical circumstances that
have turned it obsolete, who can oppose the possibility that the
same rule applies to the current Magisterium? Maintaining with
excessive emphasis that the infallibility of the Magisterium can only
be understood when applied to the Extraordinary Magisterium but
never to the Ordinary can be so dangerous as to completely do away
with all the Ecclesiastical Magisterium. In this case, it appears that
the Cardinal, in his desire to develop a *practical theology acceptable
to the modern world*, has managed to *make relative* and undermine,
even unintentionally, the Magisterium.

Someone might object that any decision of previous Magisterium
applies, of course, to the current Magisterium. Two things must be
taken into consideration. First, the Magisterium cannot contradict itself, as noted above; and second, such decisions (for example,
about whether or not certain pronouncements of the previous Magisterium were merely interim arrangements, or whether they have
been influenced or not by the circumstances at the time, etc.) *could
not be considered in turn as a magisterial act, let alone an infallible one.* Those decisions, therefore, would necessarily be entrusted
to anyone's individual judgment. Consequently, many people fear
that the Magisterium, as an indefectible bloc, is at risk of becoming
blurred (even of disappearing). Given this accumulation of present

circumstances, it is conceivable that we are dangerously approaching Protestant theology.[27]

Apropos of what we are saying, we should briefly devote our attention to a subject whose timeliness here can raise one's eyebrow. We are giving examples that can corroborate our thesis. I am referring now to the problems posed by establishing (or restoring) the institution of the *permanent diaconate.*

The issues subject to discussion about this institution, (re)introduced in Catholic life by Vatican II, have already been expounded in some detail in one of my works.[28] Here we will limit ourselves to examining some aspects of this topic which often go unnoticed despite their importance.

As everyone knows, the creation of the permanent diaconate was intended to somehow remedy the shortage of priests, with a view mainly to certain areas of the world in which their lack was felt most acutely. This purpose was explicitly stated by the Council itself.

Unfortunately, as often happens in such cases, abuses soon appeared; and with the abuses, problems whose particulars need not be repeated here. Suffice it to stress now that the remedy was not enough to overcome the disease, which, according to some people,

---

[27]It is difficult to doubt the danger of using ambiguities in matters of such importance. Choosing to dip into wordplay to justify one's own positions is to accept the use of the same procedure by those who defend opposing views, on the one hand. On the other, it is well known that, once that game in matters of such importance has been set in motion, everyone feels entitled to do the same and are willing to intervene. Something called Relativism is knocking at the door and asking permission to enter.

[28]*Commentaries on the Song of Songs, II*, Shoreless Lake Press, New Jersey, 2006, pp. 111 ff.; cf. p. 342, note 87.

was aggravated even more.[29] That is why we will limit ourselves now to discuss the delicate problem that arises in this matter, the *ecclesiastical celibacy.*

Logically and naturally, the vast majority of permanent deacons are usually mature and married men. And of course, it is also natural and logical that the problem of the shortage of priests, not only remains unsolved, but has worsened further in recent years (something that would not have been difficult to predict).

Ideas follow a mathematical logic. Given the sensitivity of the situation, and the fact that the existence of married permanent deacons is an *easily available* solution, the conclusion is obvious: the problem of ministering to so many parishes lacking Shepherds can be finally and definitely solved: just ordain married deacons priests.[30]

In this easy way to be assimilated and accepted by common Christian faithful *the proliferation of married priests* has become something normal within Catholicism.

---

[29] As can be seen, the creation of this institution was not reviewed in my aforementioned work, but the potential *abuses* which could be easily foreseen and which in fact happened. There, I simply noted that perhaps better solutions could have been arbitrated to remedy more effectively the problem of the scarcity of priestly vocations.

[30] Some may think that I hasten to report a problem which actually does not exist. A green light has not been *officially* given to the ordination of married permanent deacons as priests, nor, consequently, to reserving the rule of clerical celibacy only for those who voluntarily opt for it. This is true... until the time of this writing. But clearly this is something that is in the air we breathe, while the long–suffering flock of Christian faithful has already been psychologically prepared for it. It will not draw too much attention when it does occur. In the fierce neo–Modernist environment that is hurting the Church in these early years of this century, the fruit is ripe and it is just a matter of time. Moreover, it is not true that we are merely playing with predictions. There are already many places (the United States of America for example) where the clamor (also from the official Church) demanding priestly ordination of married deacons is being heard loudly.

It is no longer important that *ecclesiastical or priestly celibacy has become forever relegated to the background.* For what really matters now is the fact that, from a purely practical point of view, the problem has been solved once and for all.

We have now arrived at the thorniest and most sensitive point of this issue of permanent deacons —*quod erat demonstrandum.* We are referring to the fundamental point that *orthopraxis has once more displaced and replaced orthodoxy.* Or put more plainly, we have fallen again, probably without realizing it, into the arms of utopian and idealist doctrines.[31] And the fact that the majority of the flock of Christ is not aware of what is happening does not arouse excessive concern.

How did we arrive at this conclusion? Let us try a closer assessment.

The shortage of priests is a distressing fact that nobody will dare to deny. It is too obvious and painful enough to produce throughout the Catholic world —for the crisis is universal— a situation of exhaustion. To make matters worse, vocation–promoting campaigns continue to fail miserably.[32] Moreover, the solution, though not

---

[31]Here we use the word idealist in the philosophical sense. There are many who think that this is a strategically, consciously planned operation. I do not want to think so. But clearly the facts that depend on certain ideas necessarily lead, as reality clearly proves, to other facts which necessarily flow from such ideas.

[32]This is not the place to discuss this particular problem. We have already alluded to it, more or less indirectly, in other works. But it is appropriate to mention, in passing, that it would be necessary to raise a voice of alarm and denounce the substance and form of such campaigns. Not only do they lack the slightest reference to any methodology with supernatural content, they also are an absurdity no matter from which point of view you may consider them. For example, the fact that, after a *rally–like* appeal made at a religious Youth Gathering, thousands of vocations arise spontaneously, what does it mean? And how is it possible to take such things seriously and even use them as triumphalist publicity?

ideal, seems to be at hand. Since there are an abundant number of permanent deacons, who also seem to exercise well the ministry for which they were instituted, why let them stay in the diaconate and not elevate them to the priesthood, thus solving the problem...? The answer here could be: I agree. It might be a *good* solution, although it does not seem to be the *best* one (it would be appropriate to bring to mind here the old adage: the best is the enemy of the good). Everyone knows that life is full of seemingly good solutions which later on are found to be dangerous. It is a principle of common sense to be cautious with quick, easy, and expeditious fixes. Sometimes they even seem to be almost miraculous answers; nonetheless, it is always wise not to rush to accept them and use them.

Let us be calm in our reflection. What one cannot do is to give up a precious commodity in exchange for a meager bowl of stew. Ecclesiastical priestly celibacy is one of the most precious and glittering jewels the Church has possessed since her foundation. She has had this priceless treasure for more than twenty centuries, which has always been the envy of angels, the wonder and admiration of the world, the shining witness and herald of the Heavenly City, the forceful instrument to unbelievers, the first fruit and earnest of Perfect Joy for those to whom it has been granted, the priestly crown that appears almost like a halo in the face of the Lord's ministers, the hatred and terror of the devil and his associates...

Of course, I can imagine what some people will think. They will say that keeping churches and parishes properly administered, so that the faithful may have adequate care of their spiritual needs is not exactly a bowl of stew. Surely, kind people will accuse me of exaggerating; those who are not that kind, always the majority, will say far worse things. But that means back to business as usual: the logic of the world trying to supplant, once again, the logic of God.

That is why I insist and stand on what I have said, and strongly reaffirm that the solution provided by this remedy, even if recognized at first sight as a solution, is still less than a bowl of stew; of which we are going to speak next. First, we should begin by resorting to another principle of common sense. And I mean this: when one considers the possible solutions to this problem, he has to take into account advantages as well as disadvantages. Some drugs produce, as we know, healthy effects to certain symptoms of a sick organism; and yet the same drugs are dangerous to the point that they must be discarded, precisely because of the adverse impact they cause in other parts of the same body.

One more point must be made clear before going any deeper into the subject. We have said that the bowl of stew is a solution which leads nowhere. However, even assuming that in the end this prediction is totally fulfilled (as time will show), there is always the possibility that, eventually, someone may attribute the failure to a simple mistake in strategy. He would speak of finding a practical solution to a problem of ecclesial pastoral activity which, although carried out with the best will in the world, of course, nevertheless was not crowned with success.

Unfortunately, this explanation will be difficult to accept, and we will try to say why.

First, because, before resorting to the above patched–up solution, necessary and appropriate measures have not been taken; namely, those and only those courses of action which, despite their greater difficulty, would have been the only ones able to confront and remedy the crisis. And I am referring especially to the reform of the Tridentine Seminaries; outdated, to be sure, but likely to accept substantive improvements which, no doubt, would have updated them to meet the needs and demands of modern time.

Secondly, because not only has nothing been done regarding what was said in the previous paragraph, but intolerable actions have been permitted in the life of the Seminars. For example, the acceptance of trainers of dubious faith and undesirable behavior; spreading of doctrines (modernist, among others) in many ways contrary to the teachings of the Magisterium; the promotion and exaltation, before the candidates to the priesthood, of characters–idols–stereotypes who were more deserving of rejection than of receiving tributes of admiration; the acceptance and introduction of homosexuals; the relaxation of discipline; the neglect of and even contempt for interior life; the neglect and confinement to the attic of useless junk of serious study (theology of the Fathers, the teachings of Saint Thomas Aquinas and of the authentic and permanent Magisterium, etc.), and so on.

But let us go back to our subject. We said above that the elimination of mandatory clerical celibacy was not going to solve anything. There are no signs of its being a remedy capable of increasing the number of vocations, or even of maintaining the already existing ones. Not to mention the quality, height, and depth that should be expected of the clergy to get through this system.

It should perhaps be noted, before going any further, that many —if not all— of the things that we are saying —and are going to say later— seem to be misplaced exaggerations. As at the time of this writing, the abolition of compulsory celibacy has not yet been officially promulgated —let us put it this way—, we can clearly give the impression that we are playing the game of making predictions. We totally understand the reasons put forward by those who think that such a behavior is inappropriate; after all, we would be speculating about a future event which may or may not come to pass. As far as I am concerned, I have no difficulty in recognizing that the warning seems justified. In response, I will allege only two things in my defense. In the first place, to make predictions of the future is not dishonest in itself; many people make them, regardless of how successful the results are. If later on my fears happen to be unfounded and my predictions wrong, I would be the first to rejoice. Secondly, I would like to highlight the fact that since we are dealing here with predictions, the best and most practical thing to do is to wait and see what happens; giving time, therefore, sufficient slack so that it may prove correct those who will eventually be right.[33]

The abolition of mandatory clerical celibacy, even if it appears to be a practical, quick, and easy answer to the problem of shortage of priests, is not likely to result in an increase in the number of priests; rather, if one thinks things through calmly, the opposite seems to be more likely to happen.

Total Chastity was one of the most prized crowns adorning the Catholic priesthood. Today, once its denigration in the eyes of the world (and of the Church) has reached its highest levels, this virtue has become practically the last jewel left in the heap of priestly treasure. The so–called *promotion of the laity*, carried out at the expense of the prestige of the priestly state, and the destruction of the family and the institution of marriage are among the factors

---

[33]Divorce has been *de facto* admitted by members of the ecclesiastical Curiae. Of course, given that the Church has been faithful for over twenty centuries to the doctrine of the Church affirming the indissolubility of Christian marriage as a truth divinely revealed, they could not admit divorce *de jure*. It is true that they carefully avoid using the term *divorce*. But the problem is that altering the names of things does not change the reality of those things, nor can it fool anyone. Likewise, abortion, even when it is dubbed *termination of pregnancy*, continues to be the murder of a defenseless child. Therefore, if such delicate matters —and these two we have just mentioned are mere examples— are dealt with in this fashion, who will dare brand as imprudent him who thinks that the abolition of priestly celibacy is a matter of time, and not a long time at that?

contributing to such a painful discredit. One must admit that the System has outdone itself in addressing the issue of celibacy.

When one of the two terms which are reciprocally dependent —whether because one is in opposition to the other (such as paternity and filiation) or because one has greater dignity than the other (virginity and marriage)— is not properly dealt with, the ensuing negative consequences always affect the other.

It was not at all necessary to discredit the priesthood to promote the laity —we are referring to the renowned and touted *priestly identity crisis*, which is but a slogan that the System ordered liberal theologians and laboratories of advanced pastoral alchemy to mint, but which no one to date has managed to explain. After all, no promotion was ever needed; for it has resulted in disconcerting those who already had their own status and their specific charisms perfectly delimited by the sacrament of baptism. That the laity has been twenty centuries without realizing that they were not promoted seems too long, something so strange that it moves to tears.

Hybrids are a typical phenomenon that usually makes an appearance in disintegrating societies, like the various kinds of worms that appear in the body as it decomposes (*Wherever the carcass is, there will the vultures be gathered together*).[34] Say what you want, the truth is that the clerical lay person is as preposterous a product as a layman–like cleric, and both are equally harmful. The folly is more evident when one realizes that the layman does not have the charism of priesthood, just as the priest does not possess the specific charism of the layman. With the sad result that neither of them can properly perform the functions of the other, while they are forced to neglect their own. To think that the layman is *promoted* —elevated to a greater dignity and *status*— when he distributes the Eucharist,

---

[34]Mt 24:28; Lk 17:37.

is involved in one way or another in the Mass, or is exercising the function of preaching which is proper to those who have the hierarchical duty of teaching, etc., is nonsense typical of a society that has lost its way.[35]

Another hybrid example which unfortunately is quite common in our modern society has to do with the relationship between the sexes. Despite the fact that this phenomenon occurs frequently today, the tomboy woman is an aberration as degrading and unpleasant as the effeminate man.[36]

The consequences, quite successful by the way, of the fierce and global campaign organized against the family and against marriage as an institution have undoubtedly also contributed to devaluating chastity. In this case one cannot say that one side of the balance has gone down and the other up, for both scales have actually gone down. The terms referring to interrelated institutions closely linked to human nature, even when elevated to the supernatural order, are not subject to physical laws: when one term is destroyed or degraded, the other is also destroyed or degraded (if the notion of paternity, for example, is attacked or eliminated, the idea of filiation also ends up being destroyed or diffused). But this important issue needs to be analyzed more fully later on.

---

[35] On top of these strange things, there are today Societies or Associations in the Church in which the laity have jurisdiction over the priests, as, for example, Catechumenal Societies and other Associations founded later. This goes against the hierarchical constitution of the Church, which is of divine origin.

[36] Interestingly enough, the term *machismo* carries negative connotations which are lacking in its counterpart term *feminist*. The former —also regarded as taboo— takes aim directly against the male and is tantamount to a stigma which automatically affects negatively the alleged culprit. The latter, on the contrary, refers mainly to women as well as to Movements that claim women's rights, and is rather considered a mark of glory. In reality, however, both are a sad expression of the degree of corruption and distortion into which our society has fallen.

When the priesthood is surrounded by this atmosphere of disrepute, aggravated by the secularization of the supernatural and by the spreading paganism and modernist ideas, it is hard to see an increase in priestly vocations on the horizon in the near future. If, on the other hand, the difference between a Catholic priest and a Protestant minister, a Jewish rabbi, a Muslim leader, a guru, and of course a layman, is increasingly blurred... then it is easy for anyone to draw the pertinent conclusions. The Catholic priesthood has always been for the Christian people an elite group and even much more than that. But it is ridiculous to think that an elite group may increase its ranks by the process of ceasing to be an elite group; this would allow for the possibility that those who now choose to enroll are not going to be precisely premium quality members.

Unfortunately, we have not yet reached the bitterest point of this issue. Making a great effort, one could read the failure of this attempt as a simple fiasco in the procedure; after all, there have always been trees that have borne no fruit. However, it does not seem feasible to regard this failure so benignly, since we are not dealing here with the bad results of an undertaken business, rather we are looking at an *abandonment of principles*. Anguished over the shortage of priests, it has been thought, as a possible solution, to introduce married deacons into the priestly ministry, for there are enough numbers of them to solve the problem. But this answer would entail the abolition of the obligation of celibacy and ultimately —why not admit it?— the disappearance of what has been a glorious halo of the Catholic clergy for two millennia. Or to put it another way, we opted for *orthopraxis* at the cost of abandoning *orthodoxy*. Why? Everyone agrees that serious and urgent needs will admit no delaying.

But the problem is more delicate than it may seem to an inattentive glance. We alluded earlier to the abandonment of principles. It is indeed dangerous to choose *praxis* at the expense of giving up *theory*, assuming that such a thing is possible, because we must not forget that we are talking about utopias. And utopias —it must be said again— belong to the world of fantasy, that is, they have no other reality than that of lending themselves to those who make them instruments of deception and manipulation. As technique depends on and is nothing without science, there can be no practice without theory. Hence, when practice wants to become independent and live its own autonomy, all that results is practice depending on a new theory, which is always different and usually worse and inferior than the first.

Priestly celibacy has nothing to do with orthopraxis. It was not established in order to make the work of pastoral ministry more efficient or easy, as it has sometimes been thought. It is a way of existence that not only does not care about questions of practical convenience, but it completely ignores them even as a mere possibility. It depends entirely on principles —on *theory*— and only on principles. Therefore, priestly celibacy it is not a matter of better or worse performance —*Absit!*—, but of love. The priest of Jesus Christ does not remain celibate to exercise better his ministry, but to give his whole heart to Him Who has previously given His to him. In this sense, he is a living testimony of total and perfect love, which still exists in the midst of the world because it has not been permanently banished.

Consequently, it has been a serious mistake to throw priestly celibacy overboard for purely practical purposes, which are less than nothing in comparison with the real content of celibacy:

> *If a man were to offer all his family wealth*
> *To by love,*
> *He would utterly be contemned.*[37]

Thus we have arrived at a surprising conclusion. We have seen that it is meaningless to do without the glowing reality of total love —which in turn is made patent through him who has renounced everything for its sake— for reasons of practical convenience; even if such reasons are as lofty as those involving care and service to others. Hence the conclusion to which we are referring: *perfect love is the antithesis of practicality*, in that it involves surrendering everything without expecting anything. And the paradox is that this is precisely how perfect love becomes the most fruitful of all practical things; namely, through the testimony that perfect love is not interested in anything other than giving everything to the beloved. This testimony, in turn, is the only reality that pays off and which, consequently, provides the best service to others, since demonstrating —showing— perfect love, until death, is the only thing capable of convincing and tearing down the walls that the lack of love has put up among men: *Unless a grain of wheat falls into the earth and dies, it remains fruitless; but if it dies, it brings forth much fruit.*[38] And since it is obvious that these words of the Master speak of the way and manner to produce fruit, solely through love, we must urgently ask: What is left now of the practical method responsible, in turn, for displacing the supreme principle of sacrifice–out–of–love into the background? What is the use now for its touted usefulness to solve the problem of scarcity of sacred ministers?

---

[37] Sg 8:7.

[38] Jn 12:24.

Saint Paul is the great singer of the excellence of virginity (1 Cor 7).[39] In a text very much in connection with our subject, the Apostle says that *he who is unmarried cares for the things that belong to the Lord, how he may please the Lord; but he that is married careth for the things that are of the world, how he may please his wife, and he is divided in mind.*[40] It is clear that the Apostle of the Gentiles is not thinking at all of practical implications. In saying that the married person is divided, he is not merely referring to shared activities —some activities dedicated to God and some to the spouse—; Saint Paul means a surrender of the heart exclusively to God, which is the highest longing of human existence.

The same, albeit with greater truth, can be said of Jesus Christ; love is only reason that, according to Him, gives meaning to voluntary celibacy, raising it above everything else: *There are eunuchs who have made themselves eunuchs for the kingdom of heaven's sake. He that is able to receive it, let him receive it.*[41] And that is how He, Himself appearing as the supreme revelation of God's love for men, practiced it. Hence any attempt against celibacy is ultimately an attack on love. Perfect love contains in itself its own justification, and so it can dispense with any *practical* reason that seeks to *use it* for some end. Unlike what happens with the institution of marriage, which is always based on practical purposes: the procreation of children first, and then mutual aid and the remedy of concupiscence, as the Apostle noted in reference to the latter: *Now concerning the things about which you wrote unto me: It is good for*

---

[39] As he also sings the greatness of Christian marriage (1 Cor 7; Eph 5), but placing both in their proper place: *For I would that all men were even as I myself. But every man hath his proper gift of God... I say therefore to the unmarried and widows: it is good for them if they abide even as I* (1 Cor 7: 7–8).

[40] 1 Cor 7: 32–34.

[41] Mt 19:12.

a man not to touch a woman. Nevertheless, to avoid fornication, let every man have his own wife, and let every woman have her own husband (1 Cor 7: 1–2).[42]

> *Whoever does not see in this commitment the eternal source and foundation of love itself shining forth, whoever does not see this commitment as one that is inherently lovely and worthy of love (and not for the sake of its effects), has not really yet gained a Christian vision of God. He has rather distorted the purpose of love, which is its own purpose, and harnessed it for inner–worldly aims. And this inversion of the two orders —making God be there for the sake of the world— soon avenges itself in thoroughgoing atheism.*[43]

Moreover, the book of Revelation contains a text, apropos of this issue, in which two things could be highlighted. First, the passage emphasizes the intimate connection between celibacy and following the Lord wherever He goes; it certainly points to an unconditional following as a result of total and perfect love. Secondly, there is something surprising and seemingly strange; the Apocalypse seems to assign virginity in this case to men: *These are they who were not defiled with women, for they are virgins. These are they who follow the Lamb wherever he goes.*[44]

***

---

[42]An evident proof of the *practical* character of marriage, which in turn results in a transitory feature, is the fact that, just as love never fails (1 Cor 13:8), the institution of marriage is rather ephemeral to the point of disappearing with the death of one spouse: *In the resurrection they neither marry, nor are given in marriage, but are as the angels in heaven* (Mt 22:30).

[43]Hans Urs von Balthasar, *Explorations in Theology, IV: Spirit and Institution,* San Francisco, 1995, p. 303.

[44]Rev 14:4.

Sed domus hominum qui no vivunt ex fide,
pacem terrenam ex huius temporalis vitæ rebus commodisque sectatur.
Domus autem hominum ex fide viventium,
expectat ea quæ in futurum æterna promissa sunt,
terrenisque rebus ac temporalibus tamquam peregrina utitur.[45]

The *utopia of pacifism*, which we will discuss now, is no less dangerous than the Marxist utopia. This will sound strange to the ears of many people, and even to the majority of them, I should say. And the reason is obvious: can there be any evil in the effort to promote peace at all cost...? How can anybody suspect that there is any wrongdoing, or perhaps error, in the fiery campaigns striving to end, once and forever, all wars...?

Apparently all is well; but that is precisely the evil of all utopias: *it is true that they sound great; nevertheless, they are misleading, and, therefore, so terribly harmful; for lying never led to anything good.*

To understand better this problem, we will analyze it from two points of view.

First, it will be necessary to demonstrate that the utopia of *pacifism* is totally false; which, although it is sufficient to expose its harmful nature, may welcome other additional and complementary reasons that confirm the deceiving nature of this utopia.

---

[45] *But men who do not live by faith seek earthly peace in the goods and comforts of this life. In contrast, men who live by faith hope in future and eternal goods, according to the promise; they use earthly and temporal goods as ephemeral* (Saint Augustine, *De Civitate Dei*, XIX, XVII).

Then, in connection with this issue another phenomenon difficult to understand would remain to be explained. I mean the fact that this utopia has enjoyed —and continues enjoying— such a multitude of followers and propagators, despite centuries of history having amply demonstrated its utter ineffectiveness. Can we explain this circumstance by a universal reluctance to recognize its useless status? And in any case, once its ineffectiveness has been demonstrated over and over throughout centuries, and putting aside momentarily the good or bad faith of its divulgers, what exactly is intended when they try so hard to spread it?

The long history of pacifism has fully demonstrated its impotence and futility, as can be seen by studying Buddhist teachings, the doctrine of the most radical Christian sects (Quakers, for instance), and the many campaigns promoted today against war. After examination of this issue, and as strange as it may seem, one soon discovers that the main spokesman of modern pacifism at all costs has been, and still is, progressive Catholicism which seems to be gripped by a stubborn determination not to consider the alarming phenomenon of terrorism, especially the Islamic kind (despite the heinous slaughter perpetrated in the Twin Towers, New York, in September 2001). Notwithstanding all evidence to the contrary, progressive Catholics, as champions of the most extreme pacifism, maintain their stand with such a determination that it has stirred surprise and wonder in most observers. These radical pacifists (or simply pacifists, for pacifism is usually radical) oppose any kind of war and all violence in any of its forms. They argue that war is intrinsically evil and must be avoided, therefore, at any price.

Of course, no one will dare to deny that war is an evil; a disgrace to be avoided as far as possible, whenever possible. *But it is false to claim that war, always and in any case, must be regarded as intrinsically evil.*

Pacificism is based on a fallacy. Some people believe that this misleading notion has its source in a misguided sense of optimism; according to others, it derives instead from undeclared purposes which can barely conceal their ill intention. Advocates of pacifism have in their favor something that reinforces their position and that, as we have said over and over again, is characteristic of all utopias. I mean *utopia's strong appearance of truth, and even goodness.* Slogans like *we want love, not war,* and the well–known and repeated *no to war!* and others alike certainly sound good and even project an aura of integrity, goodness, and holiness on those who proclaim them. In their eyes, those who refuse to wage war are good, while those who do wage war are bad; as easily as that, as if things were that simple.

Everyone knows that evil can be considered in two ways: as absolute or relative. It is not difficult to understand that absolute evil is real evil, which must always be avoided, without exception. So we can say that, in all truth, sin is the only true evil; it cannot be justified under any circumstance. Lying, for example —be it serious or mild—, is never exonerated, and there is no exception here either.

Not so with relative evil; this, unlike the previous evil, can be regarded as evil *secundum quid.* Not being inherently flawed, it cannot be identified with sin; it even has elements of goodness of the highest degree; which are more than enough to justify its acceptance. Consider, for example, disease or death itself.

Jesus Christ maintains that illnesses are not sinful nor punishment due to sin. Let us remember, for instance, the story of the man born blind (Jn 9: 1–3).[46]

---

[46] In this episode —which we consider here merely by way of example—, Jesus not only refuses to consider the misfortune of the blind man as a punishment (to him or to his parents); He even goes on to say that the illness exists so that the works of God are made manifest in the blind man. We are, therefore, at the most opposite pole to the petty perspective of the apostles and of the many others who think like them.

Anyway, death is the consequence and punishment for sin (Rom 5:12), but not an evil in itself, as evidenced by the fact that it is natural to man. If man was delivered from it because he was elevated to the supernatural order as an additional gift, it was a matter of pure grace. In no way can punishment be confused with the malice of sin itself. In fact, God punishes (Rev 3:19), and thus punishment becomes an act of goodness. For sin, or guilt, is indeed bad, but its penalty is always good. Besides, man's death has acquired, through Jesus Christ, a redemptive character; it also has been finally conquered and transformed into glory (Ps 116:15). Hence the triumphant cry of Saint Paul, echoing, in turn, the prophet Hosea: *Ubi est, mors, victoria tua?*[47]

Jesus Christ always refuses to call death an absolute evil. He even seems to regard it not at all as an evil, and compares it to *sleep.*[48] And He takes it upon Himself.

There is a passage in Saint Matthew's gospel (26:52), where Jesus admonishes the apostle Peter, which seems to offer an objection to what has been said: *Then said Jesus unto him, 'Put up again thy sword into its place, for all they who take the sword shall perish with the sword.'* But if you look carefully to the context of those words, you soon discover that they are far from being an argument against war. After all, this passage has nothing to do with this issue. What the Master seems to be trying to teach in this case, as a lesson offered to Peter and to all of His disciples, is that no one should oppose the saving plans of the Father, and, therefore, the mode or manner in which the gentle and peaceful immolation of the Lamb must be fulfilled. Jesus Christ Himself proves this reading when He added: *Thinkest thou that I cannot now pray to my Father, and*

---

[47] 1 Cor 15:55.

[48] Jn 11:11; Mt 9:24; Mk 5:39; Lk 8:52. Also cf. Mt 27:52 and 1 Thess 4:13 in the Neo–Vulgate.

he shall give me more than twelve legions of angels? But how then shall the scriptures be fulfilled, that thus it must be?[49] For the same reason, it would not be honest to put in opposition to the passage just quoted that of Mt 10:34: *Think not that I am come to send peace on earth; I came not to send peace, but a sword.* For Jesus is speaking here not within a context of war; rather, in this particular case, He is underlining the situation of extreme fighting and tension that is always involved with Christian existence.

If there is anything clear in the Gospels it is the *total absence* of texts condemning war. In fact, Jesus Christ wishes to show His sympathy, sparing no praise in some cases, toward foreign soldiers stationed in Judea, as evidenced by what happened with the centurion of Capernaum (Mt 8: 5–13). He also speaks, as something quite natural, of the provisions of the kings to make war (Lk 14:31), and of the legality of the taxes they collect from their subjects (Mt 17:24). The Baptist, on his part, does not seem to have anything against soldiers; he merely admonishes them gently not to extort or denounce falsely, and to be content with their pay (Lk 3:14).[50]

But if to consider war as something intrinsically evil is a false approach, the second tenet of pacifism contains a greater deception and reveals more clearly its utopian nature. I mean the dream of a happy society, from which wars will have been entirely banished, and in which men will live in perfect peace and harmony. This dream is clearly contrary to Holy Scripture, History, and common sense and even denies implicitly the reality of original sin. Post Vatican II progressivist theology is proudly harping on things like

---

[49] Mt 26: 53–54.

[50] This passage was used by Saint Augustine in his *Sermon* on the servant of the centurion (cf. *Epistle CXXXVIII Ad Marcelinum* Chapter 2) to prove the lawfulness of military service and of war. Saint Thomas quoted it in his *Summa Theologiæ*, IIª–IIæ, q. 40, a. 1, *sed contra*.

The New Springtime of the Church, the *civilization of love, The New Pentecost, The Spirit of Assisi,* and a long list of niceties whose only fault is not corresponding with reality. In short, new utopias about which we can do little more than mention them briefly.

Unrealistic predictions about a happy and stable future are but optimistic dreams. But dreams, as Calderon, the dramatist, poet, and writer of the Spanish Golden Age, said, are nothing but dreams. As for the optimism of those dreams, it has nothing to do with reality, let alone with Christian hope.

The biblical texts are sufficiently clear on this for anyone who wants to read them. They speak openly about the social convulsions of increasing intensity which will fill humanity with anguish as the end of time approaches. See, for example, Mt 24: 6–8; Mk 13: 5–8; Lk 21: 6–10; 1 Thess 5:3, and 2 Thess 2:3.[51]

The dream of an idyllic era to come, along with the overwhelming triumphalism that progressivist theology is pouring into the Church today, is something that contradicts History and common sense so evidently that it needs no demonstration. To this it must be added, as the most serious of all the characteristics of this utopia, the implicit denial of original sin involved in these doctrines. Accepting a Rousseauian view of society, they seem to think that man is naturally good, forgetting his fallen, though repaired, nature. According to them, therefore, it will be sufficient to improve social structures

---

[51]This latter text even announces a great universal apostasy, which will coincide with the coming of the Antichrist and the great universal upheavals at the end of History. In this sense, any adjective could be applied to qualify these biblical texts, barring optimistic: *And except those days should be shortened, there should no flesh be saved; but for the elect's sake those days shall be shortened* (Mt 24:22). It is a condition of human nature not to see those things which are unpleasant or disagreeable, hence the loathsome feeling caused by some Pastoral work; namely, that which has placed all these evangelical passages in a state of hibernation.

to achieve the dreamt–of and longed–for happy Arcadia (which is but another reminiscence of Marxism).

The New Testament, as one would expect, is as realistic as naturally the Word of God is. So the Gospel knows well that the ideal existence that it structures for the Christian —the new man, grafted in Christ; a reality that is also true, of course, of society itself, since it is made up of men— is something which can achieve its full development only at the end of history when Christ comes again to recapitulate all things and leave them in their proper place. *Be perfect as your heavenly Father is perfect* is a precept which looks forward, or a goal to be reached; by no means is it a place for an already achieved rest: *So run, that you may attain it... I therefore so run, not as at an uncertainty.*[52] The Church is not a bearer of reassuring messages for men which are not fully grounded in the reality (soft or hard) of things. *Gaudium et Spes*, of course; but not forgetting that the real Joy has no other source of origin except the Holy Spirit. As for Hope, it is an ineffable theological virtue that is based solely on the unshakable rock that Christ is. Any joy, or hope, that sprouts exclusively from any man–made source will not be able to provide anything but the water of dismay and bitterness; while the fountain which wells up, springing up into eternal life, comes only from the heart of Christ (Jn 4:14).

This is why we have clearly said before that *it is not true that war is an absolute evil*. And so has this issue always been considered, without doubt or hesitation, by the doctrine of the Church. She has always admitted the just war doctrine and the right to self–defense, for both individuals and nations.

---

[52] 1 Cor 9: 24.26.

As Augustine says (Contra Faust. xxii, 70): 'To take the sword is to arm oneself in order to take the life of anyone, without the command or permission of superior or lawful authority.' On the other hand, to have recourse to the sword (as a private person) by the authority of the sovereign or judge, or (as a public person) through zeal for justice, and by the authority, so to speak, of God, is not to 'take the sword,' but to use it as commissioned by another, wherefore it does not deserve punishment... Such like precepts, as Augustine observes (De Serm. Dom. in Monte i, 19), should always be borne in readiness of mind, so that we be ready to obey them, and, if necessary, to refrain from resistance or self-defense. Nevertheless it is necessary sometimes for a man to act otherwise for the common good, or for the good of those with whom he is fighting...

Those who wage war justly aim at peace, and so they are not opposed to peace, except to the evil peace, which Our Lord 'came not to send upon earth' (Mt 10:34). Hence Augustine says (Ep. ad Bonif. clxxxix): 'We do not seek peace in order to be at war, but we go to war that we may have peace. Be peaceful, therefore, in warring, so that you may vanquish those whom you war against, and bring them to the prosperity of peace. [53]

We have seen that, for Saint Augustine,[54] those who do not live by faith seek earthly peace in the goods and comforts of this life. This search is only the result of confusing worldly peace (with which Jesus Christ did not want anything to do) with the peace that flows from and feeds on the heart of the Lord (Christian peace, or the only true one). We have seen that, for Augustine, who along with Thomas Aquinas is the most renowned interpreter of the tradition of the Church which has lasted over twenty centuries, war cannot only

---

[53]Saint Thomas, *Summa Theol.*, II^a–II^{ae}, q. 40, a. 1, ad 1, ad 2, ad 3.

[54]See page 123.

be just, but also necessary: *non quæritur pax ut bellum exerceatur; sed bellum geritur ut pax acquiratur*; a judgment which Saint Thomas also endorses.

All of which leads to a disturbing question already posed above: What do those who advocate pacifism at all costs exactly intend? One can, of course, kindly assume, though not without some difficulty, that those who endorse this attitude are influenced by an exaggerated sense of optimism, perhaps based more on benevolent feelings than on true understanding of the reality of the world and human nature. This assumption would help ease the problem, to the extent of discarding any shadow of ill will. Indeed, such a conjecture could be accepted as an explanation, though not as a sufficient or as an enlightening one as to settle any disquisition.

Thus a fairly large number of highly sensitive issues continues to be opened and unanswered.

Which compelling reason could be argued by pacifism to consider obsolete a twenty–centuries–old doctrine and a Magisterium...? Yet so far, at least to my knowledge, none has been brought forward.

Moreover, it is impossible not to note the *existence* of a bloody warmongering of those who wish to put an end to Christian civilization. Nor can one ignore the obvious fact that wars have changed methods in modern times; which imposes a mandatory need to study and review the procedures to be utilized in one's defense. There is a fact admitted by modern historians and sociologists, as well as military strategists, that terrorism is a new form of warfare. Granted that you cannot respond to evil with evil, neither can you forget that the old battles in the open, with kings and generals marching at the head of their armies, is one of the many useless tools that have been definitively relegated to the attic of History. But this is not, by far, the most worrisome feature of the doctrine of pacifism.

First and foremost is the fact that belief in the natural goodness of all men, which is pacifism's implicit assumption, leads inexorably, as stated above, to the denial of original sin. Maybe we
could talk about ignorance, rather than denial, but the problem,
however, would remain the same. We have already seen before that
the New Testament, like the Fathers, is remarkably realistic in this
regard.

And there is something worse: the effort to impose this utopia at
all costs (which lacks, as we have said, any basis in reality) leaves the
victims of those trying to end all vestiges of Christian civilization
unarmed and without possible defense. Some observers, after careful
examination and sociological analysis of current events, are reaching
dismal conclusions in this regard. Pacifism, they say, is suffering
from a terrible inferiority and, almost certain, guilt complex. The
International Left —to give a name to the System prevailing in the
world— has organized such propaganda, even such a blatant display
of power, that it has managed to raise the panic of many; precisely
of those who have come to be convinced, one way or another, of the
need to side with this ideology. Among these there are, sad to say,
many members of the Hierarchy of the Church.

And yet, not fear, nor the inferiority complex, or lack of faith
and certainty in one's own beliefs, nor flattery to ideologies deemed
as triumphant in the world at large, nor the naive belief that this
obsequiousness will attract the many who have gone astray or out of
the Church, are attitudes which qualify, even remotely, as specifically
Christian. The only thing a Shepherd can expect, as a result of such
behavior, is confusion and dispersion of the Flock.

Now we can understand better what has been said about the
dangers of utopias. I think that the few examples listed are sufficient to exclude the need to expand this study to others, which, in

addition to the excessive time and space that such a comprehensive study would require, does not belong in this book. Therefore, we are not going to talk about the *New Springtime of the Church*, or the *New Pentecost*, or the *Spirit of Assisi*, or the *New and Complacent Ecumenism*, or the *Anonymous Christianity*, or an alleged *Divine Infinite Goodness* incompatible with the existence of the damned in hell (Karl Rahner and his disciples), or the *New Christianity* or *Integral Humanism* (Maritain); nor are we going to talk about many other utopias, whether they are concerned with present or future life, that seem to strive to banish from men any shadow of uneasiness.[55]

The greatest misfortune of utopias is that they, because of their falsehood, take people away from the Truth, Who is Christ Himself (Jn 1:17; 14:6). And yet, to be separated from Christ is the only and deepest sorrow: *Lord, to whom shall we go? You have the words of eternal life*, said the apostle Peter.[56] But Truth is identified with Love. And without Love, neither the world, nor the sun, nor any of the stars would exist. Without Him we would not be in existence either; nor would we have come to find out that we did not know Him: a misfortune beyond measure which has no equal whatever; not even the mighty rivers of tears shed, so incessant, because of all the pains and sorrows of men of all time.

---

[55]For an in-depth analysis of what I call *Theologies of Goodness*, see my *Importunate Friend*, New Jersey, 1998, pp. 103 ff.

[56]Jn 6:68.

V

THE ISLAND OF BARATARIA

And Peter began to say unto him:
Behold, we have left all things and have followed thee;
What shall we have, therefore?
Jesus answering said:
Amen I say to you, there is no man who hath left house
or brethren or sisters
or father or mother or children or lands, for my sake and for the gospel,
who shall not receive an hundred times as much, now in this time:
houses and brethren and sisters and mothers and children and lands,
with persecutions: and in the world to come life everlasting.[1]

Neither the crude vulgarity nor his status of mere peasant was an obstacle for the character of Sancho Panza to attain an immortality almost like that of his master. After much prodding by our Immortal Hero, the good man decided to follow him, largely driven, no doubt, by the desire for the great and honorable reward promised to him despite his humble origins, which Don Quixote took good care to remind him, precisely when Sancho at last got his desired *island*.

---

[1]Mk 10: 28–30; Mt 19: 27–29; Lk 18: 28–30.

> *"If thou knowest thyself, it will follow thou wilt not puff thyself up like the frog that strove to make himself as large as the ox; if thou dost, the recollection of having kept pigs in thine own country will serve as the ugly feet for the wheel of thy folly."*
>
> *"That's the truth," said Sancho; "but that was when I was a boy; afterwards when I was something more of a man it was geese I kept, not pigs. But to my thinking that has nothing to do with it; for all who are governors don't come of a kingly stock."*[2]

If anyone tried to apply this philosophy to his own time (for human nature is always the same and the laws that govern it are immutable) he would reach more than comic conclusions bordering ridicule: from keeping pigs to being governor of an *island*; no more and no less. However, that is the rule that usually determines the distribution of prizes and rewards among men. Multitudes of literary, social, cinematic awards and those involving appointments to positions in public, social, political, and other kinds of Institutions have no foundation other than the one provided by more or less confessed political considerations or vested interests. The vast majority of literary or artistic awards are based on monetary or political motives. Which is not a problem for the common people because skillful advertising and the efficient work of the media easily supplement the absence of merit. There is no reason to doubt that a fair distribution of rewards will not take place until later, namely when divine justice finally replaces the flimsy and spurious justice of men. It is indeed very true that, judging from what we see, *all who are governors don't come of a kingly stock.*

It should be noted beforehand, of course, that Sancho Panza was moved to serve his master by unselfish motives:

---

[2] *Don Quixote*, II, 42.

Meanwhile Don Quixote worked upon a farm labourer, a neighbour of his, an honest man (if indeed that title can be given to him who is poor), but with very little wit in his pate. In a word, he so talked him over, and with such persuasions and promises that the poor peasant made up his mind to sally forth with him and serve him as esquire. Don Quixote, among other things, told him he ought to be ready to go with him gladly, because any moment an adventure might occur that might win an island in the twinkling of an eye and leave him governor of it. On these and the like promises Sancho Panza (for so the labourer was called) left wife and children, and engaged himself as esquire to his neighbour.[3]

In the twinkling of an eye. The irony of Cervantes overflows throughout his work. Here is another sarcastic allusion to the fact that rewards do not rain from the sky or usually answer to criteria dictated by equity. It would seem honest and natural that the recompense would be equivalent to the efforts accomplished and the merits achieved. Which rarely happens in human relationships, where neither logic nor justice ever finds comfortable seats. So it is no wonder that the episode of the *island* of Barataria —justly named because its purchasing turned out to be very cheap— could not possibly have a different ending.

The reader of *Don Quixote* soon realizes that this depiction of Sancho Panza as a peasant *with very little wit in his pate* dissipates as his character increasingly comes to life under the quill of Cervantes. It seems that the figure of Sancho Panza probably surpassed the initial imagination of the author. Sancho Panza shared in the madness of his master, no doubt. And it is clear that his strong desire to receive a reward contributed to making him a victim of the deceit that his master, with the best intention in the world, managed to

---

[3] *Don Quixote*, I, 7.

instill in him. However, the reader soon perceives that, as the profile of the esquire acquires consistency along the plot, his personality is taking the shape of the one character with the most common sense in the novel; not to mention the one most realistic and delightfully human of all the personages. Neither the priest, nor the barber, nor the bachelor Samson Carrasco, despite their profound realism and good purposes, ever manage to achieve the aura of grandeur and tender humanity that surrounds Sancho. Neither do they show the generous compassion or tender understanding that would have made them mirror the greatness of the men who populated the happy land of our Golden Age.

The serene joy brought about by reading it is the first thing to consider in the Gospel story that we are going to comment on. I would say that it is a feeling of excitement and joy at the same time. There is the possibility that this feeling is not too noticeable, but there is no doubt that it is there, perhaps hidden in that secret place of the heart from which normally the deepest emotions emerge. I remember the great impact that the reading of this passage had on me in my early adolescence, when I had my first forays through the gospel. And I would not dare to decide which gave me the most joy, the first or the second part of the passage. If I were forced to choose, I would opt for the first. What I mean is that the promised reward, so appealing, seemed indeed powerful enough to inspire anybody; nevertheless, as strange as it might seem, I felt more fascinated by the requisite previous condition: the possibility of giving everything to the beloved person. I suspect that my heart had the more or less confused feeling even then that this episode narrated in the gospel was dealing with love, which is intimately connected with this saying: *It is more blessed to give than to receive.*[4] That is

---

[4]Acts 20:35.

why the words of Our Lord seduced me: *There is no man that hath left house, or brethren, or sisters, or father, or mother, or wife, or children, or lands, 'for my sake, and the gospel's'...* And I confess that Jesus' reference to His own Person —*for my sake*— made an impact in my heart. I interpreted it as an exciting and wonderful challenge: Would I be able to give everything I have without waiting for anything in exchange? I must admit that even then I had the feeling, almost the conviction, that true love is entirely *selfless.* After all, the Apostle said it: At the end of the day love *seeketh not her own.*[5]

But this holds nothing against Sancho Panza's seeking his reward, or against the question that Saint Peter asked Jesus Christ. According to the text, Our Lord shows no surprise at the apparent concern of His disciple, and does not even respond with disgust; rather, it seems otherwise; for He takes this opportunity to promise an abundant reward to His true followers. Indeed, the desire for reward seems so natural to humans as to consider it legitimate. As the Apostle expressly affirms in the Apocalypse: *Behold, I come quickly, and my reward is with me, to give every man according to his work.*[6] And also an important passage of the Letter to the Hebrews: *But without faith it is impossible to please God; for he that cometh to God must believe that he is, and that he is a rewarder to them who seek him.*[7]

So, must we assume that the decision to follow the Lord is motivated by the desire for reward...? And we can advance the response stating emphatically, no. But the correct approach to this prob-

---

[5] 1 Cor 13:5.
[6] Rev 22:12.
[7] Heb 11:6.

lem, so that we can answer all questions, requires some previous clarifications.

It is evident that reward is connatural to merit. Unfortunately, human rewards are almost always disproportionate, and more often than not they do not correspond at all to any alleged merit they try to recompense and which many times does not even exist.

Nevertheless, *the matter of the reward is not the most important issue to analyze now.* The bottom–line problem that we want to investigate —it should be said once more— is love. Indeed, is there any theme —essential or marginal— in the Gospel that is not love?

Hence it seems legitimate to conclude that the question of Peter to his Master represents an early stage in the *ars amandi.* If this is true, it would mean that we are in the formational stage of the Apostles; a phase in which, since time must elapse before the coming of the Holy Spirit, they still could not understand many things. Even at the culminating moment of the Last Supper it was evident that there was much left to for them to understand (Jn 13:7; 14:26; 16:12). Therefore, we cannot say that Peter and the other disciples had already passed the initial stages of the relationship of love in their affection for their Master; hence, this relationship is still filled with imperfections such as conditions, hesitations, doubts, delays, and even setbacks:

> *Open to me, my sister, my love,*
> *My dove, my undefiled;*
> *For my head is filled with dew,*
> *And my locks with the drops of the night.*[8]

---

[8]Sg 5:2.

And who would be able to resist this request, these loving compliments from the Bridegroom? And yet, as difficult to understand as it might be, the bride responds rather evasively and elusively:

> *I have put off my garment,*
> *How shall I put it on?*
> *I have washed my feet,*
> *How shall I defile them?*[9]

The Lord knows the frailty of human nature and so He excuses it lovingly. He does not reprimand it, as its behavior would deserve; a demeanor that because of its coarseness sometimes results in bold presumptions that end up in the only way they could end. It is for this reason that, on one occasion, the Master simply let the rooster remind Saint Peter of his boasting, so that he would start learning the lesson (Mt 26: 33–35).

Hence, the words with which He responds to His disciple's question suggest more a joyful promise than a payment. And this is how the famous hundredfold plus eternal life has nothing to do with mere incentive to get a reward (no matter how sublime and elevated it could be). It is simply the promise of what awaits those who follow Him because love never thinks of giving any extra reward, a reward other than itself, to him who answers its request. Moreover, that extra remuneration does not make sense since love itself is its own

---

[9]Sg 5:3.

reward. The truth of the matter is that each of the lovers has enough with the person of the *other*:[10]

> *I am my beloved,*
> *And my beloved is mine.*[11]

....

> *There are threescore queens,*
> *And fourscore concubines,*
> *And virgins without number.*
> *My dove, my perfect one is but one.*[12]

....

---

[10]Love does not seek anything other than the beloved, nor does it expect a reward; at most an answer. Hence the meaning of the terms of the first commandment: with all your soul, with all your strength, with all your heart, above all else... which refer to the need to dispense with everything other than the beloved. The Fathers designated the Holy Spirit as the *Nexus duorum* because Love is structured as an *I*, a *thou*, and the *bond* that unites them. The ultimate metaphysical foundation of love is God as the Infinite Self–sufficient Being (One God), on the one hand; and, at the same time, on the other, as He loves Himself fully in the Trinity of Persons (Triune God). Therefore, there is not *another thing* for God because He is sufficient unto Himself as the Infinite Being He is. But, because He is Love, there are in Him diverse Persons; for Love is always a relationship between *I* and *you* (who are at the same time, and conversely, *thou* and *I*). And in Him the *Bond* that binds the two Persons is also another Person because of the true identification of the Three with the infinity of the one divine essence (the Father and the Son and the Holy Spirit truly identify with the divine essence). Hence they are three: different as Persons, but in the unity and oneness of the divine essence. In created love, however, things happen in the only way possible to an analogous sharing in Infinite Love.

[11]Sg 6:3.

[12]Sg 6: 8–9.

> *Let us get up early to the vineyards;*
> *Let us see if the vines flourish...*[13]

The Lord's words contained in the Gospel with which He invites us to follow Him, rather than promising a certain reward, refer to the *promise of reciprocity* that emerges from the *I–thou* relationship and which structures the mystery of love (Jn 6: 56–57, Mt 10:39); about which we should remember that the elements of the mysterious relationship of love are, on the one hand, the *I* of the lover and the *thou* of the beloved —where each one is, at the same time, a *thou* for the other; therefore, it could be said that each *I* is a *thou*, and vice versa—; on the other hand, there is a third element, *love*, that unites each of the two lovers and that is *distinctly* different from both, otherwise (if love identifies itself with either of them or both) the relationship of love would be impossible. From this it follows that the golden number of love is not two, but three. Thus we find a new element that give us access to the mystery of the Triune God; this third element has Personhood, in perfect equality with the first and second Persons.

One must admire the intuition of Saint Augustine when he connected the Trinity with man being the image and likeness of God (in reference to Gen 1: 26–27). But it is not so evident that this likeness, according to Saint Augustine, has to do with the three powers of the human soul. It is even difficult to dispel the feeling that his reasoning in this regard is rather gratuitous. To say that the human soul is like the Trinity because it is endowed with intelligence, memory, and will suggests an argument without much foundation... and seems even whimsical. And there is something even more important. The *likeness* or image of the sacred text in no way relates to the hu-

---

[13]Sg 7:12.

man soul but to *man as a whole* (the subconscious Manichean fear
of including the body in the notion of man surfaces once again).[14]
Perhaps it would be more consistent with the texts to connect this
likeness to the concept of love. Since man was created by Infinite
Love to love and be loved, perhaps we should look into love to understand better the issue of man's likeness to the triune God. We
have spoken before of the essential elements that make up the *trilogy*
of love, namely the lover and the beloved (in reciprocity), on the one
hand, and the bond that binds them, on the other. This bond is
as real as the reality of love, although in Substantial Love the bond
is also a Person. Man is an analogous participation of that trilogy.
Consequently, as there are Three Persons in Infinite Love, in the
reality of a single operation and one nature, likewise, man is one,
yet structured into three distinct operations and realities: to give,
to receive, and the love that makes the other two possible. Only
then is man an image (analogate) of the Triune God.

In conclusion, everything seems to suggest that in regard to Love
no higher reward can be imagined than the interchange of lives between the two lovers. For that exclusively was man created.

> *How fair is thy love,*
> *My sister, my spouse!*
> *How much better is thy love than wine!*
> *And the smell of thine ointments*
> *Than all aromatical spices!*[15]

---

[14]It is very curious, this reluctance (for centuries) of the writers of spirituality
to admit man's likeness to God in regard to the body, because the body is matter
and God is pure spirit (always the same fear of the). However, according to this
line of, the human soul would not have capacity for likeness to God; it is not pure
spirit, as it is ordained to the body and is the body's form. Moreover, the texts
are compelling. It is man, and not merely the human soul, who was created in the
image and likeness of God.

[15]Sg 4:10.

So, as *thy love is better than wine,* likewise *the smell of thine ointments is sweeter and more fragrant than all aromatical spices.* Of course, once again we are constrained here by the limitations of language, a clear example of the misery and grandeur of our condition as creatures; a condition never so clearly seen as in the relationship of love. Hence the lover is forced to turn to poetry if he perchance wants to express feelings that are beyond the means of simple prose. And poetry, in turn, requires rhetorical figures to try to speak of the ineffable. However, although neither prose nor poetry manages to achieve its purpose entirely, amid sighs and stammering, one thing is clear for both the singer of his love and for those who hear him: love is more valuable than anything else, and nothing can take its place.

Only God can say *everything* in only one Word, as the well–known dictum of Saint John of the Cross relates. But when it comes to man, words are always insufficient since what is left without being said is always more than what they actually say. Neither do concepts fit into words that are likewise incapable of expressing everything they contain (or try to contain). Yet therein lies the greatness and misery of it all. Since it is not possible for man to exhaust the depth of being (either with his knowledge or his expressions), he has been granted the power to intuit the mystery hidden *beyond what is said*; or some of it, at least. This mystery transcends language, and one feels that in it are found, in all their reality, Goodness, Beauty, and, ultimately, the magnificence of Being:

> *...Babbling I know not what*
> *Strange rupture, they recall,*
> *Which leaves me stretched and dying where I fall.*[16]

---

[16]Saint John of the Cross, *Spiritual Canticle.*

So no one can wonder at the fact that language is not always the best or even the only form of communication. Actually, beyond it is silence, which often exceeds the ability of language to express the reciprocal communication of the lovers; and the caress, filled with tenderness and loaded with feelings that would otherwise be inexpressible; and even the ardent and beaming enamored look, more eloquent than a thousand speeches and capable of killing out of love with its fiery darts.

> *You have ravished my heart,*
> *My sister, my bride,*
> *You have ravished my heart*
> *With one of thine eyes...*
>
> ....
>
> *Turn away thine eyes from me,*
> *For they have overcome me...*[17]

If the notion of *retributio* contains the idea of something owed, not so the concept of *promissio*. Love does not get along well with the idea of payment or retribution; it becomes an actuality only in liberty and without any conditions: *Ubi autem Spiritus Domini, ibi libertas. Where the Spirit of the Lord is, there is liberty.*[18] It would be useless and unthinkable to attempt to buy love: *si dederit homo omnem substantiam domus suae pro dilectione, quasi nihil despicient eum. If a man would give all the substance of his house for love, he would utterly be contemned.*[19]

---

[17]Sg 4:9, 6:5.

[18]2 Cor 3:17.

[19]Sg 8:7.

But we should continue with our analysis. The disciples have decided to follow the Master and give Him their lives. Do they do this in view of a reward...? Is it possible to accept remuneration as a possible motivation, principal or otherwise, in their decision to follow Jesus Christ...?

We had the opportunity to answer these questions before. We said that Saint Peter, by urging his Master to speak about the reward that awaited His followers, showed with his attitude somehow streaked with selfishness that he was at a rudimentary stage of love. But those who give their lives to Jesus Christ often do so out of pure love, and do not expect anything other than Him. Otherwise, that *something else* would play the role of primary object (and last) sought by their heart. Which would not fit disciples truly in love, for whom Jesus Christ is always and necessarily not just the last thing (in the sense of completion), but also the first one (in the sense of the most important): the Alpha and Omega, as the Apocalypse says repeatedly: *I am Alpha and Omega, the First and the Last, the Beginning and the End.*[20]

If we compare this decision to follow Jesus Christ out of *pure love* with what we have called the initial stage in the love of the Master, we must conclude that created love seems to evolve through an ascending path of maturity or perfection; that is: starting from the beginning, envisages further development, and ends in its final culmination. This is the way love has always been considered by centuries–old tradition on the art amatory, and even by the sacred texts (the *Song of Songs*, for example, is a mutual search and strife between lovers that takes place in time), and, as one would expect, by the authors of Christian spirituality. Suffice it to recall, among the latter, the *Itinerarium Mentis in Deum* of Saint Bonaventure,

---

[20]Rev 22:13. Cf 1:8; 21:6.

The Interior Castle or the Mansions or *The Way of Perfection* of
Saint Teresa of Ávila, the *Ascent of Mount Carmel* of Saint John of
the Cross to name only a few classics. And if we assume, as we have
often done, that created love is lived as a contest between lovers,
we must necessarily admit that there is an elapse of time. This
explains that the relationship of love not always unfolds according to
a movement of continuous improvement, but it actually is necessarily
linked to the hazards and vicissitudes of advance and retreat. The
maturing in Christ (2 Cor 3:18), which is such a characteristic of
all Christian life, is by necessity an activity that takes place over
time. It is just this passage of time with its possible contingencies
that turns the love relationship into the most ineffable, sublime,
awesome, and exciting adventure that the human being can ever
imagine or face. So much so that if created love would lack this
essential element during its phase of trial, human life would not
have any highlights or meaning. Divine–human love always begins,
develops, and finds fulfillment within the factor of time; as the *Song*
continually insinuates:

> *The flowers have appeared in our land,*
> *The time of pruning is come,*
> *And the voice of the turtledove*
> *Is heard in our land;*
> *The fig tree hath put forth her green figs,*
> *And the vines in flower yield their sweet smell.*
> *Arise, my love,*
> *My beautiful one, and come away.*[21]

According to Ecclesiastes, *there is a time and opportunity for
every business.*[22] The love of God offered to the human creature

---

[21]Sg 2: 12–13.
[22]Eccl 8:6.

and accepted by it, configured in the divine–human relationship of love, is a preliminary step that must necessarily live inside time. The present condition of man as a creature demands facing the challenge of love, which in turn entails the possibility of accepting or rejecting it. Therefore, this relationship is to take place within a period of time which, by its very nature, will be filled with vicissitudes and uncertainties. The condition of man as a wayfarer —with its *already* and *not yet*— demands this. Moreover, if the adventure of divine–human love lacked contingencies and the imponderable, it would lose the exciting thrill involved in man's acceptance of the challenge offered to him by the *Ineffable* (1 Cor 2:9): the challenge of confronting the great mystery of the possibilities that Infinite Love offers to man..., among which is to answer with man's self surrender. We are in the presence of infinite Goodness, Truth, and Beauty, which are presenting man with the chance of giving himself completely to them and to calm, by so doing, the insatiable longings of a human heart that is *rabidly hungry* for all of them.

These uncertainties present a wide variety of shapes, sometimes favorable and sometimes unfavorable. The condition of *waiting* is one of the most common, which logically derives from the element of temporality. The Husband, indeed, expected to meet His bride, and that she correspond to His love. The bride, meanwhile, overwhelmed by the anxiety and the nostalgia naturally caused by the absence of the Bridegroom, is eagerly awaiting His arrival. At the same time, both strive to be the first to find the other. At any rate, as victor or vanquished, both coincide in desiring the meeting with *promptitude*, because the feeling of rushing responds to the longing that grows, with increasing intensity, with the absence of the beloved. Be that as it may, it is clear that the situation of waiting is one of the distressing feelings imposed by the separation of the lovers:

My Love, I have walked anew
On your orchard path where lemon blooms have burst.
There I hid myself from you
Behind lemon trees from view
Just to see, My Love, if I could kiss you first.[23]

Beloved, I searched to see,
In my orchard, the path where lemon blooms burst,
There I stayed in wait for thee,
Out behind my lemon tree,
To see if, My Beloved, I found you first.[24]

My Love, dawn now shows her face,
And Aurora rocks the day in her embrace.[25]

---

[23]In the Spanish original:

Amado, he recorrido
de tu huerto de azahares el sendero,
y, luego, me he escondido
detrás del limonero
para poder besarte yo primero.

[24]In the Spanish original:

Amada, yo he buscado
de mi huerto de azahares el sendero,
y, luego, te he esperado
detrás del limonero
a ver si te encontraba yo primero.

[25]In the Spanish original:

Amada, ya amanece
y Aurora al día entre sus brazos mece.

> *The still waters of the lake*
> *Already are stealing the blue from the sky,*
> *While I weave for you and make,*
> *Under the birch trees nearby,*
> *Carpets of rosebuds and tulle to catch the eye.*[26]

Divine–human love, during its itinerant stage and as long as the wayfarer status of man lasts, unfolds itself amid the vicissitudes that take place *all through time*. Moreover, they are inherent to any relationship that expands within time.

It should be noted that man, in his present condition of repaired fallen nature, is unable to make an act of perfect love in intensity and instantaneously. After the fall, and then also in his situation of restored nature, his status as a wayfarer implies for him a period of trial. He is called to share the life and the cross of Jesus Christ, which is the way of making real his loving response to the divine request. Which is to be consolidated, in turn, through a period of maturing and growth (Eph 4:13) that, naturally, is to take place within time.

Just as the fish lives in water and cannot survive without it, man also begins, develops, and fulfills his existence submerged within time. However, in regard to his identification with Christ (which, as we said, is to find fulfillment within temporality), it must be borne in mind that, according to the Apostle, the Christian has

---

[26] In the Spanish original:

> *Ya las aguas del lago*
> *le van robando al cielo sus azules,*
> *mientras que yo te hago,*
> *bajo los abedules,*
> *una alfombra de rosas y de tules.*

already died and risen with his Master. In this connection, the
passages of Saint Paul (Rom 6: 3–9; Eph 2: 4–7; Col 2:12) are
so ambivalent regarding time that they can be expanded equally
forward and backwards. And, indeed, the *status* that the Christian
receives in baptism includes his future involvement in the death of
his Master: *Know ye not that all we who are baptized in Christ Jesus
are baptized in his death?*[27] But in such a peculiar way, according to
the Apostle, that the death with Christ that has already taken place
for the Christian in baptism must yet be made fully actual in time, to
thereby *give way* to a new life (Rom 6: 4–5; Phil 3: 10–11). We are
also here within the dialectic of the *already* that is correspondingly
a *not yet*. Hans Urs von Balthasar drew attention to a certain
sense of elasticity of time in the New Testament with its ambivalent
simultaneity of present and future. In regard to the concept of *now*,
for example, used by Jesus Christ, von Balthasar noted its *extensive*
nature; forward and backward, so to speak: *But the hour cometh,
and now is...*[28] The fact is that God has offered His own love to
man, hoping to be requited and so establish with him a relationship
of love, which necessarily has to be developed within temporality.

And because this is true, real love, it has the essential notes of
reciprocity and bilateralism: *It is enough for the disciple that he be
as his master, and the servant as his lord.*[29] A corollary of which is
that the disciple has been called not only to *complete* the death of
his Master (Col 1:24; 2 Cor 4:10) but also to follow His same way
and culminate it with his own death (Phil 3:10 and *passim*).

---

[27]Rom 6:3.

[28]Jn 4:23. Cf also 5:25; 16:32; etc. For von Balthasar does not expand neu-
trally to either side of the Resurrection of Christ. *Theodramatik: Erster Band:
Prolegomena*, pp. 27 ff. of the English translation: *Theodrama, I, Prolegomena*,
Ignatius Press, San Francisco, 1998.

[29]Mt 10:25.

The condition of temporality is but a natural limitation of the creature, referring here to the origin, development, and completion of her relationship with God. Limitation which, to the extent that it corresponds to human nature, not only does not undermine human existence but raises in it a number of vicissitudes, contingencies, and eventualities that could turn to be favorable or unfavorable, thus resulting in progress or setbacks, victories or losses; enough to provide human life with sufficient depth and importance, which it would have lacked without them (Jn 10:10, 2 Cor 4: 10–11; Col 3:3, Rev 2:10, etc.). Indeed, participation in the existence, in the suffering and death of Jesus Christ, is an opportunity given to the human race envied by the angels.

The chance of failure, even of eternal damnation, is a possible eventuality arising from the natural freedom (imperfect and weak, but not made void) of the human being. Of course the risk is more than offset, to the extent that it is worthy to assume it, given the possibility of making one's own the existence of Jesus Christ. Grace, on the other hand does the rest, in order to transform into glory what would otherwise have been pure misery (*Oh Happy Fault...!*)

It is in this sense that we can say that Protestant theology appears to be sad and distraught, as well as pessimistic. What possibilities of Joy are left to a human nature that, acknowledging itself as being deeply corrupted, cannot ever count on the goodness of its actions? Salvation by *faith alone* implies renouncing definitively the *duel* between God and man. It goes without saying that man's part in that *duel* also necessarily involves grace: *All is grace*, Bernanos said in his *Diary of a Country Priest*. But one effect of grace is precisely that *man's part in the duel is really his own*. Catholic theology is fully open to cooperation between God and man, thereby giving way to alternatives and, along with them, to the possibility of making one's own choices; and from there, man can pass on directly and simply to the chance of love. The relationship of love in the creature is not possible if she cannot choose responsibly and freely a *yes* that will make her able to assume any eventuality, including the risk of closing herself to love with a voluntary *no*.

Risk, which turns human life into an adventure, far from putting the Christian in a miserable situation, provides for him a mark of honor; for this hazard means for him the possibility of and the prerequisite for winning a crown which, otherwise, he would never earn (2 Tim 4: 7–8). When the Apostle describes in detail to the Corinthians the vicissitudes of his life, he does not adopt a plaintive or disheartened tone, but a triumphant air: *We are fools for Christ's sake, but ye are wise in Christ; we are weak, but ye are strong; ye are honourable, but we are despised. Even unto this present hour we both hunger, and thirst, and are naked, and are buffeted, and have no certain dwelling place; and labour, working with our own hands; being reviled, we bless; being persecuted, we suffer it; being defamed, we entreat. We are made as the filth of the world, and are the offscouring of all things unto this day.*[30] It is no wonder, therefore, that a little further on he adds a fiery exhortation: *Wherefore, I beseech you, be ye followers of me.*[31] The same can be said about the telling of his sufferings that he wrote in his second *Letter*, where he uses even more impassioned words: *Are they ministers of Christ? (I speak as a fool) I am more; in labours more abundant, in stripes above measure, in prisons more frequent, in deaths oft. Of the Jews five times received I forty stripes save one. Thrice was I beaten with rods, once was I stoned, thrice I suffered shipwreck, a night and a day I have been in the depth of the sea. In journeying often, in perils*

---

[30] 1 Cor 4: 10–13.

[31] 1 Cor 4:16.

of waters, in perils of robbers, in perils by mine own countrymen, in perils by the heathen, in perils in the city, in perils in the wilderness, in perils in the sea, in perils among false brethren; In weariness and painfulness, in watchings often, in hunger and thirst, in fastings often, in cold and nakedness... But nothing seems to bother the Apostle, who does not see in these adversities but an opportunity to merit a crown of glory. That is why he immediately adds: *If I must needs glory, I will glory of the things that concern my infirmity.*[32] For the author of the *Letter to the Hebrews*, risks, and consequently possible sufferings, vexations, and injustices are but a motive for joy for the Christian: *But call to mind the former days, wherein, being illuminated,*[33] *you endured a great fight of afflictions. Partly, whilst ye were made a gazing stock both by reproaches and afflictions;*[34] *and partly, whilst ye became companions of them that were so used. For ye had compassion of me in my bonds, and took joyfully the spoiling of your goods, knowing in yourselves that ye have in heaven a better and an enduring substance.*[35] And the Apocalypse is not less explicit on this issue: *These are they who are come out of great tribulation and have washed their robes and have made them white in the blood of the Lamb. Therefore, they are before the throne of God; and they serve him day and night in his temple. And he that sitteth on the throne shall dwell among them. They shall no more hunger nor thirst; neither shall the sun fall on them, nor any heat. For the Lamb, which is in the midst of the throne, shall be their*

---

[32] 2 Cor 11: 23–27.30.

[33] He means the day they received their baptism.

[34] The Greek verb θεατριζόμενοι means to expose somebody to public shame in a show which commonly took place in the theater or in the circus.

[35] Heb 10: 32–34.

shepherd, and shall lead them to the fountains of the waters of life;
and God shall wipe away all tears from their eyes.[36]

The current Pastoral activity and Theology tend to marginalize
these doctrines, apparently with the idea of advocating an easier
Christianity, able to enjoy a greater chance of acceptance by the
modern man. It seems that *Christianity involving risks is being*
forgotten to the extent that the same is being done to Christianity
of the Cross. However, it is difficult to believe, for example, that
the most successful pastoral action addressed to the youth is that
in which they are taught that Christianity is not a religion of prohibitions or constraints, but a positive doctrine with the intention
of compelling them to be themselves and to be optimistic towards
life.[37] Perhaps it should be clarified that the mentioned Pastoral
action does not fit well with the abundant evangelical teachings,
uttered by Jesus Christ Himself, about the denial of self and the
need to take up the cross daily; about the loss of one's own life, or
to give up everything to surrender it and thus acquire the precious
pearl or hidden treasure. Optimism about one's existence, welcoming and hopeful openness to those who think differently —which are
considered by some as advanced ideas and the best suited to lead
Christians today— do not seem to be consistent with the warnings
of Jesus Christ according to which the disciples are sent out as sheep
among wolves (Mt 10:16) to a world that, for that very reason and
surely, is going to make them the object of its hatred (Mt 10:22;
Mk 13:13; Lk 21:17); and we should not forget His teaching about

---

[36]Rev 7: 14–17.

[37]These and similar expressions, abundant and quite trendy today, would be acceptable if they are so explained (in the complexity of their true and correct sense,
since it is clear that Christianity is not a religion for pessimistic people, disillu-
sioned with life) that the possibility of dangerous misunderstandings is dispelled.
Relativism and debauchery are always lurking at the door.

the narrow way (Mt 7:14). All of which leads us to think that the life of the disciple of Jesus Christ is anything but an easy and euphoric existence. Regarding the opinion that Christianity is not a religion of prohibitions and constraints, it would be appropriate to recall the words of Jesus Christ, according to which He had not come to destroy the Law, but to fulfill it (Mt 5:17). Truly speaking, a doctrine that tries to make sense of human existence regardless of constraints would be an absurdity similar to a legal system that does not prohibit anything. Besides, what meaning may human life have if there is no room in it for self–denial and even for the loss of one's own life to take hold of the life of the beloved (Mt 16:25, Mk 8:35; Lk 9:24; cf Mt 20:28)?[38]

Although it may seem incredible and paradoxical, cheap and decaffeinated Christianity is not a well–selling product; too many people are not attracted to it. Like any cheap and insubstantial merchandise, it is considered a useless thing that interests no one; it always ends up in smoke; as it happened with the isle of *Barataria* of Sancho Panza —which was thought by many to be a real bargain. According to the narrative of the immortal Chronicle, within a few months of having been well beaten, disappointed, and starving, our good squire decides to finally leave his kingdom:

> *He got himself dressed at last, and then, slowly, for he was sorely bruised and could not go fast, he proceeded to the stable, followed by all who were present, and going up to Dapple embraced him*

---

[38] The legal system intends to organize society *under the law*; that is, primarily to bring order. And order means putting things in place: such a thing should be here, not there; this is first and that second; this is to be done, and that is to be avoided. Which is impossible to carry out, given the way human nature is, without imposing or forcing. Moreover, according to Jesus Christ, the only manner in which to reach the Kingdom of Heaven is to *fulfill the commandments* (Mt 19:17).

and gave him a loving kiss on the forehead, and said to him, not without tears in his eyes:

—Come along, comrade and friend and partner of my toils and sorrows; when I was with you and had no cares to trouble me except mending your harness and feeding your little carcass, happy were my hours, my days, and my years; but since I left you, and mounted the towers of ambition and pride, a thousand miseries, a thousand troubles, and four thousand anxieties have entered into my soul.

And all the while he was speaking in this strain he was fixing the pack–saddle on the ass, without a word from anyone. Then having Dapple saddled, he, with great pain and difficulty, got up on him, and addressing himself to the majordomo, the secretary, the head–carver, and Pedro Recio the doctor and several others who stood by, he said:

—Make way, gentlemen, and let me go back to my old freedom; let me go look for my past life, and raise myself up from this present death.[39]

Saint Paul feared the mere possibility of this decaffeinated Pastoral activity, based mainly on abundant babbling mixed with false optimism and supported by a *wisdom of words* that has its roots in the world's standards. The Apostle dreaded that such procedures could undermine the cross of Christ: *For Christ sent me not to baptize, but to preach the gospel: not with wisdom of words, lest the cross of Christ should be made void.*[40] The Apostle focused his care and concern for evangelizing, as we can see, on adopting the necessary attitude so that non *evacuetur crux Christi*. From this it follows that, according to the Apostle, the risk that a particular

---

[39] *Don Quixote* II, 53.

[40] 1 Cor 1:17.

model of evangelization might abandon the cross of Christ as something empty, meaningless, without content, and therefore useless, is an all too real possibility. For the Apostle of the Gentiles, the scandal of the crucified Christ (the sole object of his preaching, as said in 1 Cor 1:23), is something so essential and necessary in the work of evangelization as to induce him to rebuke, even very severely, some of his disciples: *And I, brethren, if I yet preach circumcision, why do I yet suffer persecution? Then is the scandal of the cross made void. I wish those who trouble you would castrate themselves!*[41]

Still someone might object that, given the possibility of a decline in the Christian life, or even that it may end in failure, it does not seem reasonable to believe that the contingencies which the Christian has to face are to be considered as a wonderful opportunity. Saint Augustine would respond to them with his famous explanation of the need for temptations: *How can we be crowned without victory...?* This, however, cannot be accepted as a final and definitive reply. The fundamental explanation that makes sense of the problem here revolves around the fact that the possibility of sharing the existence, suffering, and death of Christ *is the best thing that could happen to man.* If following Jesus Christ is a challenge that will give rise to heartaches, hardships, and even the possibility of failure, the Christian must welcome nonetheless that which is capable of giving him the supreme joy: being near Him and with Him; as the Baptist said *He that hath the bride is the bridegroom. The friend of the bridegroom, who standeth and heareth Him, rejoiceth greatly because of the bridegroom's voice. This my joy therefore is fulfilled.*[42] If it is true, as most theologians say, that guilt was necessary so that Jesus Christ would become our possession and we

---

[41] Gal 5: 11–12.

[42] Jn 3:29.

may share His destiny (Rom 6: 4–6; Phil 3:10; 1 Pet 4:13), then we cannot but congratulate ourselves because of the fault:

> *Oh happy fault*
> *That merited so great a Redeemer!*

The element of temporality, in the relationship of divine–human love, gives rise to a number of events that are a natural consequence of the succession and duration of things. Which provides diversity and substance to Christian life by making it a situation of exciting eventualities and passionate emotions. We have alluded above to the meaning of the condition of *waiting*, as well as to the importance of the notion of *hour* in the doctrine of the New Testament. Topics of great depth and importance, no doubt, but which we must put aside for the moment, to devote some attention to the concept of *night*.

The issue of the *Night*, indeed, achieves great importance in the Bible, as well as in the writings of mystics and spiritual writers. In terms of importance, the mysterious oracle of Isaiah seemed to echo it, with his strange repetition of the imprecation directed to the sentry and that should not be dismissed as a merely literary device:

> *Watchman, what of the night?*
> *Watchman, what of the night?*[43]

The first thing that calls our attention in this intricate issue is the ambivalent character of the concept of *Night*. Which appears sometimes with positive tones, while at others it appears to imply negative connotations (in the mystics, as we shall see, it tends to cover both aspects in the sense of passing from one to the other).

---

[43] Is 21:11.

Its ambiguity is recognized by the oracle of Isaiah, but, of course, in an enigmatic form.

> *The watchman said:*
> *The morning cometh, also the night.*[44]

For the prophet, as shown, the two moments happen simultaneously. But there is no doubt that in the *itinerarium mentis in Deum* both activities occur. Perhaps one after the other, or perhaps in a way in which it is impossible to distinguish their respective fields and moments, as can be seen in the writings of Saint Teresa, particularly in *The Mansions.*

Following the same pattern, the Night, in the lips of the Lord, sometimes has a negative character; as can be seen in these texts that are not easy to interpret: *I must work the works of him who sent me, while it is day; the night cometh, when no man can work.*[45] *If any man walk in the day, he stumbleth not, because he seeth the light of this world. But if a man walk in the night, he stumbleth, because there is no light in him.*[46] It is evident that these passages have nothing to do with the earth's orbit and the sequence of day and night; Jesus Christ is referring to Himself, the Light of the world without Whom everything is darkness: *As long as I am in the world, I am the light of the world.*[47] *I am the light of the world; he that followeth me shall not walk in darkness, but shall have the light of life.*[48]

---

[44] Is 21:12.

[45] Jn 9:4.

[46] Jn 11: 9–10; cf 12:35.

[47] Jn 9:5.

[48] Jn 8:12. These passages can actually be applied to the world and the Church of today which are increasingly shrouded in darkness, although all signs seem to indicate that we are yet far from the bottom of the abyss into which we are inevitably descending.

A clear example of the ambiguity of the notion of Night as it appears in the Bible and in the spiritual authors can be seen in this little poem of Saint John of the Cross, *Song of the soul that is glad to know God by faith*:[49]

How well I know that fountain's rushing flow
Although by night.

Its deathless spring is hidden. Even so
Full well I guess from whence its sources flow
Though it be night.

Its origin (since it has none) none knows:
But that all origin from it arose
Although by night.

I know there is no other thing so fair
And earth and heaven drink refreshment there
Although by night.

Full well I know its depth no man can sound
And that no ford to cross it can be found
Though it be night.

As can be seen, the poet is glad because of his acquired knowledge about God. Although in reality it is something deeper than mere knowledge, since, as is easily guessed, here he refers to an approach to God that eventually materializes in intimate and loving

---

[49]The ambivalence already appears in the very title of the poem: to be glad to know God, although through the Night of faith (again darkness as a paradox of Christian life). Only the first stanzas will be cited here. The italics are mine.

interaction; that is in the known *I–to–thou* (one–to–one) relationship of the lovers. Which precisely happens by and through the darkness of the Night of faith.

In the itinerant stage, which is traversed by the Christian while in this world, there is no other way to attain a *lofty* knowledge of God.[50] Neither lofty knowledge gained, nor true love: *Nox nocti indicat scientiam.*[51] Night of faith, indeed, is that which communicates the necessary knowledge to the Night or Darkness of the world, to open up access to the path that leads to God. This light and path are essential, since there is no other (Heb 10:38; 11:6). Hence, we find here again the paradox of a gloomy darkness that becomes an imperative luminaire for the road..., through which anyone can get near and make his own the Cross of Jesus Christ. In this regard, Chapter XI of the *Letter to the Hebrews*, far from merely being a text of consolation and encouragement, is a veritable hymn of glory and triumph; as was clearly expressed by the Apostle John, *this is the victory that overcometh the world: Our faith.*[52] Thus Faith and its own darkness (*rerum argumentorum non aparentium*) becomes a *necessary means* to reach the end of the road. It is evident that we must continue in the doctrine of the Christian life as risk and adventure (*iustus ex fide vivit*). Therefore it is necessary that the wheat coexist with the tares, without being removed until harvest time; likewise the fish that are useless as food must also remain in the basket, until the fishermen organize the final selection; hence the synonymy of the terms Itinerant Church, Church Militant, and Cross of Jesus Christ.

---

[50]We are not referring to the natural knowledge of God by mere reason, which is presumed here.

[51]Ps 19:3.

[52]1 Jn 5:4.

Precisely the great tragedy of today's Christians has been to prefer the guide of light (of mere reason, of course), once they rejected the security that accompanies the Night of Faith despite Its obscurity.[53] Deep down, this is tantamount to a voluntary and conscious rejection of the Cross. Modern Christianity has dismissed the sharp edges and the tremendous weight of the Cross and replaced them with welfare theology; namely: theology of this world and for this world; social justice and human rights achieved, with their own strength, by men who have dispensed with God (illusory utopia; allow the redundancy); the total absence of a realm of punishment that traditional Christianity understood beyond this world. Or putting the latter differently, as Modernism prefers it: hell merely as a real possibility without condemnation.

The *Song of Songs* seems to be clearer in identifying the Night with the absence of the Bridegroom; which agrees with the doctrine of the mystics, who attribute a purifying or purgatorial character to this episode.

> *In my bed by night*
> *I sought him whom my soul loveth:*
> *I sought him, and found him not.*[54]

This is why the bride seems to want to hasten the arrival of the Bridegroom, before the night falls. The metaphor of the coming of the break of day and the fleeing of the shadows is undoubtedly a reference to the night:

---

[53]It calls one's attention to the transformation of the Protestant notion of *sola fides* into *sola ratio*. It was bound to happen; for there is always a mania to divide the whole that man is (in need of faith and reason) and to put away, at the same time, the relational universe that God, in His goodness, wanted to establish with him (*admirabile commercium*).

[54]Sg 3:1.

> *Until the day break,*
> *And the shadows flee away,*
> *Turn, my beloved, and be thou like a roe*
> *Or a young hart upon the mountains of Bether.*[55]

The Bridegroom, in turn, also seems craving to leave the night and meet the bride.

> *Open to me, my sister, my love,*
> *My dove, my undefiled:*
> *For my head is full of dew,*
> *And my locks with the drops of the night.*[56]

It is normal that the ambivalent character that usually accompanies it affects mystical poetry which initially tends to identify the *Night* with the absence of the Bridegroom. In turn, this absence can have a character either of purification of the bride or of longing waiting, which is indeed the most appropriate time to conduct a search. This ambivalent element is easily perceived in the poetry of Saint John of the Cross, as we saw, where the searching status of the Bridegroom, serene and even joyful, seems to prevail:

> *Upon a gloomy night,*
> *With all my cares to loving ardours flushed,*
> *O venture of delight!*
> *With nobody in sight*
> *I went abroad when all my house was hushed.*[57]

---

[55]Sg 2:17.

[56]Sg 5:2.

[57]Saint John of the Cross, *Dark Night of the Soul.*

In safety, in disguise,
In darkness up the secret stair I crept,
O happy enterprise!
Concealed from other eyes
When all my house at length in silence slept.

Upon that lucky night
In secrecy, inscrutable to sight,
I went without discerning
And with no other light
Except for that which in my heart was burning.[58]

As we can see, the *Night* is not here a situation of anguish, but rather a longing search for the Bridegroom by the bride. It includes a feeling of serenity and even joy. The bride is burning with the desire of being with the Bridegroom; therefore the night is for her the ideal moment to go out and meet Him. That is why she starts her quest *secretly, with nobody in sight, concealed from other eyes.*

The mystical Night does not appear tinted with despair or uncertainty. And the bride admits that no other light except the one that fed the instinct of her heart guided her.

Sometimes, however, the feelings of grief and sorrow because of the absence or departure of the Bridegroom appear strongly in mystical poetry; although they have nothing to do with anxiety that tends to despair. It so happens that the focus is now on the fact that the Bridegroom hides Himself; or on the fact that He has disappeared, resulting in feelings of sharp pain on the part of the bride:

---

[58]Saint John of the Cross, *Dark Night of the Soul.*

> *In the dark of night my Beloved left me,*
> *As the sun drops past the hills into the west,*
> *As the waters flow from river to the sea,*
> *In the dark of night left me whom I love best.*[59]

....

> *At night he left for the distant mountain range,*
> *At night he followed the road around the bend,*
> *At night I was left in foreign lands and strange,*
> *At night I was left alone without my friend.*[60]

At other times, when she sees that night is coming and the Bridegroom is not there, the bride is carried away by fear, and her sorrow and anguish deepen. She knows that she is not with the Bridegroom and openly confesses that she wants to belong to Him; at the same time, she shudders at the mere possibility that the darkness of the night may make the absence of the Beloved more acutely felt:

---

[59]In the Spanish original:

> *De noche se perdió el Amado mío,*
> *como se oculta el sol tras el otero,*
> *como corren las aguas por el río*
> *de noche se marchó quien yo más quiero.*

[60]In the Spanish original:

> *De noche se marchó hacia la montaña,*
> *de noche se marchó por el sendero,*
> *de noche me quedé, por tierra extraña,*
> *de noche me quedé sin compañero.*

> *The fading of day is fleet,*
> *Dulcet brown goldfinch, your songs dwindle faster;*
> *As in a dream bittersweet,*
> *Night comes, we both sorrows meet*
> *You without freedom, me without my master.*[61]

However, and despite all this, what we have agreed to call the ambivalent condition of the Night (anguish/hope, sadness/joy) always ends up leaning toward the side of hopeful joy. Even the painful *Nights* of the senses and of the spirit of Saint John of the Cross are but a path that through the *Nothing* leads to *Everything*. We have said that this is precisely the condition of temporality that gives man the possibility of sharing, as an invaluable gift from above, the existence, the suffering, and the death of Jesus.

Thus there is nothing peculiar about the *Night* appearing, in both the poetry of the mystics and in their own doctrine, as the path that inevitably brings man to Jesus Christ. And so it becomes a source of intense joy and exultation:

> *O night that was my guide!*
> *O darkness dearer than the morning's pride,*
> *O night that joined the lover*
> *To the beloved bride*
> *Transfiguring them each into the other.*[62]

---

[61] In the Spanish original:

> *El día ya se aleja,*
> *dulce jilguero de color trigueño,*
> *y así otra vez nos deja,*
> *como en amargo sueño,*
> *a ti sin libertad, y a mí sin dueño.*

[62] Saint John of the Cross, *Dark Night of the Soul.*

Thus *Night* becomes a sure way and a most auspicious moment to meet the Lord. The virgins of the parable were suddenly cognizant of the arrival of the Bridegroom *at midnight* (Mt 25:6). In effect, He usually makes Himself present when least expected or when His arrival is most improbable and difficult (Mt 14: 24–25; Mk 13:35; Jn 11:17). *Night*, therefore, as we shall see at length later, cannot be an occasion for the disciple to despair, but rather the opposite. As the Hindu poet Tagore beautifully said: *If you cry because the sun is setting, your tears will prevent you from seeing the stars.*[63] The Night, with which the world wants to intimidate the disciple of Christ who refuses to belong to it, despite the obvious feelings of absence, sorrow, and labors which it implies, by paradox becomes the most direct way leading to Jesus Christ. Sometimes, the disciple may not be able, because of the night, to detect the presence of the Master anywhere. *Nevertheless, it is certain that He is there*; as someone once put it in a different way:

> *Your look is one of grieving*
> *As the light of the valley fades with your sighs*
> *But, once night steals the evening*
> *And overtakes hills and skies,*
> *One million stars brighten your face and your eyes.*[64]

---

[63]Rabindranath Tagore, *Stray Birds*, 6

[64]In the Spanish original:

> *De llanto es tu mirada*
> *cuando la luz del valle ya declina,*
> *mas, luego de llegada*
> *la noche a la colina,*
> *con un millón de estrellas la ilumina.*

In this sense, the *Night* indeed turns out to be the best and only way to find the Lord. The bride, as we have seen in Saint John of the Cross, sets out her search *in darkness and in safety*, walking *without being noticed*, and, of course, *very much in secret* and taking advantage of the moment when she is *concealed from others eyes*. Unfortunately, this solitude and silence, these hidden and unknown paths that are true routes leading directly to the Master, have been completely forgotten by modern Christianity. They have been re-placed by the deafening racket of the world that attempts by any means to disguise the emptiness of souls. Yet, it is at midnight, in the solitude and tranquility of silence, that the Lord arrives: *And behold the Lord passeth, and a great and strong wind before the Lord, overthrowing the mountains, and breaking the rocks in pieces: but the Lord is not in the wind. And after the wind, an earthquake: but the Lord is not in the earthquake. And after the earthquake, a fire: but the Lord is not in the fire. And after the fire, a whistling of a gentle air. And when Elias heard it, he covered his face with his mantle, and coming forth, stood in the entering in of the cave.*[65]

In effect, this is the age of Christianity understood as an ongoing *show business*; Cloistered Convents where religious men or women practiced the so–called contemplative life have disappeared. Thus, one does not hesitate to ask the embarrassing question: What have we really gained once the members of religious orders have aban-doned the life of prayer and have rushed out, as if carried by a wind of madness, to bear what they thought to be a necessary witness and apostolate *in the midst of, in,* and *with* the world? Where is the advantage resulting from the bride having abandoned definitely the quest to find the Bridegroom so that she could spend most of the time talking to her accompanying maids? Now we are poles

---

[65]1 Kings 19: 11–13.

apart from the instruction given by the Bridegroom, charging everybody so that nothing and no one may distract the bride or make her abandon her search:

> *I adjure you, O daughters of Jerusalem,*
> *By the roes and the harts of the fields,*
> *That you stir not up, nor awake my beloved,*
> *Till she please.*[66]

The modern time of bustle and big show of large *religious* gatherings has replaced silent prayer, humility, poverty, and abandonment of the world. But, was it for the benefit or rather for the misfortune of the Church and Christian life? For the time being, the competent authority must provide the pending answer. Continuing with our line of questioning, can anybody honestly think that those crowds, made up mostly of young people, gathered to see a show involving an expensive set up, live an authentic Christian life, or that they are going to be determined to do it from now on?

The Bridegroom's wish that His beloved be not awakened or stirred up until she please has nothing to do with any intention of leaving her immersed in a sort of somnolence or inactivity regarding her love for the Bridegroom. The sleep contemplated here in connected to the enchantment caused by the love she feels toward her Bridegroom:

> *In my bed by night*
> *I sought him whom my soul loveth.*[67]

---

[66]Sg 3:5; 2:7; 8:4.

[67]Sg 3:1.

In the *Song of Songs* sleep is the very moment when the love of the bride, who is next to the Bridegroom, culminates; when neither wants to be disturbed by anything or anybody:

> *The king hath brought me into his chambers:*
> *We will be glad and rejoice in thee.*[68]

> ....

> *I sleep, but my heart watches:*
> *It is the voice of my beloved that knocketh, saying.*[69]

It is precisely that environment of solitude surrounding the night that the bride is looking for, in the company of the Bridegroom:

> *Come, my beloved, let us go forth into the field;*
> *Let us lodge in the villages.*[70]

We must consider that this love which we have called unselfish also is *absolute and exclusive.* And this is the only convincing explanation —as we will see later— of the true meaning of the *one hundred per cent* promised by the Lord; a strange expression that perhaps has not been understood in all its depth. But let us progress from one stage to the next for the sake of clarity.

Man's answer to the love that God offers him must be affirmative and absolute. Parity and reciprocity —two essential qualities of

---

[68]Sg 1:4.

[69]Sg 5:2.

[70]Sg 7:12.

love— demand of both lovers[71] a firm and decisive *yes*. God cannot possibly understand it differently, as the all too clear and forceful corresponding scriptural passages demonstrate. It is said in them that God expects man to love Him *with all his heart, and with all his soul, and with all his mind.*[72] Other texts seem even more peremptory: *He that loveth father or mother more than me is not worthy of me; and he that loveth son or daughter more than me is not worthy of me.*[73] Still others are even more compelling: *If any man come to me, and hate not his father, and mother, and wife, and children, and brethren, and sisters, yea, and his own life also, he cannot be my disciple.*[74] The first consequence that follows from this is that the love of the creature for God must be above all other love with which the former brooks no comparison, whether it be love of father, mother, children, one's own life... On the other hand, it is important to notice that Our Lord puts so much emphasis on the love of God that when it is compared to the love of any creature, the latter seems to be paired with hatred. Which, despite the fact that we are evidently dealing with a *modus loquendi*,[75] clarifies things with regard to the relationship between these two kinds of love.

Modern exegesis is frequently set on making some passages of the Scriptures more palatable for souls prone to get scandalized. At least, that is what it seems. In most of these cases, this methodol-

---

[71]We could have properly said *both contestants*; for the relationship between two lovers can be compared to a strange and mysterious contest, as the *Song of Songs* already insinuated (2:4) and as an analysis of the Parables of the Talents and of the Mines suggests. God has taken the initiative in this contest (1 Jn 4:19; Rom 11:35) that already counts with the divine *yes* as a previous requisite.

[72]Mt 22:37 and Mk 12: 28–33; both echoing Deut 6:5.

[73]Mt 10:37.

[74]Lk 14:26.

[75]Cf, for example, Mt 5: 29–30; Mk 9: 43–45.

ogy is one more manifestation, among many others, of the wave of
Rationalism and Modernism that is currently permeating Catholic
theology. The fact that many exegetes and commentators, like Max
Zerwick, S.J. (*Analysis Philologica*) among others, consider the term
'hate' as a Hebraism and translate it as *minus diligo* has little foundation and sounds arbitrary.[76]

We must make reference here to the *Bibles of the People* of South
America. They are horrible bibliographical fabrications that have
appeared in recent times and have been unfortunately distributed
all over Europe also. As we can see, evil seems to be, in its own way,
diffusivum sui. Until now, everyone had naively believed that the
Bible was always something of the People and for the People, since
it is the Word of God revealed to all men. But the modern Pastoral
action has come out with the awesome discovery of the *Bibles of
the People*, thus posing the serious and mysterious problem of its
nature. Indeed, what are these Bibles and for whom are the other
Bibles destined, since the latter apparently belong only to an elite?
But these miscarriages of nature, given their Marxist–like language
and their equally Marxist way of twisting ideas, do not contribute in
any way to making God's Word more accessible; but that is another
story. Because we clearly find here the neo–modernist trends in

---

[76]The Greek verb μισέω has the very defined meaning of *to hate* or *to despise* as it
can be seen in other passages of Saint Luke: 6: 22.27; 16:13; 21:17. As for the other
Synoptics and Saint John, the same exact thing happens; see, for instance, texts like
Mt 5:43; 6:24; Mk 13:13; Jn 3:20; 7:7; etc., to mention only few; there is no doubt in
this regard. To claim that Hebraisms are used by a hagiographer like Saint Luke,
who was a Greek gentile and whose Hellenistic education cannot be contested,
lacks any basis and is even amusing. There is no need to resort to exegetical
or philosophical arrangements that, in addition to not solving the problem, blur
the strength of the passage and spread confusion. Whenever euphemisms, softened
expressions, or similar things are used in the biblical exegesis to *explain* the inspired
texts, then the strength of their content and meaning is weakened.

theology, shared by all those who are reluctant to welcome the world of the supernatural. They, in one way or another, are not willing to admit the existence of true love; therefore, they do not recognize either its true nature or the strength of its essence.

> *For love is strong as death;*
> *Jealousy as hard as hell,*
> *The coals thereof are coals of fire,*
> *A flame of Yahweh himself.*[77]

Unfortunately, for many people the *Song of Songs* is but a literary poem. These same people mistake human life for a *lite* existence in all its aspects, none of which is relevant for them. They have left too far afield Jesus Christ's words —which are for them like very distant and almost smothered echoes—: *Ego veni ut vitam habeant et abundantius habeant. I am come that they may have life and may have it more abundantly.*[78] This phenomenon has become more evident, in the Catholic Church, as a result of the disintegration of Theology which occurred after the closing of Vatican II.

Delving into the study of the essence of love may perhaps be the key to the problem, along with its possible answer. Divine and divine–human love, unlike merely human love (even elevated by grace) are not configured according to a more/less, greater/lower correlation, but to an everything/nothing one (Jn 3:16; 13:1; Rom 8:32). That is why Jesus Christ, Who is bound to the norms regulating our language, equates human love to hatred when compared to divine love. Not because the former has anything to do with odium but due to the *specific* exigencies of divine love, which we will examine next.

---

[77] Sg 8:6.

[78] Jn 10:10.

It goes without saying that human love is real love to the extent that it is true love. But it cannot dispense with a *quantitative* character resulting in the logical limitations imposed by the oscillations between more and less. Divine love, on the contrary, rejects any possible measure, evaluation, or calculation; it responds only to the idea of *totality*. Divine, or divine–human, love does not try to relate what is greater to what is smaller, or vice versa —in the sense of comparing greater quantity to smaller quantity; the only correlation this love admits is between everything and nothing, or the other way around.

Evidently, divine–human love, as far as the creature is concerned, is a shared love. It has been put in the human heart by the Holy Ghost, *Who has been given to us;*[79] but the creature keeps his human condition and is one of the two terms of this bilateral relationship whose opposite is the heart of God. Therefore, the creature shares, in some way at least, the character of *totality* proper to divine love. Let us keep in mind that the biblical command of loving *with all thy heart, and with all thy mind, and with all thy soul, and with all thy strength* refers to man in his relationship not with the rest of creation but only with God.

This same expression suggests that there is no idea of reward in the relationship of love. Indeed, one's self–giving out of love does not expect anything like recompense; at best, an answer of love. We have already said that love does not expect to find, as a sympathetic echo to its offering, anything different, alien, or even equivalent to

---

[79]Rom 5:5; Gal 4:6.

itself. The enamored answer to its call is its only reward; love never, at any moment, desires anything else.[80]

It is not possible to interpret *a hundred times more* in any way that may have remotely anything to do with a literal sense: one hundred houses for one house, one hundred children for one child, etc. Even if we accept this expression as a metaphor, we must aim very high to approach (and always in an uncertain manner) a somehow acceptable interpretation of the expression. It is evident that it is a trope pointing at the notion of an extraordinary overabundance, impossible to describe with words. Our Lord promises those who abandon everything to follow Him that which no human being can ever comprehend or imagine (1 Cor 2:9). It should be noted that the promise, although waiting for its complete fulfillment in the *not yet* of the future age, has begun to be realized in the *already* of the current aeon. But this beginning should not be considered as mere initiation, somewhat embryonic and incipient. Although the promise has not yet been fully consummated, its reality already has an entity of unimaginable significance.

On the other hand, the Lord Himself expressly affirms that this magnificent promise is already a reality *There is no man that hath left house, or brethren, or father... who shall not receive an hundredfold now in this time and in the world to come life everlasting.*

---

[80] *Is per se sufficit, is per se placet, et propter se. Ipse meritum, ipse præmium est sibi. Amor præter se non requirit causam, non fructum. Fructus eius, usus eius. Amo, quia amo; amo, ut amem. Magna res amor, si tamen ad suum recurrat principium, si suæ origini redditus, si refusus suo fonti, semper ex eo sumat, unde iugiter fluat. Solus est amor ex omnibus animæ motibus, sensibus atque affectibus, in quo potest creatura, etsi non ex æquo, respondere auctori, vel de simili mutuam rependere vicem... Nam cum amat Deus, non aliud vult quam amari: quippe non ad aliud amat nisi ut ametur, sciens ipso amore beatos, qui se amaverint* (Saint Bernard, *Sermones super Cantica Canticorum*, 83, 4, *Opera Omnia*, Migne, Patrología Latina, 183, 1183).

Which is not difficult to understand. The time of love arrived for a Christian at the moment of his baptism; moreover, to some extent, from all eternity when God decided to create him in time. And love is already true love from the very first moment that it commences to exist in the creature. This means that love also is for her a total self–giving which, although not yet consummated, is nevertheless rooted in her as a fundamental note of its essence. Love being the concurrent (simultaneous) *spiratio* of the two lovers,[81] it possesses from its very first moment the note of totality (and therefore perenniality) as its own. Hence, Saint Paul's proclamation that *love never falleth away* (1 Cor 13:8)[82] must be understood, according to what we said about the concept *hour* in the New Testament and if we want to comprehend its rich meaning,[83] not only in the sense of from now to the future (forward sense) but also from the future to the present moment (backward sense). As far as love is concerned, impatient as it is in its own nature, the time of loving is always at hand:

> *Rise up, my love,*
> *My fair one, and come away.*
> *For the winter is now past,*
> *The rain is over and gone.*
> *The flowers have appeared in our land;*
> *The time of pruning is come...*[84]

To understand this problem more clearly, we must take into account that the complete Joy promised by the Master to His disciples

---

[81]Saint John of the Cross, *Spiritual Canticle*, XXXIX; *Living Flame of Love*, II, 6. Cf my *Commentaries on the Song of Songs*, II, Shoreless Lake Press, New Jersey, 2006, pp. 33–34.

[82]*Caritas numquam excidit* (πίπτει means here *cadit*, or *esse desinit*).

[83]Cf note 82.

[84]Sg 2: 10–12.

is for the present moment.[85] And since Joy is the first fruit of love, Perfect Joy always accompanies Perfect Love. Hence, the overabundance of Love promised by the Lord in the *hundredfold* proportion is already real in the present eon.

It is then certain, because the Lord said it expressly, that the overflowing love of the *hundredfold* is for this world and does not need to wait for the *world to come*. In effect, one can speak of the first meeting of the lovers and of their first enamored glance,

> *The coals thereof are coals of fire,*
> *A flame of Yahweh himself,*[86]

but love is never an inexperienced beginner. As for divine–human love planted in the heart of the creature, it is oriented to look at the Beloved from the very first moment, with one's whole heart, mind, and strength. By comparison, any other love would be hatred.[87] Moreover, the beginning love of the lovers, the love at first sight that follows their mutual gaze, possesses a *special impetus* (Rev 2:4) that endows it with a special aura of lofty and sublime charm. Shakespeare immortalized this impulsive element of the rapturous love in the first meeting of his *Romeo and Juliet*. This particular note of the love between the two youths of Verona is subtlety present throughout the entire play, feeding the emotional response of the would–be spectators or readers, who almost never are totally conscious of this fact. Love ignores time from the very first moment of its birth. That is why the lover who has fallen under its influence

---

[85]There are numerous texts in the New Testament that confirm this. Cf, for example, Jn 15:11; 16: 20.24.

[86]Sg 8:6.

[87]See note 76.

does not acknowledge that his love had a beginning before which it never existed. Much less does he accept that his love will have an end, where it will cease to be. For the lovers, love exists before time... and will last without ever knowing the passing of years:

> *I sought you in the valley*
> *Where you abide in hidden mountain towers,*
> *To gaze at you lovingly*
> *Amid blackberry bowers*
> *As time gently dies in sweet cherished hours.*[88]

Nevertheless, we have not found yet the true reason for the promise of *a hundredfold* promised by the Lord to His followers for the present time before the *coming eon*. It would be a mistake to want to discover in this way of *overwhelming* His followers with love (Rom 5:5) a sort of generous compensation on the part of the Master. In reality, what totally explains this *hundredfold* granted by Jesus Christ to those who have given up everything for His sake are fundamental laws of love; in this case, the principles of bilateralism and reciprocity.

We know that love, as we have said many times, tends to place both lovers on the same level *I will not now call you servants... But I have called you friends* (Jn 15:15); that is, on the same level, at the same height: *If I wash thee not, thou shalt have no part with me*

---

[88]In the Spanish original:

> *Al valle fui a buscarte*
> *hasta el oculto vado donde moras,*
> *para poder mirarte*
> *donde las zarzamoras*
> *sin ver morir al tiempo entre las horas.*

(Jn 13:8), which is, moreover, the only possible circumstance for a real relationship of love to exist either from the *I* to the *thou* or from the *thou* to the *I*; for, given the necessary nearness in the interaction of love, the dialogue of love only takes place in the intimacy of the greatest closeness: *And if I shall go and prepare a place for you, I will come again and will take you to myself; that where I am, you also may be.*[89] And should this not be enough, we also know that mutual and total self–giving, which has been carried out voluntarily and freely by both lovers, excludes, by definition, any disparity or inequality between lovers:

> *I am my beloved's,*
> *And my beloved is mine.*[90]

Therefore, the laws of equality, bilateralism, and reciprocity in love are unbendable and immutable. Thus, if God wanted, as love demands it, to receive from man an *equivalent* amorous answer, *on the same level and with the same intensity* as His offering, then man had to be capable of that response. And since everything depends on grace, God had to overflow man's loving capacity (active and passive), so that the plenitude of His offering of love would be able to receive a loving answer of the same intensity and stature. Hence God had to make man rich and munificent, so that he, in turn, would be able to give and surrender total largesse: *For ye know the grace of our Lord Jesus Christ, that, though he was rich, yet for your sakes he became poor, that ye through his poverty might be rich.*[91]

---

[89] Jn 14:3; cf 17:24.

[90] Sg 6:3; cf 2:16; 7:11.

[91] 2 Cor 8:9.

This is not an arbitrary interpretation, as the end of the Parables of the Talents and of the Pounds demonstrate. In the first one (Mt 25: 14 ff) ten talents were given back by him who had received five; four for the two received, etc. And the same happens in the Parable of the Pounds (Lk 19: 11 ff), where the pound received to do business yielded ten or five more, etc., depending on the individual.

Consequently, if love has been given to man in the superabundant *hundredfold* ratio,[92] then man has been made able to answer in the same abounding, immeasurable fashion: ten talents for the five received; ten pounds for one given. Both metaphors express the same reality. Thus, the dialogue of love is made possible, which could not exist until both lovers were on the same plane, as the supreme laws of love demand. Now the love scales are balanced, and the possible *one–to–one* relationship of love is made real. True love implies, as a fundamental exigency, giving everything, absolutely everything, to the beloved, as a fundamental exigency; which is, at the same time, the act that the lover considers to be the most free and voluntary of his entire existence (Jn 3:35).

In this way, the possibility of the *one–to–one* relationship, in which both lovers are on the same level while each one remains being who he or she is, becomes a fundamental component of the essence of love. Therefore, since the lover is thinking more of giving than of receiving (Acts 20:35), the most perfect prayer is not petition or supplication but praise, which in the dialogue of love cannot be but mutual and reciprocal. In the Parable of the Ten Virgins, only the foolish ones beg and supplicate (although their request is not granted), for they were careless in their waiting for the Bridegroom (Mt 25: 11–12); the sensible ones, though, just entered in with Him to the marriage. For this reason, the flirtatious remark or loving

---

[92] *For God doth not give the Spirit by measure* (Jn 3:34).

compliment uttered by either of the lovers and addressed to the other is the most sublime and perfect form of dialogue ever imagined by any mind, whether it be divine, angelic, or human:

> *Behold thou are fair, O my love,*
> *Behold, thou are fair, thou hast dove's eyes.*
>
> ....
>
> *How beautiful you are, how charming,*
> *My love, my delight!*
>
> ....
>
> *Behold thou art fair, my beloved,*
> *And comely. Our bed is flourishing.*[93]

That is why one can say that the loving compliment *I love you*, is the sweetest and most tender locution that the human being has been granted to hear or utter. Generally speaking, some people usually see in the loving compliment a gentle, loving remark that a man addresses to a woman; in reality, both use it, as attested by immemorial custom. Others think that *I love you*, when spoken by a woman to a man, is something like an *admission*, a surrendering before him. But the most accurate opinion seems to be that which affirms that this expression is a free, filled–with–tenderness declaration with which man, when it is he who uses it, gives his heart to her, at her disposal. If this opinion is true, then one can see in it a thin echo of the authority over the woman that in reference to marriage the Bible grants to man, who, in turn, out of love submits

---

[93]Sg 1:14; 7:7; 1:16.

himself to her. Consequently, one can say that charity again balances things, putting them in their proper places and recognizing the worth of each one as only charity knows and can do.[94]

What could happen when the declaration *I love you* is uttered by man and addressed to Infinite Love? What can be said when, on the contrary, man is the one who hears *I love you* from the very lips of Infinite Love?

Here, more than anywhere else, we face a Mystery. In effect, we are not referring to the *unspeakable words, which it is not lawful for a man to utter* (2 Cor 12:4). We can, of course, speak about the mystery of Love —which is but the mystery of God— as much as we want. But we will always reach a limiting wall beyond which we cannot proceed. Or maybe it would be possible to pierce through it, only to discover that the horizon goes further and further away, impossible to be reached.

One could speak, for example, about the emotion and joy caused in the soul of the bride upon hearing the statement *I love you* from the lips of her Bridegroom; with the certainty, however, that one would not be doing anything other than babbling. This would be a task doomed beforehand to failure, despite having been undertaken under enormous anticipated difficulties and with the overwhelming feeling, impossible to dispel, that one is really saying nothing. For the ineffable, you know, is simply indescribable.

We know well that neither our understanding nor our imagination is able to comprehend, and much less to express, what our heart somehow *guesses*. And since we are also aware that, when all is said and done, the Revealed Word must adapt Itself to our nature to be understood, we can still resort to Scripture. What is the purpose now? Simply to try to sketch, in an almost desperate attempt, some

---

[94]The balance between authority and love in Christian existence is clearly dealt with in the New Testament: Mt 20: 25–28; Mk 9:35; Lk 9:48; Eph 5: 21–33.

idea about the joy the bride feels upon hearing the compliment *I love you* uttered by the lips of the Bridegroom.[95]

Since the utterance *I love you* is the cause of incredible joy when heard and pronounced in merely human love, it is much more so when applied to divine–human love. Some will say that even when referred to merely human love the task of speaking about it is already impossible; which is absolutely true, as we have said before. But that is not sufficient reason to not take advantage of the crumbs that fall from the table where the Word of God is distributed.

To begin with, we can recall the words of the Baptist regarding the joy brought about by hearing the voice of the Bridegroom: *The friend of the Bridegroom, who standeth and heareth Him, rejoiceth greatly because of the bridegroom's voice; this my joy therefore is fulfilled.*[96] It is, indeed, impossible not to feel overwhelmed by joy after hearing His voice; as it is also not possible to feel sorrow when one is near Him (Mt 9:15):

> *My Bridegroom's voice is for me,*
> *Like the wake of a ship deeply furrowing*
> *Like winds that stir so lightly*
> *Like a gentle whispering,*
> *Like the solemn moves of a night bird on wing.*[97]

---

[95]Pascal's phrase: *The heart has its reasons which reason knows nothing of* is better understood in the sense that some capacity of infinitude is attributed to the heart —the famous *Thou hast made us for Thyself, Lord, and our heart never resteth till it findeth rest in Thee* of Saint Augustine— which is not commonly, not even possibly, ascribed to reason.

[96]Jn 3:29.

[97]In the Spanish original:

> *Es la voz del Esposo*
> *como la huidiza estela de una nave,*
> *como aire rumoroso,*
> *como susurro suave,*
> *como el vuelo nocturno de algún ave.*

As it happens in the tale of the *Pied Piper of Hamelin*, here also there is no other way but to follow Him once we have heard the enchanting music of His voice. The Good Shepherd goes ahead of His sheep and calls them by their name, and they follow Him docilely because they know His voice, which is not the voice of a stranger (Jn 10: 3–5). *The Song of Songs*, logically, cannot but mention this issue. And, as it happened to the children of Hamelin, who felt compelled to follow the magical Pied Piper in punishment for their parents' selfishness, we are not able to put up any resistance. The only difference would be that, in our case, nobody would think that he is being punished, for he would only feel unfortunate who had not heard the enchanting music of the enamored voice:

> *The voice of my beloved!*
> *Behold he cometh*
> *Leaping upon the mountains,*
> *Skipping upon the hills.*
> *Behold my beloved speaketh to me...*[98]

And who would be able to resist the call of the enamored voice of the Bridegroom Who arrives, like a beggar, to the door of the bride to be heard and received by her? Indeed, *Behold, I stand at the door, and knock. If any man shall hear my voice and open the door, I will come in to him, and will sup with him, and he with me.*[99] The surrendering of the heart alone can answer the petition for alms of love uttered by the lips of an enamored beggar. In divine–human love this surrendering becomes following; following

---

[98] Sg 2: 8.10.
[99] Rev 3:20.

Him, staying with Him, being near Him, living with Him sharing His own life:

> *Open to me, my sister, my love, my dove,*
> *My undefiled; for my head is filled with dew,*
> *And my locks with the drops of the night.*[100]

In effect, when facing these requests that are so pressing because they spring from a heart in love, what else can be done but to initiate a blind following? A true, unconditional following, for a true lover never thinks of imposing any conditions to it. There is no room here for any *quid pro quo*; there is only and simply *take everything*:

> *Tracking your sandal–mark*
> *The maidens search the roadway for your sign,*
> *Yearning to catch the spark*
> *And taste the scented wine*
> *Which emanates a balm that is divine.*[101]
>
> *My Love, our climb goes steeply*
> *To hills with rosemary–rockrose covering.*
> *There we two will drink deeply*
> *From the pure abundant spring*
> *And taste waters fresh and clear and murmuring.*[102]

---

[100]Sg 5:2.

[101]Saint John of the Cross, *Spiritual Canticle*.

[102]In the Spanish original:

> *Mi Amado, subiremos*
> *al monte del tomillo y de la jara,*
> *y luego beberemos*
> *los dos, en la alfaguara,*
> *del agua rumorosa, fresca y clara.*

Let us go to the bowers
In the hills with myrtle there
We'll make two wreaths of flowers,
Saffron roses for our hair
And petals of azure blue tulips so rare.[103]

Rejoice, my love with me
And in your beauty see us both reflected:
By mountain–slope and lea,
Where purest rills run free,
We'll pass into the forest undetected.[104]

Then climb to lofty places
Among the caves and boulders of the granite,
Where every track effaces,
And, entering, leave no traces,
And revel in the wine of the pomegranate.[105]

It would be useless to try to explain, in quantifiable terms, the joyous feeling of the bride upon hearing the declaration *I love you* from the lips of the Bridegroom. One could speak of extreme joy; of lightheadedness produced by excessive bliss; of glare and fascination, wonder, and awe; of highest degree of delight and perfect happiness; and even of other terms we can accumulate. And yet,

---

[103]In the Spanish original:

Vayamos a las faldas
del monte florecido de arrayanes;
y hagamos dos guirnaldas
con rosas de azafranes
y pétalos de azules tulipanes.

[104]Saint John of the Cross, *Spiritual Canticle.*
[105]Saint John of the Cross, *Spiritual Canticle.*

one would not go beyond the reach of mere verbiage, and without much clarifying.[106] And although it is clear that we speak here of divine–human love in a high degree of perfection, we are not referring to mystic theology; therefore, we are not going to resort to its unique terminology. Consequently, we are left with the resource we have just used; that is, putting together a few terms, none of which is going to provide an accurate picture of the topic to which we refer; but each and every one of them can somehow *point to* signs containing clues about our topic. In this regard, terms such as lightheadedness, rapture, ecstasy, and similar others could help, rather shallowly and coarsely, our purpose. The writings on this subject, including Holy Scripture (particularly the *Song of Songs*), frequently use references to drunkenness, wine, and wedding banquets, to describe the effects of love on the lovers. As can be seen, for example, in the following verse of the *Spiritual Canticle* of Saint John of the Cross:

> *Deep–cellared is the cavern*
> *Of my love's heart, I drank of him alive:*
> *Now, stumbling from the tavern*
> *No thoughts of mine survive*
> *And I have lost the flock I used to drive.*

The help of the metaphor, allegory, or other tropes, in a deliberately ambiguous and obscure language, is a resource necessary and mandatory. It is a procedure to which Scripture can in no way

---

[106]Once again we bump into the limitations and miseries of human language. Let us recall that feelings do not fit into concepts, and the latter cannot be comprehensively expressed in simple terms.

be alien: *The Spirit*[107] *breatheth where he will and thou hearest his voice, but thou knowest not whence he cometh and whither he goeth.*[108] Clearly this is a text too deep to be easily understood. If we dare to attempt some sort of interpretation, perhaps we could say that Love *(the Spirit),* by His overflowing action upon the creature (Rom 5:5), floods man and makes him feel the embrace of His love, His caresses, and His compliments of love *(thou hearest his voice),* thus immersing him in a daze of ecstasy. In this state, man would not be able to explain or say anything about it: where his Love comes from, for example; or from which place the torrent that is flooding him is emerging; or where is the spring that generates this Love Who causes in him such an arbitration of love. Man might inquire about the whereabouts of the Beloved Who entrances him so, and where could he go and look for Him to possess Him more closely *(thou knowest not whence he cometh).* This is, of course, an intoxication of Love that induces the human soul to look longingly for the Bridegroom, although she knows well that one cannot carry out that search but through tortuous, untrodden, and unknown paths:

> *Tell me, O thou whom my soul loveth,*
> *Where thou feedest, where thou makest thy flock*
>   *rest at noon,*
> *Lest I begin to wander*
> *After the flocks of thy companions.*[109]

Once the bride has begun her hazardous search of the unknown lover through lonely and rough trails, she may find Him. And surely

---

[107]Some translate *wind.* The term seems to be deliberatively ambiguous. Nevertheless, the Greek word πνεῦμα and the context compel us to prefer rather the translation of the Neo–Vulgate: *Spiritus, ubi vult, spirat.*

[108]Jn 3:8.

[109]Sg 1:7.

then she may get a glimpse, although she cannot explain how, of that place *whence* the Bridegroom *comes*:

> *I set out to search,*
> *with quick and hurried pace,*
> *The One who enamours me;*
> *Then, in the ford, face to face,*
> *I let my deep sorrow die,*
> *While, far away, Philomel sang in the sky.*[110]

What the bride will never find out, until she has completely reached the end of the road, is *whither* the Bridegroom *goes* and whereto He is taking her. This mysterious *whither* is not merely a place, which would be, in fact, the least important thing in this case. We must understand this *whither* as something intelligently indefinite and distantly fuzzy, which can only make sense as a final end of completion toward which love is walking. However, who is able to explain, or even imagine, what this final moment or culmination of love is? Assuming, of course, that Love is heading towards a point of complete and totally satiated fulfillment. Which is impossible to prove. Therefore, there is no way of knowing *whither* Love *goes*, since His ways are as unknown, as even more hidden, veiled, and ignored is His finish line.

---

[110]In the Spanish original:

> *A la rosada aurora*
> *me fui a encontrar, con paso apresurado,*
> *con el que me enamora;*
> *y juntos ya, en el vado,*
> *dejé morir mi pena*
> *mientras cantaba, lejos, filomena.*

But, since Love is bilateral, reciprocal, and mutual self–giving (*Qui ex Patre Filioque procedit*),[111] the Bridegroom is also waiting, longing for a declaration of love on the part of the bride: *Love cannot but hope to be requited.* Hence the impatient exclamations of the Bridegroom in the *Song of Songs*:

> *O my dove, that art in the clefts of the rock,*
> *In the secret places of the cliff,*
> *Le me see thy countenance, let me hear thy voice;*
> *For sweet is thy voice, and thy countenance is comely.*[112]

> *Thou that dwellest in the gardens,*
> *The friends hearken;*
> *Let me hear thy voice.*[113]

This is the reason why the Bridegroom wants to hear *I love you* from the lips of the bride, and with the same impatience and longing with which she hoped to hear it from the Bridegroom.

In this regard, the narrative of the institution of the Primate of Saint Peter is quite telling:[114]

Jesus saith to Simon Peter, 'Simon, son of John, lovest thou me more than these?'

---

[111]To deny the procession of the Holy Spirit, that is, that the third Person of the Trinity proceeds simultaneously from the Father *and* the Son, is to spirit away the notion of God. God is Love, and, therefore, according to Revelation, He is Trinity lest He be Nothing. The concessions made to the Orthodox Churches by some Catholics with the intention of an alleged Ecumenism make no sense, either according to scripture, or dogmatically, or historically, or magisterially. Once again, the Ecumenism of surrendering, along with its derelictions, cunningness, and crafty political maneuvers, is leading to the watering down of Theology.

[112]Sg 2:14.

[113]Sg 8:13.

[114]Jn 21: 15–18.

He said unto him, 'Yea, Lord; thou knowest that I love thee.'

Three consecutive times did Jesus Christ want to hear *I love you* from the lips of Saint Peter, but why thrice? It could have been, of course, less or many more times; for love will never get tired of repeating *I love you*, whether uttered by the lips of the beloved or heard with his or her ears. But in this case there is no special reason to attribute any meaning to the threefold repetition. Many exegetes have tried to see in this episode some particular intention on the part of Jesus Christ. There would be a logical relationship, they say, between the triple denial of Peter, before the cock crowed, and the triple confession of love: something like a requirement *valde conveniens* and prior to the granting of the Primate. Which is but an arbitrary and simplistic interpretation; and even a little childish, if you will, on the part of the Lord. A betrayal like Peter's on the night of the Passion can be redeemed by one repentant, loving confession, or by three, or maybe by three hundred; for there is no fixed number set in advance. Everything depends on the offended heart and on the love shown by the offender in his repentance. I, for my part, imagine that the secret must be hidden, quite probably, in the mysterious and deep significance of the expression *I love you*. It is, as we have said above, the most terrible, wonderful, and ineffable (all at the same time) locution that the human being has been granted to hear or utter.

We have said that the assertion *I love you* has a content and a significance that can be appropriately qualified with the adjective *terrible*. And we do not have to clarify that both the word and the concept *terrible* are far from exhausting the meaning of the reality to which they refer in this case. To this declaration of love, which is the expression of total surrender to the beloved, can be attributed what the Bridegroom says to the bride in the *Song of Songs*:

Thou art beautiful, O my love...
Terrible as an army set in array.[115]

. . . .

Who is she
That cometh forth as the morning...
Terrible as an army set in array?[116]

But why ascribe the quality of *terrible* to the declaration of love, which is the confession of absolute self–surrender to the beloved person? Especially because we do not have many expressions to choose from and, of course, any that approaches what could be considered a correct meaning. It is not necessary to insist on the poverty and inadequacy of human language. Despite this, perhaps we can find a way capable of leading us to *some* understanding of the problem.[117]

The seriousness and importance of the declaration *I love you* is based on the fact that he who says it sincerely makes actual in depth the reality of love. This means the dispossession of everything that one has, including one's life, *to give it to the beloved*. He who so loves is in a state of absolute poverty so as to have given up the foundation of all other rights, that is, his own life itself. Therefore, if from now he goes on living, he does so through the life of the beloved, on which the lover depends fully. Consequently, a mysterious exchange of lives has taken place, through a process not easy to be explained by human understanding.

Any attempt at clarification by us cannot claim anything other than a certain approach to the subject. Fortunately, however, we

---

[115]Sg 6:3.

[116]Sg 6:10.

[117]"Some" must be understood here as approximation, ambiguity, and uncertainty; that is all.

can be helped in this task by the revealed texts that refer to the mystery of Love. This task we can try in the hope of providing some benefit; nevertheless, it must be taken into account the human tendency to read Scripture in a superficial way and without delving too much.[118]

Trying to find some explanation here means opening another more serious problem. We are referring to the fact that purely human love is an analogate regarding divine–human love, and much more so vis–à–vis divine love. In effect, even the purest and highest merely human love is but a participation of divine love, of which the former is an analogy. And something similar happens with respect to divine–human love, albeit in varying degrees and in different ways. Hence the different modes in which love is made factual, according to its various forms of expression. In purely human love, for example, expressions like *you are my life*, or others like this, are simple metaphors. This does not happen in divine–human love, in which there is some parity of ontological reality between its expressions and their corresponding content. And so we come to the central point of the difficulty alluded to above, since this is a hard fact for the human mind to understand due to its tendency to equate, consciously or unconsciously, both forms of love, with the disastrous, easily imagined, consequences.[119]

---

[118]This tendency, otherwise so generalized, explains the poor, barely superficial knowledge that many Christians have about their Christian condition. On the other hand, a somehow deep knowledge of the Scriptures necessarily implies a sincere life of prayer, without which everything would be reduced to an empty and useless academic exercise.

[119]Unfortunately, the wretchedness that besieges the human race goes still further. The belief that only purely human love deserves to be considered true love is quite widespread. Not to speak about the degenerate and corrupted notion of love generally accepted nowadays, which has led modern society to equate the most sublime of all human sentiments with the most abominable aberrations.

We must also refer here to another danger whose presence may hinder the correct approach to the subject; for it is more subtle than the previous ones and can become a major threat because it is more difficult to detect due to its appearance of orthodox theology and objective religiosity. I mean the distinction between *spirituality*, on the one hand, and *theology*, on the other. Or between what Von Balthasar also calls *lyric* as opposed to the *epic*,[120] which amounts to distinguishing spiritual effusions from the historical reality of past events that still, however, *keep their significance*.[121]

These theories could be accepted on condition of not admitting the intended separation between spirituality and theology. Nevertheless, it is safer not to take them too seriously. A spirituality that desires to be Christian has to be based on serious and objective theology, rooted in Revelation (Scripture and Tradition) and in the Magisterium, if it does not want to become a set of pious practices without foundation that usually turn out to be mere superstitions. In turn, what would be the purpose of a theology without spiritual implications to be followed? This theology would be tantamount to studying God and His relationship with man in the same way one analyzes the developing of anemones. It falls again into academicism or perhaps something worse. Talking about theological events that happened in the past, but which *still have some significance*, is

---

[120]Hans Urs von Balthasar, *Theo–Drama, Theological Dramatic Theory*, II, Ignatius Press, San Francisco, 1990, pp. 55 ff.

[121]According to von Balthasar, while lyric theology is addressed to God and Jesus Christ as to a *Thou*, epic theology speaks to both as to a *He*. Is it a matter of establishing a distinction between pious devotion and some objective realism? Be it as it may, avant–garde theologians (conciliar and post–conciliar) are always mulling over the same issue. Rationalistic, modernist, and neo–modernist theologies are always suspicious of the supernatural. These theologies transform human reason into an obtuse, narrow passage that considers as truth only what goes through it.

still a dangerous approach to Protestant and Modernist theologies that seek to break into today's Catholicism, according to some, or to settle definitively, according to others.

The meaning of Love in Christian existence is quite clear, despite the attempts made by secularism and today's pagan society to smudge it. It means to give up *everything* one owns in order to give that *everything* to the beloved. *So likewise every one of you that does not renounce all that he possesses, cannot be my disciple.*[122] This giving up everything is an exclusive characteristic of divine love which grace has shared with divine–human love. The nature of plain human love as mere analogate as well as participant *in the lesser degree* is most obvious here. In this sense, as we have said before, only divine–human love is not a metaphor.[123] *Totality,* of course, corresponds entirely to Divine or Substantial Love: *For God so loved the world, as to give his only begotten Son.*[124] As God, He could not give up more or greater than Himself. This explains (let us remember it again) the fact that God wanted to flood us with His wealth (one hundredfold) so that we can also give with *total lavishness*: I give you everything so that you can also give me everything. There is no other way to fulfill the fundamental law of love: reciprocity or bilateral self–giving. This law, of course, constitutes true love; the very love which God has wanted to share with His own, and which cannot exist between mere creatures. This is how Jesus Christ loved us: unto the end,[125] unto total surrender.[126]

---

[122]Lk 14:33. The expression *all that he possesses* goes beyond material goods. The Vulgate and Neo–Vulgate translate *omnibus quæ possidet.*

[123]It is a privilege which shows clearly the profound superiority of this love. In this connection, it is interesting to read again 1 Cor 7: 32–34.

[124]Jn 3:16.

[125]*In finem dilexit eos* (Jn 13:1).

[126]*Tradidit seipsum* (Gal 2:20).

Consequently, divine–human love becomes a veritable contest between lovers (Sg 2:4): who will surrender more? Divine–human love is the only place where one can give up *everything* in order to receive *everything*. Divine–human love, being authentic love, does not understand that one may keep something for himself. Contrariwise, mere human love always feeds on partial realities and vague analogies. In this regard, we can refer to the love between husband and wife as the more eloquent case; its most characteristic expression is the carnal union in which they become *two in one flesh*;[127] but where they are still two, however, if one also takes into account that their mutual surrender can never be total.[128]

Divine–human love implies the donation of the life of each one of the lovers in a way that there is nothing left to give up by each of them. When they renounce their own lives, everything they possess is also surrendered. But this *totality* is only possible in the most perfect act of love and as the greatest proof of its authenticity (Jn 15:13). Giving one's own life to the beloved person is the founding event of Christian existence. *He that findeth his life, shall lose it: and he that shall lose his life for me, shall find it...*[129] *He that loveth his life shall lose it; and he that hateth his life in this world, keepeth it unto life eternal.*[130] Evidently, the loss meant here by Jesus Christ, more than a *loss*, strictly speaking, is in reality a *change*. In other words and more specifically, what is stated here, regarding the giving up of one's life, refers to *one's particular* life rather than

---

[127]Gen 2:24; Mt 19: 5–6; Eph 5:31.

[128]In the act in which the carnal union is consummated, each spouse can never do entirely, and surely not even in part, without the search for self–satisfaction. Pursuing, exclusively and with absolute unselfishness, goodness and joy is a privilege of perfect love.

[129]Mt 10:39.

[130]Jn 12:25.

to *life* as such; without life, be it one's own (which one renounces) or the other's (for which one exchanges his own), it would not be possible to live: *As the living Father hath sent me, and I live by the Father; so he that eateth me, the same also shall live by me.*[131] Therefore, it is a matter of *living the life of the Beloved*, that is to say, the life of the other and not our own: *He that eateth my flesh, and drinketh my blood, abideth in me, and I in him.*[132] So, a veritable *exchange* of lives takes place, which must be understood in a real sense. Explaining it, however, even in some small way, is a different story.

Nevertheless, some approximation to this subject is possible, for a deeper analysis does not belong to the present eon. First of all, it should be noted that, unlike what happens in merely human love, in divine–human love we must lay aside metaphor. We are dealing here with *realities* that are supernatural and transcend us and, consequently, cannot be explained by resorting to the world of perceivable and natural things in which we live. They must be believed as they are offered to us (faith), and wait until they reach total fulfilment so that we can contemplate and understand them (hope).

We must rise above metaphor, but we cannot ignore it. Without Metaphor it would be impossible to have *expectations* or that hope we have just mentioned; there would be no means to acquire the knowledge we already have. Ignoring metaphor would be tantamount to risking understanding things as they sound, according to our normal way of knowing things, and accepting as real mere unacceptable fantasies. Now we can go back to the world of ineffable supernatural realities which have been given and revealed to us, in order to approach somehow the issue of exchange of lives which

---

[131] Jn 6:57.

[132] Jn 6:56.

takes place in love, for our understanding keeps trying to delve into the data provided by faith. In this connection we can talk, for instance, about an interchange of feelings in which each lover makes his or hers the feelings of the other: *For none of us liveth to himself; and no man dieth to himself. For whether we live, we live unto the Lord; or whether we die, we die unto the Lord. Therefore, whether we live, or whether we die, we are the Lord's...*[133] *For let this mind be in you, which was also in Christ Jesus...*[134] *But we have the mind of Christ.*[135] Once again and as always, according to the law of reciprocity, each of the lovers knows that his feelings and everything that his heart contains is owned by the other. Hence the sighing for the other, the unbroken nostalgia because of their mutual absence, and the joy of knowing oneself to be both the owner and the slave of the other, are the feelings that impel the spouse of the *Song*:

> *I belong to my love,*
> *And his desire is for me.*[136]

All of which is true but insufficient, for we can be led to think that we know enough about Love; in reality, we know so little and are still too far from the center of the mystery: at the same distance that significant expressions (metaphorical language) are from the realities they mean.

The world in which those who truly love each other live encompasses much more than the mere co–possession of feelings. The situation in which each one of those who make up the relationship

---

[133] Rom 14: 7–8.

[134] Phil 2:5.

[135] 1 Cor 2:16.

[136] Sg 7:11.

of love lives the life of the other, or lives by the other (each one integrally keeping his full personality), *is a reality* that has nothing to do with figurative language (metaphor, figure, symbol, allegory, or any trope we can imagine). The disappointing and heartbreaking fact that we cannot explain that reality does not diminish its truth one iota: *We see now through a glass in a dark manner; but then face to face. Now I know in part; but then I shall know even as I am known.*[137]

As for conjugal human love, it is necessary to keep in mind that it has some important characteristics. To begin with, it is convenient to note that this form of love cannot go beyond what is meant by expressions like *having the same feelings, share the same feelings,* or similar ones. The truth is that the universe of the hearts of the spouses remains as the property and possession of each one, and it is not possible for their love to reach, even by far, the depth of divine–human love.

The Bible carefully distinguishes conjugal love from divine–human love; which does not imply a decrease in the dignity and greatness of the former, but serves to put everything in its proper place.[138] The Bible clearly maintains the equal dignity of both sexes, the mutual belonging of each of the spouses (*But yet neither is the man without the woman, nor the woman without the man, in the Lord*),[139] and the excellent dignity of Christian marriage, elevated by God to being the analogate of the love and surrender of Christ to His Church (Eph 5:32).

---

[137] 1 Cor 13:12.

[138] We have called them respectively first and second analogate, which is but a working terminology.

[139] 1 Cor 11:11.

There is here a very interesting and apparent aporia. We have already seen that the Bible clearly affirms important doctrines such as the equal dignity of both sexes, the reciprocal possession of both spouses in conjugal society, and the sublime condition of Christian marriage. After all, conjugal love is an analogate of divine love, also frequently used by the Bible in reference to divine–human love.[140] But Scripture points out, equally clearly the differences that separate mere human love from divine–human love.

What is meant here is that, with respect to divine love, both conjugal and divine–human love need to resort to analogy if they want to be understood. Nevertheless, it is in conjugal love where *dissimilarities* are more relevant. It should be remembered that analogy encompasses an unequal proportion of similarity and dissimilarity. When it comes to relationships between God and His creatures, dissimilarities outweigh similarities to an unimaginable magnitude. Apart from that, created things also present different degrees of possible analogies.[141]

The relationship of equality and reciprocity between lovers, one of the fundamental laws of love, does not enjoy the same transcendence in conjugal love as it does in divine–human love. On the other hand, it is easy to understand that the equality we are talking about is not ontological, but the equality granted by an elevated love that is, therefore, magnanimous and condescending. God humbles Himself and comes down to His creature, in order to raise it to

---

[140]The relationship would be as follows: conjugal love as analogate of divine–human love and, ultimately, as analogate of divine love itself. Divine–human love as analogate in turn of divine love. Therefore, conjugal love would occupy the lowest place on the spectrum, followed by divine–human love, which would culminate, finally, in the Love of the August Trinity.

[141]What we are going to say has already been expounded with complementary details in my *Commentary on the Song of Songs*, II, pp. 91 ff. and 330 ff.

His own condition and make her a participant of His divine nature (2 Pet 1:4). But God is God and His creature is His creature. We will see that the degrees of *equality* as they appear in divine–human love vastly surpass those given within conjugal love; the latter have a rather *relative* relevance. In this regard, the Bible is also categorical, establishing clearly the authority of the husband over his wife in the conjugal relationship; an authority maintained in force until the bond is dissolved by the death of one of the spouses. Despite what the unfounded aspirations of the Feminist Movements may say, they absolutely ignore the dignity of women and its establishing foundations.[142] The Bible is sufficiently and abundantly clear on this issue: Gen 3:16; 1 Cor 11: 7–12; Eph 5: 22–29; Col 3:18; 1 Tim 2: 11–15; 1 Pet 3: 1–7. The identification of lives, as well as the Bride and the Bridegroom being on the same level and in mutual dependence; their mutual surrender in ownership and possession of each other so much extolled in biblical texts, do not exist in conjugal love with the prominence that they enjoy in divine–human love. The scriptural texts, indeed, do not refer to a mere communion of feelings,

---

[142]I had the opportunity to meet some nuns who seriously affirmed that, although the Bible is not *male chauvinist* (certainly a magnanimous concession on the part of the nuns for which we have to be grateful), Saint Paul is clearly affected by this most despicable scourge. One cannot but be astonished at the high level of stupidity that human nature sometimes reaches.

It should be remembered that the conjugal society, after all, is also a society. And it is known that there is no society (large or small) in the present age that can survive without a hierarchical principle if it wants to avoid falling into anarchy. It is absolutely necessary, therefore, that there be in the society established by marriage an authority that acts as the head (which is the word used by biblical texts, referring to the male). Even in Heaven there is established the Hierarchy of Angels and Blessed, although in this case it is not imposed to avoid any kind of anarchy. The reason for its existence in this case seems to be the desire of showing the various degrees of excellence among creatures, from the most humble but amazing wonders to the Sublime Height of the Creator of them all.

as we have seen above; they point at a real exchange of lives. We do not need to clarify here that only in Infinite or Substantial Love the identification of lives becomes identification in the same nature (numerically one).

The societal character is inherent to the conjugal love which is called to exist only in the present eon (Mt 22:30). Consequently, conjugal love cannot enjoy the main features of love to the degree divine–human love does because its particular characteristics and its status as inferior analogate, the mysterious features of love as they appear in the divine–human love relationships (notwithstanding the dialectic of *already* but *not yet*), cannot be found in conjugal love with the same intensity. This is why one understands better the reasons the Apostle offers in his *First Letter to the Corinthians* regarding the superiority of virginity over marriage.

We have been speaking abundantly of the characteristics of the bond of love: reciprocity, bilateralism, equality, mutual surrender and donation (in totality) of the lovers. But these qualities are properly found in perfect love alone. They also belong to the divine–human relationships of love, although in an analog degree of participation which is deep enough so as to transcend the capacity of the human mind. Going one step further down the descending scale, at a much lower and relative level, they also appear in the marital relationship, only to the extent it is structured within true love.[143]

The exchange of lives between lovers, each one living the life of the other, living because of the other, and other similar expressions

---

[143]Despite the usefulness of the concept of conjugal love; especially for its contribution to the knowledge of higher degrees in the relationship of love. We have already seen the way in which conjugal love is used in this regard in the *Song of the Songs*, and in many other places, biblical or not biblical. One more example of how human understanding usually proceeds, in its cognitive activity, from the inferior to the superior.

(Jn 6:58; Gal 2:20; etc.) are *realities* present in divine–human love. We are well aware that we can have knowledge of these realities only through faith, at least for now. True, we are entirely open to the revealed data, but, at the same time, we are equally limited and constrained by it; therefore, it is impossible to explain such *realities* with the means available to us in the present age. It would be erroneous to think that we can only hope for a purely *notional* knowledge of these mysteries. Actually it is the Holy Spirit Who is leading us to such knowledge of Jesus Christ that, although inexpressible, is sufficient to flood us with love for the Person of the Master.[144] In any case we should refer to the complicated world of mystical theology as the only science capable of providing some knowledge (limited and absolutely insufficient) about this issue.[145]

Conjugal society, by its very nature, cannot do without the authority of the man over the woman, and even over the children once the family is constituted. The fact that the revealed texts consider man as the *head* of the woman, and her as the glorious ornament of her husband and for her husband (1 Cor 11: 7–9), is one of the reasons why perfect love is not easily applicable to the conjugal bond. The qualities of perfect Love become prominent when the threshold of the supernatural world is being crossed. In this sense,

---

[144]According to Romans 5:5, the Love of God has been poured into our hearts through the Holy Spirit Which has been given to us. But since nothing is wanted if it is not first known, love is not mere knowledge without further ado. If knowledge does not *descend* and fill the heart (as the Apostle says), there is no love. Sound Philosophy has always distinguished *cognitum* from *volitum*. We are here facing the difficulty posed by the Thomistic notion of the beatific vision consisting of a mere satiating contemplation of the Truth.

[145]At this point, we must insist that one would need to have a deep spiritual life, nourished by the Holy Spirit, as an indispensable requirement if he wants to make any progress in this matter. *Practical* mystical theology has always been, by definition, more useful in this sense than merely *scientific* mystical theology.

divine–human love has been granted special prerogatives with which it reaches a much higher level than the human mind could ever have imagined.

When true love reaches a certain high status, the Bridegroom no longer wishes to place Himself on a higher and different level than the level on which His bride is supposed to be; He would rather prefer to be together with her and belong entirely to her. On the other hand, His natural superiority over her would make it difficult to realize those essential characteristics of true love: reciprocity, bilateralism, and equality; as well as His total surrender, along with His whole being and possessions. The texts are quite explicit in this regard: *I will not now call you servants: for the servant knoweth not what his lord doth. But I have called you friends...*[146] *If I wash thee not, thou shalt have no part with me...*[147]

This latter text deserves special attention regarding our subject. Jesus washing His disciples' feet has been frequently considered a magnanimous act of humility; actually, it is something much deeper: the Bridegroom, being in love, descends (*lowers Himself*) to the level where the Bride is, as something necessary to achieve the equalization desired by those who love each other with true love; in other words, they want to be together, in the same place, and in those equal conditions that make possible the relationship of love between an *I* and a *thou*. If anybody would think that this relationship is a shameful humiliation for the Bridegroom, he would have to eliminate Philippians 2:7. And our Lord also said that *the disciple is not above the master, nor the servant above his lord. It is enough for the disciple that he be as his master, and the servant as his lord;*[148]

---

[146] Jn 15:15.

[147] Jn 13:8.

[148] Mt 10: 24–25; cf Lk 6:40.

which confirms what we have been saying. The last statement is quite noticeable: *It is enough for the disciple that he be as his master*; where it is clear that the decisive thing is not that one could be above or below the other, or that either of them may consider himself as superior or inferior, but the discovery of *the tremendous and amazing reality that both are equal.* Love is mysterious, for not only does He encompass all the circumstances of human life; He also turns Christian existence into something incomprehensible in the eyes of a world which does not hesitate to consider it total madness. Thus, while society seems to consider normal that servants serve their lord, the mystery of love, however, can make something supernatural appear as the most natural thing; we are referring to the amazing fact that the lord serves his servant. This is but a logical consequence of love, which makes the lover feel happy when he descends to the level of the loved one and serves him; which is nothing strange for those who are aware that the essence of love is the mutual belonging and possession of each of the lovers. At this point, nothing matters but being together and knowing that one is the property of the other: *The Son of man is not come to be ministered unto, but to minister...*[149] *Blessed are those servants, whom the Lord when he cometh, shall find watching. Amen I say to you, that he will gird himself, and make them sit down to meat, and passing will minister unto them.*[150] It is not a question, of course, about who is the lord and who is the servant. Each one of them is who he is and retains his condition, as it could not be, or have to be, otherwise. *You call me Master, and Lord; and you say well, for so I am. If then I being your Lord and Master...*[151] *For which is greater, he that sitteth at*

---

[149] Mt 20:28.

[150] Lk 12:37.

[151] Jn 13: 13–14.

table, or he that serveth? Is it not he that sitteth at table? But I am in the midst of you, as he that serveth.[152] The only question to raise here, of which love would be the real culprit, is who comes forward first to serve whom and who is more diligent in the service. For love achieves the incredible miracle that one finds more joy in serving than in being served: after all, *It is a more blessed thing to give, rather than to receive.*[153]

The condition of submission, service, and belonging, on the part of those who love each other in perfect love, as well as the fact that each of them seems to find more joy in serving than in being served, in being the object of ownership and possession rather than being the possessor or owner, is something that does not happen by chance or accidentally; truly speaking, this condition is but a consequence of the very nature of love. *It is a more blessed thing to give, rather than to receive.* Love, indeed, is self–surrender and self–donation *before*[154] it is reception.

> *My love is a sachet of myrrh*
> *Lying between my breasts.*
> *My love is a cluster of henna flowers*
> *Among the vines of En–Gedi.*[155]

---

[152]Lk 22:27.

[153]Acts 20:35. This is another instance of the inferiority of marital love with respect to divine–human love. Despite the veritable reciprocal possession of the spouses and the husband's love for his wife as he loves his own body, the authority of the husband and the subsequent submission of the wife always remain in conjugal love.

[154]Priority of nature rather than of time, as can be easily understood. It is the same priority that exists between *active spiration* and *passive spiration* within the Trinity.

[155]Sg 1: 13–14.

Poetry again, which in this case belongs to a Poem included in Holy Scripture. And as poetry, it admits a multitude of valid interpretations; different in depth but all of them referring to the mystery of Love. In this verse, the bride is speaking echoing the charms of the Beloved; hence her expressions must be interpreted as a poetic way of referring to the Bridegroom's attractive personality: My beloved is for me *like* a sachet of myrrh... My beloved is for me *like* a cluster of henna flowers... But, clearly, equally valid is the interpretation that here the Beloved is seen as a pledge and possession of the bride: *My* beloved is a sachet of myrrh... *My* beloved is a cluster of henna flowers.

On the other hand, the way in which the Bridegroom implores His bride to *allow* him to see her face and hear her voice is equally expressive. Love does not mind imploring. For the same reason He does not mind humiliating Himself and descending, if necessary, to the level of the loved one. After all, does He not belong to her? As has always happened and continues to happen, the Bridegroom shows again His impatience to be with His bride, therefore He is in a hurry to get where she is, *jumping through the mountains and leaping over the hills*:

> *Come, my dove,*
> *hiding in the clefts of the rock,*
> *in the coverts of the cliff,*
> *show me your face, let me hear your voice...*[156]

But perhaps in no other place does Scripture speak more forcefully, as well as more beautifully and poetically, of the mutual belonging of lovers as it does in the *Song of Songs*. That is why the Bridegroom tells His bride:

---

[156]Sg 2:14.

> *Set me like a seal on your heart,*
> *Like a seal on your arm.*[157]

No wonder the bride also shows her burning impatience to be with the Beloved, anywhere and at any time; where He wants, and how and when He wants:

> *There I will go, joyfully,*
> *Wherever your love takes me, I will be there;*
> *There your true bride I shall be,*
> *And that one life we will share,*
> *There we'll leave behind us all absence and care.*[158]

One can say only very little about the exchange of lives that takes place among lovers; but it is important to stress again the fact that, despite the surrender of one´s own life that each lover makes to the other, both maintain their natural personality, without the smallest blurring or loss.[159] It could not be otherwise: if the mystery of love is to be something real then it always implies the existence

---

[157]Sg 8:6.

[158]In the Spanish original:

> *Allí iré, presurosa,*
> *allí donde el Amado me lo pida,*
> *allí seré su esposa,*
> *allí será mi vida,*
> *allí donde la pena ya se olvida.*

[159]This is another servitude and limitation of conjugal love, whose consummation through carnal union is but an attempt, no matter how exalted and ardent, to transform or lose each lover into or in the other. But, at the end of the day, it is only an attempt that knows beforehand its inability to achieve that transformation.

of an *I* and a *thou* and their mutual *distinction*.[160] If it is accepted that each lover loses his or her life, as it does happen, it must be admitted at the same time that this is so because each one finds his or her life in the other and also receives it from the other. Thus love amounts to a reciprocal and simultaneous giving and receiving that finally becomes an overflowing stream (an *impetuous wind which blows where it pleases, but you cannot tell where it comes from or where it is going*)[161] which runs into eternity. In perfect and true love, each lover *gives* his life to the other and, therefore, each verily loses his or her life. Nevertheless, in perfect reciprocity each receives his or her life again along with that of his lover. Hence, as in a paradox, the surrender of one life turns into the reception of two lives: *I am come that they may have life, and may have it more abundantly*.[162] In this way, God's creature lives divine life without losing his own. The divine Lover also makes His own the human life of His creature, like a drop of water absorbed by the ocean in the immensity of Him Who is Life (Jn 11:25; 14:6). The divine Lover receives as His possession the life of the creature *in so far as he now gives his life to Him voluntarily*. Previously He had made His own everything human, including suffering and death, in order to *experience* them, or, better yet, to know them in the human way. True friendship, authentic divine–human love, demands that these two qualities are shared *by both parties of the relationship of love*.

Obviously, it is absurd to think that divine knowledge needs experiencing anything pertaining to human nature. The Letter to the Colossians 1: 16–17 clearly speaks of the universal lordship of the Incarnated Word over all created things: *For in him were all*

---

[160]Love being a contest between two, the reality of love depends on the distinction of an *I* with respect to a *thou*. In Trinitarian theology, the distinction between Divine Persons is known as an *oppositional relationship*.

[161]Jn 3:8.

[162]Jn 10:10.

things created... All things were created by him and in him... In him all things consist; consequently, there is no absolute necessity here. But in so far as the human creature is concerned, *we can certainly speak of the convenience for him to see a "human way" in the other party of the relationship of love.* It is known that, in the divine–human relationship of love, the human creature, while still being human, loves in a human way (superhuman, if you will), although elevated by grace. On the other hand, the constant law of bilateralism and equality in love, as we have always said, requires a *certain* relationship, or level of equality, between both parties. And it is clear that, if God wanted to be loved by man in the only way man knows how and can do, it was necessary that he would maintain his own way of loving (human), on the one hand, and offer him, on the other, an object to love according to his nature. Here it would be proper to bring up the *reasons of convenience*, of which theologians speak so much, in connection with the arguments in favor of the convenience of the Incarnation. In this sense, it could be said that God became Man also in order to be known and loved by His creature, not only in the divine way, but *also in the human way.* Without this latter aspect, man's love for his God might have been deprived (as someone could have affirmed) of a problematic character.

This said, we must warn about the danger of falling, more or less consciously, into Docetism. What man finds on the other side of the divine–human love relationship is the true God, *but also the true Man Jesus Christ.* The truth and reality of divine–human love depends on the truth and reality of the statement *Et Verbum caro factum est.* It is in the light of this revealed truth that reasons of convenience for the Incarnation turn into reasons of *necessity,* when God, in His sovereign freedom, decided *to be truly loved by man.* Indeed, the idea that man could manage to love, to the point of *falling in love,* the God of the Old Covenant does not cease to be problematic; let us remember that the people of Israel thought that the mere hearing of His voice could kill them (Deut 5: 23–27). Another problem is that God is a pure Spirit, and consequently it is impossible for man to perceive Him in any way: *But the hour cometh and now is, when the true adorers shall adore the Father in spirit and in truth. For the Father also seeketh such to adore him. God is a spirit; and they that adore him, must adore him in spirit and in truth.*[163] God is, therefore, Spirit. But man is now able to reach Him through Jesus Christ (the Word made Man), but through Jesus Christ alone: *No man cometh to the Father, but by me;*[164] hence the necessity of *Per Ipsum, Cum Ipso, et In Ipso.*

In any case, the *I* of the creature would never have been able to acquire so much relevance if he had not been conformed to the divine *I*. Furthermore, it is necessary to remember that the *I* of each person becomes in turn, by the work and grace of love, into the *thou* of the other: because only through love (the *nexus duorum*) the human *self* is capable of dealing *face to face* with the divine *self* (*I will no longer call you servants, but friends*); in turn, the divine *self*, descending to the level of His creature, can now refer to him as *thou* with a realism that only exists in true friendship.[165]

---

[163] Jn 4: 23–24.

[164] Jn 14:6.

[165] Cf note 72, *supra*. Perhaps in this way some light can be shed upon the doctrine of Saint John of the Cross on the love relationship between God and the soul. Saint John speaks about the *spiration of the Holy Spirit of God into her* (the soul), *and of her to God*. It must be admitted that the terminology of Saint John regarding this point, both in the *Spiritual Canticle* (Song XXXIX), and in the *Living Flame of Love* (Song II, verse VI), is sometimes imprecise and even ambiguous; it would be unfair to demand otherwise. Otherwise, his doctrine is sufficiently clear. If the Saint alludes somewhere to the transformation of the soul in the three Persons of the Holy Trinity, in another place he makes the distinction very clear: *the substance of this soul, although it is not the substance of God, because it cannot substantially become Him...*

Summing up, when faced with such a profound and wonderful mystery, could something better be done than plunging into silence without trying to taint it with our poor speculations which would not achieve anything but to obscure it further?

We had begun this dissertation by posing the problem of the promised, and in some cases awarded, reward to the followers of Jesus Christ; which led us to wonder about the possible meaning, if any, of the reward due to love. In this regard, in order to find the most adequate response possible to such a complex question, our discourse led us to distinguish between the natural and supernatural worlds.

As for the natural world, we can go on to say that, within its own sphere, rewards very rarely respond to objective criteria of retributive justice. Humans are too used to seeing how frequently the triumphs of evil, injustice, and lies are rewarded every day. Rewards and recompenses are almost never granted to those who really deserve them, and even less in proportion to the value of their achievements. Hence, we can assure, without fear of error, that human redistributive justice is a joke; although, unfortunately, we can extend this statement to any claim of justice, of any kind, to be carried out by men. The titles of greatness and nobility that some men bestow upon themselves or others (*excellency, illustrious, majesty, highness, eminence*, and a long etcetera of egregious denominations) have no real foundation other than the occasion to smile that they provide to others. It is not surprising, therefore, that those who base their aspirations and put their trust in human rewards and promises end up in failure. That is why the farewell speeches of Sancho Panza upon leaving Barataria, the island of his dreams, (addressed to his subjects first and to Don Quixote and the Dukes later), when he was already more than disappointed, hungry, and beaten, contain such intensity of bittersweet feelings in an ingenious mix of disappointment and realism, of sadness at having succumbed to the deception of his unsubstantiated dreams, together with nostalgia and the desire to recover the peculiar and proper thing that he had so mistakenly abandoned, as to make those discourses a masterpiece (another one) within the work of Cervantes:

> *Because it was your highnesses' pleasure, not because of any desert of my own, I went to govern your island of Barataria, which I entered naked, and naked I find myself; I neither lose nor gain. Whether I have governed well or ill, I have had witnesses who will say what they think fit. I have answered questions, I have decided causes, and always dying of hunger, for Doctor Pedro Recio of Tirteafuera, the island and governor doctor, would have it so...[166]*

As for the supernatural world, as regards the reward bestowed on love, we have reason to believe that the issue has become clear enough. If we talk about supernatural or divine–human love, which is by far the true love, we have already seen that there is no point in talking about rewards regarding it. As we have said so many times, love desires no retribution outside of itself. And even in the grotesque case that one would look for it, there would not be any remuneration that could satisfy love. Hence the question of Saint Peter addressed to the Lord, about the reward to be received by those who had abandoned everything to follow Him, does not make much sense. And therefore, Jesus' answer is a human answer responding to an interpellation formulated also in a human way. The Twelve were still in an initial and elementary stage in regard to

---

[166] *Don Quixote*, II, 55.

their relationships with the Lord: *I have yet many things to say to you: but you cannot bear them now.*[167]

It is true that to a follower of Jesus it is not worthy to think of anything, except Christ Himself, that may amount to a possible prize. Following the Master is in itself the reward of rewards and the grace of graces. From a supernatural point of view, everything of this world has a merely relative value; not because things are no longer good, or are not vestiges left by the Beloved, or because they have lost their condition as possible gifts to offer to the Bridegroom. What happens is that the blinding brightness of the sun at its exit makes the faint light of the firefly disappear: *I count all things to be but loss for the excellent knowledge of Jesus Christ my Lord; for whom I have suffered the loss of all things, and count them but as dung, that I may gain Christ: And may be found in him.*[168] And Saint John of the Cross states:

> *My soul is occupied,*
> *And all my substance in His service;*
> *Now I guard no flock,*
> *Nor have I any other employment:*
> *My sole occupation is love.*[169]

The true Joy granted to man on this earth is knowing that God loves him in a very particular way. Conversely, there is no other sadness than being aware that he has not responded accordingly to that love. But man, as long as he lives in this world, lives on Hope and knows that *the fashion of this world passeth away.*[170]

---

[167] Jn 16:12.

[168] Phil 3: 8–9.

[169] Saint John of the Cross, *Spiritual Canticle.*

[170] 1 Cor 7:31.

He is certain that when what is perfect comes, what is imperfect will disappear and he will know then as he is known now. He will be able to finally begin, without veils or darkness, the loving and ineffable *face to face* dialogue with God, when things are definitively forgotten, and he will have just arrived at the shores of the wide sea that borders eternity:

> *And there my ended woes and sorrows left me*
> *There where our lives are joined as one, by the sea*
> *Rocked with gentle waves created easily*
> *By the stirred blue waters lapping lazily.*[171]

---

[171]In the Spanish original:

> *Y allí quedaron, mis penas fenecidas*
> *junto al mar do se unieron nuestras vidas,*
> *mecido en suaves ondas, producidas*
> *por las azules aguas removidas.*

VI

THE HELMET OF MAMBRINO

1. How can one make what is white appear as black and vice versa

Objects that are presented to our knowledge and events which we perceive are not always what they seem to be nor do they always seem to be what they are. This happens because of the simple nature of things; we must take into account the limitations of our understanding and perception when we try to comprehend them. We see something, consider it, classify it, and pigeonhole it; but so frequently it happens that we are just plain wrong in our assessment.

More often than not, this deception occurs because of our own stupidity, which seems to have a tendency to adhere to our already limited intellectual capacity.

But the error in our judgment is not always the result of personal limitations or defects which influence our perceptive and intellective skills. In fact, it can also be caused by some external agent foreign to us. Oddly enough, this source of confusion is the one which most frequently affects our lives.

In any case, many who are being deceived have already previously contributed to their deception with something on their own; consequently, they are to a greater or lesser degree guilty of their error; for *He who doeth truth cometh to the light.*[1] It is no exaggeration to say that any victim of deception usually has some complicity with lies. For a Christian, for example, fidelity to the Word of his Lord implies the guarantee of arriving at the knowledge of truth and, as a corollary, attaining authentic liberation (Jn 8: 31–32).

But error is not always imputable to the victim. One must acknowledge that, on many occasions, it would be difficult to determine the likelihood of guilt on the part of the victim of deception; more so when one tries to assess the degree of criminal responsibility incurred by one who culpably mistook white for black or vice versa. Is he to be accused of guilt, folly, madness, or simple naiveté...? Who can calibrate the degree of cognitive impairment or even madness, guilty or otherwise, to which human nature can descend? Don Quixote, for example, was stubbornly convinced that the basin of which he robbed the barber (*won fair and square*, according to his own point of view) was none other than the helmet of Mambrino; in the same fashion he also thought that the trappings of the barber's donkey (which also became a trophy) was a horse's harness. We must admit, though, that Don Quixote was (reluctantly) willing to compromise on this last point:

> ...*When the devil, who never sleeps, contrived that the barber, from whom Don Quixote had taken Mambrino's helmet, and Sancho Panza the trappings of his ass in exchange for those of his own, should at this instant enter the inn... and dared to attack Sancho, exclaiming,*

---

[1] Jn 3:21.

—Ho, sir thief, I have caught you! Hand over my basin and my pack–saddle, and all my trappings that you robbed me of...

Don Quixote was standing by at the time, highly pleased to see his squire's stoutness, both offensive and defensive, and from that time forth he reckoned him a man of mettle, and in his heart resolved to dub him a knight on the first opportunity that presented itself, feeling sure that the order of chivalry would be fittingly bestowed upon him. In the course of the altercation the barber said, among other things:

—Gentlemen, this pack–saddle is mine as surely as I owe God a death, and I know it as well as if I had given birth to it, and here is my ass in the stable who will not let me lie; only try it, and if it does not fit him like a glove, call me a rascal; and what is more, the same day I was robbed of this, they robbed me likewise of a new brass basin, never yet used, that would fetch a crown any day.

At this Don Quixote could not keep himself from answering; and interposing between the two, and separating them, he placed the pack–saddle on the ground, to lie there in sight until the truth was established, and said:

—Your worships may perceive clearly and plainly the error under which this worthy squire lies when he calls a basin which was, is, and shall be the helmet of Mambrino which I won from him in fair war, and made myself master of by legitimate and lawful possession. With the pack–saddle I do not concern myself; but I may tell you on that head that my squire Sancho asked my permission to strip off the caparison of this vanquished poltroon's steed, and with it adorn his own; I allowed him, and he took it; and as to its having been changed from a caparison into a pack–saddle, I can give no explanation except the usual one, that such transformations will take place in adventures of chivalry. To confirm all which, run, Sancho my son, and fetch hither the helmet which this good fellow says to be a basin.

*—Egad, master —said Sancho—, if we have no other proof of our
case than what your worship puts forward, Mambrino's helmet is
just as much a basin as this good fellow's caparison is a pack–
saddle.*

*—Do as I bid thee, —said Don Quixote—; it cannot be that every-
thing in this castle goes by enchantment...*

*Our own barber, who was present at all this, and understood Don
Quixote's humor so thoroughly, took it into his head to back up
his delusion and carry on the joke for the general amusement; so
addressing the other barber he said:*

*—Mister barber, or whatever you are, you must know that I belong
to your profession too, and have had a license to practice for more
than twenty years, and I know the implements of the barber craft,
every one of them, perfectly well; and I was likewise a soldier
for some time in the days of my youth, and I know also what a
helmet is, and a morion, and a headpiece with a visor, and other
things pertaining to soldiering, I meant to say to soldiers' arms;
and I say —saving better opinions and always with submission to
sounder judgments— that this piece we have now before us, which
this worthy gentleman has in his hands, not only is no barber's
basin, but is as far from being one as white is from black, and truth
from falsehood; I say, moreover, that this, although it is a helmet,
is not a complete helmet.*[2]

It is apparent from this humorous episode narrated by Cervantes
that there are people who, like Don Quixote, are capable of totally
convincing themselves that a barber's basin is nothing less than the
legendary and imaginary helmet of Mambrino. They are not so sure,
however, that the donkey's saddle is a horse's harness, because it
may have happened, in their recounting it, that the transformation
is due to some evil *spell* which they have witnessed in the *castle*

---

[2] *Don Quixote*, I, 44–45.

where they lodge. We leave for another occasion the attempt to determine the degree of culpability (although in reality it seems that there is none) that may have existed in Don Quixote. However, we do have to include in this group of people the multitude of naive, crazy, semi–insane, and greatly deceived persons of this world. [3]

Others, however, knew that the donkey's pack–saddle was indeed just a pack–saddle and not any horse's harness; and the same must be said about the helmet of Mambrino. But due to convenient circumstances, they would be willing to welcome this deception *as if it were real*; this situation, moreover, suited them, as it provided for them some security (that is, freedom from worries) as well as certain improvements. In other words, there are those who would be willing to accept any situation as true and real because they simply refuse to consider that it may be false. All that matters to them is that they be on the side of whoever is in command, whoever has the power, and whose word carries more weight than truth itself. This provides them with a risk–free existence, and they do not look for trouble by inquiring after truthfulness:

> *There is no doubt of that —said Sancho—; for from the time my master won it until now he has only fought one battle in it, when*

---

[3] According to Ecclesiastes (1:5), *stultorum numerus infinitus est, the number of fools is infinite,* as stated in the Vulgate —although this text is not to be found in the Neo–Vulgate, surely following the fashionable demands of textual exegetical criticism. Nevertheless, some persist in saying that, after all, this is such an obvious truth, demonstrated every day, it does not need to be revealed by God. Ultimately we must acknowledge that the discussion of the problem would be inconsequential; at best, it may be worth noting that the term *stultus* can be translated equally as *foolish* or *stupid*. In our modern society that has dispensed with God it would be difficult to determine, even approximately, the varying degrees of foolishness, imbecility, or madness which make up the atmosphere in which we live. Besides, the fact that things are so is a dish served on a platter for the opportunists.

he let loose those unlucky men in chains; and if had not been for
this basin–helmet he would not have come off so well that time, for
there was plenty of stone–throwing in that affair.[4]

Martín de Riquer notes that the word *basin–helmet* was invented
sarcastically by Sancho so as to not contradict Don Quixote, who
believed that the basin was a helmet, and to avoid betraying his
own opinion, for Sancho knew that the disputed bowl actually was
a barber's basin. It is clear that with this ambiguity Sancho got
out of his predicament before his master... while, at the same time,
he sought to ignore the voice of his conscience which was trying —
rather unsuccessfully— to assert itself. I entirely agree, although
not so much that pure mockery was, according to Martin de Riquer,
the motive which animated the squire to give such an answer.

Here we could mention, as a historical curiosity, that, in 2004,
the Spanish sectarian, atheist, socialist Government sought the con-
sent of its citizens in a referendum to approve the Draft of the European Constitution. The Government did not hesitate to exhaust all
means of propaganda. For example, it made popular a slogan, by
broadcasting it 24 hours around the clock through all the media, according to which there was no need at all to read the text of the Draft
(quite cumbersome, but this detail was concealed from the people);
the people should just follow the thinking of *those who know and*
understand best (without specifying names, of course); and these,
according to the minions and mouthpieces of the government, had
already declared the Draft beneficial and approved it. The Spanish
people, whose ancient and time–honored Christian roots are now
defunct, simply accepted the text of a Masonic and anti–Christian

---

[4] *Don Quixote*, I, 44.

Constitution, without reading its complicated text (which would have brought upon them the animosity of the Government).

But promoting error among peoples (deceiving them) by purposely making white appear as black and vice versa, is unfortunately quite a common practice. Such was the attitude adopted by the barber neighbor of Don Quixote in regard to his suffering and aggrieved colleague:

> *Our own barber, who was present at all this, and understood Don Quixote's humour so thoroughly,*[5] *took it into his head to back up his delusion and carry on the joke for the general amusement; so addressing the other barber he said...*

The barber's intention was to go along with the joke. But there are those who do the same in order to avoid problems or to prevent further complications; they are even willing to pay for it if necessary, as in the case of the curé of our Don Quixote:

...And as to Mambrino's helmet, the curate, under the rose and without Don Quixote's knowing it, paid eight reals for the basin, and the barber executed a full receipt and engagement to make no further demand then or thenceforth for evermore, amen.[6]

At other times, and most frequently, the deceivers proceed with full malice, completely determined to pursue their hidden interests; they manipulate people to think, say, or do whatever the System and contemporary opportunists want. People, because of malice, weakness, or even sometimes out of sheer naiveté, agree to be easily led, and deception eventually prevails:

---

[5] Evidently this expression refers to Don Quixote's character, not to his jovial and happy demeanor.

[6] *Don Quixote* I, 46.

By then the noise finally subsided; the pack–saddle stayed as har-
ness till the Day of Judgment, and the basin as a helmet, and the
inn as a Castle in the imagination of Don Quixote.[7]

In the imagination of Don Quixote in this case or in the imag-
inations of the people in many others, all according to the issue
in question. Let us set aside for now the obviously jovial and humorous mood of Cervantes. We should remember, however, that
the ability to laugh is not only a unique feature of human beings
which makes them different from irrational animals, it is also one of
the elements of man's soul most mysterious and difficult to explain.
While laughter is often a reaction to what is humorous or ridiculous, it can also appear as a defense against what is tragic: *I do not
know whether to laugh or cry*, for example, is an expression often
heard. Indeed, it is not infrequent to see that man, when he has to
confront horrible and unusually frightening situations, hides behind
feelings which attempt to mask those difficulties, remove them from
his mind, or possibly give them a subtle nuance; he knows that this
nuance is a façade, but at least it alleviates or numbs the anxiety
of having to withstand those frightening situations as they come.
Indeed, laughter has an ambivalent character; it can be used to disguise, to justify, to forget, or even to remove from one's mind ideas
which one does not want to recall.

There people of all ranks, who wouldn't have forgathered any-
where else, infected one another with their enjoyment, for often
the solemn man would laugh not so much at the farce as at the
sight of the easily tickled man laughing, and the sage would laugh

---

[7] *Don Quixote*, I, 45.

at the ninny, the poor would laugh seeing the great lords, usually all scowls, laugh, and the grandees would laugh at the laughter of the poor, their consciences pacified by the thought: "Poor people laugh too!" For nothing is so quickly contagious between souls as this sympathetic laughter.[8]

Of course, the actual meaning of the word *tragicomic* is more relevant these days than it may seem. Because tragedy, when it is the result of a deliberately looked–for and accepted state of affairs, is always associated with foolishness, even if it does not seem so. This explains why the tragic and anguished post–Christian society of the twenty–first century, which has rejected God so completely, appears as the most ludicrous and farcical human conglomerate that the history of the World has ever known. Saint Paul already noticed this, particularly alluding to its tragic consequences: *Do not be deceived: God is not mocked,*[9] while its ridiculous aspect had been highlighted earlier by the Psalmist: *He that sitteth in the heavens laughs at them.*[10] Ultimately, we can say that we have a society that has wholeheartedly decided to live in Farce and out of Farce, as we shall try to show directly.

Of course, as long as one simply mistakes the helmet of Mambrino for a barber's basin or the harness of a horse for a pack–saddle, no harm is done: some give free reign to their madness, which in this

---

[8] Jacinto Benavente, *The Bonds of Interests*, Prologue.

[9] Gal 6:7.

[10] Ps 2:4.

case is harmless; others have fun, nothing more.[11] But the horizon becomes bleak when *transformations* affect more important things, leading to great mistakes and wrong judgments with regard to vital issues which have to do with the meaning of human life concerning individuals and societies.

Of course we are not talking about isolated, rare, or irrelevant cases. If only it were so. The *enchantments* that affect modern society are so many and so enormously powerful in manipulating mankind that modern humanity has become a universal Puppet Show in which even those who pull the strings are part of the Farce.[12] The Devil is the Father of Lies (Jn 8:44) and the Prince of this World as well (Jn 12:31); hence he has turned it into a huge Theater in which men, wearing appropriate costumes, *represent* or try to resemble *what they are not* and to hide *what they are.*

The Devil does not always tell only lies; sometimes, although rarely, he also tells the truth when it suits him. For example, when he tempted Jesus Christ in the desert and offered Him all the glories of this world (which he claims as his own) if He worshiped him, the

---

[11]Much has been written (and will continue to be written) about the philosophy of *Don Quixote* and Cervantes's intentions in writing his immortal work. And it must be recognized that the issue and the importance of the work deserve and warrant it. But regardless of what such considerations conclude (which is not of this place), it is clear that *Don Quixote* is a novel of humor. *Knight errantry books* may have been an important problem in Cervantes' time, which justified confronting and settling it for good. Nevertheless, I do not think that this issue made many people fall into madness, except for Alonso Quijano el Bueno, or that there were many who addressed this topic with excessive worry, as evidenced by the hilarity with which the readers have always approached the two heroes of this book and their humorous adventures. Had Cervantes lived in our time, he would probably have found much more serious and troubling, as well as droller and more surprising, issues to make them the target of his sharp irony.

[12]Due to technical progress, the means for mass manipulation are more abundant and efficient than ever before.

Devil was not far from the truth. Christians would better pay more attention to reading the Gospel.

2. Where we begin to expound the state of affairs and touch upon some background that gave rise to the "show" as an expression and content of faith

Few people realize that the old problem of substituting *appearing* (or *appearances,* if you want) for *being* is the core issue here. In other words, we are dealing with an old and extremely serious philosophical quandary.

Some may think that we exaggerate and will bring up the familiar adage *it is not a big deal*; but this would be merely one way, among many others, of confronting a problem without committing oneself to anything. Therefore, nothing better than presenting an example to counter such way of thinking. Examples are illuminating in themselves and can offer a better understanding of the problem, as a practical tool to center the subject and begin the discussion.

Everyone knows the tendencies of modern theology, most of which, welcomed and embraced by the ecclesiastical Hierarchy, have sent the metaphysics of being to the attic of useless paraphernalia. Today it is not uncommon to find Shepherds who know no philosophy other than Personalism and Phenomenology. There is no sense in denying that modern theology has been invaded by Idealism, which starts with Descartes as its strong point of departure, passes through Kant and Hegel, gives rise to the *practical philosophy* of Marx, Husserl's phenomenology, and the *conciliatory* doctrines of Hartmann and Scheler —which, in reality, do not conciliate anything. The adherents to these philosophies, one must admit, are very proud of themselves.

The currents of thought which try to resist this modern theology do not pose a problem. They are simply stigmatized with the term *Thomistic*, which is universally understood as being synonymous with conservatism, obscurantism, traditionalism, and, in general, anything that can be labeled as opposed to what is now called *progressivism*. And, as everyone knows, stigmas do not need proof or explanation; they are simply attatched to the victim so that everybody considers him to be a *reactionary* and runs away from him as though he had the plague. It is, of course, assumed that progressivism need not bother at all about explaining what its claimed *progress* consists of; it is progress, and that is all there is to it. Progressivism does not have to explain the term *reactionary* either, for that would imply burdensome and useless elucidations about the meaning of the intended *reaction*, its possible motivations, and, which would be most difficult, why this position is wrong.

It is clear that many *prejudices* are involved here whose common denominator is their self–attributed dogmatism, that is, they are indisputable; therefore, their proponents can dispense with any need for proof.

This said, we can move on to analyze the example mentioned above, beginning with its background. Everyone is aware of one of the most disastrous phenomena occurring in today's Christianity along with its religious and social consequences: the lack of vocations to the priesthood and consecrated life. There are, of course, other no less dire problems affecting Christianity; but now we want to talk about this one in particular as an opening for what we are going to say next; although, we must add, we are not going to consider its causes or full consequences.

The problem of the lack of priests affects the entire Christian world. Often, their scarcety makes impossible the celebration of the Mass (now called *Eucharist*), which is the center and source of supernatural life for the faithful who make up the Body of Christ, also known as the Church.

Because many Christians (we deliberately omit the term *Catholics* in order to be more in line with modern terminology) are not able to prominently participate in the Sacrifice of the Mass, they had to resort to one of the post–Vatican II pastoral discoveries. It is some sort of substitute for the Holy Mass known as the *Liturgy of the Word*; which has the peculiar feature that a priest is not needed to celebrate it; thus, any lesser minister or even a lay person (male or female) can lead it.

We hasten to note that we have nothing to say which may impair the value and meaning of this or other similar ceremonies. A substitute is always a substitute; and, if the faithful cannot have anything else, it is always worthwhile to have something. In this regard, there are but only good reasons to gather to listen to the Word of God and praise the Lord.

But nothing, whatever it is, can easily or rashly be termed as good or bad; not even when it comes to things which offer, at first glance, upbeat and festive aspects, apparently useful, and apparently appropriate for solving some seemingly difficult problem. This is particularly so when dealing with highly transcendental issues. In this case, common prudence demands that they be examined slowly, calmly, objectively, and, of course, without prejudice. When matters affect practical conduct, it is necessary to analyze carefully the different possibilities they may offer, good or bad, as well as the various consequences to which they may lead. In short, we would better take into consideration pros and cons of the concern in question, to find the right balance and to ensure that it is a topic worth undertaking.

The Mass is the center of worship, the source, origin, and meeting place for all parameters that structure Christian life; therefore, it cannot admit any paradigm or replacement. Hence, *it is impossible to replace the Mass with a substitute.* Indeed, it is always possible to replace one liturgical ceremony with another; to carry it out in various ways —with more or less solemnity or a more or less abbreviated rite, for example); or to worship and pray according to different devotions (novenas, public or private praying of the Rosary, the recitation of the Way of the Cross, etc.). The Mass cannot be considered as merely one more appropriate act of worship among many others. The source and origin cannot be substituted by any of the distributing channels.

Of course, anyone would easily pose this objection: something is always better than nothing. It is preferable that the faithful somehow hear the Word of God, or come together to worship Him and to increase their sense of community. Nothing could be more legitimate and more logical... at least at first sight.

Unfortunately, however, as we said above, things cannot be analyzed *at first glance* only; all aspects and implications must be taken into account. And it is not uncommon to discover that, once all aspects of an issue have been weighed, there is no other course of action but to withdraw something which, although it initially appeared as good, ends up by having more disadvantages than advantages. This is exactly what may happen if the Liturgy of the Word takes the place of the Mass. For no honest realist can deny that the faithful (human nature, after all, has a certain structure and virtualities which we tend to forget so easily) will end up becoming *accustomed* to the Liturgy of the Word; with colorful and even regrettable consequences.

For it is inevitable that a time will come when the faithful mistake the Liturgy of the Word for the Mass[13] first, and *end up later on ignoring or forgetting the need and importance of the Mass*. It is impossible to prevent their believing that, after all, one and the other are exactly the same.

But unfortunately, there are further problems. Because the *ministers* of this Liturgy of the Word, laymen ordinarily, tend to take their role very seriously (often too seriously —again the weakness of human nature),[14] they organize the said Liturgy as a true *mise-en-scène*. They think that the time has finally arrived for them to show off their own importance; therefore, they emphasize, with heavy doses of solemnity and ornament, what they regard as the most essential element. Is it the consecration as the pivotal moment of the Mass? Perhaps the sacrifice of the Death of the Lord made present here and now...? *Once upon a time, long ago...* Times change inexorably. Now the sacred books are carried with uplifted

---

[13]The current religious ignorance of the Christian People is so alarming that we are dealing with an unexplained and frightening phenomenon. For never before has so much emphasis been placed upon the need for activities such as training *workshops* prior to the reception of the sacraments (for example, marriage, making it at times quite difficult to be celebrated); nor have such long periods of *catechesis* been required for Confirmation or First Holy Communion, for example. Yet never before has there been such ignorance in religious matters. I have personally known cases of youngsters who, after three years of catechetical preparation in their parishes in order to receive confirmation, do not know how many Persons are there in God.

[14]The concept of the *lay minister* is a very strange (aberrant) entity in canon law and theology in general. It is often given the surprising name of *pastoral agent*: an extravagant term to understand which one would first have to figure out how a sheep can become shepherd.

arms in a solemn procession; or the readings of the Mass are an-
nounced, read, or recited with a throaty voice; or resounding state–
of–the–art musical instruments are introduced into the *gala*... or all
of the above at once, with many ministers involved of course; not
the least among them are those charming girls who gracefully and
naturally move to and fro, animating more favorably the spirit of
the faithful.

*In short, "appearing" has replaced "being," turning a sacred reality
into a "show" to please people.*[15]

And this is not all; nor is it the most heart–rending of events.

As one can see, the bizarre and comical event in *Don Quixote*,
where the barber's basin assumed the guise of the helmet of Mambrino, is something that happened very long ago. It also was penned
by Cervantes without any particular purpose other than to make
many generations in many places of the world laugh. But here we are
dealing with something quite different whose manifold consequences
are not normally positive. And just as the medieval alchemists inevitably headed for failure in their quest for the Philosopher's Stone
(which was supposed to turn lead into gold), so modern experts con-
cocting in their laboratory of Liturgy have at last changed gold into
lead; it is not exactly the same thing, but it is a miracle after all.

But let us go back to our example, for the long list of unfortunate
corollaries is not yet ended. In effect, the faithful can easily get used
to the Liturgy of the Word, zealously carried out with pomp and

---

[15]I have before me a report, dated May 11, 2005, concerning the meeting held
by the Governing Board of an American diocese chaired by the Bishop, published
by the Diocesan Office. Among other things, it refers to the intervention of one of
the participants, whereby he stresses the need to teach the faithful that the idea of
the Eucharist as a sacred object is to be replaced by the idea of the Eucharist as
an act of worship. There is no evidence in the report suggesting that the Bishop
or any of the participants offered the slightest objection to the proposal.

pageantry by pious ministers, men or women, of good will. It stands to reason that these faithful will end up concluding, consciously or unconsciously, that *the priest is now no longer needed.* And so, there is now no longer any reason to be concerned about the lack of vocations to the sacred ministry; the problem which at first glance appeared to be worrisome has been definitively solved.

However, the proposed solution for the shortage of priests has become, perhaps without anyone's intending it, an effective tool for blocking the influx of vocations and in removing the interest in finding them.

There are other disadvantages, such as involving the laity with ministerial tasks that are not their own and for which they lack the corresponding charisma; or the risk of minimizing even more, if that could be possible, the figure of the priest. But since this is only one example among many that could be brought up, we will not insist further on this point. Although it is worth reiterating that the campaign against the priesthood intensifies as time goes on. The Barque of Peter has never before been so badly buffeted by the waves.

One of the innovations introduced by current progressivism refers to the elimination of the spiritual director. It is argued that he is an institution used for centuries by the clergy to control and subdue the laity; therefore, he must be replaced by the *spiritual companion,* preferably a lay person or a nun (the intention of displacing the priest is clear). It is argued that freedom and personal autonomy need not rely on any authority; consequently, one must do away with the figure of the priest as something unnecessary and obsolete. Farewell, therefore, to institutions of Christian Spirituality that have been in place for centuries; also farewell to another of the greatest opportunities to practice the virtues of obedience and humility... In general, bye–bye to the doctrine that for two millennia has been professed by many theologians, saints, and spiritual writers, both men and women. The words of the Qoheleth come to mind: *Woe to him who is alone when he falleth; for he hath not another to help him up* (Eccl 4:10).

3. Where a brief summary of the evolution undergone by the concept of theater in the mind of the Church, from her earliest times to the present day, is made.

The Greek classics looked down upon theater and regarded actors as people of low birth. Plato, for example, was a prominent enemy of the stage.

As for Christianity, it is known that the early Church (Councils and the Fathers in the lead) showed a continuous hostility against theater. Tertullian[16] and Saint Augustine[17] were perhaps, among many others, its most bitter critics. In fact, the enmity (including even that of famous persons such as Bossuet) lasted until after the seventeenth century, despite inconsistent periods of respect and even cooperation.[18] A careful study of the reasons for this current of thought is not relevant here. One can arguably say, generally speaking, that the high degree of immorality reached by theater since the

---

[16] *De Spectaculis.*

[17] *Enarrationes in Psalmos; De Fide et Operibus; De Vera Religione,* etc.

[18] It should be noted, as an important historical curiosity, that in the Middle Ages Saint Thomas was one of the few theologians who upheld the honor of theater and of the craft of acting, as long as morality was taken into account (*Summa Theologiæ,* IIa–IIæ, q. 168, a. 3). The Saint even defended the legality of the stipends received by the actors who acted honestly (IIa–IIæ, q. 87, a. 2, ad. 2).

classical era and early days of the Church was the cause of the multitude of prohibitions thrown against it. In effect, the complex and lascivious Dionysian milieu was involved in theater, along with its orgies, its phallic cults, and deeply obscene stage performances. Not to mention the bloody and cruel spectacle of the games at the circus. No wonder the Reformation was no less hostile than the Catholic Church to theater.

Therefore, in regard to relations between the Church and theater, it is reasonable to discuss a first period of prevailing animosity and aversion; a second interval in which condescension and cooperation alternated with strong prohibitions; and finally, in modern times, a relative calm has been achieved. Bossuet, as we said, even into the eighteenth century, still bitterly condemned theater. Since the Middle Ages until well into the Modern era, religious representations, centered on the Eucharist (*Sacrament Scenes*), on the Lord's Passion, or on other biblical events (the *Mysteries* also enjoyed great popularity), were common, involving both clergy and laity. But there were also an abundant number of representations with an obscene, burlesque, and even blasphemous character; some of them mocked the Popes and the Mass. It is no wonder that condemnations have replaced tolerance, and vice–versa. In Spain, for example, the cradle of Calderón, Lope de Rueda, Lope de Vega (and, less famously, Juan del Encina), the world of drama and comedy once reached high standards. The comedies of Lope de Vega, with a *moralizing* tone, alternated with others, rather *picaresque*; and hence periods of prohibition, imposed by the King, soon mingled with others of allowance. Finally, there is a third period, to which belong our current times and which is adorned with particularly amazing characteristics.

Amazing because, first, this relationship between Church and theater is a relevant social fact; however, *it has gone virtually unnoticed by the consciousness of modern society.* Near mid–twentieth century, technical progress and the extraordinary advancement of the media provided a new facet to religion as being a social event. Religious ceremonies became closely integrated (as an entertainment enterprise) with television networks and daily press (whose circulation had grown well over a thousand percent).

Secondly, there is no denying the fact, apparently gone unnoticed, that a conscious and calculated *playing to the gallery* has been instrumental in restructuring the content and configuration of church activities —most particularly in regard to preaching and even to the entire Christian Pastoral Ministry. It would be interesting, for example, to develop an analysis of the influence the *media* has had on the actions of Bishops. There is no intention to anticipate a negative judgment about such actions. We simply want to draw attention to the significance that such an investigation would have; in any case, it would be enlightening and useful.

We must make it clear that there is no intention of making negative criticism; it is just a critique.[19] It is not necessary to speak here of how human nature behaves, let alone of the extent to which social facts can affect (positively or negatively) man's conduct. Social facts simply are; and they have the possibility of influencing, one way or another, the psychology and actions of individuals.

Having said this, we can refer now to a current sociological event of great significance. *Opinion* and *appearance* have become so important in the modern world, even within the Church, that one can

---

[19]The substantive *critique* does not have primarily a pejorative sense. Its most appropriate meaning is to judge and evaluate things (usually to improve them). María Moliner, in her Dictionary, defines its primary and most important meaning as the *expression of a judgment*; that is all.

confirm the supremacy of *appearing* over the realm of *being*. That some may take a barber's basin for the helmet of Mambrino, or a pack–saddle of a donkey for the harness of a horse, can be considered as a merely comic and burlesque episode intended to arouse amusement. The extraordinary thing is that many of the normal occurrences in the life of our modern church, oddly enough, have the rare feature of also being perceived *as something very different from what they really are*. The comparison, though, is not completely totally valid, for now the humorous element is gone (at least at first sight, and except in what we are going to say next). Many of these events make up an important part of the sociology of the Church, but one cannot say that they have dispensed deep down with some comic element. Therefore, we should describe those events as *tragicomic* in character; especially since they are often associated with important matters of church life, thus resulting in disastrous consequences for the faithful. Since ancient times it has not mattered that the tragic and the ridiculous appear together in the *tragicomedy*; hence the intentional use of the term here, as it paves the way for the old and familiar aphorism *I laugh because I don't want to cry*.

The change of mind of the Church with regard to theater has led to the emergence of a social shift of enormous impact, as we have said. If we draw now, in order to better understand this problem, a historical sketch of this change, we find that there is first a stage of hostility on the part of the Church; initial hostility which appears to have had many reasons to justify it. Then there is a second face which is quite close to modern times; there the Church participates in the world of showbiz and alternates allowances of theater with prohibitions. Then come the years of more or less equilibrium, which gives way to the present moment we are analyzing.

We must underline the importance of a striking peculiarity that characterizes this latter stage. The Church has given the green light to theater. Furthermore, she has no qualms in welcoming it into the many facets that make up the normal development of her daily practice. But the Church has not welcomed theater as an artistic event with its proper formalities (which would have been absurd), *but rather as a structural element of her intrinsic nature.* To put it in plainer words, although they may sound rather strange: it is a fact that many of the activities of the Church which have to do with worship and, in general, with her Pastoral endeavors, *have adopted, consciously or unconsciously, a theatrical nature.* Now the reality of the Mystery does not matter so much as the feelings stirred up in the faithful. Promoting and facilitating the action of the Holy Spirit in Christian life is no longer the main objective of modern pastoral activity, which now tends to arouse feelings, usually of pleasure and entertainment, among the faithful without any real concern for their objective spiritual growth.

This statement may sound too harsh, for it implies that one must acknowledge, as a phenomenon of the modern Church, the gradual disappearance of objective, supernatural truth in favor of mere sentimentality which, in turn, as might be expected, is based on purely subjective individualism.

From this point of view, many of the circumstances that structure today's ecclesiastical life acquire a very peculiar aspect. It does not matter so much whether theater reflects ordinary life, with its varying degrees of realism and morality; for ecclesial activity has adopted the guidelines of theater. *Thus, Pastoral activity has welcomed theatricals in many of its enterprises.*

4. Where examples are provided which clarify some of the statements made above, and where the analysis of the history of the ecclesial "show" continues.

The Second Vatican Council and Pope Paul VI, who presided over most of it, made changes of greatest significance in regard to church worship.[20] The liturgy in general was endowed with great flexibility, being largely left to the discretion and responsibility of Bishops and Episcopal Conferences. Logically, and in this connection, both the Council and the Pope, exercising their legitimate powers, took into account all possible advantages and disadvantages of the changes. This done, they were left to tackle any problems which would presumably present themselves as logical consequences of these changes; which problems did, in fact, occur.

First of all, it is clear that no one can object to the right of the Church to exercise her legitimate power of governing and teaching within her competent area and when proper conditions are met; which is what indeed happened in this case.

But legitimate modifications of disciplinary rules do not eliminate the possibility that problems with ancillary risks may arise; especially when at stake are the dispositions affecting the most intimate and delicate life of the Church —as the Mass and administration of the Sacraments— and modifications of deeply rooted and centuries–old procedures and methods. And nobody should be surprised if certain human actions that are in no wise infallible are

---

[20]Constitution *Sacrosanctum Concilium.*

capable of producing outcomes not always desired.[21] Therefore, no one can consider the person responsible for making those decisions answerable for such eventualities, except when he ceased to put in place the necessary measures to prevent or reduce, as far as possible, the negative consequences that may occur in connection with his decision. This issue became more complicated in many instances because Bishops and Episcopal Conferences ascribed to themselves powers which exceeded the limits assigned to them by the Second Vatican Council.[22]

The irrefutable fact that modifications and changes in the Liturgy and Worship were, for the most part, highly beneficial to all the faithful is a source of joy. Replacing vernacular languages for Latin, for example, opened a wide field for the participation of the faithful in the Worship, particularly in the Mass.

Unfortunately, as we mentioned above, *collateral* problems immediately appeared. It is really difficult for many human actions, despite being animated by the best and most noble intentions, always to produce beneficial effects *free from any imperfection*. Although one always tends to think that things are simple and clear, the emergence of the dreaded specter of drawbacks is inevitable in the end. This reality indeed does not exempt the person concerned from the

---

[21]One might question, for example, as a merely historical judgment, the success or failure of the alliance of Saint Pius V with Spain and Venice to fight the Ottoman Turks at Lepanto in 1571; or the opportunity or lack of it of the trip of Pope John Paul II to Cuba in 1998 to visit the dictator Fidel Castro. There are many pastoral activities, throughout the History of the Church, whose questioning has nothing to do with due respect and obedience to the Magisterium.

[22]It is also fair to say that those excesses and the many abuses that have occurred since the end of the Council, on the part of some Episcopal Conferences and of many Bishops, have been orchestrated and promoted at all times by liberal theology.

right and duty of making the decisions that he deems appropriate, but it demands from him carefully weighing the circumstances and considering the possible eventualities.

The use of vernacular languages also led to the emergence of serious drawbacks; for example, the problem of translations of liturgical books. The guidelines required that *translations* of the texts be approved by the respective Episcopal Conferences and, when appropriate, by the Vatican; but, quite understandably, this norm could not be met. There are thousands of languages and dialects in this world, making it completely impossible for the Vatican to have knowledgeable experts in each of them.[23] Years of experience show that the results have been generally deplorable; for it was necessary to leave the translations to the discretion of individuals or institutions who, in addition to their incompetence, were not aware of the seriousness and importance of their task. This is how all kinds of abuses became possible: arbitrariness, inventiveness, mistranslation, and even manipulation of the liturgical texts. And to this mix we must add the extraordinary abundance of *lectors,* who often mistook their role with the performance of actors at the theater.

During the many years of the pontificate of Pope John Paul II, elements of *show business* were developed in Worship, Liturgy, and Pastoral activity, making them almost seem a part of the theatrical world. The good intentions of Vatican II for promoting the involvement of Christian People in Worship and Liturgy were generally misunderstood. The *liberalization* of liturgical norms, especially those concerning the Mass, led to the rushing in of inventiveness, impro-

---

[23]The great Masters of classical treatises *de Legibus*, such as Saint Thomas, Suárez, Vitoria, and others always required, as one of the essential conditions of laws, that they can be fulfilled.

visations, and arbitrary interpretations which sought, above all, *to dazzle and attract the attention of the faithful. Everyone tried to amaze the people with something new.*

Gradually, theater found an open door into Liturgy and a number of theatrical elements crept in: colorful *processions* with gifts during the offertory of the Mass, often accompanied by dances and rituals *typical* of each place;[24] ostentatious and pompous carrying the Gospel on high to do the readings of the day; flamboyant *recitations* of the liturgical texts by lay people, mostly by women good–looking, if possible; the *dramatic staging* of the liturgical readings of the Mass in various places. For example, everybody fell suddenly silent for the reading of the Epistle; then, a messenger entered the church through the front door with a paper in his hands and shouting: *Letter from Paul, Letter from Paul!* Not to mention the theatrical gestures of a true pacifist celebrant breaking shotguns or rifles during the homily. There were places where the biblical liturgical texts were replaced with articles of newspapers or of limelight (usually left–wing) writers, which were considered *more current and apt to awaken the feelings of the faithful.* Meanwhile, the Charismatic Movements and the like brought into fashion gestures and peculiar dances in various parts of the Mass (hands up, holding hands, voices and spontaneous screams *stirred by the breath of the Spirit*). At the same time, celebrating the Holy Sacrifice (now called Eucharist, since the element of Sacrifice has been discarded) not in the church

---

[24]Sometimes they were dances of showy young girls performing so–called *liturgical dances* while leading the procession of the offerings.

but in strange places, using sacred vessels of cheap and low–quality material, became a general practice.[25]

Of course, one can easily understand that incidents like this belong to the pre–history of the theological, ecclesial, and liturgical *tsunami* caused by the Second Vatican Council. As Modernism uncovered its face and the new condition was imposed as a reality, the value of *symbols* and what is merely symbolic put down roots in the *New Church* born along with the *New Age*. Now that *Scholastic language* and all of its terminology have been discarded, the Eucharist, for example, recovers its true value as a mere *symbol* of the Body

---

[25]We can name places where, on Christmas Eve, once Midnight Mass was over and following an immemorial custom, the Child Jesus was presented to the faithful to be kissed; only this time it was not a statue of the Child but a newborn, almost naked baby. *Enough of lifeless symbols!* Said the priest to enthuse the faithful. This is not the place to mention the snide, even scabrous, remarks that many worshipers made about this.

It would be impossible and useless to enumerate the many whims, follies, and abuses carried out in many places after the Second Vatican Council and which are still in full force with total impunity. Someone might object, however, that the old Liturgy (Solemn Pontifical Masses, Processions, the Gregorian Chant that usually accompanied so many sacred functions, etc.) also contained a lot of show. But this statement is unfair and takes things out of proportion. The ancient liturgical functions had a rather Spartan and fervent character; their main object was to honor God through a worship that was considered sacred. One has to have participated in this Liturgy (something which is reserved only for the elderly; these people do exist and can bear witness to what we are saying) to understand clearly that at no time it intended to stir up purely human feelings but supernatural sentiments of devotion, worship, and love for God. Modern forms of worship, by contrast, are mainly interested in *arousing, encouraging, and fostering among the faithful feelings of a psychological rather than religious nature.* On the other hand, secularly considered sacred music, like Gregorian Chant, for instance, is at the antipodes of meaningless noise of electronic guitars, screams, and contortions that accompany *pop music.*

and Blood of Jesus Christ. The remaining Dogmas, of course, will be next. Indeed, even heresies need time to settle definitively

Claiming that some gestures of liturgical worship, for example, raising one's hands, correspond to the most ancient Liturgy of the Church is worse than an intentional deceit. The purpose of the very primitive (and soon more developed) Liturgy was only the praising of God, whereas some modern liturgies are rather in perfect consonance with Jewish or Judaizing cults, for example, *which Saint Paul already rejected in his time because they have been made void definitively by Faith in Jesus Christ.*

Most significant in this respect, however, during the reign of Pope John Paul II, were perhaps the lavish and spectacular gestures bestowed on many occasions. They were carried out, undoubtedly, with the true ecumenical intention of attracting to the Church those who are far from her; but one cannot possibly ignore that their ambiguous tones sounded an alarm among many Catholic faithful. The flashy and showy motions performed by the Pope upon his arrival to a country; his gestures made to certain *sacred* objects of other *religions*; his visits of good will and his reaching out to political leaders considered by everybody as dictators and even criminals (in search of greater freedom for the Church in those countries), or to the heads of atheistic *religions* (Buddhism, Hinduism, or *voodoo* cults), to name only a few cases. These gestures were unsettling to many people who immediately considered them as demagogic or theatrical. But the most stunning events of the reign of this Pope were the multitudinous *World Youth Days*[26] which gathered with great display huge crowds of young people from all over the world,

---

[26]There were other gatherings which arouse greater concern among Catholics. We are referring to the well–known and controversial *Gatherings at Assisi* in 1986 and 2002, at which leaders of all *religions* in the world gathered to pray for peace.

and which sometimes began with a solemn and pompous appearance of the Supreme Pontiff as he was acclaimed dramatically. Only God knows the spiritual fruits of these Gatherings; say what you will, they are rather sparse in the eyes of men.

The case of the *Gatherings at Assisi* is much more serious. Although they have been generally considered as far–reaching ecumenical events, this appreciation is false or at least totally insufficient. These Gatherings are the culmination of the theological doctrine of Cardinal Wojtyla, which he later confirmed and preached from the Supreme Chair as Pope John Paul II. According to this doctrine, and following the theory of *anonymous Christianity*, all men, whether they know it or not, are saved by the mere fact that they are men, and thanks to the union of Jesus Christ with human nature, thus cancelling, as something superfluous, the need of subjective justification, Faith, and Baptism.

Confusion and indifference are two serious consequences which, to the detriment of the faithful, may result from this *show* mentality spread throughout the life of today's Church. One does not need to know much about human nature to realize that the stage machinery to which we have briefly alluded and succinctly summarized, soon makes the faithful forget the content and even the existence of the thing signified. All that is left is mere emphasis of psychological feelings, emptied of any supernatural dimension and extensively fed by the ambiguity used in gesture and in words.[27]

---

[27]The use of ambiguity is a dangerous resort in so far as it gives way to subjective interpretations of the mystery, blurring supernatural reality. Adding, for example, the expression *for us* to the formulas of the Consecration, along with *bread of life and cup of salvation*, can easily lead to confusion, despite its possible accuracy. The *bread of life* and the *cup of salvation* are such *in themselves* —or just *for us* (subjectively) leaving aside their content? Proximity to Modernism seems to lurk here as a real danger.

The *Show–like* Pastoral ministry alters or inverts the nature of theater. The more faithfully the significant fulfills its mission (*plays its role*, one could say) on the stage, the better it reflects what is signified. The good actor identifies himself with the character he represents; with this particularity: the more real he makes his character appear the more he fades as a *representing* actor. Or put another way: the more real the represented character is the more abstract or *forgotten* (by the viewer) becomes the person of the representing actor, who gradually *disappears* as he emphasizes the reality of the character he tries to incarnate. That is, the significant *disappears* as the reality of object signified acquires marked–out contours. The most successful actor is the one who best highlights before the public, in his role as mere significant, the reality of his character. Exactly the opposite happens in modern Liturgy, where the Signified Entity dissipates as the significant is stressed, whose sole *reality* is merely being a significant; which is the only thing left to the faithful.

The problem is understood more clearly when considering the sacraments. They are indeed signs, but they *contain and cause* the reality signified. Their character as signs is merely, as it were, pedagogical, namely, helping to understand better the mysteries they contain. Were one to insist too much on their character as signs, making more or less abstraction of their supernatural character, their efficacy would vanish and none of the sacraments would be useful, for nobody is cleansed of his stains with mere signs or fed with pure symbols. The Christian faithful understood this for centuries; so much so that it was always necessary to explain to them in Catechesis that the sacraments are *also* signs. This demonstrates that they always gave less importance to the significant than to the signified reality in the sacraments.

Someone might say that the magnificence and splendor of the ancient and traditional Liturgy, although solemn as well as Spartan, could also have contributed to accentuate the significant in detriment of the reality signified. This statement is clearly false for two main reasons.

First, because the ostentation that accompanied the solemnity of the old Liturgy was totally different in nature to the theatrical settings used in the profane world. What does Gregorian Chant, for example, have in common with secular medieval or Renaissance music? A clear proof of the truth of our assertion is the well–known fact that all the attempts to introduce profane music and singing in religious functions have resulted in total failure. The sacred music of Mozart, for instance (either a *Mass* or a *Requiem*), as everyone knows, never managed to be regarded as sacred. Undoubtedly his music is exceedingly beautiful... but only suitable for concerts.

Second, because the exclusive aim of the splendor of the old Liturgy was *purely religious and supernatural*. This is a glaring historical fact that needs no demonstration. On the contrary, the thunderous and *spectacular* scenic apparatus of modern liturgical functions, very often, as we have said above, have no other purpose than to amaze and entertain the faithful who are regarded as spectators, even *interactive* in many cases. Perhaps there is no better proof of the veracity of this assertion, should any doubt exist, than referring to the intentions and beliefs of the organizers.

With regard to the Mass, the double danger posed by this scenic setting is even more serious.

It must first be noted that the faithful may be led to forget or even totally ignore that the Mass is *the Holy Sacrifice of Christ on the Cross accomplished once on Mount Calvary and made really — not merely commemoratively or as a remembrance— present here and now thanks to the Eucharistic Mystery.* The Second Vatican Council emphasized that the two parts of the Mass, the Liturgy of the Word and the Liturgy of the Eucharist, form a unity.[28] But with the passing of time and frequent abuses, greater emphasis was given to the first part to the almost total oblivion of the second; which contributed to the profusion of all kinds of scenic settings when celebrating the Holy Sacrifice.

If this is true, only God knows its evil consequences for the Church. Casting a shadow on or forgetting the Mystery of the Cross implies the disappearance of the most essential reality of the Christian Message, indeed of Christianity itself. This dangerous outcome already frightened Saint Paul; he tried to warn Christians against it when he said that, as for him, he preached without relying on wisdom of speech, *ut non evacuetur crux Christi, lest the cross of Christ should be made void.*[29]

The second aspect is related to the first and derives from it: the fact that the Christian faithful can get the wrong idea about their necessary participation in the Sacrifice and Death of Our Lord.

Although it seems hard to believe, this participation became simply *an active involvement in the ceremonies or acts of worship.* Activities such as distributing the Eucharist, presenting liturgical readings, preaching by the laity, etc., are the only things that lay people now understand as *participating* at Mass. We must also mention the emergence of many activities —quite new and peculiar some of them— carried out by so–called *ministers* whose number and diversity, once the fever of this novelty had died down, was essentially reduced to *Eucharistic ministers.* The idea of intimate participation in the sufferings and death of Our Lord —a Mystery

---

[28] *Sacrosanctum Concilium,* II, 56.

[29] 1 Cor 1:17.

whose only vital and original source is the Mass—, along with all its practical consequences for Christian life, was replaced by external activities *coram populo, before the people,* whose significance, if any, interests nobody. Thus we are only one step away from theatrical performance. Knowledge of human nature tells us that no sooner is emphasis placed on the externals of any reality than the content of that entity fades away. Actually, attention to ceremony and to one's own performance before the people is all that remains as the only important thing. Who can be mindful, in these circumstances, of Our Lord's death and our urgent need to *share* it with Him? But participation in the sufferings and death of Christ is not an isolated event in the History of Salvation, concerned only with the personal benefit of every individual who wishes to attain the corresponding profit. Since all Christians comprise a Whole, or one *Body* with Christ as the Head,[30] such participation is necessary for the full realization of the plan of Redemption designed by God (Col 1:24). The suggestion that such a death would be a *mystical* death, something purely symbolic, could be countered with texts from Matthew (16:25), Mark (8:35), Luke (9:24), and John (12:25), to which a meaning nothing short of poetic should likewise be attributed.

In this game, *appearance* replaces *being*, and what is *real* is substituted by what is *imagined* (which Idealism esteems);[31] emotion and subjectivity displace that which until now has been considered objective (Modernism); and the possibility that symbolism should become objectivism is welcomed. This then would be the time for theater to be introduced with fanfare and pretensions of dislodging reality; the time for symbolism (otherwise so useful and necessary

---

[30] Rom 12:5; 1 Cor 10:17; 12: 12.20; Eph 4: 4.12.16; Col 2:19; 3:15

[31] Idealism reaches its apex in dealing with the issue of being: according to this philosophy, the only thing that can claim for itself the condition of reality is precisely what is imagined as such imagined.

for human existence) to demand to be used outside and far beyond its own context. This experiment could lead to disastrous consequences for the faithful's living and understanding the fundamental Mysteries of the Christian Faith; in particular, to cite one of the most important Mysteries, the Real Presence of Jesus Christ in the Eucharist. Indeed, events, as usual, rush one after another, following the rules of logical succession concerning man's behavior according to human nature.

The Second Vatican Council, in its Constitution *Sacrosanctum Concilium* (I, 7), spoke of the diverse ways in which Christ is present in His Church. The importance of this text cannot be sufficiently emphasized:

> Christ is always present in His Church, especially in her liturgical celebrations. He is present in the sacrifice of the Mass, not only in the person of His minister, 'the same now offering, through the ministry of priests, who formerly offered himself on the cross,'[32] but especially under the Eucharistic species. By His power He is present in the sacraments, so that when a man baptizes it is really Christ Himself who baptizes.[33] He is present in His word, since it is He Himself who speaks when the holy scriptures are read in the Church. He is present, lastly, when the Church prays and sings, for He promised: 'Where two or three are gathered together in my name, there am I in the midst of them' *(Mt 18:20)*.

As one can see, the conciliar text clearly expounds the various manifestations of Christ's presence in His Church, grouping them together and as if in parallel. Understandably, the document takes special care to emphasize, through the adverb *maxime*, His presence

---

[32]Council of Trent, Sess. XXII, Doctrine on the Holy Sacrifice of the Mass, c. 2.

[33]Cf. St. Augustine, *Tractatus in Joannem*, VI, n. 7.

under the Eucharistic species, thus making this presence different from the others. This is an important and illuminating precaution that is not without significance.[34]

Nevertheless, there exists the possibility that practical problems may appear (notwithstanding the authority of the Council and its clear pedagogical and pastoral intentions) precisely because the Document puts the various modes of presence in parallel. In all of them (except for the Real Presence in the Eucharist) the Document speaks of presence *by His virtue*, which can be also interpreted as *moral presence*; therefore, the danger of considering the various modes of presence as being equivalent, or as being on the same level, is more than evident. It should be noted that Christian People in general are not well–versed in theology, let alone experts on subtle distinctions; therefore, it is quite difficult to completely eliminate the risk of confusion.

The Council text refers to Matthew 18:20, which speaks about the presence of Christ when the Church prays or sings psalms: *When two or three are gathered together in my name, 'there am I in the midst of them.'* It is a fundamental rule of scriptural exegesis that biblical texts are to be interpreted according to their proper and most obvious meaning, without ignoring their context. The Council, of course, does not intend otherwise. For this reason, it is clear that the text of Matthew 18:20 cannot be interpreted in the same sense, strictly literal, as the texts referring to the institution of

---

[34]This Document also qualifies the presence of Jesus Christ in the sacraments with the phrase *virtute sua*, which is not extended to His presence in the proclamation of His word.

the Eucharist at the Last Supper or the passage of Saint Paul of 1 Corinthians 11: 23–26 about the same issue.[35]

Moreover, exegetical science has always maintained that not all biblical passages can be interpreted in the same sense. Therefore one must never abandon the guide of good doctrine and, above all, the Magisterium. There are, on the one hand, passages which cannot be understood in the strictly literal sense (for example, passages that speak about plucking out one's eye or cutting off one's hand to avoid the danger of scandal and sin); on the other hand, Scripture does have other passages —such as the Eucharistic texts which we have mentioned— whose strictly literal meaning is obvious, absolutely required by the Magisterium, and maintained by the unwavering Tradition of the Church.[36] However, risk emerges when texts that cannot be interpreted in the same sense are placed side by side equally; for then the door is opened to dangerous confusion. Obviously, physical or real presence is not identical to moral presence, if we keep ourselves to the meaning of everyday language and to what

---

[35] *Hoc est corpus meum* (Mt 26: 26 ff; Mk 14: 22 ff; Lk 22:19) is an expression which the Magisterium has always understood strictly literally. *The sacramental presence* of Jesus Christ in the Eucharist is so real as to imply the complete actualization (never symbolic), here and now, of the Humanity (His soul as well as His body) and Divinity of Our Lord. This actualization can be truly called *real presence*, although one must take into account its independence regarding all the accidents, especially the accident *quantitas*. This real, sacramental presence, according to the unshakeable doctrine of the perennial Magisterium of the Church, is different from the virtual or *moral presence* which remains in the communicant once the Eucharistic species have disappeared.

[36] The Reformation, it is well known, is an exception. Berengarius of Tours (1000–1088) is another rare one. He denied transubstantiation and (according to the majority of theologians who in this regard follow Saint Thomas) the real presence.

any normal person can understand.[37] Real life facts are quite eloquent and speak for themselves. Thus, for example, when speaking
about the real or *physical* presence of a person, it makes no sense to
talk at the same time of his *moral* presence, as if both were on the
same or similar level. What sense would it make to talk about the
moral or virtual presence of this or that person, as if he is absent,
when we actually have that person before our own eyes? Hence it
does not seem effective to place in parallel those texts whose mean-
ings are at variance or ambivalent, given the danger of confusion
and, ultimately, of equating the reality of a person's presence with
merely his virtual memory. In real, every–day language, for example, when we say of a loved one, now deceased, that *he is always with
us*, it is clear that we are speaking in a symbolic or figurative sense;
even if the influence of that person is strongly real. Human nature
is such that very often, and all too easily, it confuses Legend with
History, which is shortly afterwards thrown into oblivion. In effect,
the human being, as experience shows, passes from one to the other
as easily as he goes from the real to the symbolic. As Robert Jordan,
the American fantasy writer, said emphatically and beautifully: *The
Wheel of Time turns while Ages come and go, leaving behind memories that then become Legends. And the Legends, in turn, fade into
myth until myth is also forgotten.*[38] Therefore, everything taken into
account, it may be best to leave reality (or presence, in this case)
well established in its integrity, clearly separated with resounding
clarity from what is but a moral or virtual presence, force, or influence. Crystal clear concepts and words are undoubtedly the best

---

[37]The conciliar document perceives the difference when it distinguishes between
the moral presence of Jesus Christ (*through His power*) and His proper Eucharistic
presence.

[38]Robert Jordan, *The Wheel of Time. The Dragon Reborn*, New York, 1992,
p. 31.

safeguard of truth. When reality is displaced by the symbolic, the former ends up being considered as *merely symbolic*; and then, with simple logical thinking, as *pure nothing*; for what would be the sense of claiming to have a symbol that signifies absolutely nothing?

5. Wherein the history of the helmet of Mambrino is continued, and the odd parable of the hundred rebel sheep is told, with other accompanying trifles that add flavor to the subject

The Lord said that His Kingdom is not of this World (Jn 18:36); the Devil, however, had the nerve to assume dominion over it himself (Lk 4:6). It is true that the Devil is the Great Liar and the Father of Lies (invectives that Our Lord Himself uttered); but it is fair to acknowledge that, in some respects, the Devil was not far from the truth when he claimed world dominion for himself.[39] And since it seems that in recent History the kingdom of the Lie has expanded in no small measure, it is no exaggeration to affirm that we live under the rule of the Lie; at least in many aspects and circumstances of life. Replacing *what is not* for *what is*, and vice versa, has become normal. Modern society is no longer scandalized that a spade is not called a spade. In ancient classic theater *persona* and *coturno*

---

[39]Surely the Devil is the Great Deceiver. But sometimes, when it is to his advantage, he tells the truth: the whole truth, part of it, or a messy mixture of truth and lies. Sometimes he tells the truth in order to fool the born liars, which could seem like a paradox, but really it is not. Liars, like thieves, think that *everyone is like them*; hence the devil occasionally sees fit to tell them the truth so that they will believe the opposite. The consequence of this is obvious. Therefore, an advised person should never believe the Devil or, better yet, he should never, under any circumstances, dialogue with him.

were used as disguises.[40]   Currently, there is no need to employ
these artificial accouterments which are rather uncomfortable and
display their artificial nature too loudly. Nobody wants to appear
as a harlequin, despite the plethora of that genre among members of
society today. Most evident in the modern world is that, in a number
of areas, costumes and façades have become quite fashionable; many
people, even multitudes of people, use them. Nowadays, the tumult
caused at the inn where Don Quixote's entourage arrived would
not make sense: for the barber's basin would indeed be the helmet
of Mambrino; the saddle–pack of the donkey would absolutely be
considered the harness of a horse, without the least argument or
problem.

The members of the *setup of modern farce*, however, have something in common with the actors of ancient Classical Theater: they
also appear on the scene as heroes; but with one important difference: today's modern actors do not aspire to represent larger–than–
life, superhuman, almost (or purely) legendary characters as did the
classic actors of the world of Aeschylus, Sophocles, or Euripides, for
example. Modern times are not in favor of *representing* or recalling,
but rather of *pretending to be*, the sublime and heroic protagonist.
Hence modern farce does not present itself before the world as farce,
but with genuine claims of reality. In fact, theater has invaded and
transformed itself into ordinary life to such an extent that the latter
has become a theatrical stage.

And which role do the new actors of modern theater assign themselves? Undoubtedly the character of heroes, as we have said; but
they have a peculiar trait which sets them entirely apart from ancient super heroes. Modern paladins present themselves to the world

---

[40]The former was a mask, the latter a type of shoes; both were used by actors
in the Greek–Roman Theater.

(which looks at them with stupor and trembling...), claiming that they are authentic *rebels*.[41]

It is clear that a rebellion expresses an opposition which is usually furious and angry; ready to tear down, by any means, those obstacles that seek to prevent its purposes. But then a question immediately comes up: against what or whom do modern subversives rise up? This question is not as redundant as it may seem, since the rebels themselves would find it hard to give a straightforward answer. Should they try, they would surely respond with a long list of explanations, as evanescent and unsubstantial as they are unconvincing for many of their interlocutors: the *protest* —the rebels would tell them— is directed against the Establishment, against oppression and lack of freedom, against social injustice, against outdated and constraining conservatism, against capitalism and the reactionary bourgeoisie; and against a lot of *etceteras*. As it is, each and every one of these elements *provoking outrage and protest* do not have precise or specific meaning; therefore, all of them desperately need to be fully explained, which many people would appreciate. But this clarification will be a difficult endeavor, and we must not forget that the modern world prefers slogans and clichés to rigorous and rational explanations, fuzzy and demagogic talk to precise seriousness and reflection.

Fortunately, we believe that we now have sufficient validation of the true and penetrating reasons that have brought about these non–conformist Movements. But before satisfying the uneasiness of many inquisitors, and prior to unmasking the veneer of modern rebels and

---

[41]Heroes in ancient classical theater fought Injustice, Evil, and, above all, Destiny, but they did not seem to have thought of themselves as rebels. Even when they confronted Destiny, they never did so by claiming that they were in open rebellion against what they believed to be rather inevitable.

reformers, we must give a brief aside, a memoir, for clarification's sake.

Revolutionary Movements in the Western World seem to have begun in earnest with the fall of the *Ancien Régime*. Social revolutions carried out by the labor class reached their zenith toward the end of the nineteenth century and the beginning of the twentieth and possess peculiar characteristics which distinguish them from those begun in the middle of the twentieth century: Student Revolutions, Youth Revolutions, and those led by Intellectuals, Homosexuals, Feminists, and even the Clergy, among others; some of them have had only a fleeting passage through history before disappearing. Logically, they all claim to fight against injustice. But if this claim is true, it only means that, since Evil has been at work from the inception of the world (2 Thess 2:7), there has always been a fight for justice, although without the *revolutionary* connotations which characterize the modern struggle against injustice.

But this issue is more complicated than it seems. Generally speaking, the exposition of what we have just outlined would suffice: rebels have always fought against injustice of any kind. It is true that excesses and even abuses have been committed in the name of justice, but all that is understandable when one takes into account the legitimate yearning of rebels for putting an end to all injustice. Those abuses, we are told, are but occasional and minor evils which are necessary in order to achieve the honorable goals pursued... etc. *But this is the ominous dark bottom line of this issue.*

The only way to legitimize any protest against injustice would be that *someone is truly protesting against injustice.* In effect, as any straightforward person can notice, and we will show later, it happens that intentions are not always so pure; and the very first thing a sincere reformer should do is reform himself: *Physician, heal thyself.*[42] But to what extent can someone who has never thought seriously about justice and integrity clamor for them? To tell the truth, Jesus Christ, and no other, is the only person Who can claim for Himself the status of a true Revolutionary. Revolution and re-bellion are never authentic until they are realized in the person who pursues and clamors for them. This necessarily implies self–negation through self–immolation, in addition to a serious, constant struggle against one's own passions, concupiscence, and natural disorders: *If any man will come after me, let him deny himself, and take up his cross, and follow me. For whosoever will save his life shall lose it: and whosoever will lose his life for my sake shall find it.*[43] And there is no other way, no matter what anybody may say. And yet, can anyone seriously claim that those teeming and clamorous *rebels and reformers*, that is, those who activate the stage machinery of modern farce, are truly fighting for truth, freedom, and justice? According to Jesus Christ, sin is the only thing that takes away our freedom (Jn 8:34). On the other hand, only He can lead us to the authen-tic truth (Jn 14:6); and only He can claim to have given testimony to it (Jn 18:37). Consequently, He is also the only one Who can give true freedom (Jn 8: 32–36). Therefore, we must ask again: are these realities actually what the modern *rebels* and self–proclaimed *reformers* are clamoring for with such raucous commotion?

Unfortunately, facts, quite evident in themselves for those who want to see them, compel us to think that this is not the case. That is why we referred earlier to theatrical farce and modern actors *who disguise themselves as rebels; but the truth is that real rebellion has never crossed their minds.* If this is so, what is the actual purpose of their protest and against whom exactly is it being directed? The

---

[42]Lk 4:23.

[43]Mt 16: 24–25.

answer is obvious for those who want to see. It is possible that many of those rebels themselves are not clearly aware of the reasons for their behavior, and consequently they allow the System to control them. Nevertheless, all of them are merely marionettes cunningly manipulated from above. Once again, we find theater; this time puppet theater. The true objects of the rage of these Movements, whether admitted or not, are the *Christian roots and principles still extant in modern society.* As Peter Kreeft so very well puts it: *It is no surprise that in the culture in which philosophers scorn wisdom, moralists scorn morality, preachers are the world's greatest hypocrites, sociologists are the only people in the world who do not know what a good society is, psychologists have the most mixed–up psyches, professional artists are the only ones in the world who actually hate beauty, and liturgists are to religion what Dr. Von Helsing is to Dracula...*[44] no wonder that happens what is happening. Kreeft is directing his harangue against those who despise good books, but it is obvious that what he writes can perfectly be applied to every aspect of modern society; as he does later on. Are we or are we not immersed in the culture of a theater world? The actors have taken so much to heart their role that they have become one with their characters, forgetting that they are simple actors; and modern rebels have finally believed that they raised their swords when in reality they are but pawns moved by those who pull the strings.

What some people have called *Rebellion of the Clerics* deserves a chapter of its own.[45] The clerical *protest* began to openly manifest itself when the Second Vatican Council was is session, but the crest of the wave reached its high point during the following years and still continues nowadays.

---

[44]Peter J. Kreeft, *The Philosophy of Tolkien*, Ignatius Press, 2005, p. 14.

[45]This theme has been briefly dealt with in some of my works; but it always offers new aspects to the experts, which can help understand the problem we are talking about.

Its origin can be traced to two kinds of causes, superficial and deep sources. The latter are, logically, less known —in fact practically nobody has even mentioned them— and twofold.

First, we must mention the deficient theological and spiritual formation given in the Seminaries to the candidates to the priesthood. Run, generally speaking, by priests of good faith, these Centers were not able to adapt themselves to the World born after the First World War.[46]

The second cause is no less important: strange elements, mainly Freemasonry, infiltrated the Seminaries, especially at the beginning of the 1940s.[47] I personally think that if anyone had then had the audacity of warning the Bishops about what was happening, he probably would have been locked up in an Asylum for the mentally ill. But during the six years I spent interned in my Seminary I was a direct witness to facts that speak for themselves. Yet, even today it is not advisable to speak about this issue.

In the United States of America there was another cause, more serious, if possible. Seminaries welcomed without restrictions of any kind —which nobody yet has been able to explain— homosexuals. This remained covered for many years until finally, in modern times, it blew up with the anticipated catastrophic consequences.[48] It is difficult to explain how it was possible for both the American Bishops and even the Vatican to ignore for so long what was going on. At present, the situation of the Church in America is quite delicate; even problematic and very dangerous, to put it mildly.

---

[46]This is extensively analyzed in some of my works. One can read my brief treatise *Notes on the Spirituality of the Society of Jesus Christ the Priest*, Shoreless Lake Press, New Jersey, 1994.

[47]To achieve its goals, Freemasonry has not hesitated to use doctrinal elements of Marxist doctrine which had a powerful influence in the training of agitators within the Centers of Formation. We are referring to the aid which in this regard Freemasonry provided to the *Theology of Liberation*.

[48]Michael S. Rose, *Goodbye, Good Men: How Liberals Brought Corruption Into the Catholic Church*, Washington, 2002. This book, a serious and important documentary, caused a tremendous uproar in the U.S.A.

As for the superficial causes, obviously more easily detected and understood, they are basically two: the well–known *Promotion of the Laity* and the so–called *Crisis of Priestly Identity*. The former was a consequence born from ideas disseminated by some characters whose influence in the Second Vatican Council was most notorious; it caused a tremendous *shock* among the clergy (presbyters), relegating them to abandonment and oblivion. The world of the *simple clergy* was practically isolated between the doctrines which strove to situate the Episcopate in its proper place, on the one hand,[49] and those which promoted the Laity, on the other. This probably was one of the main reasons for the *Identity Crisis*.

Once the great importance that the role of the Laity meant for the Church was discovered —for it seemed that such an importance had so far gone unnoticed—, and *progressive* theologians propagated the idea, which was widely accepted by the people, of the lack of priestly identity — that is, that the nature of the priesthood, and consequently its usefulness, was totally unknown— it was no surprise that a great number of priests ardently endeavored to look like lay people.

This was the origin of the odd phenomenon of clergy doing profane jobs. The slogan *we* [priests] *need to bear testimony and not to appear as different from the lay people* gained momentum. Indeed, human nature is so strange, so funny if you want, that sometimes it is difficult to find a rational explanation for its behavior. For this necessity of giving testimony impelled many priests to work as plumbers or electricians, for example. Inexplicably, nobody noticed, it seems, that the only valid way for a priest to give testimony ought to be by *being a priest*. On the other hand, with all due respect for so many profane professionals, it is well known

---

[49]Until this moment, no one seemed to have been aware that the Episcopate did not enjoy the prominence that it deserved. At that time, there were some who saw in this elevation of the Episcopate an effort to cut the privileges that Vatican I had delegated to the Pope. Whatever the case, and since this issue is not of our concern, we prefer to file it as a problem to be studied by future historians. However, and given the consequences that followed the decisions taken by Vatican II on this point (especially regarding Episcopal Conferences), the results do not seem to have corresponded to the intentions sought.

that they earn much more money, and with less work, than a dedicated priest in the fulfillment of his pastoral duties. Committed priests enjoy much poorer salaries and dedicate twenty–four hours daily to their work, without holidays or paid vacations. The odd thing about all this is that not many people questioned this touted need for *not being different from the lay people*: a true ideological brainchild of obscure origin which had nothing to do with the true wishes of the faithful, who are precisely the ones more concerned that the priest be different from them.

It was this hodgepodge of ideas, among other things, that caused the identity crisis and the definitive ban of the clerical garment. In this regard, the issue was not settled by merely replacing articles of clothing. Now it was not a matter of wearing or not wearing a *secular* suit, but of donning attires as indigent and destitute as possible, bordering sometimes on the ridiculous. Thus, priests in their fifties, for example, wore gaudy outfits proper to adolescent teenagers.

During the Second Vatican Council and afterwards, Pope Paul VI exhorted the clergy to adopt priestly garments, but all was in vain. John Paul II did the same at the beginning of his pontificate, but the new fashion had by now been accepted as a done deal, definitively established.

Someone may allege, of course, that what is important here is not so much the garment as the mentality; and he would be right. In such a strange situation —the *identity crisis*— into which so many priests were tricked, it would be good to ask oneself, for example, what would happen if someone would bother to go to the jungle and try to convince the wolf, the monkey, and the elephant that they were no longer a wolf, a monkey, or an elephant. In the absurd assumption that he was believed, one can easily imagine those wretched animals, now deprived of identity, trying hard to find a disguise to look like some other animal. After all, in one way or another, *one needs to be something* at all costs (lest one prefers to be swallowed up by the nothingness mentioned in *The Neverending Story*).

But ultimately, what this vast majority of clergy were accomplishing, perhaps without many of them realizing it (again the giant puppet theater), was but the much–vaunted attitude of *protest*. If this appreciation is true, we are confronting *rebellion* again. Now, we might ask, against which or against whom has this revolt been directed in this case...? And the answer, again, for anyone with good will and a desire to know the real facts, is not hard to find. This time, the protest has targeted a set of ideas that can be summarized under the heading —also designed by these rebels— the *gentrification of the Church*. In other words and briefer: against the Church.

What *is not* appears as what *is*, and vice versa, in short, farce; consciously or unconsciously looked for, but theater after all; which in turn becomes puppet theater where puppets are moved by threads and hands, or puppet theater where puppets are manipulated by remote control. We will talk later of the shocking *Parable of the Hundred Rebel Sheep*. This parable is not found in the Gospels or even in the Apocrypha (and hence not commonly known); but it contains a good number of lessons typical of this kind of story.

Today, everyone has some idea of the connotation attributed to a flock of sheep. They are peaceful animals assembled in herds, apparently unable to live alone, which have become a symbol for what the world often calls having a *sheep–like* attitude; a near synonym of *becoming a commonplace* (which involves the loss of one's own personality) or *one–of–the–masses* (only one among a mass of citizens handled at will by the System). Indeed, the sociological concept of *mass* and the social trend to which it relates are fairly modern. But *mass* should not be mistaken for *social class*; for the notion of *mass* normally may include several social classes at once or only one. Masses, of course, have always been manipulated by Political Powers, frequently despotic to a greater or lesser degree; although some of these Powers, possibly a small number of them, have indeed worked honestly for the common good. Unfortunately, one must admit that good rulers have not been plentiful in the history of mankind. In any case, Political Powers have never before manipulated the masses so systematically, scientifically, contemptuously, and unconcernedly with regard to the welfare of the citizens, as they do today. That is why we have said that the concepts of *mass* and *social class* belong rather to modernity. The *Revolt of the Masses*, in the words of Ortega y Gasset, belongs to a utopian world. The truth is that normally masses neither rebel on their own nor govern the world — let alone themselves. It is the System and its propped-up intellectual apparatus that provoke and lead rebellions; which is precisely opposite to what Ortega thought and considered desirable. It is clear, however, that these *rebellions* are never truly such, in the sense that they are often nothing more than a concert of bleating stirred up when it suits by those whom it suits. The whole thing is but a puppet show where the puppets, of course, forget that they are stooges, for they lack the ability to think and make decisions; they simply act in accord with the wishes of those who move them, which is the only thing left for them to do.

The upsurge among the working class is one of the most important transformations of our time. Its vitality garners degrees of anger from the mid–nineteenth century and throughout the twentieth. Some may believe that its coinciding with the birth and rapid diffusion of Marxism could be regarded as merely accidental. At least that is what is affirmed by those who also think that it was then that the Church first *became aware* of the problem posed by the workers. However, others attribute this awareness to a certain inferiority complex suffered by some members of the Hierarchy of the Church which was brought on by the widespread success of Marxism. According to these, a mood arose within the ecclesiastical world acquiescing to the final and irrevocable triumph of the doctrines of Karl Marx. Be that as it may, the fact is that this state of mind resulted in the appearance of a sea of exhortations, documents, and other writings about the so–called *Social Doctrine of the Church*. Bookstores and libraries around the world were packed with the works of experts, while the Magisterium struggled to provide statements on a theme considered so transcendental.

Unfortunately, as everyone knows, it is not uncommon that the remedies provided to solve certain problems cause new ones; sometimes even more serious than those which the cure tried to solve.

Whether that was what happened here is a problem for the theologians and scholars of History to elucidate. Although one can say at the outset that it was clearly risky business for the Church to meddle in temporal matters that may not fall within her legitimate concerns: *Who has made me a judge or arbitrator over you?*[50] In fact, the obligation to *give to Caesar what is Caesar's and to God what is God's* prescribed in the Gospel has never been understood —or at least nobody has ever wanted to understand the full depth of its true meaning. The problem arises when it comes to determining clearly what is God's and what is Caesar's, which is not always easy. The Magisterium of the Church also has the right, and obviously the duty, to make judgments about temporal matters affecting the organization of Civil Society, only to the extent, of course, that those issues have to do with Christian faith and morals. The assistance of the Holy Spirit ensures the Magisterium against the possibility of error, provided it is exercised according to the appropriate conditions and circumstances. But that assistance does not protect the Magisterium from sliding into areas of temporal issues which, being circumstantial and temporary (and therefore not related to faith and morals), are open to a variety of solutions which God has duly left to the free determination of men governing the Civil Society.[51] Anyway, it is clear that, according to Jesus Christ —if His words deserve any credence—, Caesar *has rights that, being such, as long as they are exercised within their own sphere, are untouchable.* Particularly striking is the apparent contradiction between the insistence on proclaiming the autonomy and Promotion of the Laity, on one hand, and the claim on the part of some members of the ecclesiastical world that they possess the exclusive answer (with the accompanying magic recipe)

---

[50]Lk 12:14.

[51]These issues and their answers would constitute the broad field of activity for the renowned *Promotion of the Laity.* Most unfortunately, clericalism has always been the black beast continuously besetting, under different disguises, the Ecclesiastic Society.

to problems which clearly fall under the competence of civil society, on the other. Moreover, the Spirit does not guarantee His assistance against the possibility that the Magisterium may fail to keep to its duty in judging certain temporal issues when it has the clear obligation of doing so, and to the extent it should do so. This situation, in fact, occurs more frequently than the other.

In fact, many *solutions* to problems of *social justice*, which were considered at the time as promising and definitive, soon became obsolete and useless. Perhaps the mistake was not so much that they were the wrong answers, as were the stubborn and persistent demands by the Ecclesiastic Society to contribute its own solutions (believed to be sort of final and almost magical) to issues that actually were intended by God to be left to the will of Civil Society. The nature of these issues, naturally, since they can possibly be affected by contingent and variable circumstances, could admit to a variety of solutions; all of them lawful, of course, and whose success depends on the intelligence that God has given to the human race to be exercised through a whole series of possibilities left to man's free will.

In close connection with what has been said, we should not forget the risk run by the Pastoral Ministry of the Church, embroiled as it is in numerous difficult issues for which it lacks jurisdiction, of subtracting time and importance from the fundamental mission entrusted to her by her Founder; namely, leading men to the supernatural destiny to which they have been called.

Moreover, the expression *Social Doctrine of the Church* seems rather unfortunate; for everything seems to indicate, as we shall try to show, that it is a tautology.

First, the doctrine of the Church is none other than the one entrusted to her by her Divine Founder. Given by Him to men through the Apostles, the transmission throughout time of His doctrine, as well as monitoring the accuracy of its content, is guaranteed by the assistance of the Holy Spirit to the Magisterium: *Go, therefore, teach ye all nations; baptizing them in the name of the Father, and of the Son, and of the Holy Spirit; teaching them to observe all things whatsoever I have commanded you.*[52]

---

[52]Mt 28: 19–20.

The doctrine of the Church is, therefore, the doctrine of Christ, that is, *Christian Doctrine.*

It happens, however, that the doctrine taught by Christ is social by nature and necessity. After all, God wants the salvation *of all men* (1 Tim 2:4). His message, regulated by the *new commandment* of love of neighbor and designed to comprise one and the same Organism out of all believers, with Christ as its Head (the Mystical Body of Christ), could not be conceived as anything other than *social.* It is unthinkable that a Christian could think of being saved in isolation, without concerning himself with the fate of other men, his brothers: *I give you a new commandment: That you love one another, as I have loved you, that you also love one another.*[53] *We know that we have passed from death to life, because we love the brethren... He that loveth not, knoweth not God: for God is love.*[54] It does not seem to make any sense to dissociate a part of the Message of Christ as if it were something distinct because it is concerned with *the others* or with a particular group of others; that would be tantamount to speaking about a social doctrine *but now under its aspect of social doctrine.* It would not make any sense, unless the intention is to pigeonhole one particular group of men as being a special and particular *social class*, with its own characteristics so as to make it something different and somewhat distinct from the other members of the society of men. This, in addition to being not exactly in accord with the teachings contained in the Message of Christ (Gal 3:28), opens the door to the use of a peculiar terminology proper to a philosophy —the Marxist philosophy— which is quite opposite to anything supernatural. Some time ago a pronouncement from a Sacred Congregation explained that the Church *recognizes* the existence of social classes, which seems to be an innocuous and unnecessary statement —the Sacred Congregation could as well have recognized the existence of sports as a social phenomenon. But what the Church can never do is recognize the existence of class struggle, unless she be willing to accept the tenets of Marxist philosophy.

---

[53] Jn 13:34.

[54] 1 Jn 3:14; 4:8.

It may not be necessary, therefore, that the Doctrine of the Church or Christian Doctrine —a substantive— require the adjective *Social*; although difficulties still remain unresolved.

For if it is true that the Gospel Message cannot be conceived but as *social,* it is no less true that this Message cannot be imagined but as being something strictly *individual or personal.* For salvation is for people, not for classes. Hence, the Message of Salvation offered to men by Jesus Christ is both individual and social; at no time can we make an abstraction of either element in favor of the other. Talking, therefore, about a *socially oriented Christianity* would have as little sense as referring to what would be a *purely individual Christianity.*

It goes without saying that each individual human being is a person to God. Therefore he is also someone *unique* for Him: a *thou* with whom He establishes a bilateral, unique, and singular relationship (*I–thou*), for the bond of love cannot be constituted in any other way. True, God loves all men; but He considers each one as a *thou* that becomes unique for Him. God does not seem overly concerned with social classes as such. He is concerned with the salvation of all men; to this end He *loves each one of them* as a single being (person). Even the Old Testament is quite expressive on this point. It would be interesting, not to say helpful, to examine attentively each line of the most beautiful Sacred Poem of all time:

> *My dove is my only one, perfect and mine...*
>
> ....
>
> *My Beloved is mine and I am his.*[55]

The whole structure of the *Song of Songs* is based on a relationship of love which is unique, bilateral, and personal between Bridegroom and bride; her maidens and companions are a separate choir.

As for the New Testament, it seems superfluous to insist on the subject. The Parable of the Talents, for example (Mt 25), speaks of a rich man who,

---

[55] Sg 6:9; 2:16; 6:3.

before beginning his journey, distributed his assets among his servants *giving each according to his ability.* The fact that, at the return of their master, each servant is held accountable is also expressive of the character of personal individuality present throughout the parable. This point is even more eloquently made in the Parable of the Lost Sheep (Lk 15: 4 ff.), which states that the owner of a flock of one hundred sheep went in search of one that had strayed, *leaving the other ninety–nine in the field without hesitation.* In view of this fact, anyone may think that here not only is the individual and distinct person considered more important than the collectivity, but also (forgive the hyperbole) that the others matter little in comparison to the one. In the Apocalypse too, the Spirit warns the angel of the Church of Thyatira that it is He Who searches the hearts and bowels, and Who *will give to each one according to his works.*[56]

In the Pauline doctrine the indissoluble union of the individual and collective elements of the Christian Message is clearly seen: *For as in one body we have many members, but the all members have not the same office, so we, being many, are one body in Christ, and every one members one of another.*[57] Note here that Christians, for the Apostle, *are one body,* made up of many members, *albeit not all members have the same office.* Nor does the existence of particular groups within the whole of the faithful find a place in his mind (Gal 3:28). Besides, Saint Paul believes that there is a perfect interaction, which in turn implies a complete distinction, between the collective and the personal constituents: one is meaningless without the other; you cannot perform a vivisection on the Organism made up of all the faithful. If each faithful constitutes a whole with the others it is precisely because the whole is made up by each one of them. Neither is it said anywhere that someone's personality is undermined by his being bound to the totality: *But now God hath set the members of every one of them in the body as it hath pleased him. And if they all were one member, where would be the body? But now there are many members indeed, yet one body. And the eye cannot say to the hand: I need not thy help; nor again the head to the feet: I have no need of you. Yea, much more those*

---

[56] Rev 2:23.

[57] Rom 12: 4–5.

that seem to be the more feeble members of the body are more necessary. Now you are the body of Christ, member for member.[58]

Modern society is adamant in making *what is not* appear as *what is*, and vice versa. It prefers to perceive what it wishes rather than face reality: *Men loved darkness rather than the light.*[59] And the reason for this aberration is no mystery; it is explained in the passage itself: *For their works* [man's works] *were evil.* Clearly, it is a choice of the will, which freely leans towards error, rather than a lack of understanding. Modern man, led by his pride, has separated himself from God and consequently has fallen into the most spectacular ridiculousness ever imagined. The creature rejects God only because he hopes to be his own god... and the god of others; for why would a self–proclaimed god not want to exert his dominion over everything and everyone else? It is a *ridiculous* aspiration, to use the mildest, although perhaps the most appropriate, appellative. Undoubtedly Lucifer is the Great Liar as well as the most overblown Clown that World History has ever known; for nobody could make such a dreadful fool of himself as Lucifer has. Satan, of course, does not admit it, for he neither comprehends nor *recognizes* any truth; his understanding is incapable of grasping reality except in a twisted and distorted manner. He feeds on lies and lives surrounded by lies, but he does not admit this because it would mean accepting the truth. But pride is identical to lying, and lying eventually becomes a clownish stunt. Consequently, if there is laughter in Heaven then we must think of it as the place of eternal and general amusement. The inferior trying to take the place of a superior is a foolishness whose magnitude, if it could be measured, would depend on the distance between them. If that distance is infinite, then the foolishness could

---

[58] 1 Cor 12: 18–22.27.

[59] Jn 3:19.

be considered infinite as well —to call it nonsense would be to do it a favor; to regard the perpetrator of this stupidity as a clown would be an act of mercy. But be advised, one cannot mistake the professional clown for the imbecilic clown who does not want to be a clown. The former makes people laugh with absurd antics that promote merriment because that is his profession. The public laughs at his actions and facial expressions which are exaggerated, risible, and outlandish, *but their laughter is always without a trace of mockery toward the person of the clown.* One can certainly say that the professional clown is all the more respected and esteemed as a person to the same extent that he performs his job well. The unwilling clown, however, to his dismay, does not perform or act with the intent of making people laugh, quite the opposite: his nonsense flows fluently and spontaneously from a simply silly heart. The conduct of many *rebels* in modern society also borders on the ridiculous, insofar as they pretend to be what they are not at all, and only fools like them believe them.[60] Apropos of this subject, someone once offered the following parable:

Once upon a time there was in a certain place a flock of one hundred sheep. They lived happily and without problems (sheep usually have no troubles); they went from place to place in search of pasture, led by their shepherd and safe in their tranquil (and monotonous) existence. But it happened to them what happens to men: men just cannot live without problems —should they have no problems, men would invent them. And so, tired of their uneventful and rather *sheepish* existence, without excitement or any kind of contingencies, they decided to rise up against a life and an environment which they

---

[60]Nevertheless, one must admit two types of involuntary clowns: those who add a great deal of cynicism to their buffoonery (for they are to a certain extent aware of their own farce); and the simple cheap jesters, slaves of the puppet theatre manipulating them, and whose ridiculous personality provokes derisive laughter.

believed to be unfair and unworthy of their status as sheep. It is true that some of the manuscripts of this narrative, whose historical accuracy is doubted by some, also allude to the existence of a group of agitators. According to the chronicles, they were responsible, in the last analysis, for stirring up discontent and agitation among the ovine throng of our tale. Whether true or not, the fact of the matter is that this detail of the narrative did not have a great effect on the consequences. It must be acknowledged, in all honesty, that these sheep had overheard here and there comments deriding their way of life and gregarious status as *sheep* and their *sheepish* existence, etc.; all of which was convincing enough, according to the vulgar, to divest them of any personality or initiative.

It is no surprise, therefore, that one day our sheep thought it was high time for their rebellion. Some, however, claim that the decision to rebel against the injustice around them could not originate from beings so disinclined to such audacious actions; that it was actually encouraged *from above*, or perhaps *from within* (analysts disagree on this point), through infiltrating elements. Anyway, the point is that our flock, at the least expected moment, stirred up a surprisingly noisy riot in protest. And there were our sheep, shouting all at once, more gregariously than ever:

We are the rebel-l-l-l-l-l sheep!... Truly rebel-l-l-l-l-l-lious!... We are protesting against all injustices!... We want to be-e-e-e oursel-l-l-l-l-lves!... We demand shepherds with minds open to progress who are not stuck in the past! Etcetera. The content of such street outcries is well known.[61]

---

[61] As strange as it may seem, this time the familiar chant *Make love, not war...!* was not heard. Apparently, the organizers had agreed that this slogan would seem too lamb–like and stupid.

They marched in droves, firing up the admiration of the spectators who, astonished, asked themselves just what kind of injustice this protest was all about; what that strange claim —that a sheep wanted to be *herself*—, demanded in the midst of raucous bellowing, could ever mean; and where on earth can one find a shepherd *open to progress and not anchored in structures of the past,* what sort of person and how helpful could he be?

And so the chorus of the hundred sheep marched, *bleating* in unison and clamoring about their needs and demands. We must admit that never before had a flock seemed so sheep–like. But an important and astonishing detail of this story must be added: in reality, not *all* of the one hundred sheep were marching, *only ninety– nine.*

Indeed, only ninety–nine sheep. There was one among the herd that categorically refused to become a rebellious sheep. She flatly rejected the idea and there was no way to convince her otherwise. She kept saying again and again:

—*I don't want to be a rebel sheep, and nobody is going to make me yield. I'll never be a rebellious sheep, for it is my firm desire to keep on being a sheep, nothing more than a sheep.*

And there was no way to change her mind. Therefore, the *massive* remainder of the herd had to allow her to be excluded from the group of rebels. Her will finally triumphed and she did exactly what she deemed correct; even against all the rest of the sheep.

We do not need to point out to the clever reader that, according to some commentators, this last sheep was the only true rebel in the entire flock. Diversity of commentaries and discrepancy of opinions are typical among average men. In the end, the prevalent opinion, for all practical purposes, was that the rebelliousness of the ninety–

nine sheep was simply one more sheepish act, perhaps the most sheep–like of them all.

This said, each one must draw the moral and teaching of the parable. In modern society there are an abundance of rebellious stances that are nothing more than buffooneries, puppet–acting, or both things at the same time. The same, or much of the same, could be said about some classic rebellions: the rebellion of youth, of intellectuals, of feminists, of homosexuals, and of many others whose protest, apart from being sometimes ridiculous and sometimes skillfully disguised, is usually the work of some self–interested manipulating entity that handles the sheep at leisure.

Thus, there are *students* who have never studied; *intellectuals* whose *knowledge* barely surpasses that of an ass; *feminist* movements supported by women who seem to possess an excessive amount of masculine hormones; *homosexuals* whose conduct does not deserve further comment because Christian charity advises drawing a veil over the matter; *freethinkers* who were never free to think because, among other reasons, one first needs to be able to think as a precondition to enjoy this freedom.

Sometimes, as we have said, this attitude of protest may be disguised under more subtle aspects that are noiseless and even apparently heroic. Now rebelliousness is carried out against an environment which rebels believe to be *unjust*, or perhaps *conservative* (terms that are synonymous for this sort of insurgents). This attitude is usually exercised in a peaceful manner but never exempt from apparent effort and courage. This is the case, to put some specific examples to it, of some *rebel* clerics whose conduct appears quite strange, giving rise to feelings ranging from awe to laughter in those who observe them. Consequently, new and bizarre characters appear who are difficult to classify within a catalog of curiosities and whose intentions are not easy to determine: priests in their fifties dressed as teenagers; shepherds who have under their care a good number of faithful who cannot be spiritually fed because those shepherds have many other *obligations*; hospital chaplains who eschew all clothing except doctor's gowns without any religious sign to identify them as clergy; apart from that, their day is usually spent in the hallways and cafeterias of the hospital in question, and the sick people who want to receive spiritual attention are compelled to call some parish priest for help... etc.[62]

Finally, and to put it in few words: if someone wants to call things by their real name and intends to talk about true rebels, or perhaps be one of them, then he will have to deny himself, choose the narrow path and the way of sacrifice, and put the love of others ahead of the love of himself, along with other things no less important. But he is a false rebel who claims to be one while he follows the inclinations of his own likings and desires; always seeking his own comfort and satisfying himself in any way possible; seeking the applause and esteem of others; demanding rights, forgetting that there are also duties; blaming others for the ills suffered by society; trying to be regarded as a hero to hide the cowardice of never having confronted evil and true injustice, etc., etc. If anything, this false rebel is but a sad imitation and a ridiculous caricature who tries at best to imitate the Great Clown and the Great Liar, whose disciple and child he somehow is. It is the farce once again, although this time represented in ordinary life with the intention of being accepted as real: *Ye are of your father the devil, and the desires of your father*

---

[62]This insidious form of protest against the *same old conservatism*, say what you will, is the manifestation of an inferiority complex. In this case, the clergy try to appear as belonging to a social status they look upon with envy and consider as superior to their own.

*ye will do... When he speaketh a lie, he speaketh of his own: for he
is a liar, and the father thereof.*[63]

*6. Where finally the true meaning of Christian "show" is tentatively
described.*

To say that Christian existence is a real *show* may seem strange
after what has been said here about theater. However, at no time
have we wanted to inveigh against this artistic genre. Certainly not
against true theater; the theater that never tries to hide its essentially *fictional* character (even when its task is to recreate the lives
of real people or the manner of living of ordinary people). Authentic theater has little to do with distorted theatrical representations
that conceal their farcical qualities while claiming that they reflect
the real world. Or, put another way, representations that hide their
theatrical character: theater that pretends it is not theater.

This clarification made, we can affirm that Christian existence
is a true spectacle; a grand and pulsating drama whose actors must
endeavor to play their roles the best they can, even exhausting all its
possibilities. In addition, a large number of spectators are watching
this spectacle at any given time. Many of them are of the highest
class and gifted with the most acute critical spirit.

Saint Paul explains this very clearly: *For I think that God hath
set forth us the apostles last, as it were appointed to death: for we are
made a spectacle unto the world, and to angels, and to men.*[64] The
Apostle does not use euphemisms to describe this veritable drama
that ends up in tragedy: *Last, as it were appointed to death...* And

---

[63]Jn 8:44.

[64]1 Cor 4:9.

if there were any doubts, he provides more details in the following verses: *We are fools for Christ's sake... we are weak... we are despised. Even unto this present hour we hunger, and thirst, and are naked, and are buffeted, and have no certain dwelling place; we labor, working with our own hands... We are made as the filth of the world, the offscouring of all things unto this day.*[65]

It should be noted that this summary of the plot of the play to be represented does not intend to cause unrest. On the contrary, it only aims at lifting up one's spirit; as it happens with leaflets or posters advertising shows, whose main purpose is to attract viewers. Only in this case there are no relevant, deliberately exaggerated details intended to provoke the curiosity of the largest audience possible. Here there is no manipulated presentation of reality. Moreover, as strange as it might seem, the pamphlet promoting this script does not have potential spectators as the main target —in an effort to entice them—, but the actors themselves!

The apostle seeks to highlight the greatness of the mighty drama to be represented, as well as the serious responsibility of the actors who are going out on stage to perform their roles.

Indeed, Christian life, as has so often been stated, is the most sublime and magnificent, the most daring, exciting, and risky of all adventures. It is anything but an easy undertaking. The eternal destiny of the actor —the destiny that corresponds to an immortal being— and the ultimate fate of many other beings depend on the quality of his performance. There are other elements that make the play to be represented quite different from those created by man's imagination. These characteristics make it special and more exciting: the alternative final outcome, for example, which is never known in advance, may consist in either an expected *happy ending*

---

[65] 1 Cor 4: 10–13.

or something which leads to a tremendous tragedy... it is up to the actors. Everything happens in Christian existence following the general lines of the script written by the Author of the play, but the details and the corresponding execution (and even possible changes in the plot and choosing of the outcome), are left to the discretion of the actors

It is clear that the play to be represented *is extremely important*. Hence the gravity of the crime of transforming what was a dramatic and most thrilling play into a *farcical comedy*; which is the very thing done by those who despise the script of the Author and replace it with their own text. The latter develops a plot which is more suited to whimsical personal desires, and, of course, much less annoying and more apt to deceive the others and take advantage of them.

One of the major differences that separate the Christian *drama* from the worldly *show* (and often also from modern Pastoral activity and the new Liturgies), has to do with the feelings experienced by the actors with respect to the viewers. In the drama of Christian life the actors are not worried about how to please or how to *look good* before the spectators; their effort rather aims at playing their role the best possible way to please only the Author of the plot. It is true that they cannot completely ignore the spectators; the actors know that the viewers are there: *Let your light so shine before men, that they may see your good works...*[66] It is worth noting that this text of Saint Matthew ends with an important clause which gives full meaning to the entire verse: *and glorify your Father who is in heaven.* For this is what the actors of the Christian drama really worry about: the glory of God; which ultimately is proper and peculiar to love, namely that the lover seeks always and above all the good of the beloved instead of his own (Rom 9:3).

---

[66]Mt 5:16; cf 1 Pet 2:12.

Worldly show business, however, which includes much of modern Pastoral activity, tries not to appear as theater, but it really is. That is why it must be regarded as a *show*; and also because it is exclusively focused on the spectators. By forgetting the Author of the play, the true intention of worldly theater is to receive the approval and admiration of the public, in order, of course, to achieve its purposes: *All their works they do in order to be seen by men...*[67] *For they loved the glory of men more than the glory of God.*[68]

The actor in Christian drama, however, tries to pass by unnoticed, despite knowing that the drama of his existence will be performed before a multitude of spectators: *We are a spectacle for the world, for angels...*; without the presence of an audience, of course, the scenic representation would have no meaning or purpose. Greek tragedy, for example, could not be imagined without the presence of the chorus.[69] And the drama of love between Bridegroom and bride, as described in the *Song of Songs*, stands out before the backdrop of the chorus of maidens. The words of love that take place between the Bridegroom and the bride, hidden and secret, are not an obstacle to their personal dialogue with the group of companions of the bride.

The same duality is also observed in the mystical poetry of Saint John of the Cross. Both the intimate dialogue between Husband and wife and their exhortations to creatures (rational or irrational) appear in his poetry. For love, which is an enclosed garden and a sealed fountain for Husband and wife, is at the same time an

---

[67]Mt 23:5.

[68]Jn 12:43.

[69]The role of the chorus is essential in Greek tragedy. It bears witness to the presence and the part of the hero, who does not exist outside a multitude that recognizes him as such; likewise, *heroic* actions lack significance if they are not accomplished against the background of *ordinary* actions.

openness to all things. Things are thus good and beautiful because they are the fruit of the craft and workmanship of the Bridegroom; they are a reflection of their Maker, Who transforms them, in turn, into a nuptial gift for the bride.[70]

Yet the Christian, unlike those who take part in worldly theatrical *show*, does not want the drama of his existence, or his very person, to be the object of a spectacle.

What then is the meaning of the duality, which even presents itself as a paradox, between the solitude–intimacy of Husband and wife on the one hand, and the presence of creatures (people and things) on the other? For we must not forget that creatures are present as either spectators or even as part of the action of the play (as for example the chorus of Greek tragedy).[71]

The main purpose of the presence of creatures in the drama of love between the Bridegroom and the bride was just explained. They have been given to the bride so that she, in turn, enriched as she now is, may offer them, together with herself, to the Bridegroom. There is no love without reciprocal donation.

The bride, meanwhile, is in need of things to know and reach her Beloved, for they are vestiges of Him: *Invisibilia enim ipsius... per ea, quæ facta sunt, intellecta conspiciuntur. The invisible things*

---

[70]The fact that the Bridegroom enriches the bride in this way makes possible the existence of reciprocity, an essential element of love. It is now, when the bride sees herself covered with opulence, that she can give the Bridegroom the treasure of everything she has received, and which is now hers. *All things are yours; and you are Christ's* (1 Cor 3: 22–23)... *Jesus Christ for your sakes became poor, that ye through his poverty might be rich* (2 Cor 8:9).

[71]Truly speaking, there are no mere spectators in the representation of the drama of Christian existence. When Saint Paul says that Christians are a spectacle for the world and men, he is not excluding their mutual interaction. Evidently, the fact that Christian life is a drama, or even a tragedy, is intimately connected with the role that the world and other men play in it.

of him... are clearly seen, being understood by the things that are made.[72] The bride, being still in a state of *not yet*, perceives her Beloved as in an enigma only, enjoying neither the entire possession of Him nor the face–to–face vision of Him (1 Cor 13:12). So she confronts all creatures with her questions:

> *O thickets, densely–trammelled,*
> *Which my love's hand has sown along the height:*
> *O field of green, enamelled*
> *With blossoms, tell me right*
> *If he has passed across you in his flight.*[73]

The *Song of Songs* speaks about the passionate search of the bride for her Bridegroom and of her calling upon creatures to help her communicate with Him and to tell Him of her presence:

> *I charge you, O daughters of Jerusalem,*
> *If ye find my beloved,*
> *That ye tell him, that I am sick with love.*[74]

Moreover, given the itinerant and *not–yet* status of the bride, creatures are to be a test for her, as a crucible, so that she can show the purity of her love and the totality of her generosity.[75] She has to be willing to surrender them completely, along with her own

---

[72]Rom 1:20.

[73]Saint John of the Cross, *Spiritual Canticle*.

[74]Sg 5:8.

[75]It is more than evident that the bride is still in a trial period, and that her love has not yet reached the state of perfection: *But when that which is perfect is come, that which is in part shall be done away* (1 Cor 13:10)... *Sectamini caritatem* (1 Cor 14:1).

self. The Bridegroom is well aware of the weakness of the bride; therefore He rebukes creatures so that they do not burden her and are moderate in her test:

> *I charge you, O ye daughters of Jerusalem,*
> *By the roes, and by the hinds of the field,*
> *That ye stir not up, nor awake my love,*
> *Till she please.*[76]

On the other hand, nobody finds pleasure in having the tragic reality of his existence, filled as it is with afflictions and anguish, displayed as a spectacle to public curiosity. In this regard, the Master, and also Saint Paul as we have just seen (1 Cor 4: 9 ff.), described realistically what awaits the Christian (Mt 10: 17–18; Jn 15: 18 ff.; cf. 2 Tim 3:12). Despite all of this, the life of the disciple, as we have said, cannot be but the object of a spectacle, which is but a part of the fabric of his personal existence, since without spectators —we must underline this— the representation makes no sense. That is why the Master never intended to eliminate this condition of the life of His disciples: *I pray not that thou shouldest take them out of the world, but that thou shouldest keep them from Evil.*[77] Nevertheless, Christian life is a tragedy, not merely *represented*, but also quite vital and so real that it involves the loss of one's own life (Lk 9:24).

But we must say it again: the disciple of Jesus Christ has no particular interest in his life being made known, for good or for ill. He would rather be inconspicuous; as the Ancients believed: *One can say of men what is said of peoples: blessed are those without history.* Therefore, the Christian, insofar as he is able, will choose

---

[76]Sg 3:5; 8:4.

[77]Jn 17:15.

to get away from the world and be forgotten: *For you are dead: and your life is hid with Christ in God.*[78] It is as if he wanted to bring to memory with nostalgia the known stanza of Saint John of the Cross:

> *Lost to myself I stayed*
> *My face upon my lover having laid*
> *From all endeavor ceasing:*
> *And all my cares releasing*
> *Threw them among the lilies there to fade.*[79]

He does not want to be admired by any type of audience, and hence he strives to be unknown and ignored. Following the advice of his Master, he shuns being acclaimed or applauded by others: *Take heed that you do not your justice before men, to be seen by them...*[80] *Let not thy left hand know what thy right hand doth.*[81]

Jesus Christ Himself took great care to practice these same caveats. Consequently, He refused to be recognized as king by the crowds and fled from them. He imposed silence on those whom He cured from diseases and ailments, so that they would not make the miracle known. He severely admonished His disciples not to manifest in public that He was the Son of God (Lk 9:21). He prohibited His three favorite disciples from speaking to anyone about their vision on Mount Tabor until He had risen from the dead. He consented to be counted among the wicked and to appear as a reproach of men and despised by the people (Ps 22); and so on.

The consequence is inescapable: *show–like* behavior has little to do with Christian life. The grain of wheat must fall into the ground

---

[78] Col 3:3.

[79] Saint John of the Cross, *Dark Night.*

[80] Mt 6:1.

[81] Mt 6:3.

to disappear into it and die if it is to bear fruit. The applause of men today will soon turn into the obliviousness, if not the contempt, of men tomorrow. The most blatant flattery deceives the most clever men unless they diligently live the virtue of humility. Yet History tells us of many men who were initially hailed as *geniuses* or great benefactors of mankind only to be entirely forgotten later on, if not despised: *Graveyards are full of indispensable men... and forgotten,* once observed someone well acquainted with life and human nature.

But not everything falls into mere oblivion. The Shepherds of the flock of Christ who practice *show*, or those who seek the highest prominence at all costs in order to be known and applauded, will have to answer to God for misleading their sheep and have also impeded their own salvation.

One of the things that seems to have been forgotten by many Shepherds of the Church is that true liturgy can have no other purpose than the worship of God and the good of souls. The Liturgy of the *show*, on the contrary, so often practiced today in many places, intends only to entertain and amuse those who participate in it. True Liturgy seeks *directly* to worship God, contributing thus *indirectly* to the salvation of the faithful. The Liturgy of the *show*, however, tries *directly* to stimulate the emotions of the participants (a corollary of the modernist heresy), and *indirectly*... nothing else; for it is not true that in this Liturgy God remains in second place, as some naïve and good–natured people may allege: He simply disappears from the visible horizon within the reach of the human heart.

The following could be a well–known example that clarifies what has just been said:

In modern times, as everyone knows, the so–called Masses or Eucharist for children have become popular. Designed, no doubt, with the best intentions in the world, they attempt to avoid the *boredom and fatigue* of the youngest. Therefore, they are assumed to contribute to their better understanding of the content and meaning of the liturgical action.

However, we must admit that these practices are prone to forget or put into the background issues so important that cannot brook any wrong approach.

First of all, it must be noted that the Mass is not a ceremony intended to entertain anyone. Actually it is the *Holy Sacrifice*, in which the Death of Our Lord is made really present so that the faithful may participate in it; and this cannot be considered in any way as an opportunity for entertainment. In all honesty, we must acknowledge that if the faithful feel apathy and boredom in the liturgical ceremony, most of the time it is due to the celebrant.

Second, excessive emphasis on and concern for the possible boredom of children eventually results in underestimating their faith and their re-silience. In reality, it is not infrequent for children to practice the virtue of fortitude more generously than their elders. This undue emphasis brings about another more serious mistake which, no doubt, is one of the plagues of modern society: the pernicious theories advocating that children should be spared any effort. The supporters of these theories, in addition to the tremendous damage they have caused in the world today, have forgotten that children should be also educated to endure fatigue and to practice effort, integrity, and self–control; which is, after all, the only way for the children to one day become mature men: *Wars are won by tired soldiers...*

Third, it is not taken into account that children should be made aware as soon as possible that they are *part of an ecclesial community*, embodied usually in the domain of the parish; which, in turn, is part of the entire Christian community, namely the whole Church or the Body of Christ.

As for the habit of leaving the preaching of the homily to children, the least we can say on this subject is that it gives rise to a double suspicion. In the first place, we must mention the fact that children, even though *from their mouths you shall hear the truth*, do not have the charisma of preaching. A quality of such an exceptional importance —this charisma is a divine power that comes from on high, which also requires serious human preparation— is not to be mistaken with the innocent sincerity of young children, whose candid naiveté sometimes tends to cause poor and hilarious results. Next, it is difficult to dispel the suspicion that the conduct of the celebrant in question is rather the consequence of personal laziness in fulfilling his duties than the result of his pastoral zeal toward children.

7. By way of recapitulation or final summary.

And that is how the barber's basin happened to become the helmet of Mambrino, while the donkey's packsaddle turned forever into the harness of a horse.

The animators of the deception were determined to carry out a malicious mockery.[82] It is, however, fair to admit that the victims of the setup seemed to be at ease in such a situation; hence they gave no signs of wishing to abandon it.

Those suffering with madness must be counted among the duped, as was the case (almost unique) of Don Quixote; for insanity is the only justification that eliminates from guilt those who are deceived so often and in so many ways.

This does not happen in other cases, which are the vast majority, for one always has to assume a certain complicity, more or less conscious, in the victims of the hoax: *Whosoever loveth and maketh a lie.*[83]

Other participants in the event, according to the narrative of Cervantes, were not completely convinced of the truth of the farce, but were willing to accept it in consideration of their own interests. Sancho Panza, for example, was not very sure about the delusions of his master, but he seemed inclined to believe them because it suited him. In reality, the deception to which masses fall victim, or

---

[82]*Don Quixote*, I, 45.
[83]Rev 22:15.

the theater that is represented before them pretending to be something real instead of a farce, must be included within this general
acceptance, which happens to be most common:

> ...*Those transformations will take place in adventures of chivalry.
> To confirm all which, run, Sancho my son, and fetch hither the
> helmet which this good fellow calls a basin.*"
>
> "*Egad, master,*" *said Sancho,* "*if we have no other proof of our case
> than what your worship puts forward, Mambrino's helmet is just
> as much a basin as this good fellow's caparison is a pack–saddle.*"[84]

These considerations are being written in the early twenty–first
century. The years that marked the long pontificate of John Paul II
have already passed before the eyes of today's people. Nowadays, the
Church is living under the leadership of a new Pope, Benedict XVI.
It is the era of Vatican II and its closure, which has been followed
by the so–called post–conciliar times. These events constitute a
period of great import in the life of the Church because new and
far–reaching guidelines for her course have been established.

And just as one would expect of a Divine Providence that takes
care of His Church, one must also assume that the newly initiated di-
rections will guide the Barque of Peter along more promising routes.

Obviously, the Pilgrim Church in which we are living is not yet
the Triumphant Church. So it is not surprising that the Church,
because she is navigating over stormy seas, is occasionally rocked by
the elements; sometimes even too rocked —rocked enough to disturb
those who travel on it; so much so that they can feel themselves
compelled by the need to scream as the Apostles did on a similar
occasion: *Lord, save us, we perish!*[85] Although in reality there is

---

[84] *Don Quixote*, I, 44.
[85] Mt 8:25.

not sufficient reason to justify panic. The Lord, as we have said, cares for His Church, and He made her His promise concerning the ultimate failure of the attempts of hell against her. We should not want to deserve the reproach that the Master made to His disciples back then: *Why are ye fearful, O ye of little faith?*[86]

Such a fear would have as little sense as the opposite attitude; that is, to say that all is well and there is no cause for any fear since nothing alarming is happening. Objectively speaking, we must acknowledge that being overcome by panic is as bad as closing one's eyes to reality. We are sailing through a stormy sea, where an absence of storms would be considered the only strange thing. The Christian needs to keep a sharp lookout to recognize and avoid danger, on the one hand, and great confidence in the promises of the Lord, on the other. He knows that the Militant Church has not yet reached her goal, her final rest. From this the unbelievers will be excluded; that is, presumably both those who have had no faith in the Message of Salvation and those who distrusted the promises about the final triumph of the Lord. Hence what has been written: *And to whom swore he that they should not enter into his rest, but to them that believed not? So we see that they could not enter in because of unbelief.*[87]

We have been talking about the danger that both the Pastoral activity and Liturgy of the Church, influenced by theater, may have

---

[86]Mt 8:26. Nevertheless, we must take into account that the final triumph of Goodness over Evil will happen only at the end of History. Triumphalist doctrines, which incessantly proclaim the present prosperity of the Church and her inexorable march toward an even greater progress, are going against the daily experience and the teachings of Revelation which tell us that the Church is walking toward painful trials that will leave her terribly diminished. At the same time, the abundance of iniquity in the world will cause the love of many to grow cold and the almost total disappearance of Faith (Mt 24:12; Mk 13: 19–20; Lk 18:8).

[87]Heb 3: 18–19.

paved the way, perhaps unintentionally, for theatrical performances before the faithful. Which would be the case if, having lost her supernatural horizon, she would have preferred to pursue merely human objectives of whichever kind.

It is never pleasant, and always very challenging, to give examples that help explain some wrong attitudes that can be attributed to individuals or to society. However, some instances must be provided if one wants to avoid confusion and misunderstanding. Hence it is worth taking the risk of enumerating some.

It cannot be denied that our time is partial to the *Pastoral-show*. We refer, to mention a few cases, to those large *assemblies* of the faithful convoked with simply any religious motive, so fashionable today; or to the multitudinous *Gatherings* usually chaired by some senior member of the ecclesiastical hierarchy whose personal aura and the feverish enthusiasm that he arouses sometimes tend to displace the significance of the *Gathering*; or to the tumultuous canonizations[88] and the boisterous pilgrimages, both so beneficial for international tourism; or to the countless *Congresses*, to which are invited an elevated number of Shepherds and a no less bulky group of theologians and experts from all over the world, etc., etc.

Under normal circumstances, we must joyfully admit that these events, or similar ones, would have clearly helped foster the faith of the Christian people. The past jubilees, pilgrimages, processions,

---

[88]Some differences should be noted between the canonization ceremonies of the past and those of modern times. The former previously required a long and scrupulous research process which exhausted to incredible extremes the rigorous demands of Canon Law. The latter are less demanding in their probing phase, but the ceremony itself is usually well promoted and accompanied by excellently organized tourism; therefore, the prevailing feature in those attending the ceremony is curiosity, patriotic or regional emotions, and other interests somewhat foreign to religion. It is not surprising that the former ceremonies could fairly be described as *solemn* while the modern ones fit better into the category of *spectacular*.

and long journeys to shrines helped to maintain the faith of Christian society for centuries. Recall, for example, the large crowds that flocked to hear Saint Dominic of Guzman preaching (late twelfth and early thirteenth centuries), or the strange *Processions of Flagellants* who followed Saint Vincent Ferrer everywhere, almost fanatically (fourteenth century). Not to mention the devout and numerous jubilees and pilgrimages to the tomb of Saint Peter in Rome, or of Santiago in Spain. They created paths and routes that were traveled for centuries, with amazing fervor, by countless numbers of pilgrims.[89] These were also social phenomena of a magnitude that moved many crowds.

The problem is that the body and the structure may be the same, but not necessarily the spirit that accompanies them. Identical events or actions can be alternately good or bad, depending on the spirit that animates them. Jesus Christ spoke of fasting or almsgiving which, having been made in a spirit of ostentation, could not expect any reward (Mt 6: 1–4.16–18); and the same must be said of prayer devoid of humility (Lk 18: 9 ff.).

In ancient times, as always, there were good and evil, justice and injustice, holiness and sin. There were good men and bad men, just men and unjust men (one should recall here the parable of the good seed and tares). But the Christian world became considerably pagan especially since the last third of the twentieth century; therefore, the increase of wickedness has effectively contributed to the cooling of charity and the decline of faith (Mt 24:12). It would be interesting

---

[89]The many paths traveled by those pilgrims since the dawn of the Middle Ages and even before, and whose number and place of departure was always unknown, were punctuated by a multitude of humble shelters that housed free of charge those who, with unshaken faith, traveled on foot to the sepulchers of the Apostles. Today, modern highways, fast railroads, and comfortable motels and hotels have replaced those trails and shelters. Customs have improved, certainly, at the same rate that the faith and the spirit of pilgrims have subsequently diminished.

to make a serious study about the proportions of good and bad in today's world.

The post–conciliar Church has relied too much on theater. Theatrical representations abound throughout the Catholic world in high as well as in less important places. It would be unfair to say that all of them are animated by ill will. In many cases, or perhaps in most of them, they may be sincerely seeking the greater benefit of the faithful. The problem is that good will is not enough; one need examine whether the will is wrong. Good will, in itself, cannot claim to be endowed with any guarantee against error.

Pastoral activities, Liturgical Worship, and the whole of ecclesial action in general, must be accompanied by the virtues of sincerity and honest simplicity. The faithful cannot be induced to pledge their allegiance to actions and behaviors whose content is not what it seems. Nor can they be left confused as to the meaning and exercise of Christian virtues. The hype and pageantry, for example, which are often used for the exaltation of worship or of certain celebrities, may be an obstacle to the understanding and practice of the virtues of humility and simplicity. When hype and pageantry have insufficient justification, or even none, the virtue of sincerity lessens and truth disappears. And it is horrifying to think of what happens when truth fades from the horizon of human existence. Any kind of church activity that is not grounded in truth is unable to produce any improvement in the life of the Christian faithful. Rather the opposite is true, in that the smell of lies and dishonesty instills in the faithful, slowly but effectively, the poisonous venom of believing in the futility of religion.

In a well–known shrine in a Spanish city the Virgin Mary is venerated under an affectionate title that has enormous prestige among the people. There is a local pilgrimage once a year during which the Statue of the Virgin is transferred to the city, amid great expectation. A peculiar element of this procession is that those mainly involved in this act of worship, otherwise so charming and expressive of devotion to the Mother of God, are young people. When the time comes for the statue of the Virgin Mary to be transferred from the shrine, these youngsters are the ones carrying it out of the church; which they do with such a fiery enthusiasm and such an outpouring of faith and love for the Virgin that, to do it justice, one should qualify their attitude as extraordinarily *spectacular* rather than as devoutly fervent.

But the highlight of the ceremony takes place with the onslaught of the young people toward the shrine. Having waited at the entrance for a more or less long period of time, the huge crowds of youth look forward to their beloved Patroness making her exit. This delay is logical but not unfamiliar, since everyone knows that the same thing always happens every time. The prolongation of the lag is unbearable to the young, to the point that they feel unable to restrain their eagerness to see the Virgin. Therefore, at a certain point, they assault the fence surrounding the shrine in a run, like possessed men, to overtake the statue of the Virgin Mary; a veritable explosion of devotion and enthusiasm.

As might be expected, this assault is not included in the program, *although everyone knows that it will happen*. Even the time for it to occur is scheduled, thus facilitating the work of the *media*, always ready and willing to bear witness to the very expressive fact of a youthful devotion, so immensely friendly and sincere, to the Virgin Mary.

No doubt there are plenty of reasons to rejoice. Unfortunately, I have never had the opportunity of seeing such devotion translated into a better Christian life among the young. On the contrary, it grows weaker every day. Moreover, the religiosity of many, if not most of them during the entire year begins and ends with this assault on the shrine. Therefore, and much to my regret, I cannot help but notice in this behavior a certain whiff of theatrical action adorned with a bit of folklore.

The case of Mother Teresa of Calcutta, whom I have always admired, is different. I believe my feelings for her would be more enthusiastic if I could understand some events of her life. Of course, I do not mean to judge them; still much less to believe that there was anything wrong with them. I simply mean that I find it difficult to understand them and that, were it not for them, my enthusiasm for her, I must candidly admit, would be even greater.

I consider Mother Teresa to be a missionary *par excellence*; a soul dedicated entirely to the destitute and a champion of poverty and humility. My difficulty has to do with the way in which these qualities, which I do not question, harmonize with the universal favor and fame that have always accompanied them. Indeed, if anyone has always had the doors of the powerful of this world, both good and bad, opened to him, that person was Mother Teresa. Her private audiences with the Pope can be counted by the number of times she requested them. She had worldwide access to all possible means of communication, expression, and displacement without any limitation. She spoke at the UN Assembly. Some of her gestures, genius and spectacular, became famous and were publicized by news agencies around the world, such as her throwing television sets out the cell windows of one of her convents in demonstration of poverty; a gesture which could be broadcast thanks to the presence of the media, which attested to the event.[90]

A few months after the meeting of Pope Benedict XVI with the Youth in Cologne (Summer 2005), the incoming Bishop of a certain Spanish diocese made his entry into his new Diocese. Taking advantage of the coastal

---

[90]Her speech at the UN Assembly as well as her receiving the Nobel Peace Prize is something I cannot easily understand. It is well known that the Nobel Prize, especially the one for Peace, is awarded according to merely political considerations and shady manipulations. As for the UN, everybody knows that it is an inoperative Organization riddled with corruption and political fraud, and, of course, anti–Christian sentiments. To deliver a speech in that environment, no matter how much good will one may have, does not seem to make much sense. It is true that Saint Francis of Assisi, after the capture of Damietta by the crusade army (Egypt, 1219), courageously slipped himself into the Muslim camp to preach before the Sultan *al-Kāmil*, who, according to the chronicles, listened to him respectfully but did not grant him anything he asked for, except letting him go free. But those sultans of the thirteenth century have little to do with their modern counterparts who are in favor of fanaticism, petro–dollars, and missiles. True, the former *listened respectfully* to Saint Francis; but Mother Theresa was merely *heard in silence* at the UN.

geographical situation of the Diocese, the new Bishop decided to carry out his entry by sea. The event was welcomed by his enthusiastic diocesan faithful with all possible ceremony. From that port city he undertook other trips to visit the most important Dioceses, where his new flock always received him with affection and fervor.

Undoubtedly, this gesture can only be described as affectionate towards his faithful. It happens, however, that it is hard not to relate it to the triumphal entrance of Benedict XVI in Cologne, which occurred shortly before and to which the Bishop's arrival had obvious similarity. This fact, of course, far from being judged as reprehensible, should be considered as a desire to imitate the steps of the Holy Father, which is praiseworthy.

In case anyone has forgotten it, we should remember that Benedict XVI, when he was newly elected Pope, also made his entry into Cologne to celebrate World Youth Day sailing across the Rhine on a ship escorted by five smaller vessels in which there were youths from each of the five continents. Meanwhile, hundred of thousands of young people from around the globe were waiting for him and eagerly hailing him.

And because the example of the Shepherds is often imitated by the best part of the assembly, a few weeks later the new Bishop of another Spanish diocese made a triumphal arrival in taking possession of it. Only this time his entrance took place on a donkey. Perhaps to imitate Our Lord's entry into Jerusalem; which must be applauded in that the new Bishop, in his desire to emulate the best possible Model, went even beyond the Pope. He ceremoniously requested permission from the mayor to enter the city, which the magistrate granted willingly, handing the Bishop the key, etc., etc.[91]

------

[91]In the film *Gladiator*, directed by Ridley Scott, there is a very expressive sequence. Commodus, the new Emperor, is making his triumphal entry into Rome among the usual popular acclaim. His father, Emperor Marcus Aurelius, who died shortly before, had put a victorious end to his campaigns against the invading Germans, in which Commodus had not taken part. The senators were waiting for the new Emperor at the foot of the steps of the Capitol, while, in a tone of obvious disapproval, they said to one another, *He is making his entrance as a conqueror; but, what has he conquered?*

It can be assumed that these actions, insofar as they are made (as they surely are) with the desire to promote devotion and piety among the faithful, are therefore worthy of praise and approval. But we said above that good will is not sufficient. We should not forget that these activities carry in themselves a risk, that the *continent* will finally eclipse the *content*. There is in them an inbuilt possibility of facilitating, even without intending it, an obscuring of the real content and meaning of the virtues —putting them in the background— that make up the fabric of Christian existence.

The kingdom of God cometh not with observation; neither shall they say, Lo here! or, lo there! for, behold, the kingdom of God is within you.[92] The words of Jesus are categorical and uncompromising. Of course, it does not follow from them that external acts of worship should be condemned, for they are necessary for the promotion and development of Christian life. *External acts of worship, including those carried out in splendor, are not merely desirable, but essential and indispensable.*

However, it is clear that the Master's words contain some meaning and significance. They point out a path to be followed. Perhaps He wants to tell us that the existence of a disciple, or the *narrow path* to be followed and which is elected by very few (Mt 7:14), does not run through valleys or plains made ready for a comfortable and pleasant journey. Maybe what Jesus Christ is saying (in this text and in many others throughout the Gospel) is that Christian life does not consist of pomp or splendor or triumphs or applause or congratulations or welcoming... nor of anything nice and easy that implies sharing somehow in World Power, Personal Triumph, Money, or any other of the allurements that the World offers and which, in fact, do not go beyond what is ephemeral and deceitful.

---

[92]Lk 17: 20–21.

Perhaps Christians should remember more often that Freud lied when he said that the decisive impulse in man, or the one which moves man most strongly, is the sexual instinct. This instinct, even when it becomes lust, has never been the greatest or most subtle temptation to which man is subjected; *in fact, the strongest impulse has been none other than pride or the desire for power.* The demonstration of this is better understood when considering the temptation that was the cause of the first sin of man. It was committed in Paradise when man, seduced by the Serpent, would be his own god, not depending on any other.

How have we been able to forget the one path along which true Christianity flows? Which is the very path that the World despises, as one would expect:

We are weak because we no longer understand the power of weakness; we no longer understand that the greatest power is in self–abnegation, renunciation, and martyrdom. Even Catholics no longer use words like "mortification" or even "detachment." But our heart still understands this power; that is why we recognize it when we meet it in Tolkien, or Buddha, or Lao Tzu, even after our Christian teachers stopped teaching it to us in the name of Jesus.[93]

It might have been better if the helmet of Mambrino had stayed forever being what it was: a humble barber's basin. Who knows...? With it, perhaps Don Quixote would have beaten more giants, righted more wrongs, and brought more miscreants to their senses. The only force capable of defeating the pride of the World and the power of Evil is weakness assumed for the love of and in Christ Jesus: *God hath chosen the weak things of the world to confound the things which are mighty;*[94] it is clear that *strength is made perfect*

---

[93]Peter Kreeft, *op. cit.*, p. 189.

[94]1 Cor 1:27.

in weakness.[95] Hence *of myself I will not glory, but in mine infirmities.*[96] This is how it pleased God to ridicule the pride of the Great Liar: by using the weakness and the apparent failure of the Cross.

---

[95] 2 Cor 12:9.

[96] 2 Cor 12:5.

VII

THE GOLDEN AGE[1]

1. Where some detailed statements about utopias are outlined, by way of introduction to the topic.

Sheltered as Don Quixote and Sancho were by some goatherds, their stomachs filled with the rustic meal offered to them, grabbing some acorns in his hand and staring at them attentively, our hero began his famous speech about the Golden Age:[2]

> —*Happy the age, happy the time, to which the ancients gave the name of golden, not because in that fortunate age the gold so coveted in this our iron one was gained without toil, but because they that lived in it knew not the two words "mine" and "thine." In that*

---

[1] In the writing of this chapter, the observations, advises, and suggestions of Father Faustino Ruiz have been extraordinarily useful, personally and through his work: *El Estatuto Ontológico del Alma después de la Muerte: un Estudio a través de Platón y Santo Tomás de Aquino*, Santiago de Chile, 2002.

[2] *Don Quixote*, I, 11.

blessed age all things were in common; to win the daily food no labour was required of any, save to stretch forth his hand and gather it from the sturdy oaks that stood generously inviting him with their sweet ripe fruit. The clear streams and running brooks yielded their savoury limpid waters in noble abundance. The busy and sagacious bees fixed their republic in the clefts of the rocks and hollows of the trees, offering without any interest the plenteous produce of their fragrant toil to every hand...

Clearly, Cervantes is aware that, through a literary dissertation elaborated with his finest style, he is doing nothing other than describing a utopia.

Everyone knows that utopias, as long as they remain within their proper realm, which is none other than the literary world, are useful inasmuch as they serve as amusement and food for the imagination. At times, utopias even answer the secret impulses and desires of the human heart, which is so dissatisfied as to make room for the hope for a better world or perhaps to actualize the remembrance of a World or Paradise lost forever.

Utopias become dangerous only when, having forgotten their status as pure fantasy, they pretend that they should be considered as something real. Of course, nothing would happen were all reduced to a mere belief. Nothing has ever happened because the universe of children has been inhabited by fairies, elves, dwarves, warlocks, and witches —all of which are guilty of nothing more than safeguarding the fascinating world of golden childhood until the moment when these creatures abandon it, once belief in them disappears.

However, the world we inhabit seems to be filled with madmen; hence, what otherwise would have seemed unthinkable has now come to be. For nobody, aside from children, has ever taken seriously the world of warlocks, fairies, and witches... all of which are products of a wholesome imagination fed by a beautiful fantasy. Nevertheless, this issue becomes a problem —and an extremely serious one— when a utopia feeds upon an imagination that has stopped being healthy and falls prey to illness. Moreover, if the illness worsens and becomes madness, the result is nothing other than a utopia–turned–aberration attempting to impose itself on the real world, by force if necessary. The conclusion is obvious. Incredible as it may seem, the 'utopia–madness' eventually becomes accepted effortlessly by a world of madmen, a phenomenon that has taken place with utopias contrived by abnormal brains like those of Marx, Freud, or Nietzsche,[3] or by ideologies that have thrived within post–Vatican II Catholicism: namely, a varied plethora of triumphalistic, pacifist, dreamy–eyed ecumenism, etc.; all of which agree in believing in an inexorable march toward a better Church and a better world.

What is difficult to explain in this case is the fact that madness has been so easily accepted by a world which one should suppose to be sane. And this is not all, for there is something still more incredible: Madness present in imaginary characters such as Don Quixote, which is as likable as it is innocuous, has always been re-garded unanimously and universally as such; whereas the authentic madness of minds as sinister as those of Marx and Freud, real per-sons, has been accepted as a *true and salutary sanity, as even the most appropriate path for the making of a better world.*

The fact that lunacies, as abhorrent and unnatural as those of Marx and Freud or as inconsistent as those spread by the triumphal-ist contemporary Pastoral activity, have achieved the status of true doctrine, in addition to their being universally and unreservedly ac-cepted, is a phenomenon hard to explain. If one pretends to make any sense of it, even remotely, one must refer to the existence of original sin and its consequences, namely, the weakness of human

---

[3]Cf. Henri de Lubac, *The Drama of Atheist Humanism*, San Francisco, 1995.

nature attacked by concupiscence and its ensuing inclination to evil. All of which seems to be, in short, the only cause for the constant proclivity of this human nature towards lies and in favor of liars.

Something very different must be said about an imaginary character such as Don Quixote. His madness has also been unanimously accepted, and with universal fondness. This madness, however, has never sought to disguise its demented condition; therefore, it has always been regarded as what it is without any hesitation whatsoever. Nobody has ever thought that Don Quixote's delirium, with his stubborn streak to restore to the world the Order of Knight Errantry, was anything other than pure fantasy and an amusing utopia. Thus, nobody has felt compelled to become a Knight Errant, swept by the desire to follow our hero's example.

The reason for this must be found in that the adventures of Alonso Quijano El Bueno, now turned *Knight of the Woeful Countenance*, have never pretended to leave the literary domain; therefore, his grandiose and idealized enterprise may very well be regarded as a *good utopia* inasmuch as it has never pretended to disguise itself as reality. Not so with the nonsensical and irrational utopias which have endeavored to introduce themselves not only as doctrines rooted in reality but also as the only solution to understanding human nature, even to the extent of both improving it and saving it.

But there is still more. The readers of Don Quixote's adventure have always been conscious, in spite of the latter's likeability, that the enterprise attempted by our Knight was a utopia. They have fully understood that the universal Kingdom of Justice established and safeguarded in this world by the Knights–Errant was (is) an unrealizable fantasy, at least for the time being, as long as History remains. In the motley and variegated world in which Don Quixote's adventures take place, only he believes in the reality of his dream; not even his realistic and prosaic squire ever fully sympathizes with his master in this regard. Hence the Quixotic utopia, not pretending to appear as something it is not, is founded upon truth. That is why it is good and thus does not deceive anybody.

The readers who accompany Don Quixote in the progress of his foolish adventures are never induced to regard them as truthful, placing reality aside. They know that we human beings live and *will continue to live* in a convulsive and tense world, the painful condition of which will only end with the arrival of the Parousia *and never before*, no matter what the various utopias and the false prophets may say: *For the whole creation was made subject to vanity; not willingly, but by reason of him that made it subject; in hope, because the whole creation also itself shall be delivered from the servitude of corruption, into the liberty of the glory of the children of God. We are well aware that the whole creation, until this time, has been groaning and travailing in pain. And not only that: we too, who have the first fruits of the Spirit, even we ourselves are groaning within ourselves, waiting with eagerness for the adoption of the sons of God, the redemption of our body.*[4] Here we are facing the truth that places us in a position diametrically opposed to utopia. The Apostle's realism has just affirmed that we are groaning inside, *even in spite of our possessing the first fruits of the Spirit.*

Now, if this is so, how may we show affinity and admiration toward a utopia that, because of its very essence, one acknowledges as impossible to come to realization? The answer is also contained within the Apostle's words; for the knowledge of reality is not incompatible with hope; on the contrary, both call for each other. The Christian knows that the whole creation, man included, will

---

[4]Rom 8: 20–23.

someday be the object of redemption as we achieve the full fruition
of the status as children of God. Without the acceptance of that
reality, the virtue of hope is not possible; a virtue that happens to
be essential for salvation. The Apostle, alluding expressly to the
hope of the Parousia, says that the crown of beatitude is reserved
only for those who are longing with love for His coming: *Non solum
autem mihi, sed et omnibus, qui diligent adventum eius, And not
only to me, but to them also that longed for his coming.*[5]

 *2. Wherein an attempt is made to say something more about the true
meaning of Christian hope.*

 The loving hope about which the Apostle speaks seems to possess all the characteristics of an *eager waiting.*[6] And it cannot be
otherwise when the arrival of the Bridegroom is at stake:

> *I opened to my love,*
> *But he had turned and gone.*
> *I sought him, but I could not find him.*
> *I called him, but he did not answer...*
> *I charge you, daughters of Jerusalem,*
> *If you should find my love,*
> *Tell him that I am sick with love!*[7]

---

[5]2 Tim 4:8.

[6]The expression used by Saint Paul is extremely suggestive: *to long for his
coming.* The Greek original ἠγαπηκόσι, participle perfect active from ἀγαπάω,
means *diligo* or *desidero*, which seems to indicate a waiting earnestly done.

[7]Sg 5: 6.8.

This dying out of love because of the Beloved's absence —He cannot be found— fits quite well the concept of a longed–for, enamored waiting. The famous stanza of Saint John of the Cross in his *Spiritual Canticle* is a beautiful gloss of the Biblical text:

> *O shepherds, you that, yonder,*
> *Go through the sheepfolds of the slope on high,*
> *If you, as there you wander,*
> *Should chance my love to spy,*
> *Then tell him that I suffer, grieve, and die.*

Hence the cry of hope of the liturgy of early Christianity: *Maranatha!* or the longing *Come, Lord Jesus!*[8] which is uttered like an explosion of yearning surging from the bottom of the heart.

The ardent longing for the Lord's coming was the atmosphere early Christianity normally breathed. As time went by, however, the loving and impatient waiting faltered, only to reach its nadir in current times: *The Bridegroom was late, and they all grew drowsy and fell asleep,*[9] says the Parable of the Ten Virgins.

Yet in Christianity there has always existed, and will continue to exist, a *pusillus grex, little flock* (Lk 12:32) that will indeed wane as the final moments approach, notwithstanding what the defenders and propagandists of false triumphalism may say. It is not surprising that, in view of the tremendous crisis of the current situation, the small flock that still remains faithful longs with anguish for the final coming of the Lord. We are facing an unsustainable decomposition of Catholicism; meanwhile, by contrast, an enormous propaganda apparatus tries to make us believe the opposite. It is not worthwhile

---

[8]Rev 22:20; cf. 1 Cor 16:22.

[9]Mt 25:5.

to make here a description of the dissolution of Christian values; it would take too much time and space that we do not have, and it is a task already undertaken elsewhere. As a North American writer stated recently: *The hermeneutics of rupture,*[10] *if you will, arose from the desire of the Council Fathers to join the cult of youth, to 'discern the signs of the times,' to become some sort of ecclesiastical hipsters. This shift in sympathy from tradition to novelty involved jettisoning the past. As the secular culture began panting after youth, so did the Church. But the secular culture deemed itself free to pursue openly the youthful mysticism of materialism that finds its fruition in sexual license. The Church in contrast chafed under the bonds of its hoary morality: theologians could dissent from 'Humanae Vitae'; bishops and pastors could give a wink and a nod to contraception; opposition to legalized abortion could be reduced to formal and flaccid press releases; homosexuals could be given the run of the seminaries. But how to join publicly the great parade of sexual liberation under whose banner the modern world was marching? How to close the breach between the faith and modernity? Well, by simply ignoring that such a breach exists.*[11]

This longing waiting also is shared by the blessed souls that, in their present state of intermediate eschatology await the resurrection and glorification of their bodies. According to the Constitution

---

[10]The author refers here to an expression recently used by Pope Benedict XVI, according to which the Council documents can be interpreted following two ways: the hermeneutic of Tradition and the hermeneutic of rupture with Tradition. The author adds that the term 'hermeneutics' is proper to the interpretation of the Sacred Scripture, recognizing that it may have a wider use. He also expresses his confidence that the Holy Father will not extend to the documents of the Council the reverence due to Sacred Scripture.

[11]Edwin Faust, *A Pox on the New Springtime; The Latin Mass,* Vol. 15, n. 1, NJ 2006, p. 32.

Benedictus Deus,[12] the vision and possession of God which those souls already have empty out their acts of faith and hope as theological virtues (*visio huiusmodi divinæ esentiæ eiusque fruitio actus fidei et spei in eis evacuant, prout fides et spes propriæ theologicæ sunt virtutes*). But it is clear that the Constitution refers to the hope as confidence of those souls in their ultimate salvation. In no way can the papal document claim to suppress the earnest awaiting of the resurrection and subsequent transformation and glorification of their bodies as Catholic theology has always recognized it. For this *hope* of the blessed, which takes place during the interim eschatology, is, in turn, crucially important.

Primarily because the fulfillment of that hope will bring those souls to nothing less than their full identification with Christ, which will not happen until their bodies have been configured to the Body of the glorious Christ. These passages of the Sacred Scripture leave no doubt in this regard (Romans 6: 4–5; 1 Corinthians 15: 44–54; Philippians 3: 20–21). Is it possible that the Platonic tendency to overemphasize the value of the human soul, to the detriment or neglect of the body, has relegated to the background, if not forgotten, the fundamental significance of the glorification of the body in the final beatitude and its role with respect to the Parousia?

Secondly, because, until that moment comes, the blessed souls separated from their bodies actually contemplate the Divine Essence, face to face and with intuitive vision, but they will do that as *blessed human souls*; not yet in a fully human way, *as beings entirely human* in their essential structure of body and soul, as God created human nature. This, as we will explain later, will not result in an increase, either accidental or essential, in the happiness or bliss of the blessed. With respect to the beatific vision, in which takes place the

---

[12]Denz. 530 (1000).

contemplation of God face to face with the corresponding possession
and fruition, it is meaningless to talk about any kind of *increase*:
What could any kind of *intensity* be when one is contemplating God
face to face with intuitive vision? This assumption is nothing but
a sort of anthropomorphism which ends up by ultimately transfer-
ring human ways of thinking to the world of the supernatural and,
what is worse, to God Himself. When one thinks about the meaning of the mystery of the beatific vision, he often confuses *ecstatic*
with *static*. These are two terms which respond to two different
and even contradictory concepts. So much so as that the beatific
vision is not *static* at all, but a veritable *vital act* of hyper active
dynamism connected to the abundance of life about which Jesus
Christ speaks to the elect: *ut vitam habeant et abundantius habeant.*
And one should note the importance and richness of content of the
superlative adjective *abundantius*, in which it is difficult to see a
mere increase in intensity of life. It happens something similar to
what is usually said in mystic theology about the *passivity* of the
human soul in contemplation. Recall the example of Saint Teresa,
in which she compares the water that falls from the sky during the
rain (contemplation) with that which is laboriously drawn by the
waterwheel (meditation).[13] What has taken place in the blessed,
by this time, is their *final and complete glorification*: when at last
they reach the full measure of their identification with Christ (each
his own, according to Ephesians 4: 7.13), and when finally they also
see and love God in a fully and perfect human way, through the
possession of their glorified body. This does not mean, as we have

---

[13]I dealt more extensively with this issue in my book *Prayer*, New Jersey,

said, that there will be an increase, either essential or accidental, of their bliss in the beatific vision.[14]

But supernatural hope is activated the very moment that human hope is gone: *Quia contra spem in spe credidit* (Rom 4:18). It can be said, therefore, that ill–natured utopias and false triumphalism directly undermine this virtue. They want to make people see what actually is not seen and cannot be seen because it is false. While the virtue of hope, however, by guiding and leading the human heart beyond what one sees, opens for him the doors of the ineffable reality of the promises of a God Who never lies: *We are saved by hope. But hope that is seen is not hope: for what a man sees, why does he yet hope for? But if we hope for that we see not, then do we with patience wait for it.*[15]

This explains why any good man adopts a sympathetic attitude towards the Adventure of Don Quixote and his utopian delusions. He thus lives in the certain confidence that the Golden Age, so beautifully described by Cervantes in Don Quixote's speech to the goatherds, someday will become a reality, for he knows that Christian hope never disappoints: *Spes autem non confundit. And hope does not disappoint us.* (Rom 5:5). Because if there were the slightest possibility that it were otherwise, hope would be without content and, thus, no longer hope; it would not even make sense. And yet, we have seen that Saint Paul's expression is categorical and also confirmed by that strength and that compelling argument which only love provides, as the Apostle says next, when he states: *quia caritas Dei diffusa est in cordibus nostris per Spiritum Sanctum... For the love of God has been poured out into our hearts by the Holy Spirit...*

---

[14]We will speak further on in this chapter about the expression *nulla mediante creatura in ratione obiecti visi se habente* of the Constitution *Benedictus Deus.*

[15]Rom 8: 24–25.

But that Golden Age, which is now the subject of the virtue of hope, will be very different and more sublime and loftier than the one described in Cervantes' literary work; a difference that should be calculated according to the distance between heaven and earth. Such a certainty in the realization of that hope is only possible when one takes into account the reality of the world in which we live, for *the whole creation groans and travails with labor pains until now.* Without this awareness of the misery that surrounds us, it would be impossible to hope for that better world that we do not yet see: *for hope that is seen is not hope.* The frenzy of Don Quixote is indeed a utopia, but it contains a hidden hope which Christians know is not deceiving; that is, it is based in truth, although founded upon a safe promise yet to become real.

Modern utopias, however, point to a hope that is founded only on lies. They will never become real; hence they can be considered as false, wicked, and deceiving. Because they do not recognize the transience of our present city, they think that the search for another future city is meaningless, even when the latter has been invariably promised by God (Heb 13:14).[16] The modern claim that man should establish himself in the Earthly City, since there is no other to hope for, destroys hope; although, as we know well, there in so salvation without hope (Rom 8:24). This explains why the loss of hope leads to the final stride with which we go through the Gate of Hell.

Lasciate ogni speranza, voi ch'entrate.[17]

---

[16]The passage of the Letter to the Hebrews becomes a distant echo of what the ancient prophet Micah said: *Arise ye, and depart; for this is not your rest* (Mic 2:10).

[17]*Abandon every hope, all ye who enter here.* Dante, *Divine Comedy, Inferno,* III.

Don Quixote's speech about the Golden Age is perfectly consistent with the spirit of any utopia. It contains, however, an important detail for which Cervantes is not responsible, as we shall see. Of course, the author of *Don Quixote* is but using here a mere literary figure, and it would not make any sense to assume that he endorses any delusions and follies contained in this particular speech, either as a whole or in part. But everybody knows that crazy dreams may contain details or elements which are even more outlandish; that is, more extravagant aspects within a general list of nonsense. And I am referring specifically to the passage of the speech in which it is said that, for those who lived in that age, there were no concepts of *"thine" and "mine."* However, one could easily assume that the gravity of the consequences that would arise, should we admit the truth of such a statement, may escape anyone who does not think hard.

It is natural enough that Cervantes, once he decides to describe a utopia, stresses one of the topics that characterize this genre of fables. But there is nothing but literature in the adventures, speeches, and considerations of Alonso Quixano el Bueno —known as *Don Quixote,* or *The Knight of the Woeful Countenance*—-as well as in the content of his humorous dialogues with his squire; therefore, no one will dare to say that the Prince of the Spanish Literature was a Socialist. It simply happens that topics, like cherries, are easily entangled and interlocked when utilized. But nobody takes too much trouble to make a detailed analysis „ either of the topics as such or of the possible inconsistencies that often derive from them. If one takes for granted, as it does indeed happen, that the description of the Golden Age, as is depicted in the speech of the goatherds, is just the telling of a utopia, then the disappearance of the concepts of *what is mine* and *what is yours* is not surprising. Concepts which, as strange as it may seem, have never been well considered by utopias.[18]

3. Wherein incidence is made in the important concept of 'possession' within the fundamental theme of love.

This theme has more relevance than one may suppose. Although one must admit that *private property* is something inherent to the human person, *it is not, however, the most fundamental* reality of the person.

The elimination of the realities corresponding to the concepts *thine* and *mine* would suppose the *suppression of love*; love meaning essentially surrender and reception, both realized in mutual reciprocity. For such realization to happen, it is indispensable that there exist an *I* and a *you* that are entirely separate from each

---

[18]This issue has always been present in every utopia, including the one Thomas More* wrote about. The funny thing here is the unanimous commitment of these ideologies to ignore private property, although this concept is one of the most inherent and substantial characteristics of human nature. And yet, its denial is intrinsic to utopias in general and to Socialist fantasies in particular. In the latter, the collectivity takes precedence over the individual: what is social overrides the individual as a person. And because private property is inherent to human nature and the only guarantee of individual freedom, it is logical that it is fought by the eternal enemy of all sorts of freedoms, namely, Socialism.

*More actually coined the word *Utopia*, as the name he assigned to his imaginary island. His work, written in Latin and published in 1516, contains a fully communist philosophy. The experts still debate whether it was a serious study or perhaps a mere vagary unpretentious of reality (Thomas More was justly canonized by the Church). Perhaps the author wanted to express a protest against the lawlessness that existed in Europe at the time, without trying to give prominence to the solutions he proposed in his work. In any case, the most important utopia within the realm of political philosophy is the *Republic*, by Plato, supplemented in more detail by his dialogue *The Laws*.

other, and each one able to surrender *whatever belongs to self* so
that the other may receive it. Revelation is sufficiently clear as to
be understood without further difficulties.[19] It is worthwhile to look
to the testimony of both Testaments:

I am my Beloved's and He is mine.[20]

In a time like ours, in which love has been reduced to sex in its
merely animalistic form, once love has been stripped of its essential qualities of perennial nature and totality, the idea of *possession*
of the other by each of the lovers has disappeared from modern
thought; nevertheless, it is impossible to surrender something to the
other person, so that the other may make that thing his or her own,
if that thing does not first belong to the giver. Hence, the concepts *thine* and *mine* are just as essential to love as those of *you*
and *I*. Therefore, without surrender and reception —both carried
out mutually between distinct persons— there would be no possibility that love exist. Thus one could conclude, with due logic, that
in the case that during the Golden Age the concepts of *thine* and
mine would not have been known, then love would also have been
unknown completely therein. Yet a hypothetical *Golden Age* devoid
of love would be simply unthinkable, even if that age would be considered as the most fantastic and utopian notion the imagination
could have ever conceived. Can a *Golden Age* be conceivable without love, perchance? When it so also happens that man was created
by Infinite Love to His image and likeness, just so he could love and

---

[19]This theme as a whole has been analyzed in various places of my books *Commentaries on the Song of Songs*, Vols. I and II, New Jersey, 1995 and 2006; and
more in depth in Vol. I, pp. 111 ff.

[20]Sg 2:16; 6:3.

be loved! In this sense, as an ingredient substantial to love, private property is also an inherent quality of the human person.

The idea of *possession* in love has been eradicated from modern thought. The new ideologies that have somewhat to do with love, such as, for instance, feminist, machismo, or homosexual *Movements*, reject it flatly. The concept of *possession*, so fundamental in love, seems to oppose the flowing verbiage connatural to the licentious conduct now called freedom: the autonomy of the individual, women's liberation, the right to self–fulfillment according to individual criteria, the right to be oneself, etc.; in short, anything under the banner of a sort of *liberation* that is nothing else, after all, than the rejection of God —or the most recent echo of the Fallen Angel's cry of *Non serviam!*

Nevertheless, all doctrine about love revolves around the concept of *possession*. The interchange of lives, an essential quality of love, presupposes the total and reciprocal surrender of the lovers. This means, if words signify anything, that the life of each one of them now *belongs* to the other. It goes without saying that the surrender of life is tantamount to the donation of the whole person: *Vivo autem iam non ego, vivit vero in me Christus. Nevertheless I live; yet not I, but Christ living in me.*[21] With this, a true interchange takes place in which the life of each one now becomes the property of the other: *Whoever eats my flesh and drinks my blood lives in me and I live in him. As the living Father sent me, and I draw life from the Father, so whoever eats me will also draw life from me.*[22] In love, the lover is not at peace until he is certain that his life *belongs to the beloved.* It is in this way that the concept of possession becomes a reality, although in a double sense: Whoever loves ardently desires

---

[21] Gal 2:20.

[22] Jn 6: 56–57; cf Mt 10:39.

to belong to the beloved, yet, at the same time, in what may appear as the strangest of paradoxes, the lover, in turn, equally longs to *possess the beloved.* That is why the *Song of Songs* says:

I am my beloved's and he is mine.[23]

The concepts of *thine* and *mine*, which in turn are correlative with the concept of *possession*, are fundamental in the doctrine of love. In turn, since all theological doctrine derives from the mystery of the Divine Trinity, and given that the Theology of Love exactly coincides with the Mystery of God, it seems logical that the scriptural texts alluding to this fundamental Mystery of Christian Faith abundantly support what we have being saying until now. The Mystery of the Trinity of Persons in the Unicity of Divine Essence would be completely unintelligible without the concepts of *thine* and *mine*, and thus, without that of *possession* —and the same applies to the concept of *Love.* Let us see some primary texts, all of which have Jesus as speaker:

Everything has been given to me by my Father...[24] *I am in the Father and the Father is in me...*[25] *Everything the Father has is mine; that is why I said: 'all he reveals to you will be taken from what is mine...'*[26] *All I have is yours (He talks to the Father) and all you have is mine.*[27]

From these texts follows the mutual, reciprocal, and total surrender of all that belongs to one to the other. In these texts the concept

---

[23]Sg 2:16; 6:3.

[24]Mt 11:27.

[25]Jn 14: 10–11.

[26]Jn 16:15.

[27]Jn 17:10.

of *possession* as well as those of *thine* and *mine* is also clearly contained, all of it made possible through the *bond of love* that unites them.

The doctrine of the mystics, as it could not be otherwise, has understood very well what the idea of (mutual) *possession* means in love; as Saint John of the Cross said:

> *Why then did you so pierce*
> *My heart, nor heal it with your touch sublime?*
> *Why, like a robber fierce,*
> *Desert me every time*
> *And not enjoy the plunder of your crime?*[28]

One must take into account that we are speaking of the greatest of all Mysteries, namely, that of Love —God is love— about which questions issues could accumulate and their possible answers would entail new questions in turn, each time more difficult to answer.

Understanding the deepest recess of the Mystery of Love, should such recess exist, would be for man as impossible as understanding the Mystery of God. In which case the Mystery would cease being a Mystery, Love would cease being Love, and God would cease being God, for nothing would exist, then... not even The Nothing. Created love is, however, a participation of infinite Life and Love; that is why created love also *participates* in this infinitude that could be referred to with the misnomer *relative* but which, in any case and in a manner impossible to explain, would be infinitude insofar as love (participated love included) is an unfathomable abyss. For the love created and granted to creatures loses itself at a given moment in the Abyss of Infinite Love, as a river flowing into the sea. Although

---

[28]Saint John of the Cross, *Spiritual Canticle.*

it is also true that, even though both loves *melt* into one, in no way do they *mix*. In reality, they remain the love of God for His creature and the love of the creature for his God, since bipolarity and reciprocity are essential to love: *Because the love 'of God' has been poured into 'our hearts' by the Holy Spirit 'which has been given to us.'*[29] Or, better stated yet: if the love between both is one, it follows that God is always God and the creature is always a creature; the two loving each other and the relation uniting them —indeed the golden number in love is three.

Since we have been reflecting upon the Mystery of Love and its essential components revolving around the concepts *mine* and *yours*, one could ask about the possible precedence of one regarding the other. According to which, the question could be formulated as follows: In regard to the surrender of self that the lover wishes to make to the beloved with the ensuing possession, can one say, perchance, taking into account reciprocity, that the lover desires to become a possession of the beloved, rather than possessing the beloved in turn? Furthermore, no one will doubt that simultaneity *in time* is no obstacle for priority in nature.

Concerning which it seems that the act of *surrender* should be given preference to the act of *reception*. Hence, the lover would first and foremost desire to become a possession of the beloved, namely: becoming the other's possession rather than —or prior to— possessing the other in turn.

In truth the words of the Lord seem to confirm this: *There is greater joy in giving than in receiving.*[30] As for the rest, the Holy Spirit is known as *The Gift*, one among His diverse names. And as for the New Testament texts, they always speak of total surrender,

---

[29] Rom 5:5.

[30] Acts 20:35.

of renunciation, of forgetting and denying oneself, etc. This is a problem which, if viewed from the right perspective, introduces us fully to the rather intricate question of whether love is disinterested or not. For, indeed, what would it mean for man to love God *disinterestedly*? Is it perhaps possible for man to place his surrender to Uncreated Love as something with greater priority or importance than man's desire to possess Him?

The answer, should an answer be found, would have to lead us to the very essence of love. And as always, given that God is Substantial Love Itself and that the love of the creature is but a participation in It, one must depart once more from this fundamental truth.

God is *Disinterested Love* by essence. Hence, created love, granted by God to His creature as participation in His own life, *must also necessarily be disinterested love*. The words of Jesus Christ cited above are conclusive: *There is greater joy in giving than in receiving*. On the other hand, love necessarily presupposes that the lover prefer the beloved to self; therefore, the lover desires the well being of the beloved before that of self, even with scorn of self well being or yet of self if that were possible: *I could pray that I myself might be accursed and cut off from Christ for the sake of my brothers.*[31] Of course, the creature cannot but love and desire God, something which is true above all. Yet, what does it mean to desire God necessarily...? Doubtless, to love Him necessarily, but it is here where the fallacy of those who think in *a disinterested love* of God by the creature lies. Where has it been demonstrated that to love necessarily may involve any constriction whatsoever? For the fact that the creature may feel compelled to love God means nothing else than... the creature loving Him effectively. Yet, *what is to love, except to desire disinterestedly, above all, the well being of the beloved?* To

---

[31]Rom 9:3.

say that someone feels compelled to love by necessity is not only a statement devoid of sense, but also a supposition that would destroy the very essence of love *because nobody may be 'forced' to act freely and voluntarily.* The truth is, however, that there does not exist in the whole Universe something both more free and voluntary than love: *Where the spirit of the Lord is, there is liberty.*[32] The affirmation that love is free by essence and nature is compatible with the fact that Supreme Love draws irresistibly in an act of perfect freedom.[33] In this way, the love of God, inasmuch as it is the most perfect act of love granted to the creature, is by this very reason *the most disinterested act* it has been granted the creature to perform. What the creature longs for when loving God is that *God be*, in such manner that in this sense it would not matter to the creature not to be what it is, even to become anathema if that were necessary. *God is*, Saint Francis of Assisi would indefatigably repeat in the summit of his joy. For the creature, God is before it and God is above all. For indeed the creature prefers God before self so deeply that the creature loves God above self and more than self: *You shall love God 'above all things.'*

To explain the mystery of *selfless love* would involve elucidating another related mystery which is equally impossible to be fathomed by any created intellect. We are referring to the fact that the lover

---

[32] 2 Cor 3:17. The perfect freedom of God, and to some extent that of the blessed in Heaven, is in no way incompatible with their inability to sin. Here, and in many other issues, the error lies with the initial approach, which is really nonsense.

[33] We have said that in perfect freedom, that is, freedom free from the shackles that would have made it deficient, it *does not make sense* to raise the possibility of a *no* to Perfect Love. How could anyone suppose that the possibility of such *no* would be something *better and more perfect* than the fact of not even admitting that possibility? And true love, and especially perfect love, always chooses what is most perfect. It would be impossible to make room in it for an alternative aberrant in nature.

prefers the beloved before himself; which shows clearly that the love impels the lover to go out of himself and go towards the beloved.[34]

These notions also are described in the *Song of Songs*, the Poem of divine–human love; but in a way as only Poetry (divinely inspired in this case) can do it; for poetry reaches levels of depth and beauty which simple prose is unable to reach:

> *A bundle of myrrh is my beloved unto me*
> *Lying between my breasts.*
> *My beloved is unto me as a cluster of henna flowers*
> *In the vineyards of Engedí.*[35]

The outpouring of affection with which the bride speaks, in so far as she can express herself, somehow manifests what the Bridegroom means for her.

---

[34]It goes without saying that Uncreated Love is not moved by anything outside Himself. There is in each Divine Person a reference to the other (or a mutual reference), without going beyond the ineffable simplicity, unity, and infinity of the Divine Essence. Therefore, God cannot want something that He does not possess because it was out of Himself —it would be meaningless. What God loves in creatures, which are distinct from Himself, is the goodness in them which He Himself has granted them as a share of His own. God loves the being and goodness of things which He Himself has placed in them moved by His own good will: *Hence, although God wills things apart from Himself only for the sake of the end, which is His own goodness, it does not follow that anything else moves His will, except His goodness. So, as He understands things apart from Himself by understanding His own essence, so He wills things apart from Himself by willing His own goodness.**

[35]Sg 1: 13–14.

Unde, cum Deus alia a se non velit nisi propter finem que est sua bonitas, ut dictum est, non sequitur quod aliquid aliud moveat voluntatem eius nisi bonitas sua. Et sic, sicut alia a se intellegit intelligendo essentiam suam, ita alia a se vult, volendo bonitatem suam (Saint Thomas, *Summa Theologiæ*, Iª, q. 19, a. 6, *ad secundum*).

Of course, as always, the bride cannot do more than *try* to say what she feels. Therefore, she insinuates things through poetic figures of speech, struggling to say *something* which otherwise she could not express through mere prose. All too often, and more especially on issues related to love, human language cannot go beyond an attempt to *suggest* something of what the soul experiences; a task for which poetry clearly enjoys greater possibilities than plain prose. It is not that poetry is able to say everything. Actually, since man is never able to say *everything that there is* about any of the realities of this world, he is even more powerless to do so in regard to love; he can only hope to stop at the threshold of mystery.

Of course, even poetry, as we have said, cannot but suggest or imply. It is exactly what happens here. Man is not allowed to know in this world the Mystery of Love beyond what he has received as first fruits (Rom 8:23; 2 Cor 5: 2–5). And even those first fruits are too much, since they overflow upon him (Rom 5:5) with a strength that would be impossible to calculate: *non enim ad mensuram dat Spiritum, for God gives not the Spirit by measure.*[36] Hence, poetry itself, which knows quite well its limitations, strives to make use of all its resources: tropes, metaphors, synonyms... only to end up by recognizing its inability to express what it feels, and also admitting that it cannot go beyond what would merely be tantamount to *stammering*:

> *And those who haunt the spot*
> *Recount your charm, and wound me worst of all*
> *Babbling I know not what*
> *Strange rapture, they recall,*
> *Which leaves me stretched and dying where I fall.*

---

[36] Jn 3:34.

Thus expressed himself, once more, Saint John of the Cross in his *Spiritual Canticle*. And indeed, what can the bride do but break into apparent foolishness filled with tenderness? Like comparing the Bridegroom to a *sachet of myrrh*, to end up by saying, in a frenzy of love, that he *rests between her breasts*. It is true that love's poetic language will seem insanity to him who has never felt himself in love. And indeed that language presents some indications which may confirm this statement. At least in the sense that this language recognizes its inability to say what it feels and even its being very far from the realities which it tries to express. Therefore, its terminology seems spoken out of context, irrational, inappropriate, and incoherent.

And since we are dealing with a number of apparent inconsistencies, let us note that the expression *unto me* used here by the bride,

A bundle of myrrh is my beloved unto me,

seems to want to declare, first, the sweet wonder that the Person of the Bride means for her; and then also the fact that such an ineffable Reality, that the Bridegroom *belongs to her*, is hers. And, in perfect reciprocity, she also recognized herself the property of the Bridegroom, as we will say later.

Some may think that the expressions *bundle of myrrh* or *cluster of henna flowers* are but poor metaphors, rather unable to provide much light on the reality of the Mystery to which they relate; which is indeed true. But they forget the essential limitation of human language due to its exceptional poverty, narrowness, and shortcomings to refer to any of the created things. Besides, when it comes to Love, even the language of angels is insufficient, similar to the unfitness of the human mind when it tries to go deeper into this Mystery; which ultimately is none other than the unfathomable Mystery of God. It should also be noted that both characteristic of poetic language, its

uncanny ability to go *beyond* where mere prose can reach and its
undeniable beauty, do not exclude its limitations. At the end of the
day, poetic language, including the one God uses in Scripture, still
remains human language (*Song of Songs*); otherwise it could not be
understood by man.

Moreover, it should be said again, the ubiquitous law of reciprocity in love is present here. The Bridegroom, in turn, equally
feels Himself to be the owner of the bride, recognizing her as His
own, as something that belongs to Him. For the idea of possession,
as stated above, constitutes the very essence of love; hence love
cannot be conceived without (mutual) possession. A study of the
poetic language of the Song of Songs clearly shows these realities,
as evidenced, for example, by the speech of the Bridegroom:

> *I am come into my garden, my sister, my spouse*
> *I have gathered my myrrh with my spice;*
> *I have eaten my honeycomb with my honey;*
> *I have drunk my wine with my milk.*[37]

---

[37]It seems that the traditional mystical doctrine has not insisted enough on the
idea of reciprocal love.

First, the concept of *possession* in this doctrine is often too restricted to the
owning of God by the soul; as if the reaching and possession of God by the soul
were the only important thing, and, therefore, the reciprocal reality would not
matter as much. If this is true and taken to its logical conclusion, it would imply a
unilateral concept of love completely unacceptable in that it would be meaningless.

Moreover, when it comes to highest degrees of union of the soul with God, this
doctrine overemphasizes the *passivity* of the human counterpart: *contemplative
prayer* would be the rain falling heavily from the sky which, unlike the one extracted
with no little work by the water wheel, floods the human soul which cannot do
anything except receive the *gift* from God, etc.

It may be necessary to insist on the idea of *bilateralism* as part of a deeper and
complete sense of love. In addition to which, we must also place more emphasis
on the role of the Person of Jesus Christ, especially through His humanity, in the
relationship of divine–human love.

Again poetry says too many things; many more than those which a cursory reader would be able to appreciate. The kaleidoscope of the mind and heart could be applied to this verse of the *Song*, and to all the others —and in general to any kind of true poetry— to extract from it a multitude of readings. Each one would be filled with an endless supply of suggestions, since no one has managed to spot where the depths of the abyss of Poetry reach. So much so that Poetry comes to life, and the *intuitions* and feelings consequently evoked escape even the perception of its own author.[38]

As any one can see, the Bridegroom stresses, in poetic language (an esoteric language for the uninitiated, those lacking sensitivity, and those with a shrunken heart), that He goes to meet His bride and to what is His: *my spouse, my sister, my garden, my myrrh, my spice, my wine, my milk...* a veritable literary outpouring of possessive adjectives to express satisfactorily that His bride belongs to Him in absolute possession and total ownership. The garden here is, without doubt, the common place where the lovers will meet, once distances have vanished for both of them and the absences have ceased: *I shall no longer call you servants...but I have called you friends...*[39] *After I have gone and prepared a place for you, I will come again, and receive you unto myself; that where I am, there you may be also.*[40] Surely the Bridegroom comes hurrying after hearing the tender and tempting voice of the bride:

---

[38]In this sense, the language of true Poetry shares *quodammodo* the characteristic of the reveled word: always ancient and always new; always actual and alive; it even reaches, somehow, *the dividing asunder of soul and spirit.*

[39]Jn 15:15.

[40]Jn 14:3.

Your sweet words of love to me
Are coverlets weaved with soft threads in tandem
On fields where flowers blow free.
Come to my side, whisper them
Here in my garden of rosebud and linden.[41]

The bride is convinced that there, at last and forever, the two of them will be for each other; so she hastens to prepare the site. The Bridegroom comes, and her very longings will be fulfilled and satisfied at last. The anxious waiting ceased, and the yearning nostalgia ended forever.

Awake, O north wind; and come, thou south;
Blow upon my garden, that the spices thereof
　　　may flow out.
Let my beloved come into his garden,
And eat his most exquisite fruits.[42]

She then promises Him that she will be there, awaiting Him with restless and nervous impatience; looking and watching, in the high and isolated peaks where everything has been left behind and forgotten, to make way for a love that will never be disturbed by anything or anyone:

---

[41] In the Spanish original:

Son tus dichos de amores
como una tela de suaves hilos
en un lecho de flores;
ven a mi lado, y dilos
en mi jardín de rosas y de tilos.

[42] Sg 4:16.

> *There I will be joyful,*
> *There where you robbed me of my life;*
> *There where prideful*
> *The eagle is nesting;*
> *There where everything is forgotten.*[43]

Chapter 10 of Saint John's gospel, concerning the doctrine of the Good Shepherd, is one of the passages of the Gospel in which *possession* appears as an essential ingredient of the typical love relationship, and very particularly of the divine–human love.

It is said there that the Good Shepherd goes before the sheep and calls each one of them by name. And the sheep follow him and know his voice because they are his own sheep: *Et propias oves vocat nominatim... Cum propias omnes emiserit, ante eas vadit, et oves illum sequuntur, quia sciunt vocem eius* (vv. 3–4). The Master also contrasts the Good Shepherd with the mercenary, *qui non est pastor, cuius non sunt oves proprie... quia mercennarius est, et non pertinet ad eum de ovibu. He is not the shepherd, whose own the sheep are not... because he is a hireling, and cares not for the sheep* (vv. 12–13). And Jesus declares that He is the Good Shepherd and knows His sheep, and they also know Him because they are His: *Ego sum Pastor Bonus: et cognosco meas, et cognoscunt me meae. I am the good shepherd, and know my sheep, and my own know me* (v. 14).

---

[43]In the Spanish original:

> *Allí estaré gozosa,*
> *allí donde robaste tú mi vida;*
> *allí donde orgullosa*
> *el águila se anida;*
> *allí donde ya todo se olvida.*

It is noted that, according to the text, the friendship, intimacy, tenderness, and love that spring from the heart of the Good Shepherd to His flock depend on the fact (on which the text insists repeatedly) that they *belong* to Him, they are His own. This distinctive feature, however, puts the sheep at the opposite pole to any imaginable situation in which they could feel themselves subdued. The truth is that they could not be happier because of such intimacy and such tokens of love: the Shepherd goes before them, calls them each by name, leads them to the best pastures...and is even willing to give His life for them, if necessary, at the moment of danger... Who could say then that the condition of belonging to another merely amounts to being subjected and, therefore, in a position of detriment and harm? Did not the Master say that to win and find one's own life one needs to lose it...? Consequently, it is no surprise that the sheep docilely follow their Shepherd, as they listen and recognize His voice with joy; which will never happen when they are led by a hireling, because they know that they *do not belong to him, and, therefore, he cares not much for them* (v. 13).

Obviously, and according to reciprocity —another fundamental law of love which we have mentioned repeatedly here— the Shepherd, in turn, *also belongs to the sheep*. And this interpretation cannot be considered arbitrary, for it clearly follows from the passage. In the words of Jesus Christ Himself, the Good Shepherd gives His life for His sheep: *Bonus Pastor animam suam ponit pro ovibus* (v. 11). Now if He is willing to give up His life for them, and in fact He does, can He then perform an act of greater love and a greater act of *self-surrender to them* (Jn 15:13)? And if He gives Himself to them even to the point of His own death, does this not mean that He becomes entirely their possession? This patent and obvious fact is evidenced over and over again by the Master's very words; for

He establishes the love relationship between Him and His sheep in parallel to the one existing between Himself and His Father: *As the Father knows me, even so know I the Father, and lay down my life for the sheep* (v. 15). The sheep know this fact well, to the extent that only the absence of love could ignore it. They finally have known that, in their mutual relationship with their Shepherd, any component that might be the consequence of a superior–inferior bond has disappeared, because *Henceforth I call you not servants* —the Good Shepherd told them—*but I have called you friends* (Jn 15:15). It is something normal, therefore, that the sheep, unlike the way they would behave toward a hireling, obediently attend to the voice of their Shepherd and get ready to listen and to respond to it with great joy: *The friend of the bridegroom, who stands there and hears him, greatly rejoices because of the Bridegroom's voice: this my joy therefore is fulfilled* (Jn 3:29). In short, the same joy which makes the bride in the *Song* exult with ecstasy:

> *The voice of my beloved! Behold, he comes*
> *Leaping upon the mountain,*
> *Skipping upon the hills.*[44]

Back to our analysis of love relationships, we should remember that the biblical texts are quite expressive. Speaking of men and women at the time of their creation, it is said of them that *the two shall be one flesh.*[45] The union originated in the love relationship of the two, from which married life derives, is clearly expressed by the statement that the two who make it up will become *one flesh.* At the same time, the personal individuality of both of them is also

---

[44]Sg 2:8.

[45]Mt 19:5, quoting Gen 2:24; Cf. Eph 5:31.

evident when it is said in the passage *the two shall be.* In effect, there must be two persons perfectly distinct as such persons for love to exist; two that are even *opposite* to each other, if one wants to apply analogy to the Trinitarian mystery. We are contemplating the self–surrender of an *I* who gives what he is to a *thou* who receives it and who, in turn, gives his own in reciprocity and closes definitively, by so doing, the circle of love.

Unfortunately, when we speak of love among created human beings, theology and even the documents of the Magisterium rarely go deeply into the very essence of its character; and it is not uncommon that they do not value it for what it is: a participation in Substantial Love. Love tends to be reduced to irrelevant topics: solidarity, commitment to others, due consideration for the marginalized, etc; which are only practical and legitimate derivatives of love, if you will, but which remain on love's outward layers, and so far from its original nucleus that they eventually become reduced to nothing. As the waters of an exceedingly long river which become dirtier and less transparent as they move away from their source. It is clear, nevertheless, that a serious and in–depth analysis of love would have led to important conclusions of which the modern world needs to be strongly reminded: such as, for example, the need to recognize the dignity of the human person, the ongoing desecration of the concept of love, along with the oblivion of its essential features and notes, etc.

The text of John 16:15 concerning this subject is conclusive: *Everything that the Father has is mine;*[46] which apparently can be

---

[46] The doctrine about life in the Holy Trinity concerns and illuminates Theology as a whole. Nevertheless, when dealing with love, it is fundamental and of the essence to make reference to this most profound Mystery of Revelation. After all, *God Is Love* (1 Jn 4: 8.16).

interpreted in two ways, though both ultimately come to mean the same thing.

All that the Father possesses has been given to me and, therefore, belongs to me. Or: Everything that I am and possess I have given to the Father.

The latter interpretation, although it may seem more convoluted than the former, is nevertheless correct. And both come to show that in love relationship everything comes down to mutual giving and receiving. So much so that love would not exist should either one of these two elements be absent.

From this it follows that within the Trinitarian life there is a *mine* and a *yours* whose reality is as absolute as the actuality of the Persons from whom they come. The oneness of nature in God is compatible, as is clear from the revelation of the Trinitarian mystery, with the existence in that nature of an *I* and a *Thou* both united by Love. *All mine are thine, and thine are mine,*[47] says Jesus to His Father. Hence *mine* and *thine* correspond here to an identical reality that belongs, however, to *two distinct Persons.* Here perfect reciprocity in love is also demonstrated, because if either of these two concepts, *thine* or *mine* —which as such concepts are different—, would respond to different realities, then an absurd conclusion would ensue: that one of them, either the Father or the Son, would be greater than the other.

It goes without saying that both concepts, *thine* and *mine,* are a mystery as difficult to explain as it is impossible to exhaust the mystery of Love, Who is God (1 Jn 4: 8.16). Had the latter been clarified thoroughly the other two would also have been explained, for the concepts of *mine* and *thine* belong to the very essence of love. Both in turn, as is easily seen from what has been said above, are

---

[47] Jn 17:10.

equivalent to the concepts of *self–giving* and *receiving,* which also constitute the intimate nature of love.

Having established that the two concepts, *thine* and *mine,* correspond exactly to each other, one question still remains: Is it possible to appreciate, despite what we have seen so far, any priority *of intention* or of nature in one of them over the other? The question, contrary to what it may seem, is not idle, since it was the Lord Himself Who said, *It is more blessed to give than to receive.*[48]

In order to achieve a better and deeper understanding of the problem, we should bear in mind that Jesus Christ did not say that the act of giving was more important than receiving, but that *it is more blessed* to give than to receive. Nor should one forget that happiness or joy, far from being identified with love, are but the first result that follows from it (Gal 5:22). I think, unless the teachings of the Magisterium lead us to believe otherwise, that the ultimate end of the human person does not have so much to do with the *Beatitudo,* nor even with *Satiating Contemplation of Truth,* as with the *Possession of God through love*; from which the other two immediately result.

4. Where is made a bold, tentative approach to the daunting problems of the beatific vision and double eschatology necessarily related to the theme of love; along with the no less arduousness issue of the entity of the soul separated from the body.

According to the teaching of the dogmatic Constitution *Benedictus Deus* of Benedict XII, heavenly bliss or *Beatitudo* consists

---

[48] Acts 20:35.

essentially and primarily in the vision of God, which takes place immediately after death (for those who have no need of purification). This is the common doctrine of the Fathers also taught by Tradition, which confirms, again, the doctrine of intermediate eschatology.

As Candido Pozo says,[49] it is curious that the document does not mention explicitly the *love of God* as a component of eternal life. *However*, he continues, *love is implicitly in several sentences of the document.*

For my part, I see no contradiction between the elements which, according to the Magisterium, make up *Beatitudo*, the ultimate end of man. It is clear that some priority of nature should be recognized to the *vision of God*. Without prior perception of beauty and goodness of the loved object there is no possibility of love nor, therefore, of the ensuing beatitude. However, as common logic apparently demands, it seems that the possession and the fruition of God by the blessed *follow* the *vision*. What would be a *vision* that is not consummated, ultimately, in *possession*? Is it possible to limit the bride's desire to only the possibility of contemplating the Bridegroom? Candido Pozo quotes these words of Miguel de Unamuno (*Tragic Sense of Life in Men and Nations*): *A beatific vision, a loving contemplation in which the soul is absorbed in God and lost in Him, appears to be either a self–annihilation or a prolonged tedium according to our natural way of feeling.*[50]

Moreover, according to *Benedictus Deus*,[51] the souls that are in no need of purification, and *immediately after their death... see the divine essence with an intuitive vision and even face to face, without*

---

[49] Cándido Pozo, *Teología del Más Allá*, Madrid, 1980, p. 403.

[50] Cándido Pozo, *op. cit.*, p. 406.

[51] The dogmatic character of this Document of Magisterium cannot be questioned; the teaching, therefore, cannot be changed; but we are not concerned here with this issue.

the mediation of any creature by way of object of vision; rather the divine essence immediately manifests itself to them, plainly, clearly and openly, and in this vision they enjoy the divine essence. Moreover, by this vision and enjoyment the souls of those who have already died are truly blessed and have eternal life and rest...

So far the doctrine is plain, clear and unambiguous. Although we must recognize the need to address several delicate issues which remain unresolved.

The question arises about what theologians call the *dual phase* of eschatology, namely intermediate and final eschatology.

If the souls of the righteous that have nothing to purify, from the time immediately after death, enjoy the vision of the divine essence intuitively and face to face with the consequent fruition, which does the final eschatology add to their bliss?

Ordinarily this issue has been resolved by saying that the blessed are awaiting the resurrection of their bodies. Once this resurrection takes place, when the time for the Parousia arrives, these souls will receive an *accidental* or extensive increase of beatitude or joy.

It happens, however, that in no way the events taking place at the end of History, that is, the Parousia, the Resurrection of the dead and the advent of a *new heaven and a new earth*, can they have a merely *accidental* meaning in History or Economy of Salvation; quite the contrary, because the Resurrection of the dead, the Second Coming of the Lord, the Universal Judgment, the Redemption of creation (that is until now groaning in labor pains), and the advent of a new heaven and a new earth, are essentially important according to both revealed texts and Tradition. It is impossible, therefore, merely to recognize them as purely *accidental*.

There have been many (especially in modern times) that have attempted to resolve the difficulty by assuring that, for the just, the resurrection has already taken place at the time of their death: once the passage to eternity has occurred, temporality does not count, but only timelessness. Others prefer to resort to some psychological explanation which states, as they say, that the separated soul would have no perception of duration.

But what these doctrines actually do, expressly or implicitly, consciously or unconsciously, is to deny the intermediate eschatology. However, both the Resurrection of the dead and intermediate Eschatology are *doctrines of faith*; they cannot be denied or put between brackets.

Candido Pozo, to name one among modern theologians, rightly rejects the explanations that opt for an *accidental* increase of bliss in the final eschatology. However, after dancing around the subject, he is compelled to maintain the transcendence of everything involved in the *Parousia*, and goes for an *intensive increase* of the final beatitude.[52]

Thus the issue remains unresolved. What Candido Pozo actually proposes is *changing the words while keeping the same concept*. To talk of intensive increase and accidental increase is to talk about the same thing, because the former is equally accidental. The difference, for example, between 3 and 1, and that between 5 and 1, is purely arithmetical and therefore accidental. It cannot be considered as an essential difference since it is merely quantitative, and quantity, everybody knows, also is an accident. The problem, as one can see, is not easy to solve. On the one hand, the reality of intermediate eschatology must be maintained; on the other, the no less real transcendental character of the Parousia and the Resurrection of the dead in the Economy of Salvation must be upheld.

---

[52]Candido Pozo, *op. cit.*, pp. 319–320.

Probably there is but one way to find possible solutions to the problem: to explore its relationships, if any, with the equally difficult and delicate issue of the *ontological status* of the separated soul. Saint Thomas, and most of doctrinal tradition along with him, denies personhood for the separated human soul. He establishes his approach on the fact that, while the separated soul enjoys the status of a subsistent immortal being, it does not possess a perfectly complete intellectual nature, in that the soul is destined to be joined with the body.[53]

The problem however, as might be expected, is so difficult and delicate that is gives rise to many questions that have not yet been answered.

It is *de fide* that the separated souls of the blessed, as the papal Bull *Benedictus Deus* clearly teaches, enjoy full bliss in the intermediate eschatology. They see God face to face, which is the contemplation of the Divine Essence, and thus enjoy the ensuing fruition. Moreover, there is no doubt about the dogmatic character of this Bull.

And here is the problem. If separated souls already enjoy in this state complete beatitude, what is it that they may yet lack? What can be added to that *complete bliss*? What sense can there be for such souls to be awaiting the Parousia, which is, moreover, rightly regarded as fundamental? What will these souls receive *by way of addition* when this momentous event arrives...? And we have already mentioned above that to admit an accidental increase of their joy would result in also granting accidental importance to the Parousia.

---

[53]Cf. *Summa Theologiæ*, Iᵃ, q. 29, a. 1, *ad quintum*.

The blessed souls already enjoy the fullness of beatitude during the intermediate eschatology. As *Benedictus Deus* clearly and forcefully states *vident divinam*

   essentiam visione intuitiva et etiam faciali, nulla mediante creatura in ratione obiecti visi se habente, sed divina essentia immediate se nude, clare et aperte eis ostendente, quodque sic videntes eadem divina essentia perfruuntur... But the blessed separated soul is a subsisting being that reasons, contemplates, knows, wants, loves and is loved, and feels such a complete joy as can reasonably be expected once it possesses Perfect Love. What, therefore, is lacking, and what can the waiting for the Parousia mean to that blessed soul?

   According to which, as has been said and amply demonstrated, the blessed separated soul enjoys the qualities of a rational being: it knows, contemplates, reasons, wants, loves and is loved...

   Things being thus, the problem can be posed in the following terms: It appears that these activities, which properly and exclusively belong to a rational individual, *cannot be exercised, therefore, but by a personal "I."* Is it possible to think of a subsisting being who understands, reasons, dialogues, loves and is loved, and who does not hold, however, the condition of a personal *self*...? Should we admit that such an entity, being able to exercise such *rational* (and seemingly exclusively personal) activities, far from being a *who* would have to be considered merely a *what*?

   Aquinas already considered it necessary to improve and refine Boethius' definition of person. Therefore, it should not seem impossible to admit the option of a new approach to the concept of *person*, despite the tremendous difficulties that this task might pose, even if one might finally conclude that it is an impossible mission.

   Perhaps one may attempt, just as a hypothesis, to outline the following conjecture. Since the human soul (even without the body) is capable of such *rational* activities and, of course, love, it can be said therefore that the separated soul is a being *essentially open and capable of self–giving to the other*. Consequently, it may not be too risky to hold that it is a relational being. One must resort to analogy to try to explain this statement.

The three Divine Persons are constituted by so–called *relations*, which actually differ from each other. It is clear that since there are no accidents in God, such relationships are necessarily *subsisting* because they really identify themselves with the Divine Essence, even though they distinguish themselves from that Essence with a mere *distinction of reason*.

Analogically there is a relational character in relational creatures inextricably linked to their created being which, therefore, is not an accident.[54] This relational character is not identified with the creature's essence or nature but with its participated act of being. Such a relational condition set by God as foundational perfection in the creature, and by which it is capable of self–opening to the other, is then inherent to the human soul, whether it is attached to the body or separated from it, to the extent that this relational condition is inherent to the act of being which constitutes the soul *ex nihilo*. The relational condition would be like that perfection which necessarily accompanies the other rational qualities and which would

---

[54]Millán Puelles speaks of the existence of a *transcendental relation*, which is the reference that every created being has towards his Creator. This transcendental relation is not a secondary or adjective element of the creature's nature; it is present in the created substance as one of its fundamental and primary characteristics (Antonio Millán–Puelles, *Léxico Filosófico*, Madrid, 2002, pp. 513–414). Cf. *Summa Theologiæ*, Iª, q. 45, a. 3, *Respondeo*.

constitute self of the rational creature; a perfection which would not necessarily disappear when the soul separates from the body.[55]

Man, created as a person into the image and likeness of God Who is Love, was made to love. This means that he has been destined to forget himself (self–negation) and to give himself, thus establishing a *relationship* with the other and with others: *You made us, Lord, for you...*, said Saint Augustine.[56] Accordingly, man is a person insofar as he has the ability to love (and therefore also to be loved); which is to say that man has the capacity to give as well as receive.

The Divine Persons are constituted by the *Trinitarian relations*. But relations in God are not accidents, for they are really identical to the Divine Essence, in which accidents are unthinkable. Relations in God can not be considered, therefore, within the category of accidents, given that God is Pure Act. Therefore He is never in *potentiality* to love, for He is absolute and perfect *actuality*. Simply put, God *is* love.

Things are different with creatures. To affirm that man has been created *to love*, is tantamount to saying that *being in potency* to love is a constitutive element of his own person. But it is clear that the potentiality to love can only be the *possibility* of establishing relations with others. Or put another way, the possibility of going out of his self in order to give himself; and consequently the possibility

---

[55]The problem of the real distinction of the three Divine Persons despite their identification also real with the Divine Essence, seems to have been a source of confusion for Suárez, who thought he saw in this issue a contradiction with the principle of identity (two things equal to a third are equal to each other). The problem, however, was solved by Saint Thomas with his doctrine of the distinction of reason with foundation *in re* between the Divine Persons and the Divine Essence (*Super Sent.* Lib I, dist. 2, q. I, a. 3, *ad sextum*; *Summa Theologiæ*, Iª, q. 13, a. 4; q. 28, a. 2).

[56]We are obviously referring to the Other as the Supreme Being. Nevertheless, it is clear that man needs to come out of himself to give himself to the other.

of receiving in reciprocity. This means that man, because he is a person, has the potentiality to establish a relationship, which in this case is clearly not an accident.[57]

So the possibility we are discussing here is indeed potentiality. However, since it has been given to man as a constitutive element of his being a person, it must be clearly something more to him than a mere possibility. In fact man is called to make it actual; in such a way, however, that one may even say that he *needs* to... lest his nature be diminished or truncated; *not realized*, if you want to use a more current expression. Of course, man can refuse to love and thereby not to actualize this essential potentiality. In this case, he will not be able to know God (1 Jn 4: 8.16), which is the same as saying that he will not know himself. To say it more emphatically, man will not be able then to know anything at all: *If thine eye be single, thy whole body shall be full of light. But if thine eye be evil, thy whole body shall be full of darkness.*[58]

Consequently, as regards relationship between creatures, it is evident that there must be previously an *I*, capable of actualizing his power to love. For this to happen, the existence of another correlative term, the *Thou*, also is necessary; capable of being loved and making it possible in turn, under the laws of reciprocity and bilateralism proper to love, that the other opposite end, or *I*, be a *Thou* for him; and vice versa. It also must be stressed that *mine* can only exists if there is a *thine*, for love is *self-giving* as much as it is *receiving*, and at the same time.

---

[57]We must take into account that what we are saying has nothing to do with modern theories of Personalism and Phenomenology, which are but an outgrowth of Idealism and therefore end up by reducing the reality of man to nothing.

[58]Mt 6: 22–23. Cf. Lk 11:34; Eph 5:8; Rev 18:23; 1 Thess 4: 4–5; Jn 12:35; 1 Jn 1:6.

Given the importance of this issue and its impact on broad sectors of our society, we should consider now some of its practical aspects.

The considerations just made, although sketchy, show the futility of certain expressions which under the guise of slogans target certain sectors of the faithful, as for example the youth. Some slogans aired in speeches and harangues, like *be yourself* and the like, have no content and even are sometimes incompatible with the doctrine of the New Testament. The truth is that man is never a complete self, according to the maturity in Christ to which he is called, if he does not *lose his life*; if he does not *deny himself* and *come out of himself* to give himself to others. The cluster of topics which often intend to flatter the young are nothing more than a set of vague statements that seem to have no justification other than their *sounding good*. Although if we want to be consistent, we should say that this kind of topic does not sound right. For the simple reason that falsehood can not look good, which is the same as saying that it can not be grasped or perceived as good, except by people prick–eared for lies and inane things. It is true that an empty jar or pitcher sounds better than when they are full, well understood that theirs is an *empty* and *hollow* sound which does not mislead anyone about their lack of content.

As we have been saying, what may the blessed soul without the body still be lacking? It is a dogma of faith that it enjoys beatific vision and fruition of God. But we have already talked about the difficulties that arise when the operations of the soul —intellect and will— are not recognized as referred to a person.

And the answer, as far as it is possible to elaborate one, maybe could be more or less constructed as follows: *As a soul, nothing is missing.* The separated soul is still a subsistent being —although now blessed—, sees God face to face, knows God as it is known by Him (1 Cor 13:12), and enjoys, therefore, the ensuing fruition.

The following observation does not claim to solve the problem. It is curious that the first thing that comes to mind, naturally and logically, when confronted with the text of 1 Corinthians 13:12, is that the Apostle employs both *I* and *we* (in the same verse he uses the singular and the plural); so that he seems to be referring (that is certainly the impression the reader gets) to the human being as a person rather than merely to the *blessed souls*. Of course, the Apostle has the final eschatology in mind, but can it be said with certainty that he intentionally excludes at this time any consideration of the intermediate eschatology? To assume this (which would not make much sense) would mean the rejection of the doctrine of the *Benedictus Deus*.

However, during the state of intermediate eschatology, the blessed soul *is a separated soul and therefore is still waiting for the recovery of its body, though now a glorified one.* Because the human being is constituted as a unity of nature by the union of the two substances which are the body and soul, it must be recognized that, once they are separated by death, man no longer has a complete human nature. This is a strong and safe doctrine that no one apparently contradicts.

The question to pose here is this. According to traditional and safe doctrine, man loses his status as man after death. The body becomes a corpse. The soul goes on living and conducting its own operations as a subsisting being, spiritual and immortal; but it is no longer a person, for it is separated from the body.

The human soul separated from the body is not, therefore, a complete human being; despite which, *it undoubtedly remains being a human soul.* In connection with this the following important question can be asked: things being so, *can it be said that this soul has also lost its personality?* It goes without saying that if we accept Boethius' definition of person, nuanced in turn by Saint Thomas, such as it has been accepted by the common doctrine, the affirmative answer is evident. To say otherwise would face the delicate task of elaborating an alternative concept of person.

Nevertheless, as we have said before, the difficulties derived from denying the separated soul its character as person cannot be put aside. At this point, the least one can say is that this issue remains an open question.

It cannot be denied that the blessed human soul during the estate of intermediate eschatology is indeed missing something, or is waiting for something. What is that something which this soul is missing or is still expecting to receive? Obviously, its body, but now risen and glorified. Without the already transformed body, the blessed soul has not yet become *a complete man fully conformed to Christ*; which is not fulfilled until its flesh is like the flesh of the risen and glorious Christ. For that, and for nothing else, man was baptized: *Know ye not, that so many of us as were baptized into Jesus Christ were baptized into his death?... For if we have been planted together in the likeness of his death, we shall be also in the likeness of his resurrection...*[59] *He shall change our vile body, that it may be fashioned like unto his glorious body, according to the working whereby he is able even to bring all things under his mastery...*[60] *And as we have borne the image of the earthly man, we shall also bear the image of the heavenly one...*[61] *So when this corruptible body shall have put on incorruption, and this mortal body shall have*

---

[59]Rom 6: 3.5.

[60]Phil 3:21.

[61]1 Cor 15:49.

put on immortality, then shall be brought to pass the saying that is written...[62]

The complete restoration of man with his definitively glorified soul and body is a *transcendental* event because of what that means to both History and Economy of Salvation and each Christian in particular: The triumph and final completion at last of God's Plan; the Design which created things, and man as the crown of them all, were placed in Eden to participate and enjoy divine life. This Plan, however, apparently plunged into failure because of the original fall of the first sin... if we can speak of frustration regarding God's plans. The reality, however, is quite different. For not only was the Divine Plan not disrupted; it reached its complete fulfillment and final triumph that had always been foreseen by God: *The mystery which has been hidden for centuries and generations and has now been made manifest to his saints.*[63] It is now that the New Adam is more glorious than the Old, for he has been configured to Christ and has participated in His victory and His glorification: *O felix culpa!* Now at last —once he has been made participant of the existence of the New Adam Who is Christ— man shares everything with Him Who has undergone testing and experienced the cross and has overcome them, with the outcome of the final defeat of the devil. The victory of Christ is now his as well. Man is no longer merely *saved*; through his participation in the existence of the New Adam, and through the grace and strength received from Him, *man himself is now a winner.* Can we say that Parousia, and all of these events which it entails and means, can be regarded as a merely *accidental* event with the rather limited consequence of giving man just an accidental or intensive augment of his blessedness?

---

[62] 1 Cor 15:54.

[63] Col 1:26.

The glorification of the human body, in like manner and according to its model and cause which is the glorious Body of Jesus Christ, together with the redemption of the whole material creation (which is still now suffering labor pains), represent a *transcendental* event, that is, the completion of the History of the Universe; the crowning and ultimate fulfillment of God's Plan for His Creation and of the whole Economy of Salvation: *Then comes the end, when he shall have delivered up the kingdom to God the Father... And when all things shall be subdued unto him, then shall the Son also himself be subject unto the One who has subjected everything to him...*[64] *We are citizens of heaven; from whence also we eagerly await a Savior, the Lord Jesus Christ, who shall change our vile body, that it may be fashioned like unto his glorious body, through the working of the power which he has, even to bring all things under his mastery.*[65] This is the mysterious and benevolent divine plan, foreseen from all eternity and finally fulfilled: *...The mystery of his will, according to his good pleasure which he has purposed in himself. That in the dispensation of the fullness of times he might gather together in one all things in Christ, both which are in heaven, and which are on earth.*[66] Meanwhile, in eager anticipation until the time arrives when the most glorious of all events is carried out and accomplished, *the earnest expectation of the creature waiteth for the manifestation of the sons of God.*[67] The definitive moment will finally have come. The grand culmination of a History in which, *when Christ, who is your life, shall appear, then shall ye also appear with him in glory.*[68] The History of Creation and Salvation of man; the History of the

---

[64]1 Cor 15: 24.28.

[65]Phil 3: 20–21.

[66]Eph 1: 9–10.

[67]Rom 8:19.

[68]Col 3:4.

love of God towards His creatures and of His own glory manifested in them, will have reached at that moment the glorious culmination which had been planned *since before all time.*

Speculating about an alleged *increase*, either essential or accidental, in the bliss proper to beatitude *does not make any sense at all.* Of bliss itself, either essential or accidental, it makes no sense. Talking, for example, about the increased volume experienced by the waters of an ocean when one throws a bucket of water into it would still have some meaning; the augment would be as tiny as you like, but it would always be measurable. But it is difficult to imagine an *increase* —more or less, measurable or immeasurable— in fruition resulting from the contemplation of the infinity of the Divine Essence. The contemplation and fruition of the Divine Essence by the blessed souls will bring about in them, no doubt, a stream of varied and deep feelings for all eternity. But it is almost impossible to assume an *increase* of joy in the blessed souls that are in no need of purification, and *immediately after their death... even before the resurrection of their bodies and final judgment... see the divine essence with an intuitive vision and even face to face... and that once this intuitive and face to face vision, and also its fruition, have been or will be initiated, the same vision and fruition continue without any intermission.*[69]

The Parousia and the Resurrection will certainly imply the consummation of their glory for the blessed souls; which would mean their full identification and configuration to Christ, *with a glorious body like His.* Finally man will be restored to the fullness of his nature and will see himself entirely identified with Christ: a long–awaited moment for the realization of which, according to Saint Paul, the Christian had been baptized. Finally, once his waiting

---

[69]Constitution *Benedictus Deus.*

has finished, he will also be able to know and love through his bodily senses naturally according to his own natural way, even if this way is to be supernaturalized and elevated by grace; which not even in Heaven overrides nature. The possession of their own bodily senses will lead the Elect to know and love the Person of Jesus Christ through His Humanity, albeit this time in a peculiar, specific, and somewhat new way, that is, in a *human manner*, with the quallifications pointed out above. Things being thus, how is it that one is not to consider here an event that undoubtedly is *critical* even for the blessed?[70]

5. Where an attempt is made to recover the rightful doctrinal place for the Humanity of Christ. About the expressionx 'nulla mediante creature in ratione obiecti visi se habente,' of the Constitution 'Benedictus Deus.'

One important issue in connection with what has been said above must be discussed: the way in which the blessed souls see God.

For Revelation, the answer to this fundamental issue is clear. The blessed souls see God face to face and know as they are known. The Constitution *Benedictus Deus*, nevertheless, adds an important qualification. According to the Document, the vision of God that those souls will have takes place without the mediation of any creature by way of object of vision: *nulla mediante creatura in ratione obiecti habente.* Based on what emerges from such a statement an

---

[70]If man is a being essentially composed of body and soul, it is evident that he will not reach his definitive state until he has regained his body; even if beatitude has already been granted to him. He will not think he has achieved his full identification with Christ until he is clothed again with a *glorious body like His.*

important and decisive question can be asked here: What is the role of the Humanity of Christ in that vision, if It plays any?

It is clear that a quick reading of the Document gives the impression that the Humanity of Christ is not necessary in the beatific vision. If one accepts the assumption that the Humanity of Christ, interposed between the Divine Essence and the blessed soul in the beatific vision, plays a mediating role, then this assumption seems to be against the doctrine defined; consequently, one could logically conclude that the Humanity of Our Lord is superfluous (perhaps even an obstacle?) to the beatific vision.

This issue is perhaps more delicate than what it seems; important consequences are derived from accepting or rejecting the logical consequence of the mentioned assumption.

Much has been said about Platonism and Neo–Platonism; the opposition between Dualism and Monism in reference to the nature of man; the suspicion against matter and consequently against the human body; etc. It is known that discussions on the subject have been held since time immemorial, and that their impact, in one way or another, in the form of a more or less clear acceptance or rejection, has survived to this day. It is necessary to recognize, nevertheless, a certain preponderance of Platonism in the History of Christian Spirituality. The great masters, including Saint Augustine and even Saint Thomas, not to mention such great mystics like Saint John of the Cross, allowed themselves to be imbued with Platonism; although this influence is less prominent in Saint Thomas, probably due to his dependence on Aristotle.

However, the theory which maintains that the Humanity of Christ is superfluous to the beatific vision is hard to accept. Not to mention another even more serious possibility: to consider His Humanity an obstacle for such vision. It is common doctrine among mystics, like

Saint John of the Cross for example,[71] regarding the need to dispense with such Humanity once the soul has achieved a certain high degree of contemplative prayer and union with the Divine.

Nevertheless, everything seems to demand the *absolute necessity* of the Humanity of Our Lord with respect to both the beatific vision and, in general, all that has to do with the enjoyment and possession of God in Heaven. This statement, as we shall see, can prove its compatibility with the doctrine defined in the Constitution *Benedictus Deus.*[72]

Those who lived with Jesus Christ and saw Him with their own eyes, they actually *saw* His Humanity and more specifically His Body. At least that was the *direct* object of their vision. But what they actually *perceived* was precisely the *Person* of Jesus Christ; and in It, of course, His divinity: *Philippe, qui vidit me, vidit Patrem.*[73]

This is how the human way of knowing works. When we speak directly with someone who is before us, such as, for example, a friend, we *directly* perceive his body with our corporal senses. In effect, *we do not see his soul, let alone his person.* Yet it is precisely

---

[71]We should refer here to the differences between the spirituality of the Saint from Fontiveros and that of Saint Teresa of Ávila. Hans Urs von Balthasar already alluded (in his *Herrlichkeit*) to the discrepancies between these two great Mystics and Doctors of the Church.

[72]According to Hans Urs von Balthasar, *Even the Church's definitions, though infallible and assisted by the Holy Spirit, do not share this special quality of scripture, for their significance is mostly to put an end to a period of uncertainty, to solve a point of doubt or controversy, rather than to engender a fresh perspective.* Von Balthasar quotes Scheeben's *Dogmatik* (I, 122): *A diligent comparison and reflection on the expressions and indications of holy scriptures affords... a fuller, deeper, and more comprehensive understanding of revealed truth than is given in the authoritative dogmatic teaching of the Church.* Hans Urs von Balthasar, *Explorations in Theology, I, The Word Made Flesh,* San Francisco, 1989, p. 25.

[73]Jn 14:9.

his person whom we perceive, so that we would never think that his body is, with respect to us, *a mediating or interposed object*: a screen or an obstacle of some sort *between us and him*. No one would think that he has been speaking with the mouth or ears of just any person, *but with that particular person*; or that he has seen the face of this or that person, but *that he has seen that person*. Hence the difficulty in considering the Humanity of Christ *interposed* between the blessed soul and the Divine Essence in the vein of a creature acting as a mediating object: *nulla mediante creatura in ratione obiecti vis se habente*.

To dispense with the need of the Humanity of Jesus Christ in connection with the vision of the Divine Essence by the separated soul is a source of major problems; which are even more serious than those resulting from recognizing the compatibility of this need with the teachings of the Magisterium.

First of all, it would be necessary to explain the role assumed by the Humanity of Our Lord in Heaven, after His Resurrection and Ascension, where He has even kept the wounds received during His Passion. Are we to think that, once our redemption has been accomplished, His Humanity would be relegated to the role of producing *some increase* of joy in the blessed? And that, after His Humanity has accomplished the mission entrusted to It by the Father, an accidental meaning is all that is left for that Humanity, as if It were a glorious object, a trophy of victory, to which a place in the house has been assigned for decorative purposes only?

Also, it would be more difficult to explain the permanence of the righteous of the Old Testament in the Bosom of Abraham wherefrom they were not released to enter into heaven until the time of Christ's Ascension, at which moment they did enter together with Him already risen and glorious. The theory of the need of the Humanity of Our Lord to make possible the vision of God facilitates a better understanding of this event, otherwise so fundamental in the History of Salvation.

The scriptural texts seem to favor this interpretation: *No one knows the Father except the Son and those to whom the Son chooses to reveal Him...*[74] *No man comes to the Father but by me...*[75] *The Father is in me, and I in him...*[76] *Without me you can do nothing.*[77] Etc.

Someone might object, and probably rightly, that these texts are not decisive (apodictic) in order to solidly sustain this theory; but it is also clear that they support more than oppose it. The truth is that they seem most favorable to the theory of the necessity of Christ's Humanity for the beatific vision.

The tendency to consider both man as a fallen soul enclosed within a body (which would then be a kind of prison of the soul) and matter as an evil principle, is a mysterious Manichean constant background of human thought which has endured through the centuries. This tendency has rendered possible the aberration of considering the human body, even in the minds of the mystics, as a burden which should be let go as soon as possible.

But the Word of God did not consider assuming a human nature as an infamy: a body and a soul, therefore, which He took entirely as part of His own unique divine *Self*. Saint John uses a strong phrase to express this reality: And *the Word became flesh*;[78] where the term *flesh* does not allow any doubt or leave room for any appearance of Docetism. Moreover, the Evangelist goes on to say that, precisely

---

[74] Mt 11:27; Lk 10:22.

[75] Jn 14:6.

[76] Jn 10:38.

[77] Jn 15:5.

[78] Jn 1:14.

because He was made flesh, *vidimus gloriam eius, gloriam quasi Unigenity a Patre, we beheld his glory, the glory as of the only Begotten of the Father*. It is impossible to detect in this expression any vestige of His Humanity constituting an obstacle for us to *behold His glory, the glory of the only Begotten of the Father*. Also, far from appreciating here any trace of *mediation*, one rather notices that what Saint John has in mind is the belief that, because of His Humanity, we have seen (directly) His glory; the glory of the only Begotten Son, who is the very glory of the Father (Jn 17: 22.24). Similar considerations could be made in regard to the beginning of his First Letter (1 Jn 1: 1–4).[79]

Moreover, the resurrected and glorified Jesus Christ does not seem to think that there is any kind of buffer between His physical body and His *Self*. It is true, as is clear from the revelation of the mystery of the hypostatic union, that the two natures of Jesus Christ (divine and human) are not mixed together, *although both belong properly and equally to the Person of the Word*. In this sense, there is a very expressive text which tells one of the apparitions of the Lord, already resurrected, to the Apostles, who thought they were seeing a ghost: *Why are you troubled? and why do thoughts arise in your hearts? Behold my hands and my feet, that it is I*

---

[79]It is clear that Saint John draws here a line of distinction–parallelism between those who saw the Word of God made Man with their own bodily senses (the apostles and disciples) and those who have known Him only by faith through the testimony given by the former (*ex auditu*). However, he seems to gather both within the same group, as if all of them had been partakers of the same perception and, of course, the same consequent joy (to which the first person plural is referred): *We are writing this to you so that our joy may be completed*. It is difficult to interpret these texts in the sense that the Humanity of Christ merely means something mediating (or even an obstacle!) with respect to the contemplation of the glory of the Only Begotten Son.

myself;[80] a text in which the last paragraph is quite convincing: *Behold my hands and my feet, that it is I myself.*

6. Where the author stubbornly continues to insist on the content of the terms 'self–giving' and 'receiving,' as well as those of 'mine' and 'thine,' for he understands that they are essential to the mystery of love.

Going back to the Lord's words to the effect that *there is more joy in giving than in receiving*, we ought to affirm that they must obviously have a meaning which, as usual, will be deeper than appears at first sight; although not easy to explain, unless the text is read superficially and thus deprived of content.[81] Moreover, with respect to the Holy Spirit, Who proceeds at the same time from both the Father and the Son, the Fathers have a tendency to refer to Him with the notion of *Gift*. To Him also are attributed the source of all graces, fruits, and supernatural gifts that God gives to man. This suggests the existence of a certain *intentional priority* of giving in regard to receiving in the mystery of love; well understood, of course, that full reciprocity and mutual need of both concepts are maintained intact.

According to this, and once mutual reciprocity, correspondence, and equality of both concepts of giving and receiving are granted, is it possible to establish in love some priority of intention of *thine* over *mine*? Or put another way: Is it possible to think of a preference of intention which affects *giving* rather than *receiving*?

_____

[80]Lk 24: 38–39.

[81]One should take into account that we are dealing here with the Mystery of Love, which is as unfathomable as the Mystery of God; both are one and the same.

If the answer is yes, one can explain more easily the fact that the lover thinks of self–giving (oneself) to the loved one before (or rather than) receiving from that person. And Our Lord's words seem to confirm it: *Greater love hath no man than this, that a man lay down his life for his friends.*[82] Jesus appears to be in favor of the option of *surrendering* rather than *receiving*, as is also clear from other texts: *For even the Son of man came not to be served but to serve...*[83] *If I wash thee not, thou hast no part with me...*[84] *I am among you as he that serveth.*[85] The texts therefore, and in general the doctrine of Love, seem to lean rather toward *self–giving* than toward *receiving*.

But it happens that one cannot give or surrender without first having something. No one gives what he does not have. For there to be *thine* there must before be *mine*. Besides, *thine*, according to the lover, is verily *mine* of the beloved; and vice versa. This is true at least in the order of nature, which is different from the order of intentions. And this is the nuclear reality of the play and mystery of love.

Therefore, due to the trichotomy of thine–mine–reciprocity, both biblical and extra–biblical texts about love often revolve around certain versatility; particularly those expressed in poetic language, which is certainly more appropriate in speaking about love. Hence, those texts sometimes clearly and expressly refer to one or the other of the two lovers; at other times, they seem to have an ambiguous meaning, so that they can refer to either one. But in all of them, the concepts of *thine* and *mine* imply each other, so that each gets its meaning because of the other. From which it follows that if there

---

[82]Jn 15:13.

[83]Mk 10:45.

[84]Jn 13:8.

[85]Lk 22:27. Cf. Mt 20:28; Phil 2:7.

is no reciprocity then *thine* and *mine* cannot even be thought as different, independent, and distinct entities constituting a person as such. This could perhaps open up another avenue of research and study of the mystery of the *person* as the subsistent, rational, and perfect being and, at the same time, the most enclosed and independent universe; or as the *I* that also is totally opened to the *other*, without which opening his existence as such *I* would not make any sense. *Mine*, or *I*, is unthinkable without *thine* and *thou*. Thus, the enclosed (or rather *complete*) universe of *mine* is inconceivable without its *opening* to the *thine*. Consequently, the *I* could be considered a person to the extent, and only to the extent, that he be open to the *thou*; likewise, *mine* would be meaningless without *thine*. It seems clear that the created person, made into the image and likeness of uncreated Love, is meant to give his self, be opened, to the *other*: that is the same as saying that the human person was made to love and be loved. According to which, perhaps it could arguably be said that the damned in hell, unable to love in any way, should be considered as mere *beings* rather than persons. In fact, it seems that even the demons have lost their status as persons, as evidenced by the statements of the gospels which refer to them using more often the plural than the singular (or either number alternatively), as if they were part of an undifferentiated *massa*.[86]

Now we understand that the loving dialogue (archetypal) taking place between Bridegroom and bride, as it appears in the *Song of*

---

[86]That the damned have lost their status as persons means here that they have been dispossessed of the nobility and excellence of their beings which set them apart from mere creatures. They in no way cease to be (annihilation). As Saint Thomas puts it, their annihilation is possible, but, in fact, being is more fitting to them than not–being (*Summa Theologiæ*, Iª, q. 104, a. 3–4; *De Potentia*, q. 5, *ad sextum*).

Songs, takes the form of a contest (Sg 2:4) as well as of mutual compliments and flattery; which apparently is a paradox difficult to explain, as anything that has to do with love. The Bridegroom and the bride appear as *two* persons courting each other; which they do, as is normally done, through questions, answers, complaints, praise, apostrophes, and even dithyrambs. In this setting, an *I*, a *Thou* and a *Mutual Relationship* are combined. In Substantial Love these three terms are three really distinct relationships that constitute also three different Persons. And the three really identify themselves with the one and same divine nature.

We can examine some examples that may contribute to a better understanding of the problem. While not forgetting that, ultimately, we face the greatest of mysteries offered to human understanding, the great Mystery of God:

> *The fading of day is fleet,*
> *Dulcet brown goldfinch,*
> *Your songs dwindle faster;*
> *As in a dream bittersweet,*
> *Night comes, we both sorrows meet.*[87]

This stanza is addressed by a person in love to his beloved. The former could be considered as the acting subject and the latter could be imagined, in this case, as a passive subject or the object of the

---

[87]In the Spanish original:

> *El día ya se aleja,*
> *dulce jilguero de color trigueño,*
> *y así otra vez nos deja,*
> *como en amargo sueño,*
> *a ti sin libertad y a mi sin dueño.*

other person's love; although we know that, thanks to the essential element of reciprocity, the relationship could be reversed. In the field of mysticism, this verse should be seemingly attributed to the bride; but we cannot exclude the option of assigning it equally, if necessary, to the Bridegroom. Here, however, conventionally, in order to facilitate its commentary, we will assume that it has been pronounced by the bride.

Thus the stanza could be interpreted approximately as follows. It plays with the idea of the loving possession exerted by the beloved, once the act of total self–surrender out of love has been carried out by the loving person. Although in reality, to be exact, we should be speaking here more specifically of *dispossession*, namely: the lover complains that the loved one did not want to be her owner, for he has refused to accept her as his possession (we put aside for now the possible reasons for 1this). Now we have a new problem: the idea of *possession* is inherent to the concepts of *thine* and *mine*. To be sure, at least with respect to the Divine Persons (ultimate term of reference for all created things), the gospels seem to support this correlation: *Omnia mihi tradita sunt a Patre meo...*, *All things are delivered unto me by my Father...*[88] *Omnia, quaecumque habet Pater, mea sunt, All things that the Father hath are mine.*[89]

The bride would have liked to see herself transformed into the property of the Bridegroom. Instead, it seems that He has decided to disappear, leaving her alone. Nevertheless, she does not give up —why should she?— consequently she longs to go out in search of Him, so that she can be together with the Beloved of her heart:

---

[88] Mt 11:27.

[89] Jn 16:15.

> *...And waiting no longer the bird took to wing*
> *In search of her Bridegroom, her Love, her Dearest,*
> *Leaving forever her comfort, her soft nest,*
> *Without any grief, nor pain, nor sorrowing.*[90]

To insist on not belonging to anyone; not denying oneself; not surrendering one's own life..., is to be condemned to never bearing fruit and to being alone forever *ipsum solum manet, it abideth alone.*[91] Therefore, talking about being yourself, being all one can be, independence, autonomy, emancipation, freedom understood in a worldly way, and so on, is ultimately tantamount to speaking of selfishness and *loneliness,* which are synonymous to those terms. The selfish person ignores the duality *mine–thine* and only keeps *mine,* thus closing himself to any possibility of love.

The bride, on the contrary, feels completely joyful when she sees herself being the property of the Bridegroom; when everything that belongs to her —actually she herself— finally belongs to Him.

> *My beloved is gone down into his garden,*
> *To the bed of aromatical spices,*
> *To feed in the gardens, and to gather lilies.*[92]

The Bridegroom, for His part, by ratifying and corroborating such property and possession, fulfills the happiness of the wife:

---

[90] In the Spanish original:

> *...Y ya sin esperar alzó su vuelo*
> *en busca del Esposo tan querido,*
> *dejando para siempre el blando nido*
> *sin pena, sin dolor, sin desconsuelo.*

[91] Jn 12:24.

[92] Sg 6:2

> *I said, I will go up to the palm tree,*
> *I will take hold of its clusters of dates!*
> *May your breasts be clusters of grapes,*
> *Your breath sweet–scented as apples.*[93]

Let us note the joy of the bride upon seeing herself the *property* of the Bridegroom. For in this case, it is not so much to possess, at last, the Bridegroom as to be His possession. Hence, one can already infer that any attempt by someone to obstinately belong to oneself, or to circumvent the donation of one's life, *is to renounce forever knowing Joy.* And we are here at the antipodes of the way the world characteristically thinks.

Of course, both the Bridegroom and the bride are well aware that they cannot be owned without being at the same time each one owner of the other. And the two of them agree to confirm both realities. We have just seen how they have been corroborated by the Bridegroom, who adds elsewhere:

> *I come to my garden, my sister, my promised bride...*[94]

And also equally the bride, on her part:

> *I am my beloved's, and my beloved is mine.*[95]

If I wash thee not, thou hast no part with me...[96] The Apostle Peter was very far from understanding the secrets and profundities

---

[93]Sg 7:9.

[94]Sg 5:1.

[95]Sg 6:3; 2:16.

[96]Jn 13:8.

of love..., but one thing was sure, that he would sometime: *What I do thou knowest not now, but thou shalt know hereafter.*[97]

Unfortunately, modern man is willing to recognize love as an opportunity to gain mastery over someone, but certainly not as a reason for him be the object to be possessed. He sees himself as capable of possessing, but he is not willing to belong to another. That is why he is incapable of recognizing one essential element of love, namely, the *equality status* of the two lovers. We saw this in the *Song of Songs*, and we could see it again in many places in the Gospels. Also, we should remember this passage of the Apocalypse: *Behold, I am standing at the door, knocking. If any man hear my voice, and opens the door, I will come in to him, and will sup with him, and he with me.*[98]

If we ascend through analogy to the first Source and Origin of all love, we realize that, within the Trinity, the Father loves the Son *because the Father sees in Him His exact and same Image.* And the same happens between the Son and the Father: *Ego et Pater unum sumus.*[99] Created or participated love can claim only an equality mediated by analogy; for it is the case that, in one way or another, *if there is not a certain level of equality, there can be no love.* It was Love Who made God to be able to take to Himself a human life, and Who gave man the ability to become a partaker of divine life. God became human out of love so that man, also through love, may become divine: *Henceforth I call you not servants, but I have called you friends.*

---

[97] Jn 13:7.

[98] Rev 3:20.

[99] Jn 10:30

7. Where the author finally discusses some futile considerations about the Golden Age.

The Great Liar and Father of all Lies who is the Devil, Satan, has not only managed to plunge the world, and in particular the Church, into the most severe crisis ever known in their history, he has also succeeded in presenting this crisis as the Era of the highest splendor and grandeur that Humanity has so far experienced. In the modern World, and more specifically within the Church, it is held as something indisputable that this present moment in History is an irreversible stage of light and progress, with no importance given to some minor, still–lingering shadows because it is assumed that they are on their way out. Their disappearance will finally happen —it is said— at the very moment that the widely proclaimed and universally praised Universal Peace, which seems to be so imminent, is imposed everywhere. We are, at last, on the threshold —practically almost within, according to many— of the state which human beings have been craving for millennia: *The Golden Age.*

On this point, however, there is still one sole discrepancy between the Church and the World. While the latter, as we have said, admits the stubborn persistence of some minor shadows —but those which are already about to fade away— the Church, on the contrary, in her optimism, goes beyond the World: on her horizon, as far as her life and development are concerned, there is no cloud to hinder her sunny brightness, which has lasted until this historic moment. The Second Vatican Council, and even more so its aftermath, has marked the zenith of a History which during centuries has witnessed a great number of vicissitudes —although unfortunate events have been predominant—, but which now sees a splendor and maturity that many consider a veritable Grandeur.

Of course, as always happens in all the events that mark human existence, and despite this alleged optimism *universally agreed to*, there are still some voices that proclaim their disagreement regarding such euphoria. Of course, it is an insignificant number of non–conformists, whom, moreover, the powerful sound of the *media* takes good care to silence. It does not matter that facts appear sufficiently evident, patent, and notorious and speak entirely in favor of such dissidents. It has been said above that we face the great Golden Age, wisely assembled and led by the Grand Liar. Probably not even Lenin himself (a great disciple and ardent supporter of the Father of Lies) was aware, when he said it, of the enormous force of the slogan that he invented and also ordered to disseminate and put into practice, according to which, *if facts are against us, too bad for the facts.*

If we restrict ourselves to the circles within the Church, it soon becomes obvious, to whoever wants to see it, that facts do not follow any logical consequences of the so–much–heralded post–conciliar *Golden Age* —to the extent that they almost seem to run in the opposite direction; which would certainly surprise anyone who is not aware of the power of seduction, of farce, and of the histrionics that The Lie has.

It is an obvious fact that what was the Christian West has become de–Christianized. Or at least it is obvious to people who honestly want to recognize the truth. It is also obvious and patent that Christianity (and here we refer especially to the Catholic Church) has been emptied of supernatural content and that a large number of Christian people, consciously or unconsciously, have stopped believing.

There are many Bishops who seem incapable of preaching the Gospel. Silenced by their cowardice, moved —many of them— by their financial interests, dedicated to adulation for no other reason than that of climbing posts or keeping their *status quo* undisturbed, they have become collaborators of the System and have forgotten the mission they were being called to fulfil. Meanwhile, the Christian People have ceased to practice the sacraments, have lost faith in the Eucharistic Real Presence, have been confused regarding the sense and significance of the Mass, have lost sight of the importance of the role and necessity of the Hierarchy within the Church, have forgotten about the notion and sense of sin, and consequently, have stopped thinking about the need for penance. If that were not enough, the great masses of the Christian People have been induced to believe that Morality is a mere relativism in which each one depends upon self–will, only to become stripped of all consideration toward the meaning of values (both natural and supernatural). If we must cite some concrete results, one could speak, for instance, of the almost total abandonment of attendance at Mass, of the neglect of the practice of confession, of the emptying of seminaries and novitiates and of the total depreciation, and almost disappearance, of the consecrated life. And thus follows a long etcetera upon which it is not worthwhile to insist.

Meanwhile, Pastoral practice seems to have adopted *drama* as its main instrument. Theatrical *demonstrations* happen frequently, regarding both small domestic liturgy in parishes and extraordinary assemblage in *fare–stage* or great show liturgy. It is not easy, on the other hand, to understand well what the pretension may be with these puppet–show liturgies, even presupposing the good intention of many of them. Since in the *fare–stage* and great show the *media* collaborates assiduously, the goal appears to be that of triggering feelings among the faithful —maybe with the idea of preventing the apparition of a consciousness of crisis or of creating a sensation of

euphoria and triumphalism favourable to certain situations. One
way or the other, an excessive worry regarding whether such feelings have supernatural content or whether they lead or not to the
fomentation of Christian life does not appear to exist. The issues of
welfare and human relations have displaced the Gospel in preaching,
to the point in which Theology has been reduced to Sociology and
Politics: *They are from the world; that is why they speak according
to the world, and the world listens to them.*[100] Although Jesus Christ
had already said this clearly: *whoever is from the earth, belongs to
the earth and speaks as one from the earth.*[101]

It is appropriate to make an observation that could be important regarding these texts, for if the existence of Pastors who *speak
according to the world, for they themselves are from the world* is already a distressing fact, the statement that *the world listens to them*
is no less worrisome. Doubtless, this last observation refers to the
Christian People, or the great mass of those to whom the preaching
of the Word should be addressed: a People who listen to Falsehood
knowing of its Falsity, since they have already chosen beforehand to
turn away from the Truth.

It is understood that all this is but the tip of the iceberg, since the
enumeration could extend itself quite a bit more, even pointing to
situations and hypotheses graver than those indicated here. However
sometimes it is not possible, or expedient, to uncover the wound too
much, perhaps for a number of varied reasons, among which one
should not forget the delicate state of the patient.

Nevertheless, it is a firmly admitted belief in the world of Catholicism that the authentic *Springtime of the Church*, or the true *Golden
Age* of a triumphal resurgence that has replaced a Dark Age at last

---

[100] 1 Jn 4:5.

[101] Jn 3:31.

happily forgotten, has arrived. And woe to him or those who dare to raise the slightest objection regarding this belief, since they will be treated as traditionalists, fundamentalists, conservatives, enemies of progress and of looking forward, nostalgic, unsupportive, preconciliar and even enemies of the Council, if not of suffering from an acute tendency to paranoia. The least attempt from these unfortunate ones to defend themselves will not achieve anything but will rather confirm their state of proximity to insanity. In the great epoch of *Dialogue*, its greatest advocators are not willing to establish one with those who do not share their *monologuing* way of proceeding.[102]

The fact that the crisis suffered by Catholicism, undoubtedly the most serious throughout her history, has been able to be presented and unanimously accepted as the Springtime and *Golden Age* of the Church is an evident proof of the incredible seductive power of the Great Deceiver: Iniquity has turned to goodness; destruction, to progress; cooling of the faith, to rejuvenation of religion; and falsehood, to truth. The annihilation of the faith and the retirement of the Magisterium are considered as the cure–all regarding the evils of the past, and as the elixir of youth for the future of a Church that hitherto —or so they say— struggled among the throes of decadence and senility.

That the situation to which we are referring was made possible is one of the mysteries of History. Perhaps God has allowed it in

---

[102]It is clear that *to look back*, even occasionally, also offers advantages. First and foremost, it is well known that *Histoiria est magistra vitae, History is the teacher of life*. Secondly, though not least, you can not forget the fundamental value that Tradition represents regarding the content of Christianity and the life of the Church: *Nihil innovetur nisi quod traditum est, Let nothing be innovated upon; accept what has been handed down* was the famous dictum of Saint Vincent of Lerins which has been accepted without question for so many centuries.

view of the metamorphosis of Christian life into paganism. That is why the words of the Apostle are current, and more poignant and relevant than ever: *What fellowship has light with darkness? What concord has Christ with Belial?*[103] Nevertheless, the *reverse* phenomenon seems to have occurred, but without any harmony or having anything in common: it just happened that darkness has replaced light.

Then is there no hope for the *pusillus grex, small flock?* Of course there is, but only because now is precisely the time for hope and confidence in God. The suffering and prayers of the tiny flock will not go unanswered: *And will not God revenge his elect who cry to him day and night, though he bear long with them?*[104] *In the world you will have sufferings, but be confident; I have overcome the world.*[105]

The Golden Age, projected into the past or allegedly made real in the present, is nothing more than a tremendous lie. But, some day in the future it will become a reality —although not now and never before the second and definitive coming of the Lord: *We look for new heavens and a new earth according to his promises, in which justice dwells.*[106] The Golden Age, whether we try to make it real in the present or we believe that is has been accomplished in the past, is only a Utopia. But if, according to Saint Peter, justice will finally dwell in that Joyful Age that is yet to come, then the Apostle recognizes that *now there is no justice among men.* And the same happens with Jesus Christ, as we have seen before, Who also promises that at the appointed time He *will avenge his own elect.*

---

[103]2 Cor 6: 14–15.

[104]Lk 18:7.

[105]Jn 16:33.

[106]2 Pet 3:13; cf. Rev 21:1.

Therefore, we cannot try to find now those things that have been promised us for a future time.

That is why the Christian lives always with an eye to the future, which is the same as saying that he lives on hope. And because the present time, *to the extent that it outlines and decides the future,* is decisive for him, the Christian cannot fall into past utopias, much less into those utopias which claim that they are destined to shape the present time. Hence, those who attempt to make a Christianity that is *only good for this world* because they do not believe in another are terribly mistaken. They no longer raise their eyes to Heaven because they believe that they have reached the end of the road, when, in reality, they are still at a provisional inn.

In the future and authentic Golden Age, of course, contrary to what Don Quixote said in his speech, there will continue to exist *mine* and *thine*; but then more real than ever because both are part of the content and essence of love; the very love that has always existed and that one day was given to men as a present, so that it would fully fill and flood human existence for all eternity.

The Golden Age is indeed a reality, but a future one. That is why the Christian lives with a hope and an impatience which become a longing for the One Who is to come: *Qui est et qui erat et qui venturus est, He who is and who was and who is to come;*[107] therefore he cries: *Come, Lord Jesus!*[108] The Apostle, in a text which evidently refers to the Parousia, interprets the coming of the future Age as the moment when the definitive glorification of the One Who is to come takes place: *Cum Christus apparuit, vita vestra. When Christ appears, and He is your life...,* along with our own glorification: *tunc et vos apparebitis cum ipso in Gloria, you will*

---

[107]Rev 1:4.
[108]Rev 22:20.

also appear with Him in glory.[109] Then, and only then, *the fulfillment and definitive completion of God's Plan, which had been established and determined since eternity* will take place.[110] In the meantime, said the Apostle, *if ye then be risen with Christ, seek those things which are above... set your affection on things above, not on things on the earth.*[111]

This last exhortation encourages the Christian to live in *tension*: are created things to be despised... are we facing again the *contempt of the things of this world*?

All created things are good. God made them as a wedding present beautifully arranged for the bride. Without them, the bride would not be able to offer them, in turn, to her Bridegroom. How else would she be able to surrender everything out of love? Or to become totally poor if she had not first been surrounded by riches? In every relationship of love, poverty is never an *a priori* condition, rather poverty is a situation which has been *voluntarily sought and willed* (a *virtus*) and through which he who loves surrenders everything to the beloved person.

If things were not good and beautiful, or their language were not similar to that of the angels, they could not be a mirror image of their Creator, and then they could not serve us as a reminder of Him, nor could they speak to us about Him. We can turn them into

---

[109]Col 3:4.

[110]Thus the Parousia does not refer so much to what could be accidental or essential increases of Beatitude as the ultimate goal of man, as to the supreme and ultimate glorification of Christ; and also the glorification of man, definitely identified with Jesus now also in his body. And also the glorification of the whole Creation, which has been suffering the pains of childbirth until this final moment of its total liberation: This is, nothing more and nothing less, the *transcendental* meaning of the Parousia.

[111]Col 3: 1–2.

an offering made out of love (including our life and death along with
them) only to the extent that they have been given to us.

> *There is in our orchards an abundance of all kinds of delightful*
> *fruits;*
> *The new and the old, my beloved, that I have kept for you.*[112]

---

[112]Sg 7:14.

VIII

THE GREAT TEMPTATION

(AMAZING STORIES)

Several years ago, the American producer–director Steven Spielberg produced a relatively successful television series entitled *Amazing Stories*.[1] Rather than amazing, these *Stories*, which actually suffered from a depleted imagination, should have been called implausible and even impossible to be believed. One clearly saw that they could not be real. The worst part was that since it was not possible to believe them in any way, these stories immediately ceased to be amazing. Why would anyone be astonished at what is known to be only fiction and a mere product of the imagination? It is clear that for something to be truly amazing it must be, above all, *real*; after that, it must be extraordinary, not recurrent, or never seen before, unusual, difficult to explain or to equate to the ordinary or commonplace, something which may cause admiration and

---

[1]They are available in DVD format, released through *Universal Studios*.

fascination, etc. It happens, however, that these characteristics of what makes something really amazing tend to be minimized, for the simple reason that people cannot believe things that really are amazing.

We can admit, surely against general opinion, that truly amazing stories are always real; for the reason that reality far surpasses the human imagination; which, when it wants to walk the paths of the fascinating and portentous, is forced to resort to the unreal and the fake. This is a deplorable mistake, since it is sufficient to look closely at the real world, if one has (at to some extent) first learned to delve into the depth of being, to perceive truly amazing consequences and results. But ordinary human beings, in general, consider themselves content with a superficial looking at the sea, without at all considering the waters beneath the surface.

The most painful thing about this matter is that the truly amazing stories —precisely because they are real— are usually not believed by most people; either because they have never learned to see the world and reality in depth, or because they are unwilling to accept conclusions which, although true, can contradict a human existence that does not want to confront its own reality. Complete truth (Jn 16:13) is often the privilege of the few. As for the world, it does not know the Spirit of Truth, neither is it willing to receive Him (Jn 14:17). Not uncommon is the human attitude according to which the greater the abundance of truth, the less willingness there is to receive it: *The light shines in darkness but the darkness did not comprehend it.*[2]

This said, we can anticipate that the story, or stories, to be told here will not be believed by virtually anyone. Does it make sense then to insist on telling them? Frankly, it is hard to know. At any

---

[2]Jn 1:5.

rate, it may be worth trying, although it is impossible to guess the practical consequences that may result from this endeavor. Jesus Christ often spoke with full awareness of the ineffectiveness of His discourse, even knowing that it was only going to cause the perdition of many: *If I had not come and spoken to them, they would not have sin. But now they have no excuse for their sin.*[3] However, given what human nature is now, and according to what is happening in the History of Salvation, it seems that *voices that cry in the wilderness* are also necessary.

What is going to be told here is truly incredible and, of course, amazing. This means that it is absolutely real, although no one, or hardly anyone, will want to admit it. Which is explicable to some extent, because it affects many personal interests that are at stake, and also because it is prone to stirring up deep and delicate human feelings.

It's amazing, for example, that huge set–ups, capable of stirring up enormous amounts of money and power, can appear before the world as archetypes of heroism and sacrifice, namely, of poverty, sacrifice, human solidarity, self–giving to others... without raising any surprise in anybody's mind. Or that the caricatures of the most sublime and lofty Christian virtues (poverty, heroic charity, humility, sacrifice) are being dramatized on the world's *stage* and acclaimed to the sound of fanfare and considered as authentic and even as the paradigm of true holiness... and yet no one seems to raise any objections. Or that certain Spiritual Families, created to defend Catholicism and to spread the Faith according to the intentions of their founders, find themselves involved in the handling of political, often turbid, interests, and controlling huge business investments, while being blessed by the media; and that they end up promoting

---

[3] Jn 15:22.

purely naturalistic doctrines which are utterly alien (if not hostile) to Christianity... and yet no one raises a wee complaint or the slightest protest. Or that the means and methods of Evangelization, as proposed by the New Testament, have been forgotten, only to be replaced by others whose practical philosophy, besides being purely naturalistic and often mundane, is completely alien to the teachings of Scripture... whose disastrous results don't seem raise alarm or concern in anyone. Or that the Church, after twenty centuries of constantly establishing, by divine right, the doctrine of the indissolubility of marriage, has accepted divorce (although it has been given a different name). Or that the immense crisis the Church has been suffering during the last fifty years, which is arguably the worst in Her history, is unanimously considered as nothing less than the *Springtime* of the Church.

Clearly, all these things and many others are quite able to amaze. Undoubtedly, however, the most amazing thing of all *is the fact that they do not arouse amazement!* Here we will discuss only one of them. Not because it is the most serious or the most important, but because this one is to such an extent the consequence of the most subtle and deceptive of all the temptations that almost always tend to go unnoticed by even the most enlightened minds. While it may be said that it is difficult to detect its origin, it is even more so in regards to acknowledging its consequences, or that one has been the victim of its deception. All seems to indicate that some of the most brilliant characters of the Church's Calendar of Saints have succumbed to it; although their giving way was never attributed to their guilt or implied an attenuation of their holiness.

Although later we will address the issue of potential liability, which is imputable to external circumstances directly connected to a particular historical moment rather than to particular persons, it is good to put forward that we are not going to question here the merits of those who have been raised by the Church to the honor of the altars. Actually the problem occurs mostly because of the peculiarity of this temptation, and also —why not say it— because of the serious consequences that it can bring about.

This temptation, in addition to not appearing as such (which is normal in all sorts of temptations), in this particular case coats itself so gloriously under the guise of virtue that it is almost impossible to detect it (which is not so common). And that is why we consider it *extremely subtle.*

Of course, evil always presents itself under the appearance of good; and falsehood always adopts the guise of truth —a servitude to which both are forced to submit, but that is what makes it possible for men to accept them. But the case of which we speak is different. And it is this difference which we are going to deal with in the present chapter.

1. From this it follows that the death of a human being can be as expressive, at least, as his life has been.

We can almost ensure that the most exciting moment of the great adventure of Don Quixote is his death. Battered and beaten, our hero, back home again and already with his wits recovered, abhors his past madness:

> *"Good news for you, good sirs, that I am no longer Don Quixote of La Mancha, but Alonso Quixano, whose way of life won for him the name of Good. Now am I the enemy of Amadis of Gaul and of the whole countless troop of his descendants; odious to me now are*

*all the profane stories of knight–errantry; now I perceive my folly,
and the peril into which reading them brought me; now, by God's
mercy schooled into my right senses, I loathe them."*

....

*"Sirs, not so fast, said Don Quixote, 'in last year's nests there are
no birds this year.' I was mad, now I am in my senses; I was
Don Quixote of La Mancha, I am now, as I said, Alonso Quixano
the Good; and may my repentance and sincerity restore me to the
esteem you used to have for me..."*[4]

And so ended the dreams and enthusiasm of Don Quixote, now
mere nostalgia and memories; and, with them, his desire to undo
and destroy the multitude of wrongdoings and outrages that are
loosed in the world.

*I, master barber, am not Neptune, the god of the waters, nor do I
try to make anyone take me for an astute man, for I am not one.
My only endeavor is to convince the world of the mistake it makes
in not reviving in itself the happy time when the order of knight–
errantry was in the field. But our depraved age does not deserve
to enjoy such a blessing as those ages enjoyed when knights–errant
took upon themselves and placed on their shoulders the defense of
kingdoms, the protection of damsels, the succor of orphans and
minors, the chastisement of the proud, and the recompense of the
humble.*[5]

The ill–fated and pestiferous books of knight–errantry have received a tremendous and well–deserved beating, rather a *coup de
grace*; but there is still something that seems to have eluded the

---

[4] *Quixote*, II, 74.

[5] *Quixote*, II, 1.

analysis of the scholars. One can still wonder whether this gibe means simply the end of knight–errantry books or if it can also do away with something else.

It is difficult to know whether Cervantes was totally aware that, along with the end of such bibliographic monstrosities, his work also certified the end of a Legend; and a beautiful Legend at that, according to which the multitude of wrongdoings, outrages, and injustices which fill the world could be thwarted by the actions of some kind of Knight–Errantry.

But, was it really a Legend, or was it simply a wonderful dream? Irrespective of whether or not —at least for the time being— that dream had the possibility of becoming a reality.

We know that Cervantes did not solve the problem; very probably he was not even aware of its existence. As for us, we must admit that, at first sight, we would readily reject the Legend: no Knight–Errantry would be able to put an end to the enormous pile of injustices that roam throughout the world.

Nevertheless, there are too many ideologies willing to think otherwise, despite the abundant number of objections that could be raised. Let us consider, to name only one which may be the closest to us and the most current, the *Marxist Paradise*, designed for this world and in which so many deceived people still believe. The fact that this madness has found universal acceptance could have become one of the great mysteries of History; had it not been for Theology, which with its contribution to the knowledge of human nature has provided a good number of answers. But this is not the aspect of the problem which we are going to discuss here.

Accordingly, to what was stated above, the attempt to put an end to the injustices and the evil of this world, as Don Quixote intended to do in his own way, should it be construed as a chimera, doomed beforehand to failure?... Or perhaps as a new utopia which, properly speaking, is but another Legend?

If one answers yes, then one must accept the fact that there is no explanation for the purpose of the Incarnation; it would also be impossible to understand Saint Paul's statement to Timothy: *God wants all men to be saved and to come to the knowledge of the truth.*[6] The adventure of Don Quixote seems indeed outlandish, but *never because of the enthusiasm that animated it.* The fact that people have been able to portray this adventure as crazy is due to nothing other than the *wrong approach of the motives which propelled it, as well as the lack of consistency in the means employed to carry it out.* You may say what you want about the contention that Knights Errant have never existed outside the hapless books about knight–errantry; or about the anachronous task that Don Quixote tried to accomplish; or about the weakness and insufficiency of the means for his quest; and about many more things —all of which bring us to the focal point of our problem: namely, what can happen when the means employed to perform a task are inappropriate, useless, or even unsuitable, or when the motivations that serve as encouragement for the enterprise respond for the wrong reasons.

2. Where it begins to explain the reality that, as happens in Hell, Heaven is also full of good intentions.

The question we are dealing with becomes complicated when Evangelization is the task at hand. Of course, the claim that *one must evangelize at all costs* is not admissible.

---

[6] 1 Tim 2:4.

First, because that would not conform to God's wishes —at least, that is what seems to be gathered from Revelation.

Secondly, because it would be neither practical nor proper; centuries–long experiences have amply demonstrated that such an attempt would be useless.

"Go ye, therefore, teach all nations, baptizing them in the name of the Father and of the Son and of the Holy Ghost; teaching them to observe all things whatsoever I have commanded you.[7] This is the command of our Lord; therefore, so far, everything is clear and there is no problem.

But as often happens with missions too broadly worded, there remains the task of finding ways to implement them —an enterprise that can be difficult and risky, since an error in the choice of the means can lead to disastrous results; as in our case which, no doubt, is the most important and momentous of all human endeavors.

Before proceeding we must first undo three misunderstandings that could lead to confusion.

First, it must be noted that, although the principle of Christian morality according to which *the end does not justify the means* constitutes the essence of the problem, this principle is not going to be considered here as the direct object of our reflection.

The second explanation has to do with the so–called *self–evident truths*. Traditionally, as is known, Hell has been designated as the place of good intentions, no doubt influenced by the proverb stating that *the road to Hell is paved with good intentions*. Of course, it is not a matter of doubting the veracity of the adage; we just want to remember the fact, somewhat forgotten, that Heaven is also filled with benevolent intentions; as we will show in this chapter.

---

[7]Mt 28: 19–20; cf. Acts 1:8.

The elimination of the third misunderstanding, though, is the most urgent of all. First, because it is the most difficult to detect, and, hence, it *almost always* goes unnoticed by even the shrewdest minds; and also —probably due to that difficulty— because it is fairly widespread; most particularly, curiously, in certain circles from which this misunderstanding needed have been completely erased. We refer to the existence of human intentions which can be at the same time (or at least so it seems) as honest and sincere and just as they are wrong and misguided and misdirected. The most interesting thing is that these kinds of intentions, which in no way constitute a *rare species*, are also in Heaven —we mean, of course, that they came alive once when practiced by people who are now living in such a blessed place. And something even more surprising: despite their being welcomed into the Heavenly Halls (and no one would dare to consider it unfair), and despite the goodness that once drove their intentions (after all, they were good intentions), *even so, these intentions brought, and still bring, about disastrous and counterproductive effects*. Which is logical, after all, if you consider that error, even though it may not be always found at fault, is nevertheless an error. And it never happens that falsity produces anything good.

No one can doubt that the phenomenon of good (although misguided) intentions is also frequent in the Church; here we are interested only in their influence on the Spiritual Families that have, over time, emerged in Her bosom.[8] And here is precisely where the

---

[8]We use here the generic term *Spiritual Families*, without being more specific, for sheer convenience. We include in it the various groups of faithful, religious or secular (Orders, Congregations, Institutes, Prelatures, Communions, Associations, etc.), approved and canonically erected by the Church according to the Constitution, Statutes or By–Laws of each of these groups. The purpose of these Societies of the faithful is twofold: first it points to the common life (in general) as a means of greater and easier sanctification; on the other hand, it seeks to achieve the particular goals peculiar to each Family regarding the Gospel.

surprise of some and the outrage of others begin. Indeed it seems, judging by appearances, that the works of evangelization carried out by these Families have been animated by an erroneous political philosophy... with disastrous and logically expected results.[9]

Spiritual Families have been established in the Church with a view towards the highest end —how could it be otherwise?—, which is the sanctification of its members and Evangelization: general motivations which then have to be translated according to the specific purposes and charisms of each Family. At the same time, they must also receive the appropriate sanction from the Church (without which they lack legitimacy), who is the one to recognize the authenticity of the charisms received by the respective founders. The reason for their number and diversity is based on the fact that the Church, because of the richness and depth of the Gospel's teachings, admits the possibility of the existence of different and varied paths to carry them out: *In my Father's house there are many mansions.*[10] And here is where the opportunity and advantage of the various distinct charisms come into play.

And it is also here, of course, where problems start. After the Incarnation and once the work of our Redemption was accomplished, Evangelization has been given the task of bringing that work to fruition, which God wanted to entrust to men (Mt 15:24; 24:14;

---

[9]It must be taken into account that we do not try to make here a thorough study of the problem, neither historical nor theological. We simply outline some considerations rather general in character and eminently pastoral in purpose. This issue was addressed (although also superficially) in A. Gálvez, *Commentary on the Song of Songs*, Volumes I and II., Shoreless Lake Press, NJ, 2000 and 2006. For details on this subject, see especially Volume I.

[10]Jn 14:2, interpreted in a wide sense as Doctrine has frequently done. One must admit that the Church usually shows, regarding this issue, a broader and deeper vision than that which the Spiritual Families habitually display.

28:19) as the most important, risky, and difficult of all tasks. Any wavering or hesitation in carrying it out or any error in the methods used will lead to results that can qualify as disastrous —to give them a name.

Once Spiritual Families have been born and sanctioned, their development and expansion begin; which, generally speaking, take place in a rapid and successful manner. Based on a charism supposedly firmly established in the Gospel, and taking also into account the sincere love for God and enthusiasm which usually adorn the personality of the founders, it is not surprising that the number of disciples soon increases. We can consider this initial stage a triumphant one, for true problems have not yet surfaced. Generally speaking, this is a *stage of the offensive approach* and of easy conquests.[11]

It should be noted, however, before proceeding further, that these considerations are not intended as a negative criticism of the Spiritual Families that through the ages have appeared within the Church. Some have been for her a veritable crown of glory and a bright firmament of Saints, as well as an inexhaustible source of goods (natural and supernatural) for mankind. The intended rationale here has no purpose other than to draw attention to certain risks that threaten Spiritual Families and that, despite their imminent dangerous character, seem to go unnoticed.

Similarly, these reflections have no consideration other than the spiritual benefit to men of good will who so desire it. In no way do they try to judge people; moreover, we have no objection to assum-

---

[11] This is not always the case, as we shall soon see. It is certain that the moment chosen by the Devil to carry out his *counter-offensive* has been carefully planned; it will depend on various circumstances, among which one cannot rule out his will to allow (and even encourage) a rapid expansion... with a view, of course, to precipitate the onset of the first difficulties. We shall soon talk about it.

ing a hypothetical good will in all and sundry. These reflections will try to adhere strictly to the facts. Only God judges with complete truth and absolute certainty; whereas the historical judgments of men, like it or not, will always be subject to some uncertainty and to the possibility of review.

Unfortunately, it cannot be said that Spiritual Families are much in favor of self–criticism, and even less of the negative assessments carried out by strangers —which is an attitude easy to understand, given the condition of human nature, though it is not always justified. We cannot deny the possibility of the existence of assessments and judgments of facts made in good faith, even though they may be painful and onerous because they respond to situations not easy to understand. The fact that it is extremely difficult to find absolutely objective historical judgments, devoid of prejudice and marked by honesty and love for truth, does not justify one's persistence in rejecting historical criticism. We must always assume —need we repeat it?— that true History, absolutely true and worthy of total acquiescence, will only be definitively written, signed, and stamped by God when Humanity sees that History, as men have seen it so far, has come to its end. Any human institution, including the Church (which despite being divine is also human), is far from being completely perfect. *Regarding the latter*, it is convenient to recall the old name, *Casta Meretrix*, which has sometimes been applied to her. Speaking of which Hans Urs von Balthasar said: *When Luther dares to equate the Roman Church with the whore of Babylon, it strikes us as the height of blasphemy. But he was not the first one to coin the phrase. Similar things can be found in Wycliffe and Hus, and their language was not a complete innovation but the violent simplification and coarsening of a very old 'theologoumenon.' This in turn has its origins in the Old Testament, in the words of*

judgment spoken by God, the betrayed Husband, against the arch-
whore Jerusalem, and in the New Testament's application of these
texts, which are so fundamental to the Old. Now it is true that the
Church regards herself as profoundly different from the unfaithful
synagogue; in her there is at least one identifiable place where she is
perfectly pure and unchangeably faithful. No believer, no Christians
theologian (including Luther), would ever doubt these truths. But is
that the only thing she has to be? Could the real 'Ekklesia,' made up
of 'these' particular believers, be something different? Christians of
other times have unhesitatingly acknowledged that it would be rash
to deny these possibilities a priori.[12] The Church has always acknowledged herself as Saint and Sinner at the same time (*Ecclesia*
semper reformanda), which has not ever been a scandal to anyone;
after all, *veritas liberabit vos,* truth will set you free.

Saint Paul recognized himself as a sinner (1 Cor 15: 8–9;
1 Tim 1:15) and even admitted candidly that he was the victim of
shameful temptations (2 Cor 12:7). Jesus Christ, for His part, spoke
harshly against the bad Shepherds, whom He rebukes as mercenaries
because they are not concerned about the sheep but only about taking advantage of them and unhesitatingly abandoning them when
danger is looming (Jn 10). The issue of bad Shepherds has been
denounced since ancient times by the Prophets of the Old Testament and was dealt with no less acrimoniously by the Fathers of the
Church, especially by Saint Augustine.

However, at the present time, regarding this issue, the System
plays a double game. On the one hand, it does not hesitate to use
flattery, not to mention establishing a cult of personality; while, on

---

[12]Hans Urs von Balthasar, *Esplorations in Theology*, Ignatius Press, San Francisco, 1991, p. 193.

the other, it seeks to undermine the authority and prestige of the Shepherds.

The first has helped the System to stifle any attempt at raising justified reservations regarding some actions of the Ecclesiastical Hierarchy. Because of this state of anarchy and confusion experienced by the Church today (caused by wide–spread Modernist doctrines), any attempt to contact the Hierarchy to present reasoned reservations and friendly objections is instantaneously eradicated by the System; which has not hesitated to brand such attempts as rebellious, and even as contumacy against the alleged *spirit of the Council* —an ambiguous expression whose meaning nobody has cared to specify.

At the same time, as contradictory as it may sound, and taking advantage of the universal worship of *democracy*, the System has worked, using all means at its disposal, to destroy the monarchical constitution of the Church. And we should not exclude from those means the manipulation of the Conferences of Bishops to dilute the authority of Bishops within their own dioceses, nor the resurrection of old conciliarist doctrines to weaken or annul the authority of the Pope.[13]

It seems that far behind are those times in which the Councils of the Church did not hesitate to condemn doctrinal error, and even wrong actions of the Hierarchy which could be harmful to the Faith, merely to defend the sound doctrine, without taking into account rank or persons. The Third Council of Constantinople (VI Ecumenical), approved by Pope Leo II, for example, condemned Pope

---

[13]In fact, the spirit of democratization of the Church has spread to all her structures, extending even to the organization and operation of parishes.

Honorius I on charges of monothelitism.[14] It is not necessary here to remind that *papal infallibility* requires certain conditions and that it does not extend to *all* declarations or actions of the Pope.[15] On the other had, History does not tell us that the faith of the Christian People has wavered because of events of this sort. A well–intentioned comment or warning, made constructively and taking into account the rules imposed by charity and mutual respect, should not be carelessly rejected. Jesus Christ recommended fraternal correction as something normal (Mt 18:15),[16] and Saint Paul did not try to hide that he had sharply rebuked Saint Peter (Gal 2:11). The bias of not considering different and even opposite criteria brought with good will before the pertinent person can lead to tyranny and despotism.

Modern times are as inclined to talk about democracy, human rights, freedom of thought and expression, respect for all ideas, etc.,

---

[14]In the Session XIII of the Council (March 28, 681) the Fathers pronounced the following sentence:

Having found that these writings are entirely in disagreement with the apostolic teachings, with the definitions of the holy councils and the Fathers worthy of approval, and that they agree, instead, with the false doctrines of heretics, we absolutely reject them and vomit them as the poison they are for the soul. As for the men whose impious dogmas we reject, we think that their names should also be eradicated from the Holy Church of God, which are the names of Sergius, Cyrus of Alexandria, Pyrrhus, Paul and Peter who have succeeded Sergio in the See of Constantinople, and Theodore of Pharan. All of them have been named in the letter of Pope Agathon and rejected by him for thinking contrary to orthodoxy. We also share the opinion (συνείδομεν) of banishing from the holy Church of God and also of anathematizing Honorius, former pope of old Rome; for we have founded in letters sent by him to Sergius that he has followed completely the opinion of those whose impious teachings he sanctioned. (Mansi, col. 556; DS., 550–552).

This condemnation was later endorsed and confirmed by succeeding Popes.

[15]If the Pope, for example, makes a trip (whose political implications perhaps cannot be excluded) to a country with a particular political regime, it is evident that convenience or inconvenience of the trip does not fall within the field of infallibility, even if one admits the good intentions which may has motivated it.

[16]Cf. Lev 19:17; Gal 6:1.

as they are unwilling to put such proclamations into practice. As far as the Church is concerned, the cult of personality (powered by the Pastoral practice of *show*) skillfully used by the System, makes it virtually impossible for the common faithful to try to bring before their Shepherds any doubt, difficulty, or suggestion, no matter how friendly they may be, which does not seem to be entirely in accord with established slogans. To this purpose, she even uses, if necessary, the accusation of disobedience and lack of harmony with the *spirit of the Council.*

The Church founded by Jesus Christ is neither merely divine nor merely human; she is divine and human. She has not been established for angels but for men, who become part of her and form a unity with her. Therefore, one has to allow for the fact that *deficiency* be part of her composition. Such deficiency on the part of the Church amounts to something faulty, incomplete, imperfect, and even a sinful condition as far as her members are concerned. As the Master Himself said: *Only one is good.*[17] And so He assured Peter: *But I have prayed for you, that your faith fail not; and you, being once converted, confirm your brethren.*[18] This text shows that Jesus Christ conceded the *possibility that Peter might fail.* And it was not a mere possibility, as would soon be demonstrated by events that Peter experienced and because of which, according to Jesus Christ Himself, Peter would be in need of *conversion.* Which conversion accomplished, Peter would, in turn, *confirm* his brothers, no less in need of help than he was.

It is strange that many Spiritual Families refuse to acknowledge any shortcomings in things that concern them —whether it is their way of life; the behavior of their members, how to implement their

---

[17]Mt 19:17.
[18]Lk 22:32.

own charism; or the composition of their Constitutions, Bylaws, or Regulations. With regard to the founder, his possible canonization only guarantees that he has practiced all the Christian virtues to a heroic degree. Also, the positive sanction of the Constitutions or the Bylaws is limited to ensure their ecclesiastical sense, but in such a way that this sanction has nothing to do with the way they will be applied, the political or social consequences they may give rise to, or the interpretations that the followers may give to them and to the charism of the founder.

Man is a being who can easily become a victim of mirages; and the Devil, who knows this well, takes good care in promoting them.

As for Spiritual Families, the spiritual fervor of their first members, in addition to their normal early success, contributes to the promotion of the idea that the practice of their charism appears as happily viable. At such times everything seems to depend on how authentically the members live their lives according to the Gospel, the apostolic momentum that springs from their sincere love for God, and the ability of the firmness of their Christian witness to impact men. Thus a time comes when they are convinced that more followers are needed, in increasing numbers, able to assimilate the spirit of the Spiritual Family and spread it everywhere (*Euntes ergo docete onmes gentes.* Go, therefore, and teach all nations); which implies the need for sufficient means, essentials of course, for meeting the demands that operating a large Group of people entails.

It is easily understandable that the three evangelical counsels of chastity, poverty, and obedience, which are considered essentials when one follows and imitates Jesus Christ, have always been a key ingredient of the spirit of Spiritual Families. These counsels have been lived with different binding force according to the various Constitutions or Bylaws, but they are an integral part of any spirit;

which is not surprising when one considers that these Groups, or Spiritual Families, constitute what might be called an *Avant–garde* Christianity.

But it often happens, however, that any one of these evangelical counsels —for instance, that of *poverty*— becomes problematic when the time arrives for it to be adapted to the life and expansion of the Spiritual Families. For centuries, this has brought about a set of really disturbing tensions, in that everything seems to happen as if difficulties arise in direct proportion to the desire for practicing such a challenging counsel. The problems that this adjustment has given rise to throughout the history of the Church have been the subject of many treatises, but have never been fully resolved. Just remember, as an example, the old discussion about the distinction between *material poverty* and *spiritual poverty* —a thorny issue that has already produced many headaches, and even quite a few reasons for slander.[19]

Poverty, as opposed to *wealth*, is one of the key points that can wreck the best intentions of a Spiritual Family.[20] The problems, difficulties, and dangers that can result from the incorrect practice of the evangelical counsel of poverty —to the extent of distorting it

---

[19]In reality this problem has always been solved... for those who have dealt with it with goodwill. There is no contradiction between *material poverty* and *spiritual poverty*. For it is not difficult to understand that poverty in spirit is either *real* poverty or not poverty at all; in effect, the authenticity of the adjective *spiritual* implies the reality of the substantive *poverty*. Anyway, this is not the problem being treated here, since neither the content nor the meaning of evangelical poverty will be the object of our reflection; the issue will be considered from a different perspective. Cf. A. Gálvez, *The Importunate Friend*, New Jersey, 1995, pp. 98 ff.

[20]Another key point closely connected to the first one, which will not be discussed here, refers to the acquisition of Power and Influence as a means *to do good and to facilitate* the task of evangelization.

and turning it into something else[21] —could be systematized more or less as follows, which we present in outline form for the sake of clarity.

a) If evangelical poverty is feasible or not. Actually, and above all, this is where the whole problem lies.

b) If considered viable: if evangelical poverty is to be understood in a strict or perhaps in a more or less mitigated sense.

c) If understood in a strict sense: if evangelical poverty can be practiced collectively (in community), or perhaps only as an individual virtue and in isolated cases.

d) If the so–called *spiritual poverty* is susceptible of being misunderstood, to the point of becoming a chimera replacing real poverty and making it disappear as a virtue.

e) If a certain *spiritual poverty* is compatible with the acquisition and possession of property, which may be so abundant as required (apparently) by the needs of a more effective and extensive Evangelization.

f) If a spirit of poverty which has been distorted and made compatible with the possession of substantial means (considered necessary for an effective work of Christianizing people) can disrupt the charism and the foundational spirit of a Spiritual Family. Which aspect of the problem seems to be decisive and probably the merging point of all the others.

Is it possible that, because of some mysterious sleight of hand, poverty could become wealth...? Can original intentions, whose sincerity and honesty cannot be doubted, produce an opposite, or at least different, result than the one intended?

---

[21] It is true that problems are to be solved and dangers are to be avoided. Few, if any, human endeavors exist that can stay clear of them altogether. But the biggest and most serious problems arise precisely when dangers are not perceived as such, and, therefore, they are not properly, or not at all, confronted.

At least initially, the answer seems to be in the affirmative. Nevertheless, we will try to reply to these and other issues as well as possible, albeit in a rather unsystematic manner.

3. Which speaks, with the best possible intention, about the wonders of Christian poverty as well as of the problems which, by a strange paradox, this virtue is capable of causing the Spiritual Families that try to practice it.

The virtue of poverty is so much at the heart of Christian existence that without it one might not even consider the possibility of following Jesus Christ: *Whoever of you does not renounce all his possessions cannot be my disciple.*[22]

Logically, given the character of what we have agreed to call Spiritual Families in the Church, all of them hoist this virtue as one of their flags; which takes in them two facets:

First of all, this virtue appears as an integral and essential part of their spiritualities; therefore, it is considered as a key element in the sanctification of the members themselves.

Second, it is a basic factor in bearing witness to evangelical life; a witness which is expected to be effective to the extent that it is eloquent (attractive). We must note here that this latter character of poverty becomes in practice the most important, at least in certain respects, as we shall see.

These two facets reach their most brilliant moment in the early stages of the life of Spiritual Families. Poverty is now practiced with

---

[22]Lk 14:33. Cf. Mt 5:3; 19:29; Lk 6:20; 9:58; 12:33; 18:22; etc.

sincerity and intensity as a normal thing; its character as a witness becomes even suggestive, attracting many people who can, in turn, become either new members or maybe fans and collaborators of the Spiritual Family.

However, paradoxical as it may seem, this last character (being a witness) of poverty soon takes on a condition of serious ambiguity. It can lead to a bright promise of holiness and apostolic fruitfulness..., or it may mean the announcement of the appearing of disturbing problems for that Spiritual Family.

The best way to address this problem, so important as well as exciting and captivating, is to examine it where it originated and evolved in the most singular and paradigmatic way. For a considerably long time, the whole Church was aware of the question posed and developed, with numerous incidents, within the Franciscan Order, or Friars Minor. Its eminent Founder, Saint Francis of Assisi (the main actor of this drama) undoubtedly is one of the most glorious and illustrious sons that the Church has had throughout her history.

It is common doctrine that the saints lived all the Christian virtues to a heroic degree, and that each saint distinguished himself in practicing some of them most particularly. With regard to poverty, perhaps no one has ever practiced it in such a strict and sublime manner as *The Poverello* of Assisi. In the life of Saint Francis, it would not make any sense to raise the distinction between *material* poverty and *spiritual* poverty. It would be a useless distinction that Saint Francis, more than anyone else, would not have understood. His poverty *was simply there*, as a faithful reflection of the teachings of the Gospel: so sincere and real, and, at the same time, so human and so divine that it needed no explanation; its evidence was the manifestation of true holiness, capable of arousing a deep sense of fascination and nostalgia at the prospect of those realities which surpass everything of this world, according to the statement of Saint Paul: *Seek the things that are above... set your minds on things that are above, not on things that are on earth.*[23]

> *The man who has a lily–like heart,*
> *Cherubic soul, heavenly speech,*
> *The minimum and sweet Francis of Assisi...*[24]

As it could not be otherwise, the exciting holiness of Francis attracted a circle of disciples; few at first, but very eager to imitate Jesus Christ as the Saint was doing. Soon, however (perhaps too early), the number of disciples grew and became quite large (perhaps too large). Thus began what seemed inevitable: success was as the prologue to the tragedy.[25]

---

[23]Col 3:1.

[24]Rubén Darío, *The Reasons of the Wolf.*

[25]It is a situation whose dangers are often invisible and which the Devil, who always *circuit quærens quem devoret,** is on the prowl, looking for somebody to devour, perhaps has some vested interest in promoting because it predisposes people to deviate from supernatural parameters; or to do without them, which amounts to the same thing. Success is pleasant to human nature which, consequently, not always thinks of stopping to consider (actually, it almost never does) as to whether success will be beneficial or possibly harmful. And yet, it is not easy to associate success (at least understood in a human way, which is how it is most often considered) with the idea of the Cross, although the latter is the only thing that leads to apostolic fruitfulness and eternal life. This should be reason enough to become suspicious of early, tumultuous success which is spectacular, easy, and applauded... if you make more use of common sense and right reason; but that would obviously be expecting too much from human nature. There is something which Christians are quite contumacious to understand, the fact that Christian life is an incredible series of paradoxes. Success as a possible prelude to failure? However, the dialectic strength–weakness, wisdom–folly, belongs to what is most central in the New Testament (1 Cor 1: 25–28).

*1 Pet 5:8

The few disciples of the first moments, like Saint Francis, found no difficulty in meeting strict poverty, since it was not anything other than following, to the letter, evangelical doctrines; who could have difficulty with that?

Note, however, that the mere statement of this question already poses the problem in all its crudeness; or, put another way, in all its gravity and importance: Can the implementation of the teaching of the Gospel be called into question...? Do some sayings from the mouth of Jesus Christ Himself (usually called *evangelical counsels*) presume in advance the possibility of their realization in real life...? Or, on the contrary, are they utopian idealizations aimed at a certain minority (a strict minority) because their being put into practice by communities with many members is impossible —which already was more or less implicitly envisaged...?

The historical fact is well known to all. As soon as Francis' disciples became numerous, the important question was posed: *Would the norms of life elaborated by Saint Francis not be too strict (meaning unrealizable), most particularly those referring to poverty?*

This problem never existed for Saint Francis. His *Rule*, which he thought to have been inspired to him by Jesus Christ Himself, was a simple and accurate (*sine glossa*, without commentary) copy of the Gospel; and does the Gospel need additions or perhaps cuts...? Certainly not for Saint Francis; to him, a passionate love would have been incompatible with mitigations, conditions, or circumstantial changes. Since poverty (absolute detachment) is identified with total self–giving or perfect love; and since Saint Francis was *totally* in love with Jesus Christ, it would have been impossible for him to understand anything other than *perfect poverty*.

For Saint Francis, of course, but not for ordinary mortals. Thus began the long struggle of the different *Rules*, with their many and various *touch–ups*, whose complicated history is not of this place.[26]

Suffice it to say here, as a summary, that the First Rule approved orally by Pope Innocent III in 1209, suffered frequent changes in the Chapters which Saint Francis convoked every year. After his last trip to the East (1219), the Saint introduced several texts of the Gospel in the primitive Rule (which, as stated above, had already been quite touched up), the writing of which was finished by brother Caesarius of Speyer. That text was then known (inaccurately) as *First Rule*, or better yet, as *Rule of 1221*, which is the date of its composition. In the absence of ecclesiastical approval, it appears that Saint Francis sought the advice of Cardinal Ugolino (given to Saint Francis as his Protector by Pope Honorius III), who induced him to modify and shorten the text of the Rule prior to its submission to the Pope. It was then that the Saint, says Saint Bonaventure, retired with two companions to a lonely hermitage where, after intense prayer and severe fasting, the Saint wrote what he thought the Holy Spirit inspired him. Upon completion of the work, the Saint gave it to Brother Elias, who was already practically running the Order. After a few days, Saint Francis asked for the Rule. Strangely enough, however, Brother Elias *had lost* the manuscript, so it was necessary to write it again. Finally, to cut this complicated story short, definitive approval was granted by Honorius III by the Bull *Solet annuere*, on November 29, 1223. We should still mention here the issue of the famous *Testament* of the Saint, along with the protracted and debated question of its legally binding condition, which was settled negatively by Gregory IX in 1230. A synopsis of the whole problem can be provided as follows: *The total renunciation to property and possession of goods, both collectively and individually, and the prohibition of receiving money, in person or by proxy, are distinctive features of the Franciscan rule. It is precisely about this issue of poverty that disputes will arise which will lead to divisions and bring about reforms. Innocent III would have said*

---

[26]For a more in–depth study of this issue from an historical point of view, see *DTC*, article *Frères Mineurs*, VI–1.

to Francis: The kind of life you want to embrace seems to me to be too difficult. It certainly did not intimidate the first disciples, but among the large number who joined them soon appeared those who kept on repeating that the life chosen by Francis and ordered by the Rule was too austere, and even impracticable. The last years of the Saint were saddened by this opposition, which he perceived around him and especially in the provincial superiors. This motivated his ending up by resigning; which he tried to hide under the pretext of his illness.[27]

But, as we said above, this is not the place to insist on the careful complexity of historical events. Rather, it seems preferable to turn our attention to considering the human pathos that motivated those events and which ultimately led to one of the most important historical and curious events in the history of the Church.

Men pass away, but ideas remain and even take on a life of their own. Thus, they grow up, mature, develop their potentialities, and spread everywhere. Saint Francis had accepted that the initial small group of his disciples would gradually increase; which is totally logical because who would not want the perfect practice of the Gospel, materialized in the following and imitating of Jesus Christ, to spread to the greatest possible number of men...? It so happens, however, that organizing a large group of men involves a series of needs which there is no choice but to tend to and for which the required means must be provided. *And this does not seem to fit very well with the absolute poverty that the Saint wanted.*

We must also take into account what has been said above with respect to perfect poverty: it can only be understood and practiced by true lovers, who, as is well known, are never found in abundance. There is no need to see anything strange in this: there are many texts of Scripture that confirm the known fact that charity admits of degrees; therefore, even within a small circle of souls close to each

---

[27] *DTC*, ibidem.

other and so dear to the Lord as to sit with Him on thrones on the Day of Judgment (Lk 22:30), even there the intensity and depth of love can reach higher or lower levels (*Simon, son of John, lovest thou me more than these?*[28]).

Hence, discussions about the appropriate relaxations and mitigations of the Rule soon began to appear within the Franciscan Family (*Friars Minor*, as Saint Francis wanted his friars to be called). And, although the Saint did not understand the problem, it *seemed reasonable* to think that there was no other way but to accept them. So much so that even the likes of Saint Bonaventure[29] and Saint Anthony of Padua, not to mention Cardinal Hugolino and many others, were in favor of making a more practical and accessible Rule. Considering the circumstances, they were probably right, but the problem is much more complex than what it seems.

Considering this issue with the greatest serenity possible with the passing of time, it appears that Saint Francis was right; and equally so were those who did not think as he did. Because the key to the problem is the point of view adopted, or the situation in which one places himself. Thus, while total poverty is essential to perfect love, to the love which has not yet reached such a degree the virtue of poverty admits *compromise* with human nature. The most curious and even the most interesting thing about this famous and important issue, which has also gone unnoticed by historians, is the fact that Saint Francis made a *serious mistake* —divine, like everything he did, but a mistake after all, as we shall try to explain. This is one of the most profound paradoxes as well as one of the greatest ironies that the history of the Church has ever known: the

---

[28] Jn 21:15.

[29] For the stand of Saint Bonaventure regarding the need of *making more reasonable* the Rule, see Étienne Gilson, *La Philosophie de Saint Bonaventure*, Vrin, Paris, 1943, pp. 9–75.

man who seems to have understood and lived better, more perfectly, the poverty of Jesus Christ —*The Poverello of Assisi*— was caught in a situation that necessarily involved the management of *wealth*; an extraordinarily odd situation as well as a very real one. However, as with most unusual historical facts, here we can also find an explanation.

First, the Saint was convinced that the evangelical counsels could be put into practice and have nothing to do with utopias. Jesus Christ, *who had married Poverty on the Cross*,[30] raised this virtue to a rank which is beyond the sublime; and that is how Saint Francis understood it. For this Saint, the ownership of assets (or wealth, which amounts to the same thing) was in contradiction to the Gospel. He understood to the letter, in all their depth, the teachings of Jesus Christ; like this one: *you cannot serve God and riches*,[31] or that one, no less categorical, in which Jesus Christ said that *any of you who does not renounce all his possessions cannot be my disciple*.[32]

But the same thing happens to these sentences of Jesus Christ (which possess a forcefulness that makes them problematic) as happens to the others contained in the Gospel: Christians often *look the other way*, that is, they try to conceal them, to pass on them as on hot coals, or, better yet, they proceed to *interpret them*; this latter is accomplished from their point of view, of course, but it runs the risk, in the end, of making human reason judge faith, and not vice versa.

---

[30] This phrase, the beauty and deep thinking of which deserved a place in History, belongs to Saint Francis himself.

[31] *Non potestis Deo servire at mammonæ* (Mt 6:24; Lk 16:13).

[32] *Sic ergo omnis ex vobis, qui non renuntiat omnibus, quae possidet, non potest meus esse discipulus* (Lk 14:33).

In the beginning of the Thirteenth Century (which is when this chapter of our story occurs), neither Saint Francis nor his first disciples considered the problem of distinguishing between material poverty and spiritual poverty. For them poverty was simply poverty, literally understood; which was, as we have seen above, the abnegation and dispossession of all goods. This was the way Saint Francis and those advocating for a reading of the Gospel *sine glossa*, without gloss, understood poverty; for them the dispossession of property had to be radical, or, in any case, excluding only what is indispensable for living. Even Saint Paul himself seemed to be not too far from this understanding when he counseled his disciple Timothy that *having food and wherewith to be covered, with these we are content.*[33]

Soon we will see, though, that the ambiguity of the concept of *indispensable* is going to be the cause of early problems.

Truly speaking, the notion of *indispensable* applied to poverty is more than ambiguous and subtle; it is also dangerous: it runs the risk of becoming a pun deprived of any content and nearly becoming something simply *empty*. In effect, when it comes to deciding what man needs to live, which things must be considered indispensable in attending to human needs (minimal and peremptory) for subsistence? Economic Science stands by an axiom that is universally valid: the needs of men are unlimited in number but limited in capacity. It can be verified that, in fact, if the answer to this problem is left in the hands of the experts, there will immediately appear a diversity of opinions equal to the number of experts studying the issue. Therefore, the concept of *indispensable* is useful *in so far as it is not subjected to discussion*: in other words, when this concept is simply accepted at face value, as it presents itself to the intuition

---

[33] 1 Tim 6:8.

of a sincere, clear... and enamored mind. Which is what sometimes happens with ambiguous concepts: the best thing to do is to leave them as they are, so that they may not lose their expressiveness should one try to specify them. Neither Saint Francis nor his first companions found any difficulty in applying the term indispensable to their needs of subsistence. They never thought that it could give rise to a *quaestio disputata*, disputed question, and very disputed at that. In spite of this, not many people have realized that the famous problem of Franciscan poverty, along with its endless discussions, dissentions, and separations of the early times (and those that followed) has always hinged upon the concept of what is indispensable, that is, that which can be considered as *reasonable and apt for life in common*, or that which can be considered as *according to the Gospel*. Which of the two interpretations responds to the correct meaning of what is indispensable and, therefore, more in harmony with the concept of evangelical poverty?

The evangelical teachings are for everyone. The saying of Jesus Christ: *Be perfect as your heavenly Father is perfect*[34] is valid for all Christians —at least in principle— because, although God dispenses His grace generously without missing anyone, every man is for Him a particular and unique being. Hence, although all Christians are one Body and share in the same Spirit (Rom 12:5), each of them is a different story to God, to the point that for each one of them He has paid the price of the blood of His Son (1 Cor 6:20; 1 Pet 1: 18–19).

This explains that while God distributes His gifts generously and sufficiently without omitting anyone, yet not all receive the same amount; just as not everyone responds equally to the divine goodness. After all, God created a polychrome world of free beings capable, all of them, of immense possibilities and variable reactions.

---

[34] *Estote vos perfecti, sicut Pater vester cœlestis perfectus est* (Mt 5:48).

Saint Paul exhorted the Christians in Rome to estimate each other soberly, *according to the measure of faith that God has given to each one.*[35] And he reminded the Corinthians that, *although each is given the manifestation of the Spirit for the common good,* different gifts and charisms —the Apostle insisted— are things *of the one and only Spirit who distributes them to each as he wills.*[36] But perhaps the most expressive text about this issue is contained in his letter to the Ephesians: *To each of us, however, has been given grace according to the measure that Christ wants to give his gifts.*[37]

Although the Message of Salvation preached by Jesus Christ has a universal content and scope, the Master knew that not everybody would follow it, and that the deepest meaning of the evangelical teachings would be understood by only a very few people. He did speak about His *little flock* (Lk 12:32), and the first seventy–two disciples sent to preach, in the end, were reduced to only twelve. On the other hand, His words speak for themselves: *If any man wants to come after me, let him deny himself, and take up his cross, and follow me;*[38] here the expression *if any man wants* is quite eloquent regarding the small number of those who would undertake a true following.

Things being thus, it is not surprising that the notion of evangelical poverty, taken in its most pure and primary sense, has been understood by only a few; in reality, as we have said above, only by those who are more in love, for only *total love* is able to understand what *total poverty* is. In this sense, it can be said that the issue of practicing evangelical poverty, as Saint Francis understood it, is

---

[35]Rom 12:3.

[36]1 Cor 12: 7.11.

[37]Eph 4:7.

[38]Mt 16:24; Lk 9:23.

an ill–posed problem because its answer is found through different ways. The possibility of putting into practice evangelical poverty —as well as any other practice contained in the Gospel— must, of course, be admitted; otherwise we would have to consider Jesus Christ to be a dreamer or an idealist. The divine mistake of Saint Francis we have referred to before is a different thing, as we will soon see.

Undoubtedly, the evangelical poverty which Saint Francis practiced seems to be an exaggeration, and many of the ways in which he behaved strike us as equally extravagant. But we must not forget, nevertheless, that this judgment is usually uttered *from the point of view of human reason and not of faith*; conclusions of this sort can only be termed as *merely rational*, and not as supra–rational or supernatural —taking into account that these terms are not synonyms with irrational. And since it is not possible, through unaided reason alone, to know exactly where faith can lead us, it is not licit to speak lightly of exaggerations or extravagant behaviors within the supernatural field.

According to what we have just said, judgments which consider the primitive way of Franciscan poverty an exaggeration, which is tantamount to saying impractical, can appear (be) as reasonable as you want, but only from a perspective which does not take into account (as a method) faith. It is risky to term as an exaggeration or as extravagant certain things or attitudes which human reason cannot grasp; unless one wants to term divine conduct as irrational, as has indeed been done regarding the mystery of the Cross, which has been considered *a stumbling block to the Jews and foolishness to the Gentiles... but the power of God and the wisdom of God. For the foolishness of God is wiser than men; and the weakness of God is stronger than men...*[39] And the Apostle added: *For, seen that in the wisdom of God, the world, by wisdom, knew not God, it pleased God, by the foolishness of our preaching, to save them that believe.*[40] In fact, from of old, God had already warned us through the prophet Isaiah: *For my thoughts are not your thoughts; nor your ways my ways, says the Lord. For as the heavens are exalted above the earth, so are my ways exalted above your ways, and my thoughts above your thoughts.*[41]

The mission of every apostle is that of continuing the work of Jesus Christ. This was the task —the establishment and spreading of the Kingdom of God on this Earth— which this man of great holiness called Saint Francis tried to carry out. But the saving mission of Jesus Christ is universal and includes all men. Consequently, it was not strange that *The Poverello* wished to reach all of them (including the Sultan *al–Kámil*) in order that his spirit (which is not different from that of Christ and of the Gospel) could be spread to the largest possible number of those who would become his own disciples: *Going therefore, teach all nations... As the Father has sent me, I also send you.*[42] And, indeed, his followers could be counted by the thousands shortly after the Saint started his venture.

However, Jesus Christ, despite having an absolutely universal mission in view, *only instituted twelve of His disciples as Apostles.* Founder of a Church that would have to assemble all His followers (Christians, as they soon were called), at no time did He ever think of creating a great Organization in the manner of a huge Administrative Body. The Mystical Body, or the εχχλησία, given its

---

[39] 1 Cor 1: 23–25.

[40] 1 Cor 1:21.

[41] Is 55: 8–9.

[42] Mt 28:19; Acts 1:8; Jn 20:21.

singularity and uniqueness, transcends all forms of human Organizations. Notwithstanding this, Saint Francis, undoubtedly driven by an unquestionable apostolic zeal, *created a huge Organization which was integrated, in turn, within the Church* —with all that this entails and its relevant consequences.

The appearance of Franciscanism led to two important consequences which personally affected Saint Francis.

We have already mentioned one of them when we referred to the fact that a human Organization which includes a large number of people needs resources for their livelihood and expansion: food and accommodations for the members who make it up, means and training sites, travel and transportation of personnel, etc. All of which requires the necessary management of a considerable amount of money.

On the other hand, to believe that such a human Organization would be able, or willing, to live the evangelical poverty in the strictest sense... while it may be true *in theory* it is evidently a mere dream *in fact*. As we said before, not everybody is given the grace to surrender to a perfect and total love.[43] Repeated attempts by the Saint of Assisi to convince the crowds of his disciples during the numerous *Chapters* he convoked always ended in failure. *The Poverello* proved himself to be as much an expert on the ways and mysteries of God... as he was little versed in the nature of human behavior. Anyway, as expected, circumstances imposed upon Franciscanism the need of possessing and managing money (read *wealth*). It is not surprising that, ultimately, we have no choice but to understand Saint Bonaventure when, a few years later, he found it necessary to

---

[43]The fact that traditional Doctrine has always distinguished, in regard to the teachings of the Gospel, between *counsels* and *precepts* speaks volumes about this issue. Those terms do not seem quite fortunate, but they contain some truth which must be justly recognized.

fix the mess as best as possible; there was no other solution than *to put order in the horde.*

Back to the Seraphim of Assisi, the second consequence affected him personally more than the previous one.

The faculty of managing such a great number of people who are subject to the strictest obedience[44] is ultimately tantamount to the wielding of power; whether one admits it or not. It is true that 'power' here must be given the most benign nuance possible; in the sense —by applying to it some kind of analogy— of divesting from it any idea of imperfection. And, if that is not enough, one can also think that both, the subject to whom this power is immediately attributed as well as the obedience that is given to him, are motivated by strictly supernatural considerations: obedience out of love for God in imitation of the Obedient Christ. In this situation, the person to whom obedience is given (Father, Superior, Responsible, or any other name used to call him) accepts a heavy burden of great responsibility that makes him, following the teachings of the Master, the servant and slave of all (Mt 20:27).

All of which, nevertheless, does not negate the undeniable reality that the person to whom obedience is given *has a power of decision over others (who can be many) which is somehow absolute.* The accompanying evangelical connotations to the Christian notion of *authority*, despite all their loftiness and transcendence, cannot eliminate its consequent (necessary) idea of *power*. The fact that subjection to obedience implies a situation which has been freely accepted and exercised for love's sake does not negate the real duty of *subjection* that has been established.

---

[44]The Feminine Branch of Franciscanism soon also appeared, under the leadership of Saint Clare, the spiritual daughter and favorite disciple of the Saint of Assisi. The *Poor Clares* soon also had a quick expansion.

It is only in Jesus Christ that the idea of power appears in perfect con-
junction or identification with the notion of service. *Auctoritas* (the power
to subject) is found in Him in a perfect equivalence with *oboedientia* (will
to be subjected). For the attitude of (absolute) obedience is in Him but
the fruit and the result of a perfect and absolute act of love: *Having loved
his own who were in the world, he loved them "unto the end."* [45] Hence
Jesus Christ's authority, contrary to the human authority even elevated
by grace, has to be contemplated under the focus of analogy, that is, eliminating from it any possible imperfection: *You call me Master and Lord,
and you say well, for so I am. If then I being your Lord and Master, have
washed your feet...*[46] *Even as the Son of Man is not come to be ministered
unto, but to minister and to give his life in redemption for many...*[47] *I am
in the midst of you, as he who serves.*[48] Only Jesus Christ could exercise
with absolute perfection the office of *Lord* because only He, out of love,
humbled Himself to nothingness (semetipsum exinanivit) becoming *obedient unto death, even to the death of the cross* (Phil 2: 7–8). Therefore,
authority, which in Him is identified with perfect love, excludes from itself
imperfections of any sort. It is evident that the notion of *authority* in God
cannot contain any imperfection.[49] Since the exercise of human *authority*
is not the consequence of an infinitely perfect act of love, it cannot eliminate all hints of imperfection in an act which, in the end, cannot renounce
to be *potestas* (read *dominion*)

---

[45] Jn 13:1.

[46] Jn 13: 13–14.

[47] Mt 20:28; Mk 10:44.

[48] Lk 22:27.

[49] It is evident that the concept of *auctoritas* when applied to God cannot include
any imperfection, which does not happen when human authority is exerted, for
the latter is not capable of eliminating all kinds of *dominion* that does not imply
imperfection. Regarding the Kingship of Christ, see A. Gálvez, *Meditaciones de
Atardecer*, Shoreless Lake Press, NJ, 2005, pp.135 ff. The mission of *feeding* the
sheep entrusted to the Hierarchy of the Church (Jn 21) will be a more perfect task
the more it resembles the office of Christ as Supreme Shepherd (Jn 10; Heb 13:20).

This explains the mutual identification, according to Jesus Christ, of the situation lord–servant or that of master–disciple (Mt 10: 24–25; Lk 6:40); in the sense that this identification places both lord–servant, master–disciple on the same level. It is a relation of bilateral opposition which, because it loses its specific character of *opposition* as such, would become a mere *relation* between two who are on an equivalent level, that is, just what is needed for the conditions of perfect love to be ushered. The (absolute) *authority* of Jesus Christ becomes, through love, (absolute) *self-giving*.

Needless to say, this situation would be unintelligible should it be taken out of the context of Christian existence. And we must add here another restriction: this situation is only valid within the field of divine–human loving relationships and not of merely human relationships, even though these may be elevated by grace; for only divine love is able to place the *other* in a situation of perfect equality and reciprocity.

My beloved is for me and I am for my beloved.[50]

The power to order others (who can be many, as in the case we are considering) is nothing but power. At any rate, although it is based in love for Christ, it is not yet, properly speaking, a relationship of divine–human love. Love of neighbor, even as a derivative of the love for Jesus Christ, cannot materialize itself in a relationship of equality, mutual self–surrender, and ownership; which is exactly the way a relationship of divine–human love would manifest itself.

---

[50]Sg 2:16; 6:3. And also, *I will not now call you servants... But I have called you friends* (Jn 15:15). We must be careful, though. As we have said above, the relationship of perfect love does not at all eliminat the relation lord–servant, master–disciple: *You are my friends if you do the things that I command you* (Jn 15:14). And yet, it still is a relationship of absolute and perfect love: *Blessed are those servants whom the Lord, when he comes, shall find watching. Amen I say to you that he will gird himself and make them sit down to meat and passing will minister unto them* (Lk 12:37).

You shall love your neighbor as yourself... but no longer *above all things.* It is not possible, under any circumstances, to address oneself to our neighbor, as the Apostle did, thinking of Christ: *I live, now not I, but Christ lives in me.*[51]

Saint Francis, carried by the most ardent and sincere love of God, created a situation that we now call *franciscanism.* It is obvious that the Saint was only thinking of communicating the divine fire which was consuming him, and he never would have cared about franciscanism as such. He was encouraged by the love of Jesus Christ and the possibility of extending the Kingdom of God to all men... And the Holy One of Assisi is one of the towering figures in History, as well as having been established forever as one of the greatest Luminaries Christianity has ever known. Have there been many who have loved Jesus Christ as much as he did?

But facts are facts; and reality is the way it is; and the laws of Logic are but the very Laws of Nature.

As we have been saying, a human Organization needs the means to survive and to expand, which will necessarily be numerous if the Organization is too large. We are also saying that the power of decision over others is tantamount to power; a power which would inevitably be included within the category of what men call *goods* and sometimes *riches.* This former term is too broad and includes, therefore, all those things which are beyond what is strictly necessary, including not exclusively material goods. This issue must be dealt with.

In order to do just that, we must keep an eye on the forceful words of Jesus Christ: *You cannot serve God and riches.*[52] Indeed, as incredible as it may seem, what happened here was least expected. The Poorest among the poor, the angelical man known

---

[51]Gal 2:20.

[52]Mt 6:24; Lk 16:13.

as the *Seraphim of Assisi* that was Saint Francis, was committing himself to the Powers of this World. We are referring, of course, to *riches*, understood in the broad meaning which we have agreed to grant them and which properly belong to them. All this happened precisely when the intentions of the Saint, undoubtedly the most sublime and lofty in nature, were totally the opposite... and when the outcome was quite clear, although completely conflicting with the one Saint Francis would have envisioned and desired.

If the words of Our Lord must be taken seriously —if we grant that they mean anything and go beyond the poetic and allegorical language— then we must admit as real that service to (of) *riches* is incompatible with service to God. And we have said above that the complexity of this term embraces equally Money and Power; as Quevedo identified them in his well–known sentence: *Mr. Money is a Powerful gentleman.* And both, as the Gospel points out and as experience amply proves, can corrupt human beings to the roots.

What is truly subtle and dangerous with this issue is how easily it disguises itself. It seems logical to suppose that goods cannot but yield other new and abundant goods... if the former are used, of course, *for a good end.* We must consider also that those goods become necessary when the time comes for new and ambitious projects whose character, in this particular case, would be apostolic, charitable, or any other beneficent way in which goodness (to expand the Kingdom of God) can be done to others. With these enterprises or projects two factors come undoubtedly into play which justify the acquisition or the increase of goods (riches): the mere *possibility* of carrying them out, in the first place; and greater *expediency* in accomplishing them, on the other.[53]

---

[53]The problem, therefore, has two facets: the danger of riches in and of themselves to salvation and the employment of riches for the purpose of Evangelization.

What is most incredible in this complicated issue is the remarkable ease with which certain things are relegated to oblivion or are willingly ignored that, nevertheless, are elementary and very well known.

One of them, perhaps the most important and which contains all the others, is that the end does not justify the means.

The second thing that has been forgotten, which is no less important and is connected with the previous one, is that one cannot argue the fact that we are not dealing here with intrinsically evil means and that, consequently, according to some people, the well–known and fundamental principle of Christian Morality previously mentioned cannot be applied to this issue.

But the truth is that this principle also is valid in this case; even despite the possibility of admitting that the means used in the [quite laudable, indeed] undertaking at hand have no malice at all; which is, moreover, ordinary and normal.

But from the very moment that those means are disproportionate to the end pursued, they turn the whole issue into something inappropriate, to say the least. Here the fundamental principle is usually forgotten that the means must be proportionate to the ends. A supernatural end necessarily demands the use of supernatural means. Not in the sense of absolutely excluding the natural means —which can be suitable end even convenient for the proposed supernatural undertaking; after all, technology and its products also belong to God. The problem arises when the stress and trust is laid upon the natural means, which is the first step to discarding the supernatural ones and ends up by building a religion which is totally human in nature. However, the determining objections against

---

Although Scripture clearly includes both, we are going to refer here only to the second.

these procedures are based mostly on the very clear teachings of the New Testament— while not forgetting the experience drawn from the lessons that History has taught us. As far as this issue is concerned, the striking reality is that the use of *riches*, with the purpose of Evangelizing or extending the Kingdom of God, *is incompatible with the teachings of the New Testament*. And we can say even more. This incompatibility, far from being merely constrained to what would be a simple error in procedure, ends up bringing about results which may be unexpected but which are always contrary to the lofty and noble ends pursued.

Surely many will think that these affirmations are exaggerated and out of place; but there are facts to confirm them. These facts are so varied as well as patent that they can convince anybody of good will moved by the desire to know the truth. It is true that the decadent civilization in which we live does not care too much about facts; neither is it willing to admit the evidence which seems to contradict its materialistic and pagan principles. *Darwinism* is a case at hand, which is admitted by Atheism as a dogma despite the lack of scientifically reliable data which, moreover, rather contradicts it; as Lenin said: *If the facts are against us... it will be worse for the facts.* All of this is but a consequence of having rejected *being*, having turned our backs on *truth*, and having affirmed the *I* as the only and supreme arbiter of all things. As for the Church, who is suffering a crisis of catastrophic proportions since the Second Vatican Council (surely the most serious in all her History and which seems to be reaching its zenith), she has to face a number of facts that are so tremendous and painful as to be blinding with their evidence; nevertheless, according to what the propaganda of the System proclaims everywhere, the Church is enjoying, more than ever before, the triumph of a veritable *Springtime*.

The first and main fact of our consideration, which nobody can deny, has to do with the attitude which Saint Francis himself adopted. He did not hesitate to walk away from and have nothing to do with the enormous setup that arose about him, as soon as he saw the direction to which things and events were turning. Many and varied explanations have been furnished about his retirement into solitude, accompanied by a few intimate disciples, and leaving the multitude of *Minor Friars* in somebody else's hands. In fact, he alleged his illnesses; but the only reason which moved him to do such a thing was his desire to live the Rule —and more particularly the chapter on poverty— in a stricter way. He left behind the mitigated Rules that allowed the Brothers a more viable and *rational* way of life... which was where the whole problem existed; for Saint Francis believed (say what you will) that this more rational way of life was incompatible with the one God had inspired in him, or with what he wanted: a *super–rational*, or perhaps a quasi–evangelical way of life. But the way of existence the Brothers crave now —more reasonable and adapted to a more bearable existence— would end up extinguishing the spirit with the passing of time (so the Saint surely thought): *Do not extinguish the Spirit*; something that subsequent events confirmed.[54]

The debate about whether the way of life which Saint Francis intended was viable or perhaps suitable for a few people but not for communities with many members becomes irrelevant and we are not going to press this issue. The best thing we can do now, contrary to the way modern ideologies proceed, is to confine ourselves to the facts which, in this case, are as expressive as they are patent.

The decadence which appeared early within the Friars Minor, only to continue later among the various branches of the Francis-

---

[54] 1 Thess 5:19.

can Order (Friars Minor of the Observance, Conventual Friars Minor, Capuchin Friars Minor), grew with the passing of time until it reached its zenith in current times as another manifestation of the universal crisis which the Church and Western Civilization are suffering. Obviously, we are not going to blame the obliteration of the evangelical poverty which Saint Francis wanted as the *sole* culprit for the crisis within the Franciscan Order; but it is sufficiently clear that their option for wealth was one of the main *determinant* factors that caused the disaster.[55] Neither would it be true to consider such a decline as one more manifestation of the crisis affecting the Church and Western society. We cannot deny that there are reasonable interdependence and interconnections between the former and the latter; but in this crisis, as it always happens in any other singular crisis, there are also particular and concrete causes which can be known. For the rest, to deny the existence of deterioration within the Franciscan Order would be nothing short of a senseless denial of what is evident.

At any rate, the spirit of Saint Francis lives and will go on living until the end of time. There will always be men and women so enthralled by the Saint's personality as to try to live, more and better each time, the spirit of the Gospel; which happens inside and outside the Franciscan Family, since true *franciscanism* does not usually coincide with the official limits of the Order: not all its members are able to practice it, and many who live it have never thought of joining the Order.

The disappearance of the spirit of Saint Francis would be tantamount to the disappearance of the spirit of the Gospel. In this sense, the ques-

---

[55]As we have already said above, it is well known that the term *riches* in Holy Scripture has a broader and more comprehensive meaning than it has in ordinary language.

tion about the viability of the poverty and the way of life that the Saint intended is completely inane. When Jesus Christ exhorted His disciples to be perfect *as your Father in Heaven is perfect*,[56] He probably was not concerned about the feasibility of His refrain. The goals are always there, to be pursued rather than reached. When one arrives at them, they are no longer objectives to *aim for* and become realities already *achieved*; for *hope that is seen is no longer hope*, and yet hope is such a fundamental virtue that *in hope we are saved.*[57] A wish that becomes true is a culminated wish which, precisely because of it, is no longer a wish. Nevertheless, Christian existence inexorably flows between wish and longing, being consummated only after having fought *a good fight and reached the end of the road* (2 Tim 4:7). Many *goals* which configure the horizon of a Christian existence as aims to be achieved are not reached except at the end of the journey; then they cease to be something searched for and become something found and possessed. In the meantime, they are there, like a lighthouse which illuminates and points at the road that has to be trodden. Perhaps it is no longer a matter of thinking of those goals as already achieved bur rather as always fought for to be accomplished; for that was the true content of the combat: *Well done, good and faithful servant; you have been faithful over a little, I will set you over much.*[58] No Christian faithful will question the realism of the precept which compels him to be perfect as his heavenly Father is perfect; and yet, no one thinks to have achieved in this aeon such a perfection, which, despite everything, is there as a goal to be pursued.[59]

---

[56]Mt 5:48.

[57]Rom 8:24.

[58]Mt 25:21.

[59]Obviously, the precept does not try impel people to attain a perfection equal to that of the Heavenly Father. It is really not hard to understand: Your heavenly Father is perfect; therefore you have to *continually* tend toward perfection. This puts the existence of the Christian faithful in its proper condition of being an itinerant and longing search for God; ultimately a condition of living hope, *thanks to which he is saved* (Rom 8:24).

Things being so, one cannot confine within fixed and well–defined parameters a condition of hope and yearning for what one does not yet possess, nor a condition of itinerancy and searching which tries to accomplish what has not yet been achieved. It would not make any sense to say, for example, that evangelical poverty must be to have this but not that; and that much of this in particular: exactly this amount, neither more nor less (not more because it would destroy poverty, not less because it would lead to rendering life impractical). In a situation that claimed to be truly evangelical nobody could ever say that *this* is Christian poverty; simply because poverty, far from being a reality that is already lived, cannot be but a goal for which to fight. Only Christ espoused Poverty and only He could say that He already was really poor (2 Cor 8:9). But for a Christian poverty is always a road to trod and a goal to reach: And who could say that he is poor enough...? Therefore, in this sense, the amount of energy deployed in the discussion of the various Franciscan *Rules* was but a waste. That was perhaps the reason why none of them satisfied or convinced. Would it not have been better to leave Saint Francis alone, allowing him to live simply the existence which, he said, had been inspired to him by Jesus Christ...? Would it not have been better for the Saint himself simply to *let things be*, without worrying too much about something so unviable as to be imitated by a large group of disciples...? Did not any one realize that real poverty, or evangelical poverty, would cease to be the Poverty of Christ the very moment that someone wanted to pigeonhole it in a *Rule*?

Up to this point, we have been talking about franciscanism as an archetype because of both historical convenience and the singularity of the personal case of Saint Francis. But franciscanism is neither the most recent nor the most striking example of the issue we are dealing with in this chapter. There are a number of other modern and powerful Spiritual Families which could be offered as a more patent case in point of the problem... and the serious consequences which could arise. In reality, the very fact of considering those Families as *powerful* is quite telling.

What follows will address a delicate issue which could stir feelings of animosity and rejection. Nevertheless, we do not want to hurt anybody's feelings, much less offend people or Institutions. We only want to search for the truth as a possible useful means for people of good will. We do not want to denounce behaviors or to judge intentions, which would be a task totally beyond our competence. We simply try to point out ways of doing things which, because they show signs of being apparently out of focus, perhaps derive from and are the consequence of misguided intentions. It is evident that these misguided intentions, because they have to do with activities of Spiritual Families aimed at evangelization in general and at the personal sanctification of their members, can lead to unfortunate and perhaps unforeseen results. Of course, we can be partially or totally wrong in what we are going to say. Should that be the case, we must hope that good–willed people will take into account our right intention and will judge us with benevolence. Otherwise, and to the extent that there is some truth in these reflections, they can be helpful to whoever wants to make good use of them. In turn, the reader will have understood by now that this reflection is in no way a historical essay or study. Since its aim is only at spiritual usefulness or benefit, references to the facts of History are necessarily brief, without mentioning all the events (nor even the most important ones) or thoroughly expounding their evolution and consequences.

Saint Ignatius of Loyola founded the *Society of Jesus* in 1534. It must be conceded that this *Society* has been one of the greatest mysteries in the history of the Church ever since then. Of course, we are not using the term *mystery* in a pejorative sense. Rather we are referring to the number of complex phenomena —often very important from a political and social point of view— which the *Society* has given rise to throughout History. These events have not always been free from relatively ambiguous or equivocal connotations, so it is no wonder that at times they have been the subject of discussions and topics not easy to interpret.

It would be more than unfortunate, however, to try to discredit, in the least, such a prominent and exalted figure as Saint Ignatius of Loyola. His beneficial influence, both in the last centuries of the Church and in the development of the historical events of the Western World, is beyond any discussion. The constellation of Saints belonging to the *Society*, its role as an important instrument in support of the Popes, its work of evangelization throughout the whole world, its positive and universal influence in the world of culture, etc., are evident facts which cannot be doubted.[60]

The problem arises when one considers other events that also appear in the history of the *Society* and which are, as we have said before, susceptible to misinterpretation. Perhaps the fact that these events are so extraordinarily complex and that their multiple consequences —religious as well as social and political— do not always seem to have a positive character makes them subject to discussion. Nevertheless, if we cast an honest glance to the reality of life, it is no surprise that a Religious Order as widespread and influential all over the world as the *Society of Jesus* has always been should be subject to such occurrences.

Once Saint Ignatius decided to change his life radically, he wanted to make available to the Church an important instrument of Evangelization which, at the same time, would be a powerful weapon against the Reformation (which, at that time, was spreading dangerously throughout Europe). As the military man he had been, with

---

[60]For a better understanding of what follows, see A. Gálvez, Commentary on the Song of Songs, Shoreless Lake Press, NJ, 1995, pp. 411 ff.

a strong character and a spirit of adventure, the Saint undertook the task with more than fiery enthusiasm. The very act of giving his Association the name *Company* [*Society*], taken from military jargon, speaks a great deal about the military spirit, the charging militancy that would characterize his disciples in their implacable struggle against Evil. And so it was, indeed. For the *Society of Jesus*, in addition to the many benefits that it brought to the Church, played an important part in containing the Reformation. The intentions of the Saint could not have been better.

Alas, *good intentions* and *well–chosen intentions* are not synonymous notions. Unfortunately, good intentions can be wrong; and the fact that they are the result of personal goodness does not necessarily imply that they are the most appropriate ones for achieving the goal in mind. The well–known adage *the road to hell is paved with good intentions* makes reference to right intentions which were never accomplished; it is also known that the road leading to Eternal Life (the *narrow road*) does not merely consist of wishes, no matter how good they might be. But this is not the present case. We are referring here to totally realized intentions, where the problem has nothing to do with ill will but rather with error. Everything seems to indicate that it happened to Saint Ignatius as it happened to Saint Francis many centuries before: he made a mistake. It is a mistake that does not in the least diminish the greatness of the Saint, but a mistake, nonetheless, with its logical consequences. The same thing happens with ideas; they seem to have a life of their own which develops accordingly, but always with sufficient internal logic as to make it impossible to attribute their outcome to the arbitrariness of any alleged *Destiny*.

Saint Ignatius wrote concrete instructions on how the Society should accomplish its mission, which later were completed by his collaborators and closest followers and came to the conclusion that it was desirable to win over the trust and cooperation of the most exalted powers —an objective that was even given a character of relative priority. The intention, as anyone can suppose, was simply to obtain the right means for evangelizing and better serving the Church. The objective to be accomplished, quite clear of course, was to take advantage of the influence of the most powerful people of a given society; in short, *ascendancy and economic power*, but now focused on and used for achieving the highest goals. It is very clear that the intentions of the holy Founder of the *Society* could not have been more righteous or more in keeping with pure logic.[61] But historical facts prove that the ensuing results were not foreseen by Saint Ignatius, and that, had he anticipated them, they would surely not have pleased him. As we have said before, ideas are determined to have their own life and become independent of the intentions of their progenitors.

After the death of the Saint, not too many years had to pass for one of the major objectives —the intention of influencing the higher echelons of society for the purposes already mentioned— to become a problematic issue... to put it as gently as possible. The truth is that the machinations and political intrigue by leading members of the *Society* started to emerge as a regular *modus operandi*, first in Europe (especially in Spain) and later in colonial America: a set of activities that eventually led to important political consequences.[62]

---

[61]The expression *pure logic* here does not connote any negative critique which, we must insist, is alien to our purpose, but it certainly contains a special intention. By using this expression we are referring to the existence of an entirely honest purpose, but one which nobody cared to compare to the teachings of supernatural Revelation.

[62]The most notable of these consequences is that they are likely to be analyzed from many different perspectives, religious and political and social, with very dif-

But since we are only outlining a summary as short and concise
as possible, and we are not judging historical facts, we will not go
into the controversial and complicated problem of the *Reductions*
in Paraguay and Argentina;[63] nor will we examine the reasons, also
much discussed by historians, which led to the suppression of the
Society.

By modern times, the actions of the *Society* were gaining quite
ambiguous tones. On the one hand, an abundance of missionaries
and Saints, a rain of blessings and spiritual benefits for the Christian People... and, on the other, continuous, increasing, and purely
temporal —even highly suspicious— activities. As regrettable as
it is to say this, one has to point out that roughly from the time
preceding and following Vatican II, this second aspect of the work
of the *Society* was gaining in notoriety and ended up by attaining
supremacy.

It should be kept in mind that the development and enormous
diffusion that *Liberation Theology* reached in the whole universal
Church, especially in Hispanic America and some European countries, was mainly the work of the *Society*. This made possible the
Marxistization of a wide area of Catholic theology and a good part
of the life of the Church.

---

ferent conclusions. Whilst acknowledging the extreme difficulty of establishing
(and finding) an objective History without bias, one must recognize the existence
of highly questionable actions in that *modus operandi*.

[63]It seems that between 1610 and 1670, and only in the region between the
Paraguay and Paraná rivers, the Jesuits converted more than 700,000 Indians;
more than 150,000 of them lived in the *Reductions*. The problem presented to the
Jesuits by organizing the life within these Reductions, of which much has been
written, does not belong to this book. Let us just point out that there is a prolix
historical controversy about it.

This was but one step on the path to implementing neo–modernist trends within the Catholic world. These lines of thought had been trying to impose themselves in the Church, both in the times leading up to Vatican II and in the aftermath of its conclusion; and even more so in later years. Only God knows the havoc that these naturalist–horizontal ideologies (still in full force) are causing to the life of the Church and to the Faith in the Catholic world. It is well known that their procedure consists of calling into question a considerable number of dogmas and everything supernatural. While one cannot lay the whole blame —perhaps not even most of it— solely on the activities of the *Society*, it is honestly impossible to deny its decisive influence on the present crisis. Also today, most of its universities, both in Europe as well as in America, continue to spread freely and widely neo–modernist doctrines.

The *Society*'s cooperation in spreading Darwinian theories is well known; not to mention its giving shelter —both were Jesuits— to such doubtful and extremely influential persons as Teilhard de Chardin[64] and Karl Rahner,[65] for example. Besides, its contribution

---

[64]Teilhard de Chardin, well known for his famous theories of the *Cosmic Christ* or *Christ Omega*, and whose whole doctrine, though not easy to summarize, leads to naturalistic Christianity and very *consistent with science*. At least with science as understood by Teilhard, who gave himself airs of a recognized paleontologist, but who never was taken seriously by the real scientific community. Admittedly, he managed at least to blur Christology and dilute the Person of Christ in an alleged *Final Point* which coincided with nothingness. Apart from his contributing to eroding the faith of the Christian people, his beliefs are more pantheistic and gnostic than anything else. He is much celebrated among non–Catholics. Oddly enough, the historical summary that the *Encyclopedia Britannica* makes of this character is notable for its absolute lack of objectivity.

[65]Karl Rahner was the most influential person in the discussions held during Vatican II and in its development. His doctrinal intrigues before the Conclave and during it are impossible to hide, for there is historical documentation. Karl Rahner was the prophet of the doubt. If one were to write a brief summary of his work one

to propagating in the West the Eastern cults and prayer methods (naturalistic or pantheistic, and always entirely alien to Christianity) is impossible to deny, for it is all too obvious and with sufficient public domain.

There are also well–known theories of some modern historians, whose seriousness and intellectual honesty cannot be doubted, about the strange bonds of rapprochement and cooperation between the current *Society of Jesus* and Freemasonry. This is a sensitive charge with respect to which we will not pronounce ourselves; nevertheless, those who maintain this allegation claim to possess the corresponding documentation on the subject. Whether these connections affect only some members or isolated groups of the *Society,* or whether perhaps they have to do with activities of the Order as such, is an unknown issue but no less puzzling.

As we have said, ideas are like living beings. After a period of gestation, they are born at last; then they grow, unfold, stretch... and end up themselves giving birth to the consequences that are contained in their wombs. Logic, like Mathematics —with which the former identifies deep down— carries in itself strict exigencies which are given no choice. In this regard, suffice it to recall what happened in the world of philosophical doctrines with the Cartesian *cogito* and its consequences. With respect to our case, all seems to indicate that those who choose to gain Influence and Power (which, after all, are mundane and worldly realities), whatever their intentions may have been, become in the end just another instrument that the World handles to its purposes. *It is impossible to serve God and mammon.*

---

would have to say that it consisted mostly of questioning all of the main dogmas of Catholicism. Even today, many years after the closing of the Council, Karl Rahner, besides being the Grand Patriarch and Definer of all Catholic Theology, is also, precisely for this reason, the primary responsible for the dissemination of Neomodernism in the actual Church.

It goes without saying that not everyone will be willing to admit what has been said here. Rather, many will deny it: mainly the same Spiritual Families which may feel that they are being indicated, to begin with.

There will also be some who may agree to recognize the facts but deny, however, any relationship of cause and effect in this case. They will allege that the original intentions or foundational projects of a Spiritual Family — usually blameless and beyond dispute— have nothing to do with the status and operation of that Spiritual Community today. They will insist on saying that, although the events could have happened as described herein, a causal relationship between those events and the practical philosophy and intentions of the Founder does not follow.

This argument is consistent with a saying that went around after the Second Vatican Council in the crucial moments of the crisis that is chastising the Church ever since. The saying, which may seem clever to a superficial approach, is concerned with the disasters which the post–conciliar Church is suffering, intending, no doubt, to exculpate the Council from them. In order to do that, the aphorism merely assured ambitiously that the catastrophe happened *post hoc, sed non propter hoc*, after it (the Council) but not because of it.

It is possible that the authors of this foolishness were convinced that with such a display of wisdom, and so profound an argument, the problem was finally solved. But let us dispense, at least for now, with the truth or falsity of such a farsighted locution. The truth is that once this issue has been attentively examined, despite the amount of good will that one may want to exhibit here, one always reaches the same conclusion, namely that it is impossible not to feel intense anxiety. Trying to dispatch a very serious and extremely important problem by merely using a pun is an indignity. It does not seem honest to assume in the others an IQ that low.

But we can concede the *post hoc*, for there is no doubt as to its veracity. The facts are there, and you can not deny them nor is it necessary to prove them.[66] But what about the *non propter hoc*? It is evident that here the problem becomes complicated.

Unfortunately, there is no evidence about it. The mere assertion that the facts did not happen because of the Council could be true or false. But the mere assertion proves nothing, since the mere fact of pronouncing it alone is not a demonstration. Obviously, such a statement requires additional proofs which have not been provided so far. Indeed, it is curious to notice what certain Systems (usually all of them dictatorial) claim: everybody has the obligation (they presume) to believe what they say as if it were a dogma of faith and *simply because they say it*; which is like an echo of a famous maxim of Lenin: *The more strongly you lie the more firmly you will be believed*. It is certainly astonishing the tendency of people to *just believe what they hear simply because they hear it*; they even more openly believe the more deceitful the speaker is. While it is true that Lenin was a crafty criminal, it is also necessary to recognize that he knew human nature well.

With regard to the issue we are analyzing here, it goes without saying that the relationship between the acquisition of Power and Influence (wealth) by a Religious Order or a Spiritual Family and its situation of decadence or corruption can be either recognized or denied. Normally, of course, the discussion ends with an outright denial of the facts and a dismissal of the problem as non–existent; or at most as a mere vagary without any basis, fabricated by people of ill will.

It should be noted, however, that merely denying the alleged relationship proves nothing. However, since the cause–effect relationship could be a reality, it would become necessary to provide convincing evidence to disprove it. Unfortunately, as anyone can understand, any evidence that could support a denial is, of course, hard to find, if not practically im-

---

[66]In more recent times (we are talking about the first ten years of the twenty–first century) the System has changed the orientation of its strategy. Instead of recognizing and openly proclaim the *post hoc*, it rather tends to blatantly deny the facts and to assure the faithful of an alleged *Springtime of the Church*. But such a fruitful expression continues to be used, if the opportunity presents itself and advises it.

possible. What possible argument could convince someone that there is no connection between the acquisition of Power and Influence and corruption...? Should that argument be found, it would clearly be as interesting as it would be reassuring for everyone.

Obviously, the position that supports the existence of the aforementioned relationship also needs to provide arguments. Anybody could say that it is not acceptable here to affirm something for the sake of affirming it or to negate it for the sake of negating it; this is so obvious that everybody will agree to it.

First of all, let us say, as a necessary introduction, that the arguments which support this belief do not intend to be decisive or conclusive. This does not mean that they do not exist. They do; and they are strong enough to convince anyone who honestly wishes to know the truth. If human life always had to follow absolutely incontrovertible arguments, existence would be impossible.

The first proof to be brought here is empirical. When a given reality produces a particular result over and over again, without variation or exception, it is evident that it is permissible to consider the extremely probable existence of a cause–effect connection. Here we are not in the world of Physics,[67] but in the world of human behavior and relationships. It is true that man is a being endowed with freedom who has somewhat unpredictable reactions, but it is also true that human nature is governed by fixed trends, or at least regular enough trends as to be considered standards or guidelines of conduct. Hence, certain branches of knowledge, such as Anthropology, Psychology, or Sociology are classified, with good reason, as true sciences. To deny its character of cause to a reality whose effects are always the same, without any known exceptions, would be to show a remarkable lack of prudence or a considerable determination to not accept the truth.

With regard to our case, an occurrence which spans many centuries of History and includes our present moment and is, therefore, easily verifiable, it clearly demonstrates the cause–effect connection between the *Wealth–Power–Influence*, acquired by Spiritual Families..., and the corresponding *Decline* —if not corruption— of those same Families.

---

[67]Much less are we in the world of sub–atomic particles. Therefore, there is no reason to think here about the principle of *indetermination.*

Of course, you can always deny the truth of these conclusions as, in fact, the majority of people will do. The world in which we live (the beginning of the twenty–first century) is not exactly a world which is fond of truth. The lies, manipulations, and control of the masses by the System, using the means of modern technology, have reached their apex in the History of Humanity. Due to which there is less freedom now than ever —and precisely now, when we talk about it more than ever before. At the end of the day, as Jesus said, truth is the only thing that makes man free (Jn 8:32).

But the second argument to advance in support of our theory is even more important than the first one.

This second argument has to do with the undeniable fact that the New Testament is clearly against *Riches*. And, with respect to using them for Evangelization (which is what pertains directly to our analysis), the New Testament not only discards them entirely but also encourages, openly and without hesitation, the practice of Poverty and Detachment for making that evangelization efficient and effective. This is what we will try to clearly and comprehensively demonstrate in the following part of this essay.

According to this, and if what has been said so far is true, the only *accountability* that could be imputed to some Founders —regarding certain objectives embodied in their Statutes, Constitutions, or Instructions—, or to the Church that approves them, would be their marginalizing, or bracketing, those teachings which, regarding this issue, have been manifestly established and stated in the New Testament. Of course, we are not talking here about *moral* responsibility. He would be suffering hallucinations who would doubt the good intentions of irreproachable Founders, most of them now raised to the honors of the altar, or of the Church in Her office of Magisterial Teaching. In any case, perhaps we could speak here of *intellectual* responsibility, free from any subjective *blame*, which could be attributed to individual persons or institutions, although not without some *objective* accountability whose exact nature would be difficult to pinpoint. Why were certain warnings and teachings contained in the New Testament not taken more into account...? And to what extent were practical —and not always beneficial— consequences predictable; consequences which could occur in the future as an inescapable corollary of the established premises...?

In modern times, with the appearance of new and vigorous Spiritual Families, the problem has become more topical and important. Some of these Families have displaced the *Society of Jesus* in influence and resources, as well as in the number of members. The *Society*, however, in addition to experiencing a decline in the number of vocations, has had to endure the affliction of numerous desertions.

Undoubtedly, the increasing success of new Spiritual Families in the Church has complex causes which would deserve an analysis of its own, if that were possible. None of them would hesitate to attribute its rapid flourishing to its own peculiar *charism* which, having been inspired by the Spirit to the respective founder, they intend to wield to respond to the new challenges and needs that Christian existence must face in our modern times. This belief has been endorsed by their approval from the Church; an approval which we cannot but suppose is true.

So much for the study of the problem as far as its supernatural dimension is concerned. But a more secular analysis would easily find other causes for the phenomenon. This time they would not belong to the supernatural order, but they would be as equally decisive and worthy of reflection. As to which of these two types of causes has been more important, or if one of them is incompatible with the other and to what extent, that is something known only to God and whose study is not for this place.

In honor to the truth, we must recognize that some of these Spiritual Families, which are so booming today, have made a substantial collection of what we have been calling *Riches*: Power, Influence, Material Means, and Money. Some Families even seem to resemble powerful Multinational Organizations.

Given the way human nature is, some will feel affected and hurt by these claims, which consequently will often be rejected in spite of the evidence. However, we state again that *we do not want to judge intentions*. That is not our mission; moreover, should it be the case that we had to decide regarding this issue, we would willingly acknowledge that such intentions were entirely honest. We are just trying to examine History, with the full intention of providing a service to the truth that can be useful to people of good will.

The problem is, as was already mentioned above and as we shall see later more broadly, that such ways of proceeding by the corresponding Spiritual Families do *not seem to agree well with the teachings about this topic contained in the New Testament*.

If we accept as true what was said about the accumulation of Power and Influence, everything seems to indicate that these two factors, equally important, had a part to play in this issue. To explain this, we will also try to stick to the facts.

In the first place, some degree of *denaturalization* with respect to some of the most important Christian virtues seems to have occurred. Paradoxically, this has contributed to the extraordinary expansion of some of these Spiritual Families.

Regarding our case, the most important and distinctive of those *metamorphosed* virtues is poverty. The fact that it easily lends itself to being the subject of some shady deals makes it the crux of the problem.

Oddly enough, since poverty is the virtue most amenable to histrionics, once it is disguised and suitably made up, it can become a significant source of *wealth*.

Poverty is a strange and singular, as well as sublime, virtue. However, if it is not firmly rooted in a most solid Christian existence, it produces unexpected effects that detract from it completely. One of them, for example, is what we might dub the *calling effect*.

When poverty loses the most enchanting and quirky of its charms, that is, the contempt that it constantly endures from the world, it quickly becomes a virtue of *show* —despite its being the most opposite thing to a performance, or *show*, imaginable. Poverty is neither made for the theater nor does it ever enjoy the approval or the applause of a credible audience. Its most distinctive aspects would be to go unnoticed and unknown, never to be applauded by anyone, nor envied or desired anywhere. The truth is that if anyone wishes to understand this virtue he should first approach the Mystery of the Cross. Despite which, if poverty chooses to leave its own place of misery, hardships, and silence..., and forgets that contempt on the part of the world is a quality peculiar to its essence... and seeks to present itself all dressed–up, with the proper make–up, and redolent... then poverty becomes, as by a marvel, a virtue of *show* —and, by now, the object of all the applause. Of course, it also needs the element of propaganda, as always happens whenever one wants to make something widely known to the public. The consequence of all of this is that, once the stage has been set, and thanks to the *calling effect,* what we have come to call *wealth* arises as if by magic. The many goods at the disposal of the world start to pour in from everywhere. At the same time, the prestige and influence of those who now are considered charmingly poor increase. Finally, the least expected change has happened: the wonderful, indescribable, incredible, and divine Christian Virtue of Poverty has become something as eccentric as the peculiar triad of Influence–Money–Power; although now accompanied, it could not be otherwise, by the applause and admiration of the World.

And it is at this point when the decline begins. Soon deviations appear relative to the purposes and the charism of the founder, but usually at a uniformly accelerated speed. At the end, it could happen that a particular Religious Order, Institute, Congregation, or any form of Association whose aims are the sanctification and evangelization of people and which has been approved by the Church, eventually becomes something that looks little or nothing like the blueprint of the founder and the enthusiasms of the first beginnings. Once wealth has been accepted as the best means to achieve the aims pursued, the process becomes irreversible. One does not need to assume that the result has been sought, or even planned, within the framework of the original purposes. But still, once the cause has been brought into play, the effect is produced accordingly as if it were an *ex opere operato* consequence.

This process gives rise to apparently confusing actions which sometimes are ambiguous while at other times are clearly wrong. Moreover, unfortunately sometimes one cannot exclude occasions when intentions are difficult to qualify. When those who were meant to evangelize the World through the *startling* witness of Christian virtue lived in fullness and in total opposition to the criteria of that World, they choose to use the weapons and means proper to the World... *The failure of the alleged witness and the victory of Evil are fully insured.*

It should be noted that, over the centuries, Religious Orders, in addition to the purpose of the sanctification of its members, have aimed at providing the World with a testimony of Christian life. This testimony should be so obvious, evident, and manifest (*shockingly* overwhelming) as to serve as a lever, in order to prepare the World for conversion. As to how to carry it out, there could not be a more appropriate means than practicing, strictly and rigorously, the three evangelical vows or counsels.[68]

---

[68]This is the main feature that would differentiate, within the Church, *religious* from *secular* members (the latter in both of its components, priests and laity). And if it is true that the *spirit* of the evangelical counsels applies equally to all Christians who aspire to be holy, it is obvious that, *formally* speaking, those counsels have always corresponded more strictly to the religious, that is, those counsels

Salt is good, but if the salt shall lose its savor, wherewith shall it be seasoned? It is neither useful for the soil nor for the dunghill; it shall be cast out. He that has ears to hear, let him hear.[69]

What happens when a testimony of Christian life, called to be as thorough and convincing, through rigorous practice of the evangelical counsels, as to serve as a salutary lesson to the World in order to *aggressively* drive that World to conversion (*compelle intrare, ut impleatur domus mea,* compel them to come in, that my house may be filled with guests[70]); what happens when that testimony is weakened to the point that combatants come to the contest with the same weapons and in the same arenas as those of the World? The answer has been given by Jesus Christ Himself in a clear enough language: If the salt shall lose its savor it is no longer good for anything; neither for the soil nor even for the dunghill.

Some Spiritual Families seem to have reached this point we are talking about. Not only do they claim that they live the virtue of poverty, but they even boast about it and announce it everywhere. They begin by assuming as certain that they live this virtue with admirable (and novel) authenticity and end up by allowing the *media* to be in charge of the advertising; which brings about immediately,

---

are practiced by them in a *blatant* and defiant way before the World and its criteria. At present, because some groups (Secular Institutes and others) have also sought to live the vows (with different and varied legal characteristics regarding their mandatory, temporary, etc., nature), without considering themselves *religious* because of it; and also because canon law is still not too clear about this matter, it has not yet been possible to completely dispel every hint of confusion between *religious* and *secular* members of the Church. But it remains clear that the spirit of the evangelical counsels, lived more or less compulsory and under various legal forms (although always *manifestly*), is the hallmark of all Spiritual Families of consecrated souls.

[69]Lk 14: 34–35.
[70]Lk 14:23.

as we have said above, the *calling effect*. As *extraordinary poverty*, absolute unselfishness, and dedication to the marginalized by such a Spiritual Family are more widely known, the means made available to it overwhelmingly increase. Always present among these are Prestige and Fame, whose glories are famously proclaimed and spread with added din by the spokesmen of the World.

It is important to realize that the salutary effects of *scandal*, intended primarily to contradict (in order to convert it) a World which has drifted apart from God, gives rise to a strangely opposite effect. What that *scandal* now causes is admiration from a World that celebrates enthusiastically the glories of Poverty, as if the World had finally reached a stage of accepting the existence of a Christianity which someone can live with sincerity. Wouldn't such a thing be worthy of praise and honor, along with an outpouring of the means to contribute to it?

Definitely we need to recognize what would happen if human beings were not so easily blinded; they would soon experience an acute sense of suspicion. *Because it so happens that poverty (the true Christian virtue) has never been applauded (and certainly not by the world); much less has it been a source of new wealth, fame, or power.* Actually, this evidence of the applause of Christian poverty by the World surpasses the boundaries of what is outlandish and becomes extraordinary and unusual. Everything seems to indicate that, thanks to this situation, the World finally recognizes the greatness of the Gospel... and so applauds it.

How can something so unheard of be possible, and how did we arrive at a situation where someone who speaks the language of the Gospel is heard by the World, not only with admiration and accolades, but even with an enthusiastic spirit of collaboration? And the answer, as hard as it may seem, is not difficult to find. Such a language is accepted and celebrated by the World *because it is no longer the language of the Gospel,* but rather something different and mundane: *They are of the world; therefore, they speak of the world and the world listens to them.*[71]

When a virtue as important and sublime as poverty is denaturalized, situations arise about which the least you can say, using euphemistic language, is that they are *ambiguous.* It is very possible, and even probable, that the World applauds them enthusiastically; which is enough to prove that such situations (perhaps introduced unconsciously by those who caused them) have been stripped and emptied of their Christian content: *If you were of the world, the world would love its own.*[72] Indeed, those situations *seem to be* Christian, but they are proportionally less Christian the more they appear to be (again the *show* effect, cf. Mt 6:1). The testimony they provide is nonexistent, at best; there is the possibility that their testimony even be negative. For we must consider, with respect to Christian life, that a non–existing testimony, not only does not make sense: *Nisi granum frumenti cadens in terram mortuum fuerit, ipsum solum manet,* Unless a wheat grain falls into the earth and dies, it remains only a single grain,[73] it actually presents a dangerously negative content: *I am the vine and my Father is the husbandman. Every branch in me that bears no fruit he cuts... If anyone does not abide in me he is cast forth as a branch and withers; and they gather him up and throw him into the fire, and he burns.*[74]

Without intending to adopt a stance that corresponds only to God, that of judging intentions (it is essential to repeat it once more), it seems unlikely that anybody was converted by the gesture of Mother Teresa of Calcutta, so aired by the *media* as being previously prepared for the occasion, of throwing television sets out the window of one of her convents. It is hard to believe that such a spectacular demonstration of poverty, or of any virtue, can serve as Christian witness to the World. Maybe someone wants

---

[71] 1 Jn 4:5.

[72] Jn 15:19.

[73] Jn 12:24.

[74] Jn 15: 1–2.5–6.

to argue that in such cases it is not a matter of bearing testimony, but simply of demanding the enforcement of a particular virtue. This claim, however, is impossible to maintain, for such an obvious advertising gesture can not give up its essentially testimonial aspect.

In this connection, it is clear that we Christians should adopt a suspicious attitude toward spectacular gestures. We easily forget that, on principle, Jesus Christ always shunned them. He hid when they tried to make Him king; He forbade touting the miracle to those He cured; He forbade His disciples to say He was the Messiah; He strictly refused any demonstration of Power when someone called for it; and so on, etc... It is true that the Apostle says that we have been made a *spectacle* to the world and to angels and to men (1 Cor 4:9). However, reading this verse and the ones following it in their entirety is all one need do to be immediately convinced that in this case the term has an absolutely disparaging and painful sense. Christians also were thrown to wild beasts in the Roman circus as a bloody spectacle for the crowds. In the same way, in the Letter to the Hebrews, Christians were exhorted to remember those early days of their conversion *in quibus illuminati magnum certamen sustinuistis passionum; in altero quidem opprobriis et tribulationibus spectaculum facti...* wherein, being illuminated, you endured a great fight of afflictions. And on the one hand indeed, by reproaches and tribulations, you were made a gazingstock...[75]

Mother Teresa of Calcutta, whose status as an extraordinary woman is not being called into question here, displayed throughout her life various gestures which one can willingly admit as being well intentioned, but whose character as Christian testimony is rather questionable. For instance, her address for Peace at the United Nations.

It is true that such an important and universal woman, who earned the Nobel Peace Prize, was easily and frequently received by Heads of State, or in audience by the Pope; she could always contribute favorably with her words to such a beneficial cause. But the set of circumstances that often accompany these types of events (and this one in particular) make them

---

[75]Heb 10: 32–33.

questionable, at least, as to their objectives and quite weak, at best, in terms of their testimonial value.

Everyone knows, for example, that the UN is an infected cesspool and a bottomless pit of corruption where nobody is interested in Christianity and where everybody would deride any claim to recognize the simplest value based on any ethics, even merely natural ethics. Not to mention that the vast majority of those who heard her are even open enemies of Christian values.[76] To believe that someone there would listen to the words and exhortations of Mother Teresa or that he would feel moved or convinced by them, is to believe in fairy tales or in ghosts of castles.

What is certain is that nobody in his right mind, and with a modicum of common sense, would be willing to believe that such a discourse would have a positive outcome. It would take an immeasurable dose of naiveté to believe that, from that moment on, the leaders of the World either would accept Peace or would start immediately working to achieve it. Some might think that, at least, the paths which lead to such a happy and desired conclusion would have been smoothed out to some extent. That would be akin to trying to win the first prize in a lottery, but not even bothering to buy tickets to participate in it.

That said, one must admit that an event like this conference presents a totally ambiguous significance. What could have been intended by it...? To convince world leaders...? Obviously not; and anybody who thinks rationally cannot but recognize this fact. Another explanation, therefore, must be sought. Was the purpose to give a testimony of Christian faith, expounding before the Powers of this World the need to achieve Peace —a need which can be clearly seen in the teachings and admonitions of the Gospel...? And again, the answer cannot but be strongly in the negative, since it is also impossible to accept this second justification at all.

---

[76] Clearly, they *heard* is a way of speaking, but it is said here with some irony. It was possible that perhaps they *heard* her, but it is very doubtful that they *listened* to her. Would it not be closer to the truth to think, as painful as it may be to say this, that Mother Teresa was seen on that occasion as one who assists at a circus act?

First, because Mother Teresa of Calcutta could not speak on that occasion *but of a peace as understood by the world and never as Jesus regarded it* and left it to His disciples and followers (Jn 14:27).[77] To claim otherwise would have caused a raucous laughter in the auditorium. But if this is so, what meaning could the presence of Mother Teresa at the UN have...?

But there is something still more important. It so happens that *the New Testament never speaks of peace as understood by the World* (no wars), except in order to open the eyes of the enthralled idealist who, dreaming of utopias, thinks that it is possible to end the wars before the second coming of Our Lord (Mt 24: 6–7, Mk 13: 7–8; Lk 21: 9 ff.; 19: 43–44). Or even in order to simply speak ironically about naïve people who, at the end of time, will still be talking about peace, and yet, at the least imaginable moment and when they are clamoring most intently for it, they will be surprised by the most dreadful disasters (1 Thess 5:3). If what we have said is true, and we are now speaking plainly, a question inevitably follows: What was Mother Teresa talking about, and what exactly was she announcing at the UN...?

There is no other option but to think that Mother Teresa, despite the good intentions which undoubtedly encouraged her, had to be another victim of the strong winds of *show* that have been lashing against the Church since Vatican II. We can be sure she was not aware of the maneuver, which

---

[77]What emerges from this text is that Jesus Christ seems to completely ignore peace as understood by the world. The Gospel is already a Doctrinal body sufficient in itself to teach men how to live in loving harmony. Moreover, texts such as Matthew 10: 34–35 and Luke 12: 51–53 (*non veni mittere pacem, sed gladium*, I have come not to bring peace, but a sword, etc.), cannot refer indeed to war or to the absence of war, but they evidently make it clear that Jesus Christ has not come to establish exactly a situation of calm. Saint Augustine understood peace as *tranquillitas ordinis* (in his *De Civitate Dei*, book 19, Chapter 13), which seems to coincide, as far as order is concerned, with the well-known saying *iustitia et pax asculatae sunt*, righteousness and peace have kissed each other, of Psalm 85:11. But such an order and justice, along with the ensuing peace, so longed for by the human race, will not be true for men until *a new heaven and new earth* are created (2 Pet 3:13).

perhaps cannot be said to the same extent about those who might have encouraged her. There are still Christians who think that the *show* carries strength as a demonstrative argument, believing that power is always convincing. They forget that Jesus Christ died on a cross, convicted by a human race that, for the most part, keeps on despising Him today. These Christians do not want to realize that the true strength of Christianity, as the sole Power to oppose the power of the World, is weakness (*My ways are not your ways*). The true disciple of Jesus Christ, contrary to those who live according to the World —*who do all their works to be seen by men*[78]—, acts always looking to God and never keeping in mind what men may think or say.

We have said, regarding the acquisition of *Wealth* with the purpose of Evangelization, that the procedure could be carried out in two ways, seemingly different but basically matched: through the accumulation of Money or through the acquisition of Power. Both procedures converge at the same point, as stated above when we remembered the saying of Quevedo: *Mr. Money is a Powerful Gentleman*; which could be turned around to say that Money always aims at Power. One does not need to emphasize here that we are referring to concepts and values such as money, power, influence, and so on, in their most purely mundane sense. But in the same way as we have already spoken of money as being opposed to poverty and as the *first goal* to be achieved, now we will do the same thing, although this time changing the perspective: that is, the *immediate objective* to be accomplished now is the search for Power. One can easily understand that both ends are looking for one and the same thing, namely Power; and we do not have to insist that all this is allegedly being done with a view to better and more effective Evangelization. It is only a matter of choosing one of them as the shorter

---

[78]Mt 23:5.

and easier path. Let us now try to say something about the second one.

You can gather a group of people, as numerous and influential as possible, for the purpose of Evangelization. If the attempt is successful, you end up accumulating a set of important and *powerful* people; a large army which, in this case, would belong to Jesus Christ, if we stick to the stated intentions of the organizers.

It would be something similar to what Saint Ignatius of Loyola attempted and to what, many years before him, Saint Francis of Assisi tried. Although one important difference between the two should be noted: *The Poverello* did not primarily intend to form a *powerful* group, but rather a *large* group of faithful imitators of Jesus Christ; he did not realize then, or perhaps it was too late when he did, just how easily a large group of people could become powerful.

But we are dealing here with something different: the greater abundance of modern resources and procedures allows for more ambitious projects than those of which the Founder of the *Society of Jesus*, in his burning love for the Church, ever dreamed; projects of a much higher calibre than those which the naïve enthusiasm of the Saint of Assisi could ever reach.

However, it is precisely because of this latter reality that the problem acquires more serious significance, which would certainly deserve a thorough and deep reflection that does not belong to this study.

Now it is not easy to presume that such projects involve *a priori* purely evangelizing intentions, although Spiritual Families following such procedures proclaim this apriority very loudly. However, we immediately find the first stumbling block, for *now the aim is indeed to bring together a powerful Army*, although this aim is not clearly and explicitly admitted. In fact, there is already a Spiritual Family in the Church that has achieved it.

The difficulty in admitting the above *apriority* is based mainly on how these Spiritual Families proceed when recruiting new proselytes, which is achieved in great numbers by following a successful *modus operandi*. The first step is to make a clean sweep of Revealed Truth and everything that signifies an impediment to the new ideology, namely, Doctrine, Tradition, and the Magisterium of the Church.

Needless to say, this procedure raises a new problem, even more serious and difficult to resolve; for now the question is to know exactly what is the objective pursued: to raise a large army as an effective instrument and weapon of the Church (Ignatian *Society* style, but with more power) or to destroy her from within; another new mystery whose explication does not belong to this study.

Recruiting large groups of people within the Church is not difficult. To this purpose, two methods, seemingly antithetical but quite effective, are mainly used.

The first one, which has led to a tremendous growth and a rapid expansion of certain Spiritual Families, consists, in general, in the dissemination of dazzling and appealing programs whose difficulty levels are below the minimum requirement. These programs tout a *trifling* spirituality, sufficiently watered down, which usually has great success with those who like to feel committed through a spirituality that actually demands nothing. But it sounds nice, and is well regarded in the international market of *progressive* theology and *liberated* Catholicism. Moreover, the organizers of these Movements tend to write books on a rather unsubstantial spirituality, *soft to the palate*, and somewhat diluted, in whose fashion clichés abound: love (meaning one without problems and to the liking of today's people), solidarity, commitment to the poor, human values... and so on. All of which have the particularity, how could it be otherwise, of attracting supporters of a religion which is not at all demanding and uncompromising. The real truth is that, ultimately, these Groups lack import and content, except for their extraordinary ease in bringing people together to get involved (and swell the numbers) at meetings, parades, and liturgical and pastoral settings of massive scopes (*shows*). To which we must add the many privileges and perks that, of course, their organizers enjoy: they tend to be appointed Chieftains; Members of the Board of Commissions of High Ecclesiastical Bureaucracy; Presidents (with honor or without it) of a hubbub of useless Associations; etc. A quality, however, which provides them with enough prestige to be summoned from everywhere to provide others with the benefits of their *spirituality* and apostolic *experience Urbi et Orbi*.

The second method of recruitment, with more practical results than the previous one, has much to do with the methods used by the sects and heresies throughout the ages. Apparently, contrary to the foregoing, this method is characterized by professing vigorous beliefs and demanding strong commitments. The followers are challenged to hold to those beliefs and commitments with a blind faith which, however, bears little relation to the corresponding theological virtue.[79]

Under the banner of a Christianity which allegedly is all the more authentic the more radical it is, these Groups preach a Catholicism —genuine and demanding, according to them— which soon accrues from everywhere scores of hardcore fans. They are usually well-

---

[79]The faith we are referring to in no way is the virtue mentioned in Heb 11:1: *Est autem fides sperandorum substantia, rerum argumentum non apparentium,* Now faith is the substance of things hoped for, the evidence of things not seen. The faith of these Groups is rather an unconditional belief or trust, very close to fanaticism, in their founders.

meaning, simple people, convinced of having found at last the true expression and experience of a faith that they believed lost forever. It can easily be understood that these Movements take advantage of the state of crisis in the Church, for which sake simple people, otherwise almost hopeless, feel themselves compelled to find something safe, wherever it may be.

These Groups propose, as an alternative, a Catholicism that actually becomes a new religion. Their success among great masses of Christians is based, as we said above, on methods and procedures that resemble those practiced by sects and heresies and which lead to the implementation of a new set of beliefs seemingly more genuine, more in line with a supposedly *primitive* Christianity, but at whose bottom is the use of tricks and methods which seem to better accomodate human nature and which, therefore, are more easily accepted by it. We are referring to fallen human nature, of course; which, although repaired by grace, is still exactly the same victim of lust and still retains its tendency to sin. This makes it possible to erect a set of dogmas and practices whose primary contingency is none other than the removal of the Cross. To achieve that, they do not hesitate to fabricate the idea of a new God, more of a Father, more Good–natured and Merciful, less Righteous and Avenging; the author of a religion more in line with human beings who instinctively flee from sacrifice and effort. Finally, the message of Jesus Christ is left far behind, according to which *narrow is the gate and strait the road that leads to life, and few there are that find it!*[80] Not to mention the Apostle's exhortation to take care not to leave without content (not to empty) the Cross of Christ.[81] In the end, this approach leads to a Catholicism characterized by guitars and

---

[80]Mt 7:14.

[81]1 Cor 1:17.

pop music, extolling a Community that needs no priests, practicing a worship which substitutes the idea of Solidarity between men
and women for the notion of Sacrifice, proclaiming Joy in the Holy
Spirit (Who is now converted into an instrument for personal use)
now transmuted into the revelry and *mystical* outcries of an *ecstatic*
community in which the God of Joy has ultimately been replaced
by the God of Whoopee.

The *Neo–catechumenal Way* Movement is beyond a doubt the most
influential Religious Family that exists in the Church today, far beyond
any other established and extensively widespread Family. Some say (we
do not know to what extent they are exaggerating) that its founder, Kiko
Argüello, is more powerful than the Pope, since he has a huge number
of followers around the world, all *hardcore* devotees, with a confidence in
the founder so blind as to not call into question, in any way, any of his
instructions. Cármen Hernández is the co–founder of the Movement; Both
Cármen and Kiko are equally regarded as the brains of the Organization,
although Kiko Argüello normally operates as the visible head.

There is still not enough literature, at least known to us, about the
spirituality of the Movement. Moreover, the documents issued by the Organization itself are closely guarded, and it is impossible for non–members
to access them; something rather esoteric, which seems pretty much —
one must admit— in accord with the procedures of sects. Sects like the
Neo–catechumenal Way Movement have always kept their writings and instruction manuals for the *initiated*. Hence, it has been impossible for us
to consult firsthand the *Catechetical Guidelines for the Training Phase*,
seemingly a capital Document about the spirituality of this Movement.[82]
So we have had to resort to the various declarations of Kiko Argüello
(and some of his close collaborators), scattered here and there in maga-
zines and testimonial press conferences. As for in–depth studies, we have
only been able to consult a series of articles by Mark Alessio[83] published

---

[82]Henceforth *Catechism.*

[83]Mark Alessio was for many years a prominent member of the Neo-
catechumenal movement.

in the American journal *Catholic Family News*, plus the references that we have obtained from two books by Enrico Zoffoli: *Heresies of the Neo-catechumenal Movement* and *Neo-catechumenal Catechesis and Orthodoxy of the Pope*.[84] Some of these testimonials we have had to translate from English ourselves, but we can attest to our fidelity to the originals and the accuracy of both.[85]

In his Apostolic Letter *Ecclesia in America* 1999, Pope John Paul II explained the principles underlying the New Evangelization as the *commitment to carry out not a re-evangelization but a new evangelization; new regarding its enthusiasm, its methods, and its expression.*

Here it is worth noting the danger of ambiguity that surrounds some words uttered, no doubt, with the best of intentions. In fact, there were some who interpreted this *new evangelization* to the letter. Although, in reality, everybody knows well how easily one can transfer the Logic of the *new (novel)* to the *different*; entirely different, say some, unless we are prepared —so they say— to resign ourselves to more of the same.

But, for more than twenty centuries, the Church has been insistent on keeping the *Deposit* of what has always been considered an intangible Revelation.[86] It is true that the good scribe timely draws out of his treasure things *nova et vetera* (Mt 13:52); with much care, however, to ensure that *nova* does not drown or dislodge what is *vetera*; otherwise both would be invalidated. Moreover, Saint Vincent of Lerins already said in the fifth century that *nihil innovetur nisi quod traditum est*. Even before him, it seems that Saint Paul was concerned about this issue: *O Timothee*

---

[84]The works by Father Enrico Zoffoli were given to high-ranking Bishops and Cardinals, even to the Pope himself, but nobody took them into account.

[85]Let us add the important caveat that the present writing is not intended as a comprehensive study, not even a fairly summarized one, about the spirituality of this Movement. It tries to be a simple and brief summary, by way of illustration in this chapter of the book, by which we intentionally attempt to extend ourselves to the least possible degree; among other reasons, because of the unpleasantness of the subject.

[86]Note that the word "deposit" evokes the notion of something that has to be guarded and kept untouched, both in its integrity and in its essence.

depositum custodi.[87] The serious warnings of the Apocalypse, therefore, do not surprise us: *If any man shall add to these things* [the words of the prophecy of this book], *God shall add unto him the plagues written in this book. And if any man shall take away from the words of the book of this prophecy, God shall take away his part out of the tree of life.*[88]

As for the determination and precise content of *vetera* and *nova*, the mode and manner of handling them, and their correct interpretation, these are things that come under the jurisdiction of the authentic Magisterium of the Church only. Therefore, no individual, absolutely no one, can claim the right to carry out such a function, no matter how much that person may feel himself or allege himself to be inspired by the Holy Spirit; so much so that even assuming the (absurd) hypothesis that such a thing were true, it would still be something impossible to authenticate, and, consequently, no one could feel compelled to accept such changes.

However, the Movement called *Neo–catechumenal Way* did not have any trouble in developing a new concept of the History of Religion; and of something even more important yet: nothing less than the Holy Sacrifice of the Mass.

> *Primitive man, say Kiko and Carmen, "has always met phenomena, things superior to him: storms, illness, death, etc., and he found it necessary to find shelter, to stop in some way these powers which were superior to him." In an effort to appease these superior forces, man "created a religion, and he built a temple and an altar and put a priest there." With the acceptance of Christianity under the Emperor Constantine, hordes of improperly catechized pagans swarmed into the Church, bringing with them their pagan beliefs, particularly the idea of fear–induced blood sacrifice to gain the favor of higher powers. These examples of "natural religiosity" infected the celebration of the Mass, so that it, too, became an example of offering things to God to appease Him. As a result, say the NCW founders, "there's one thing that this mass of pagans are going to see in*

---

[87]1 Tim 6:20.

[88]Rev 22: 18–19.

the Christian liturgy: the idea of sacrifice. It's a total regression to the Old Testament which Israel itself had outgrown."[89]

In case these notions of Religion and the Mass as understood by the Neo–catechumenal Way has not been made clear, let us see some other texts of the *Catechism*, their main document which expounds the spirituality of this Movement:

"So we see a whole series of ideas entering the liturgy from the natural religions: offering things to God to placate Him, sacrifices, lambs, offerings, etc. Israel too did this sort of thing in their sacrificial cult, but little by little God had brought them from sacrifices and temples toward a liturgy of praise and glorifying, and to the great spirituality of the Passover. The new people in the Church then returned to what the people of Israel left behind, the pagan rites appear in the Christian liturgy."[90]

The *Neo–catechumenal Way* totally rejects the notion of the Mass as an *unbloody sacrifice*:

"Perhaps God requires the blood of His Son, His Sacrifice, to appease Himself? But what kind of a God have we done [sic]? We have arrived to think that God appeases His Wrath in the sacrifice of His Son in the manner of the pagan gods."[91]

In the world–view of the *Way* founders —Mark Alessio goes on to explain— the Mass quickly degenerated from a fervent and inspired banquet of praise to a static, superstitious routine filled with destructive images of *sacrifice*. Thankfully, the NCW founders happened along in the

---

[89] *Catholic Family News*: "Where do Rome and the Neo–catechumenal Way Stand in 2006?" April 2006.

[90] *Ibid.*

[91] *Ibid.*

twentieth Century to take over and set the Church back on course, especially via recovering, among other things, the supposed joy of the primitive Christian *banquets*.

A description of the Neo–catechumenal *Eucharist*[92] would take us out to a more detailed knowledge of the core of the spirituality of the Way. But given that this would exceed the scope of the present chapter, we will merely list a brief summary of the key points about this issue.

Overall, it is a matter of substituting an anthropocentric Liturgy for a God–centered one. To that purpose, everything has been studied and prepared in great detail. The *eucharists* are extremely noisy and bustling festive assemblies; never held in the temple (and the uninitiated are not allowed to participate in them). The figure of the priest has lost all relevance in them (according to the doctrine denying the hierarchical constitution of the Church). Preaching has been replaced by spontaneous interventions of almost all of the people present at them, in endless succession of long duration, while only a few words at the end are reserved for the priest, whose mission is merely to put the finishing touch to the speeches of the laity. The Presence of Christ in the Sacrament of the Eucharist is no longer a belief held in these assemblies, and hence the sacred character of that Presence has been lost in them; the faithful receive the Eucharist sitting, without any concern for the meaning of sin, in the consciousness that they are celebrating merely an act of solidarity.[93] In short, every vestige of sacredness has been removed from these assemblies; it has been replaced by the joy of a Community (guitars, songs, pop music, etc...) which claims to be animated by the Spirit, but which actually has turned the Sacrifice of

---

[92] The Neo–catechumenal Movement very carefully avoids using the term *Mass*, which it has replaced with the word *Eucharist*. We must admit, nevertheless, that, in doing so, it follows the tendencies of the modern *progressive* theology that is associated with Modernism. The ultimate goal pursued here is to erase any notion of the Mass as the memorial of the Sacrifice at Calvary made real *here and now* in an unbloody manner —which is never merely a remembrance or a symbol.

[93] For Kiko Argüello, without the assembly proclaiming the Eucharist there can be no Eucharist, and the Eucharist received outside the Mass is but a *canned communion*.

Calvary into a boisterous revelry. Man, so it seems, no longer needs God for his agapes: he can organize his own going out on the town, and to his own liking.

However, since the specification of each of these points would take us too far, we must confine ourselves to writing a cursory but pretty accurate list of some of the propositions that establish the foundations of the Neo–catechumenal spirituality. The list is mainly based on the Neo–catechumenal *Catechism* and is not intended to be exhaustive:

> 1. *Christ has not attained any redemption.*
>
> 2. *Sin is not possible, since man can not help it.*
>
> 3. *Jesus cannot have satisfied the mercy of God, since He is only pardoning mercy.*
>
> 4. *Jesus has not offered Himself as a victim for the sins of the world. No "sacrifice" was carried out on the cross.*
>
> 5. *The Church is not a legally constituted hierarchical society, but a charismatic society.*
>
> 6. *There is not a priesthood conferred within the Church and derived from the sacrament of Holy Orders, since Baptism is sufficient to incorporate everybody into Christ, the one high priest.*
>
> 7. *No "sacrifice" is offered on the altar, for no sacrifice has ever been accomplished by Jesus Christ.*
>
> 8. *There is no Eucharist without an assembly to proclaim it... It is this assembly that gives rise to the Eucharist.*
>
> 9. *"Transubstantiation" is not a dogma of faith, but simply an attempt by theologians to explain the "way" of Christ's presence.*
>
> 10. *The true, real and substantial presence of Christ in the Eucharist can not be accepted, nor is the alleged miracle of "transubstantiation" believable; the extant particles or those which fall from the altar do not contain such a presence and are therefore not worthy of worship.*
>
> 11. *Confession is public and communal.*

Etcetera. As we have said, this list is not intended in any way to be exhaustive. And this is not the place (nor are we the ones called) to carry out a critical study of the spirituality, or theology, of the Neo–catechumenal movement; assuming that the notions of spirituality and theology can be applied to this ideology. We are concerned here only with the connection of this movement to the content of this chapter. Because the development of a man–made religion for the sake of man, in which one dispenses with supernatural motivations and especially with the indictment of the Cross, and in which one appeals to most peculiar trends that emerge from fallen human nature that disregards Grace (despite its claim to possess the Spirit)... is obviously a great tool for the acquisition of Power; as facts demonstrate unequivocally.

Something that forcefully calls one's attention, at first glance and regardless of any critical spirit, is the fact that it has taken more than twenty centuries —until the coming into the world of Kiko Argüello and Carmen Hernández— for Christianity to get to know itself. Millions of Christians have lived throughout this time deluded and living in the greatest of all mistakes. One wonders whether God has done right in delaying the appearance of such Guides of True Christianity, thus preventing many human beings of good will from knowing truth, and savoring and enjoying authentic Christianity —for more than twenty centuries! One must face it: without a doubt, the History of Humanity is full of insoluble mysteries.

Another reason for the extraordinary admiration aroused by the Neo–catechumenal movement, in its efforts to root out of Christianity every vestige of the *Cross* or *Sacrifice* —*thus turning the Suffering Servant of Yahweh into the Christ of Revelry*[94]— is the unbelievable but veritable fact that Christianity has considered for such a long time that a man as wrong as Saint Paul was an inspired Apostle. The Apostle of the Gentiles occasionally became annoyed, and even reacted with impatience. Facing some who accused him of insisting on circumcision practices and of reverting to obsolete doctrines (which sounds familiar if you think about the topic we are dealing with), Saint Paul exclaimed angrily: *As for me, brethren, if I yet preach circumcision, why do I yet suffer persecution? Then is the*

---

[94] *The Christ of Revelry* is not a new name given to Jesus Christ venerated in Andalusia or a new Brotherhood of Holy Week; he is the Christ of the New Evangelization entrusted to the Neo–catechumenal movement.

scandal of the cross made void. I would they mutilate themselves, who trouble you![95] There are still around some *exegete* nuns who claim —on the subject of feminism— that the Bible, of course, is not male chauvinistic, but that the Apostle actually was. That is all right, because there are people for everything: they are an opportunity for others to exercise patience and ignore their nonsense. But the present issue is much worse: to staunchly defend at all costs *the scandal of the Cross*!... Furthermore, the Apostle was also extremely wrong, that is, in his way of carrying out his ministry: *For Christ sent me not to baptize, but to preach the gospel; not in wisdom of speech, lest the cross of Christ should be made void.*[96] Some speak of what they call *historical fate*, referring to the fortune of having been born earlier than others (or, contrariwise, of having been born too late). Therefore, with regard to this issue, there is only one option: to pity an Apostle like Saint Paul who, having suffered the misfortune of having been born twenty centuries too soon, could not know that the cross and sacrifice are pagan concepts that have nothing to do with Christianity. A pity, because in his madness he even considered as *enemies of the Cross*, and even as *opportunistic*, those who despised it: *For many walk, of whom I have told you often (and now tell you weeping) that they are enemies of the cross of Christ: whose end is destruction and whose God is their belly.*[97] And yet —unheard of—, there are still people who believe that his writings are inspired...

As we said above, it does not correspond to this essay to make a critical–theological study of the *Way*. It would be inappropriate, however, to fail to mention the canons of the Council of Trent, which contain *dogmatic definitions entirely opposed to the doctrines of the Neo–catechumenal movement*. One can refer to the XXII Session of the Council (DS., 1738 et seq.), paying particular attention to canons 1 through 9 (DS., 1751–1759). And let us also point out an important caveat. If someone dares to say, as *progressive* theology now frequently does with impunity, that the formal statements of Trent correspond to temporary and historical circumstances

---

[95]Gal 5: 11–12.

[96]1 Cor 1:17.

[97]Phil 3: 18–19.

that now are obsolete or have no justification or that those declarations used a language, now outdated and rejected by everybody, that belonged to the philosophy of that time... *the consequences would be disastrous.* For the same considerations could be made in the future regarding all of the Councils of the Church, including the most modern ones. Consequently, *the entire Magisterium of the Church would no longer have any credibility and, as a result, it would be made void.*

In view of this, even taking into account that what is said here is but a brief synopsis of the ideas of the *Way,* a question must be asked which, in turn, also calls for a mandatory response. The doctrines held by the Movement called *Neo–catechumenal Way,* can they be regarded as orthodox, or rather are they heretical in character?

And the answer, obviously a delicate one, however, is clear and categorical: If we abide by what theologians have always termed *material heresy,* the answer is in the affirmative. The facts are so clear and emphatic that whoever insists on denying them is doing so simply because he wants to.

As for what theologians also know as *formal heresy* (heresy stubbornly held and subjectively guilty), it is not for us to decide, insofar as it is a function that belongs exclusively to the Hierarchy and the Magisterium of the Church.

Moreover, on November 19, 2005, Pope Benedict XVI personally received Kiko Argüello and Carmen Hernández in a private audience. The Neo–catechumenal Way subsequently issued a statement, on November 22, 2005, in which both founders stated that *the Pontiff had expressed his support for their efforts, especially a project to spread the Gospel in the most de–Christianized regions of the world, and in particular in Europe.*

Also, on December 1, of the same year, Cardinal Francis Arinze, then Prefect of the Congregation for Divine Worship and the Discipline of the Sacraments, published a Document addressed to the Neo–catechumenal Movement. It makes several concessions, clarifications, and observations to the spirit and the liturgy of the Movement. Such concessions, always with a view to possible future approval of the Movement, have been granted *ad experimentum* for two years. The official response to the Document, carried out as an interview with the magazine *Zenit* (January 1, 2006), was provided by Giuseppe Gennarini, the main *person in charge* of the Movement in the United States; it has, in general, a congratulatory and triumphalist air, and, as expected, it tries to make the provisional approval from the Holy See appear as definitive.

To which it is fair to add that the Movement enjoys the sympathies of many Cardinals and many Bishops throughout the world; in addition to currently maintaining numerous Seminaries, both in Europe and America, for the training of ever–increasing numbers of candidates to the priesthood.

As can be seen, and as always must happen, the final word lies with the Hierarchy of the Church, the only entity that is responsible for the delicate Magisterial Mission. It is true that, in the meantime, given the evidence that such tangible facts are seemingly opposite, both in doctrine and practice, to twenty centuries of Christianity, the attitude of many Catholics of good will is a perplexity.

Apropos this issue, it is perhaps useful to recall the events that shook the Church in connection with a priest from Aragon, Spain, Miguel de Molinos (1627–1696), founder of *Quietism* and in the end condemned as a heretic by the Roman Inquisition and Pope Innocent XI. Before his condemnation, he enjoyed immense fame and was highly favored by the uppermost ecclesiastical circles. Given that those events are quite revealing and exemplary,[98] it may suffice to quote a text of Marcelino Menéndez Pelayo (in his *Historia de los Heterodoxos Españoles*, V, I–VIII, where one can find abundant historical documentation which we will not repeat here); after all, *Historia est Magistra Vitæ*.

---

[98]Not to mention how rapidly the Arian heresy spread throughout the Universal Church (*one day the whole world woke up and realized that it had become Arian*), or the Priscillianism heresy in Spain, or the Protestant Reformation all around the world with the tremendous, shocking events that ensued.

*Not everybody discovered, neither at first sight, the poison contained in
the "Guide."*[99] *The Archbishop of Palermo did not hesitate to praise and
recommend it to his diocese in a pastoral letter issued in 1687. Molinos
became regarded as an oracle by his devotees of Rome and Naples. He
continually received letters in support of his method. Cardinals Coloredi,
Ciceri and, above all, Petruzzi, Bishop of Lesi, known as the "Timothy" of
Molinos, openly declared themselves in favor of Molinos. Other cardinals,
for instance Casanate, Carpegna, Azzolini and D'Estrees, without any
detailed examination of the book, considered his friendship as an honor.
Many ecclesiastics came to Rome to learn his method from him, and almost
all of the nuns, except those whose confessors were Jesuits, gave themselves to practicing prayer of "quiet" as explained in the "Guide." Cardinal
D'Estrees, to add more credit to the doctrine, had translated into Italian
a book by Francisco Maraval: "Practique facile pour éléver l'ame a la contemplation, en forme de dialogue"; a work which had been often printed
in France and seemed consistent with the doctrine of St. Teresa. At the
same time, Petruzzi published many treatises and letters in support of
Molinos. If we were to believe some reports at that time, the Pope himself
was advised in favor of Molinos, and thought of giving him a Cardinal's
hat.*

In short, concerns about what the Gospel regards as *Riches*,
with which one can achieve better Evangelization, accomplished, in
turn, with good or bad intentions (always with good intentions, if
we are to believe those who manage to secure *Riches*), often end
up in disaster. It seems that the sentence of Our Lord, pronounced
as if it were a curse, hangs over such attempts: *You can not serve
God and mammon.* It seems that Power, Money, Friendship with
the world and the use its procedures, do not square well with the
Gospel.

---

[99] *Spiritual Guide Which Disentangles the Soul and Brings It by Inward Way to
the Getting of Perfect Contemplation.* It is the Ascetic Manual written by Molinos,
a veritable *Catechism* of Quietism.

It's as if you were contemplating a strange phenomenon. On the one hand, man is determined to make things more *humane*, easier, and more comfortable, including salvation —not hesitating to make a salvation solely *for this world*, in the case that the salvation which could lead to the other world would be too difficult. On the other hand, there is the Gospel preached by Jesus Christ, whose principles like the scandal of the cross and the narrow and steep path as the only ways of salvation cannot be dismissed.

Of course, the search for a second pathway, or the easy way, has its origins in much more remote times than it seems. It is as old as Christianity itself, even earlier; and the Devil himself had already offered it to Jesus Christ:

The Devil took him up into the holy city, and set him upon the pinnacle of the temple. And said to him "If you are the Son of God, cast yourself down, for it is written:

> *He has given his angels charge over you,*
> *and in their hands shall they bear you up,*
> *lest perhaps you dash your foot against a stone."*[100]

Clearly, the Devil, from his point of view, was right. A spectacular miracle, performed in the very Temple at the time of greatest concourse of people, would cause such astonishment and wonder that it would be compelling on its own. No need for more sacrifices and difficulties. Ultimately, the miracle would seek to make things easier for people in order to avoid making faith something as problematic and as *dark* as it is now. In other words, salvation for everybody, and without effort, not even for the Savior.

---

[100] Mt 4: 5–6, quoting Psalm 91.

And yet, would such a miracle be indeed convincing...? Can you convince of things that are above by using solely and exclusively instruments that are of earth...?

The most amazing thing about this issue is that the suggestion of the Devil at the pinnacle of the Temple and attempts to put confidence in worldly instruments —with the best intentions, of course— agree on the same point: the determination to make things easier and more reasonable, removing from the scope of human activity everything that might seem annoying, hurtful, or hard to do. *That simple.*

In the last analysis, since man has become his own master, he does not need anything which, as an alienating element, could hinder. At last, religion has become reasonable and *rational*; therefore, the Cross and Sacrifice are no longer needed. *My ways are not your ways, saith the Lord.* Indeed; although for many men, their own ways are the best.

Searching for *Wealth*, or the commitment to employ the same tools that the world uses with such *effective* results, may be done with the good intention of also making Evangelization easier and more productive. In effect, men have always had a predilection for choosing what is more convenient and simple. Hence, the majority of them always opt for the broadest and easiest paths, those along which one may walk more comfortably; a sociological observation already made by Jesus Christ referring, once again, to man's behavior. And to complicate matters further, He added a clever warning, that this is precisely the path that leads to destruction; and He went on to say, as if that were not enough, that the only one leading to life is so narrow and steep that very few are walking on it.

The truth is that, ever since then, we men should have been wary of what is easy; at least with respect to the road or path which each of us travels in our existence. Ever since the mischief that took place in the Earthly Paradise and since God had the idea of Himself personally intervening to fix it, things got pretty difficult, which by no means implies that they became unfortunate. The word *difficult* can also refer to things that are risky, exciting, enrapturing, dynamic, daring, courageous, bold, resolute, fearless... in short, a series of conditions that, when integrated within the whole of human life, can make it *abundant* (Jn 10:10), full of meaning,... and strangely joyful: now man can share the existence, life, death, and the unprecedented and mysterious *Adventure* of the destiny of Jesus Christ; the only event which, in this world and in the other, is able to bring to man the most immediate fruit derived from Love: Perfect Joy.

4. Where, with simplicity but not without some naiveté, we talk about the methods of evangelization that Christ considered the best.

But let us definitively set aside the problem of the evil or goodness of *Riches*. Riches *in themselves* cannot be bad. After all, it was the Apostle who said *I learned to be content with whatever I have: I have learned how to live in poverty, and I have learned to live in abundance; everywhere and in all things I am instructed both to be full and to be hungry, both to abound and to suffer need. I can do all things in Him who strengthens me.*[101] It seems, therefore, that to determine the morality of Riches it is necessary to add some specifications to them; and to legitimize them as a means of Evangelization, to add still more.

Perhaps the main problem lies in whether one trusts them or not. Jesus Christ provides certain identification keys: *You cannot*

---

[101]Phil 4: 11–13.

serve God and mammon.[102] Some are particularly hard: *It is easier for a camel to go through the eye of a needle than for a rich man to enter into the Kingdom of God.*[103] And there is still another key, specifically dedicated to Evangelization, which contributes to further complicating our problem: *Behold, I send you as lambs among wolves;*[104] which may refer to the apostle's weakness against the strength of the world to which he has to go. It is possible that Paul tried to echo this dictum when he said: *For I think that God hath set forth us the apostles last, as men condemned to death... We are fools for Christ's sake, but ye are wise in Christ; we are weak, but ye are strong; ye are honorable, but we are despised.*[105] Hence, perhaps, the bottom line comes to serving or not serving money; to put it more clearly, to use Riches as a fulcrum and lever... or not.

If we do, the danger would ensue if we attempt to make them a sufficient means of human existence; the same existence which has previously forsaken any aspiration to a supernatural end. Or perhaps (which would be worse) if we try to use them as an important (or perhaps primary?) means to achieve supernatural ends.

And everything indicates that the *rich* of whom Jesus Christ speaks is the one who adopts such attitudes.

According to all we have just said, can a Spiritual Family possibly make use of Riches *without putting its trust in them?*

There are situations in human existence which might be asked, of course, embarrassing questions, but to which it may not be convenient or even possible to provide a categorical or forthright answer —at least *from the outside.* Perhaps they are peculiar questions,

---

[102]Lk 16:13.

[103]Mk 10:25.

[104]Lk 10:3. Mt 10:16.

[105]1 Cor 4: 9–10.

specifically configured to be asked and answered by the ones who are affected by the problem and under their sole and exclusive responsibility. Therefore, if they honestly want to provide a full response to the question formulated above, they will have to shed beforehand all prejudices, selfish views, human standards... , and anything else which, in one way or another, may become an obstacle to a clear and loving opening of oneself to truth.

After all that has been said about Spiritual Families in connection with using or not using *Riches*, we might dare to make a final observation *from outside*, and as an *Epilogue* to this writing; taking into account, of course, the warning we have just expressed. For we are concerned only with a provisional conclusion, as a possible warning inspired by charity and, of course, subject to revision since, in reality, the final word on this issue belongs only to the Spiritual Families themselves.

This established, we would be in a position to formulate our own conclusions, which would more or less comprise the following:

We would encourage Spiritual Families to use happily the assets at their disposal —especially more so since they employ them with the good intentions by which they profess to be motivated. After all, God created all things good and for the benefit of mankind.

But allow us to formulate, as a final note, three warnings. Two of them are cautionary in nature; the third has a totally positive character filled with hope.

First of all, it is always advisable to take a glance at History, since it is *Magistra Vitæ*. It is always salutary and beneficial to consider what has happened in the past to those who have put their trust in *Riches* and what is happening to those who still do. At the same time, it would be highly dangerous to ignore the obvious facts provided by History.

Secondly, it is also healthy to read and consider Scripture. Turning only deaf ears to the serious warnings of Jesus Christ about *Riches* would be the greatest of follies. Spiritual Families should always have them before their eyes... and draw pertinent lessons from them.

Thirdly, while taking the Scriptures into account, why not consider the Master's teaching on the ways and methods to be used in Evangelization? Let us momentarily put inside parentheses His warnings about the danger of *Riches* and focus our attention on the words of Jesus Christ on how to evangelize: Is it possible that we do not know how to draw from those words the best, most practical, most intelligent, and effective way of carrying out Evangelization...?

The first thing that comes to mind in considering them, as so often happens with the Master's words, is their striking and unique character. As for us, it seems as if they would have been the last advice we would have offered in a similar situation: Was it really so necessary, or at least so important, that the apostles marched on to their task devoid of what seems so essential? Once again, His words come to our memory: *my thoughts are not your thoughts, neither are your ways my ways.* If someone is sent to fulfill a mission, it seems only reasonable to provide him with the necessary means. The Gospel, however, formulates a way of acting alien to common thinking. One should ask some modern evangelists if perhaps they would be willing to undertake their task *devoid of means.* And yet, here is His prescription: *He sent them to preach the Kingdom of God, and to heal the sick. And he said to them:*

—*Take nothing for your journey, neither staff, nor haversack, nor bread, nor money; neither have two tunics apiece. Whatever house you enter, there abide, and depart from there. And whosoever will not receive you, when you go out of that city, shake off the very dust from your feet as a testimony against them.*[106]

Admittedly, this seems exaggerated, and even bizarre: *Take nothing, neither staff, nor haversack, nor bread, nor money; neither have two tunics apiece...* Ah, but this is too demanding!... Not even two coats? Are we not even to consider our hygiene, Master...?

However, after a careful consideration of things, we can soon discover what the Master is aiming at. He gives us a warning, *a very serious one*, about the necessity, with respect to the obligation of evangelizing, of never putting our trust in human means —no matter how very convenient, effective, and even indispensable they may seem to be. Our human condition is such that in particular circumstances we need somebody to speak to us in a very resolute way. Clearly, this is not about simply proscribing extravagance; it is about being made aware, through the use of strong words, of an issue that can become serious.

So much so that the Master Himself, Who knows our perplexities, took upon Himself the charge of telling us that *nothing adverse will happen* when proceeding in this way: *And he said to them:*

—*When I sent you without purse or haversack or sandals, did you lack anything?*

—*Nothing —they replied.*[107]

Evidently, this is a warning which tries to dispel beforehand all fears. *When I sent you without any means, did you lack anything...? Nothing*, answered the disciples. Here we have a terse question and response which by themselves are a treatise on Evangelization. From that moment on became unnecessary and superfluous the great number of Pastoral Documents concocted in laboratories issued throughout the ages (more abundantly in modern times) by many Ecclesias-

---

[106]Lk 9: 2–5.
[107]Lk 22: 35.

tical Curiae and Offices, written by those who typically have never
done any pastoral work.

It would be interesting to know what would happen in that
Springtime of the Church —so often promised and stridently proclaimed since the Second Vatican Council, but which so many Christians are still earnestly looking forward to seeing— if someone with
ardent desires for Evangelization (Spiritual Families, men and women
in love with Jesus Christ...) would seriously believe in the words of
the Lord. We do not know what would happen, because, again, it
is business as usual: the narrowness of the human understanding
when facing the greatness of the heart of God. But one thing is
certain: if the promised *Springtime of the Church* ever happens it
will be made possible precisely thanks to those who firmly believe
in the roads mapped out by the Gospel.

That this form of Evangelization is not feasible...? That it is
impossible to *organize* a Spiritual Family with such criteria...? It
may be true. And yet, we have already heard the words of the
Master. Words about which He Himself said *are spirit and life.*[108]

Obviously this is a challenging problem. Because it is even possible that it may not be necessary to *organize* a large set–up and
that, instead, the procedures to follow are different ones. Of course

---

[108] Jn 6:64. Some people will accuse us of advocating for the ideology espoused by
some *spiritual* Movements of the Middle Ages which in the end were rejected and
condemned by the Church. However, these Movements emphasized certain virtues,
such as poverty and total detachment, while ignoring others equally important,
such as obedience and humility. In fact, Christian existence is an organic whole
that can be summarized in the participation in the *immolation of Jesus Christ.*
Accordingly, poverty without obedience is nothing. And one and the other, or
both together, or even all the virtues, without charity, are less than nothing. We
are not considering here Christian life from only one side of the prism, but from
the point of view of the *entire* Gospel. Neither are we encouraging a certain type
of behavior; we are simply advocating that people should let themselves be filled
with the *spirit* of the Gospel Message.

it would be foolish on our part to try to come up with a magic formula, especially one to solve a problem that has existed for many centuries. Besides, had we put one forward, there would be no challenge; it being the case that in a Christian existence nothing has value unless it is permeated with the aroma of the Cross.

Don Quixote failed in his dreams of improving his *depraved age*. In the end, he realized his folly. The pettiness and insignificance of his person; the trifle of a few weapons quite obsolete and inoperative; the inanity of an old nag that the owner considered a horse; the company of one rustic squire who had never seen battle... In addition, there was no longer any Knight Errant, if they had ever existed. In short, *ways and means absolutely inappropriate* for a task which, just because of what has been pointed out, if for no other reasons, seemed farfetched. Hence, no one has ever doubted Don Quixote's madness, his own creator least of all.

But his dream could not die with him. A Christian cannot ever admit that a *depraved age* does not have a remedy; such a thing would mean that he gives up the fight and admits a fatalistic defeat. The *Springtime of the Church* might be, perhaps, a slogan of fantasy for deceiving unwary people; and it could easily end up being so if the Church does not decide to be true to herself. But the struggle will continue until the end; an end that will be a total and definitive victory when God *makes thine enemies thy footstool.*[109] In the new Age of the Saints, no doubt soon to come, New Champions will rise again, for they are the only ones who have always saved the Church. They will go down into the arena to beat the world and humiliate it, with added embarrassment and ridicule, by using means that the world would regard as absolutely inadequate: *no haversack, no sandals, no bread, nor money, nor two coats, no staff...* Yes, indeed,

---

[109]Heb 1:13.

because these are the means, methods, and ways that, being entirely inadequate according to the world, are the only guarantee of final victory in the eyes of God.

The Church is currently facing a deep crisis, likely the greatest throughout her History; a crisis which is shared, despite their Power and Influence, by the Spiritual Families within her bosom. The Church, steeped in modernism, blinded by the veil that the propagators of Lies have spread over her, not only seems incapable of seeing the immense danger that she faces, but she has even come to believe that she is enjoying a flourishing *Springtime.* Don Quixote, in his madness, saw the windmills as if they were horrible, evil giants, while the Catholics of our time, properly manipulated and blindfolded, see dangerous Giants as friendly and practical Windmills.

But the long–awaited *Springtime* will become true at last; despite its being falsely advertised by some who were consciously lying, in the end their lie will turn against them and will become truth. And this will come to pass as all things concerning God always occur: in ways that men deem to be folly: *For the foolishness of God is wiser than men, and the weakness of God is stronger than men.*[110]

Don Quixote died having regained his sanity, but the spirit of his *madness* is not dead, if by chance one should consider madness the attempt to save his *depraved age* by means which in the eyes of the world and of human common sense were, more than inadequate, ineffective. However, once the futility of Power, Influence, Money, and Strength has been demonstrated, the Church will come through, as she has always done; this time, though, thanks to one or more new Quixotes who, brushing aside the means which the world regards as efficient, will take pride in using instead those means that

---

[110]1 Cor 1:25.

the world believes inoperative. Wearing instead the *armor of God* (Eph 6: 11.13), and the *breastplate of faith and love* (1 Thess 5:8), they will rescue again the integrity of the Truth.

Meanwhile we will continue hoping and praying that this time will come soon. Of course, the world will consider our expectation vain and useless, like dreaming a fantasy that will never come true. But we Christians have learned to *hope against hope* (Rom 4:18). And so we look to the horizon. Until one day, when the world least expects it and our longings are about to be overwhelmed, the new Knights Errant will reveal their figure on the horizon, riding down through the hills, making us realize that our hope was not in vain.

Index of Quotations of the New Testament

Matthew

4: 5–6, **453**

5: 3, **391**

9, **98**

15, **51**

16, **280**

17, **157**

29–30, **173**

43, **174**

48, **400, 414**

6: 1, **285, 433**

1–4, **292**

3, **285**

16–18, **292**

22–23, **341**

24, **174, 398, 408**

33, **73**

7: 14, **157, 297, 441**

15, **80**

8: 5–13, **127**

25, **289**

26, **290**

9: 15, **185**

24, **126**

37–38, **71**

10: 9–10, **81**

16, **156, 456**

17–18, **284**

22, **156**

24–25, **206, 407**

25, **152**

34, **98, 127, 130**

34–35, **436**

37, **173**

39, **143, 198, 316**

11: 27, **317, 352, 358**

12: 19, **49**

13: 52, **443**

14: 24–25, **169**

15: 24, **381**

16: 24, **401**

24–25, **260**

25, **157, 251**

17: 24, **127**

18: 15, **386**

20, **252, 253**

19: 5, **330**

5–6, **198**

12, **121**

17, **157, 387**

27–29, **135**

29, **391**

20: 25–28, **184**

27, **405**

28, **43, 157, 207, 355, 406**

22: 30, **122, 204**

37, **173**

23: 5, **281, 437**

24: 6–7, **436**

6–8, **128**
11, **80**
12, **290, 292**
14, **381**
22, **128**
28, **116**
25: _, **270**
5, **307**
6, **169**
11–12, **182**
14, **182**
21, **414**
26: 26, **254**
33–35, **141**
52, **126**
53–54, **127**
27: 52, **126**
28: 19, **382, 403**
19–20, **268, 379**

MARK

3: 13–14, **54**
5: 39, **126**
6: 8–9, **81**
8: 35, **64, 157, 251**
9: 35, **184**
43–45, **173**
10: 25, **456**
28–30, **135**

44, **406**
45, **43, 355**
12: 28–33, **173**
13: 5–8, **128**
7–8, **436**
13, **156, 174**
19–20, **290**
35, **169**
14: 22, **254**

LUKE

3: 14, **127**
4: 6, **256**
23, **260**
6: 20, **391**
22, **174**
26, **80**
27, **174**
40, **206, 407**
8: 52, **126**
9: 2–5, **459**
3, **81**
21, **285**
23, **401**
24, **157, 251, 284**
48, **184**
58, **391**
10: 2, **71**
3, **456**

22, **352**
11: 34, **341**
12: 14, **267**
32, **307, 401**
33, **391**
37, **207, 407**
51–53, **436**
14: 23, **431**
26, **173**
31, **127**
33, **197, 391, 398**
34–35, **431**
15: 4, **271**
16: 13, **174, 398, 408, 456**
17: 20–21, **297**
37, **116**
18: 7, **367**
8, **290**
9, **292**
22, **391**
28–30, **135**
19: 10, **37**
11, **182**
43–44, **436**
21: 6–10, **128**
9, **436**
17, **156, 174**
22: 19, **254**
26–27, **43**
27, **208, 355, 406**

30, **397**
32, **387**
35, **459**
23: 11, **37**
24: 38–39, **354**

JOHN

1: 5, **372**
11, **46, 50**
14, **50, 352**
17, **133**
3: 8, **190, 211**
16, **175, 197**
19, **80, 272**
20, **174**
21, **220**
29, **159, 185, 330**
31, **365**
34, **182, 323**
35, **182**
4: 14, **129**
23, **152**
23–24, **213**
5: 25, **152**
41–44, **42**
6: 56, **199**
56–57, **143, 316**
57, **199**
58, **205**

470

60–71, **5**

64, **460**

66, **8**

68, **133**

7: 7, **174**

18, **42**

8: 12, **161**

31–32, **220**

32, **426**

32–36, **260**

34, **260**

44, **95, 228, 278**

50, **42**

9: 1–3, **125**

4, **161**

5, **161**

10: _, **384, 406**

3–4, **328**

3–5, **186**

10, **68, 78, 153, 175,
211, 455**

11, **329**

13, **329**

14, **328**

15, **330**

20, **37**

30, **361**

38, **352**

11: 9–10, **161**

11, **126**

17, **169**

25, **211**

12: 24, **78, 120, 359, 433**

25, **198, 251**

31, **228**

35, **161, 341**

43, **281**

48, **56**

13: 1, **175, 197, 406**

7, **140, 361**

8, **181, 206, 355, 360**

13–14, **207, 406**

34, **269**

14: 2, **381**

3, **45, 181, 326**

4, **48, 63**

6, **78, 133, 211, 213,
260, 352**

9, **350**

10–11, **317**

17, **372**

26, **140**

27, **98, 436**

28, **45**

15: 1–2, **433**

5, **352**

5–6, **433**

11, **179**

13, **66, 198, 329, 355**

14, **407**

15, **180, 206, 326, 330, 407**

16, **54**

18, **284**

18–19, **45**

19, **433**

22, **56, 373**

16: 12, **140, 216**

12–13, **57**

13, **61, 372**

15, **317, 331, 358**

20, **179**

24, **179**

28, **45**

32, **152**

33, **367**

17: 10, **317, 332**

11, **46, 50**

14, **45**

15, **46, 49, 284**

18, **42**

22, **353**

24, **181, 353**

18: 36, **256**

37, **260**

20: 21, **42, 403**

21: _, **406**

15, **397**

15–18, **192**

ACTS OF THE APOSTLES

1: 8, **379, 403**

20: 35, **138, 182, 208, 319, 333**

ROMANS

1: 19–22, **74**

20, **283**

4: 18, **51, 311, 463**

19–20, **51**

5: 5, **176, 180, 190, 205, 311, 319, 323**

12, **126**

6: 3, **152, 344**

3–9, **152**

4–5, **152, 309**

4–6, **160**

5, **344**

8: 6–7, **10**

17, **14**

19, **346**

20–23, **305**

23, **323**

24, **312, 414**

24–25, **311**

32, **175**

9: 3, **280, 320**

11: 33, **74**

472

35, **173**

12: 3, **401**

4–5, **271**

5, **251, 400**

14: 7–8, **64, 200**

1 Corinthians

1: 17, **158, 250, 441, 449**

18–20, **9**

18–25, **38**

21, 11, **403**

23, **64, 159**

23–25, **403**

25, **62, 462**

25–28, **393**

27, **298**

27–28, **71**

2: 5, **8**

9, **149, 177**

14, **79**

16, **200**

3: 19–20, **9**

22–23, **282**

4: 9, **53, 278, 284, 434**

9–10, **456**

10, **56**

10–13, **154, 279**

16, **154**

6: 20, **63, 400**

7: _, **121**

1–2, **122**

7–8, **121**

31, **216**

32–34, **121, 197**

8: 1, **74**

9: 22, **49**

24, **129**

26, **129**

10: 17, **251**

11: 7–9, **205**

7–12, **203**

11, **201**

23–26, **254**

12: 7, **401**

8, **74**

11, **401**

12, **251**

18–22, **272**

20, **251**

27, **272**

13: 2, **74**

5, **139**

8, **122, 178**

10, **283**

12, **201, 283, 343**

14: 1, **283**

5, **74**

18–19, **74**

15: 8–9, **384**

24, **346**

28, **346**

44–54, **309**

49, **344**

54, **345**

55, **126**

16: 22, **307**

2 Corinthians

1: 5, **44**

7, **44**

3: 17, **68, 146, 321**

18, **148**

4: 10, **152**

10–11, **153**

12, **65**

5: 2–5, **323**

6: 3–10, **76**

14–15, **367**

8: 9, **181, 282, 415**

11: 23–27, **155**

30, **155**

12: 4, **78, 184**

5, **72, 299**

7, **384**

9, **72, 299**

10, **72**

Galatians

2: 11, **386**

19, **14**

20, **197, 205, 316, 408**

3: 28, **269, 271**

4: 6, **176**

19, **64**

5: 11–12, **159, 449**

22, **333**

6: 1, **386**

7, **227**

14, **51**

17, **51, 52, 64**

Ephesians

1: 9–10, **346**

17, **74**

2: 4–7, **152**

4: 4, **251**

7, **310**, 401

12, **251**

13, **151, 310**

16, **251**

5: –, **121**

8, **341**

21–33, **184**

22–29, **203**

31, **198, 330**

474

32, **201**

6: 11, **463**

13, **463**

17, **57**

1–2, **369**

3, **153, 285**

4, **78, 346, 369**

15, **251**

18, **203**

PHILIPPIANS

1: 20, **63**

21, **65**

2: 5, **200**

7, **50, 206, 355**

7–8, **43, 406**

3: 8, **65**

8–9, **216**

10, **44, 152, 160**

10–11, **152**

18–19, **449**

20–21, **309, 346**

21, **344**

4: 11–13, **455**

1 TESSALONIANS

4: 4–5, **341**

13, **126**

5: 3, **128, 436**

8, **463**

19, **412**

2 TESSALONIANS

2: 3, **128**

7, **259**

COLOSSIANS

1: 16–17, **211**

24, **44, 152, 251**

26, **345**

2: 3, **74**

12, **152**

19, **251**

3: 1, **393**

1 TIMOTHY

1: 15, **384**

2: 4, **269, 378**

11–15, **203**

6: 8, **399**

20, **444**

2 TIMOTHY

3: 12, **284**
4: 3–4, **57**
7, **414**
7–8, **154**
8, **306**

TITUS

2: 13, **14**

HEBREWS

1: 13, **461**
3: 18–19, **290**
4: 12, **57**
5: 1, **42, 44, 49**
4, **44, 54**
9: 22, **43**
10: 32–33, **434**
32–34, **155**
38, **163**
11: 1, **51, 440**
6, **139, 163**
9, **50**
13, **50**
12: 4, **50**
29, **82**
13: 14, **101, 312**
20, **406**

JAMES

3: 15, **9**

1 PETER

1: 18–19, **400**
2: 11, **50**
12, **280**
3: 1–7, **203**
4: 13, **44, 160**
5: 8, **393**

2 PETER

1: 4, **203**
3: 13, **367, 436**

1 JOHN

1: 1–4, **353**
6, **341**
3: 1, **77**
14, **269**
4: 5, **365, 433**
8, **8, 269, 331, 332, 341**
16, **331, 332, 341**
19, **69, 173**
5: 4, **163**
4–5, **51**

Revelation

1: 4, **368**
   8, **147**
2: 4, **179**
   10, **153**
   23, **271**
3: 19, **126**
   20, **186, 361**
7: 14–17, **156**
9: 12, **15**
11: 14, **32**
14: 4, **122**
18: 23, **341**
21: 1, **367**
   6, **147**
22: 12, **139**
   13, **147**
   15, **80, 95, 288**
   18–19, **444**
   20, **307, 368**

Books of the Bible

Acts, Acts of the Apostles

Amos, Amos

Bar, Baruch

1 Chron, 1 Chronicles

2 Chron, 2 Chronicles

Col, Colossians

1 Cor, 1 Corinthians

2 Cor, 2 Corinthians

Dan, Daniel

Deut, Deuteronomy

Eccles, Ecclesiastes

Eph, Ephesians

Esther, Esther

Ex, Exodus

Ezek, Ezekiel

Ezra, Ezra

Gal, Galatians

Gen, Genesis

Hab, Habakkuk

Hag, Haggai

Heb, Hebrews

Hos, Hosea

Is, Isaiah

Jas, James

Jer, Jeremiah

Jn, John

1 Jn, 1 John

2 Jn, 2 John

3 Jn, 3 John

Job, Job

Joel, Joel

Jon, Jonah

Josh, Joshua

Jud, Judith

Jude, Jude

Judg, Judges

1 Kings, 1 Kings

2 Kings, 2 Kings

Lam, Lamentations

Lev, Leviticus

Lk, Luke

1 Mac, 1 Maccabees

2 Mac, 2 Maccabees

Mal, Malachi

Mic, Micah

Mk, Mark

Mt, Matthew

Nahum, Nahum

Neh, Nehemiah

Num, Numbers

Obad, Obadiah

1 Pet, 1 Peter

2 Pet, 2 Peter

Phil, Philippians

Philem, Philemon

Prov, Proverbs

Ps, Psalms

Rev, Revelation

Rom, Romans

Ruth, Ruth

1 Sam, 1 Samuel

2 Sam, 2 Samuel

Sg, Song of Songs

Sir, Sirach

1 Thess, 1 Thessalonians

2 Thess, 2 Thessalonians

1 Tim, 1 Timothy

2 Tim, 2 Timothy

Tit, Titus

Tob, Tobit

Wis, Wisdom

Zech, Zechariah

Zep, Zephaniah

Contents

WAITING
FOR
DON QUIJOTE

Prologe 7

I. Logic, The Great Unknown 13

II. Power to the Laity 21

III. The Promotion of the Priesthood
   (The Greatest Story Ever Told) 35

IV. Utopias, Scourge of Humanity 83

V. The Island of Barataria 135

VI. The Helmet of Mambrino 219

VII. The Golden Age 301

VIII. The Great Temptation
   (Amazing Stories) 371

CPSIA information can be obtained
at www.ICGtesting.com
Printed in the USA
LVHW010533021122
732067LV00008B/400